KV-013-503

Work, Urbanism and Inequality
UK Society Today

Edited by
Philip Abrams

Professor of Sociology at the
University of Durham

Weidenfeld and Nicolson

London

© 1978 by Philip Abrams,
Brian Elliott,
Richard Brown,
Hilary Wainwright,
Anthony Giddens,
Paul Corrigan

All rights reserved. No part of this publication may be
reproduced, stored in a retrieval system or transmitted,
in any form or by any means, electronic, mechanical,
photocopying, recording or otherwise, without the prior
permission of the copyright owner.

ISBN 0 297 77469 7 cased
ISBN 0 297 77470 0 paperback

Weidenfeld and Nicolson
11 St John's Hill, London SW11

Text set in 10/11 pt IBM Press Roman,
printed by photolithography,
and bound in Great Britain
at The Pitman Press, Bath

Contributors

Introduction

    Philip Abrams
Professor of Sociology, University of Durham

Chapter 1

    Brian Elliott
Lecturer in Sociology, University of Edinburgh

Chapter 2

    Richard Brown
Reader in Sociology, University of Durham

Chapter 3

    Hilary Wainwright
Research Assistant in Sociology, University of Durham

Chapter 4

    Anthony Giddens
Lecturer in Social Sciences and a Fellow of King's College, Cambridge

and

    Philip Stanworth
Lecturer in Sociology, University of York

Chapter 5

    Paul Corrigan
Lecturer in Sociology, University of Warwick

Contents

Tables

Chapter 3

Figures

Acknowledgments

The publishers wish to thank the following who have kindly given permission for the use of copyright materials:

The *Archives Européenes de Sociologie* and F. Bechhofer and B. Elliott for material from 'An Approach to a Study of Small Shopkeepers', vol. 9 (1968);

G. Bell & Sons and H. Land for a table from *Large Families in London*;

The British Journal of Industrial Relations for tables from 'Union Growth Re-visited' by R. Price and G. S. Bain;

The British Sociological Association and J. H. Goldthorpe & C. Llewellyn for material from *Sociology*, vol. 11, no. 2;

The Bulletin of the Oxford Institute of Economics and Statistics and H. F. Lydall and D. G. Tipping for material from 'The Distribution of Personal Wealth in Britain';

Cambridge University Press for material from G. Salaman, *Community and Occupation*;

Cambridge University Press and the National Institute of Economic and Social Research for tables from pages 104–107 of *Occupation and Pay in Great Britain 1906–1960* by G. Routh;

The Child Poverty Action Group for tables from *Poverty: the Facts* (1975);

The Controller of Her Majesty's Stationery Office and the Office of Population Censuses and Surveys for tables and text reproduced or adapted from the British Labour Statistics *Yearbook*, the Department of Employment *Gazette*, the *General Household Survey*, the *New Earnings Survey, Occupations and Condition of Work, Social Trends* nos 5, 6 and 7, *Reports* nos 1 and 3 of the Royal Commission on the Distribution of Incomes and Wealth, the *Report* of the Commission of Inquiry on Industrial Democracy, the *Report* of the Committee on One-Parent Families and the *Report on Social Insurance and Allied Services*;

Counter Information Services for data from *Women Under Attack*;

Granada Publishing Ltd for data from *The British Political Elite* by W. Guttsman;

Heinemann Educational Books Ltd for tables from D. Donnison and D. Eversley, *London: Urban Patterns, Problems and Policies*;

Macmillan Ltd for figures from C. Clark, *The Conditions of Economic Progress*;

The Manchester School for material from T. Lupton and C. Shirley Wilson, 'The Social Background and Connections of Top Decision Makers';

New Society for material from 'Landlords' Slow Goodbye' by D. Eversley;

The Open University for material from DE351, Unit 6;

Penguin Books for material from K. Coates and R. Silburn, *Poverty: the Forgotten Englishmen* and J. Westergaard and H. Resler, *Class in a Capitalist Society*;

Pluto Press Ltd for tables from *The Hazards of Work* by Patrick Kinnersley;

Princeton University Press for data from M. Abramowitz and V. F. Eliasberg, *The Growth of Public Employment in Great Britain*;

H. W. Richardson and Teakfield Ltd for a map from Professor Richardson's book *Housing and Urban Spatial Structure*;

Routledge & Kegan Paul Ltd for material from G. D. H. Cole, *Studies in Class Structure*;

The Scottish Journal of Sociology and G. Payne, C. Ford and C. Robertson for data from 'Changes in Occupational Mobility in Scotland', vol. 1, no. 1;

Spokesman Books for tables from F. Field, *Are Low Wages Inevitable?*

The publishers would like to point out that every effort has been made to obtain all relevant permissions but that if anyone has been overlooked they apologise and will make amends in future editions.

Introduction

Social Facts and Sociological Analysis

It seems sensible to begin by saying what this book is not. It is not an expanded version of *Britain in Figures*. [1] Although it contains a good deal of statistical evidence, quantitative information and tabulated data it is not meant to be any sort of definitive presentation of that type of evidence. It is not, for example, an attempt to emulate the invaluable series published annually by the Central Statistical Office, *Social Trends*. [2] There would really be no point in trying to improve on the way in which the CSO gathers official statistical data and, letting the data speak for themselves, offers a year by year commentary on the directions of social change. One of the things this book seeks to do is to talk about official statistics while deliberately *not* letting those sorts of 'facts' speak for themselves. Again, the book does not offer an alternative to A.H. Halsey's *Trends in British Society since 1900*. [3] Halsey and his colleagues have done one of the jobs that *Social Trends* has never yet quite achieved in assembling a genuinely long range and comprehensive digest of quantitative information about British society, together with a series of critical and politically alert commentaries on the social problems indicated by that evidence. But here, too, the evidence is for the most part not itself questioned; the assumption again is that 'the data' do provide a more or less reliable picture of British social relations and social structure. This book is more sceptical than that. Where Halsey is comprehensive we have been selective; he has something to say about virtually every aspect of British society while we have concentrated on exploring a selection of the key aspects of that society in rather greater depth. On the other hand, while we are concerned to apply sociology as a system of theory and interpretation to the available 'facts' about UK society, the book is not a guide to applying social research methods to the study of practical social problems; it is not a companion volume to Albert Cherns' *Sociotechnics*; [4] nor do we discuss in detail the methodological issues involved in the sociological interpretation of 'given' empirical data in the way that Barry Hindess has done in *The Use of Official Statistics in Sociology*. [5] Nor, finally, is this another attempt at 'the sociology of modern Britain'.

A vital function of sociology as an intellectual discipline is to open the fortified windows of commonsense knowledge and let the gales of uncertainty blow through. Determining what sociologists can claim to know about UK society is in large part a matter of freeing ourselves from the uncritical trust in 'facts' to which we are all too readily disposed, and trying to rediscover the social reality of the relationships and conditions to which the 'facts' refer. We start therefore by putting 'facts' in question — especially statistical 'facts'. A principal object of this book is to suggest the sociological meaning of the sort of information about UK society which we normally take on trust. As Paul Corrigan points out in his discussion of juvenile law-breaking, our problem is not that the information presented to us in statistical tables and official reports is totally misleading; it is simply that, for the sociologist, it is not totally correct either. It is, as he puts it, a peculiar type of 'refracted', or partly distorted, knowledge. The task of sociology is to seek a more reliable image. The problem is two-sided. On the one hand there is a meaningless fascination about a great deal of 'factual' information which grips the imagination and tempts us to believe we have learned something significant: in 1975 beer production in Britain totalled 40 million barrels; there were 52,000 confectioners' shops and 47,000 hairdressers; 75,000 children were taken into care by local authorities; and 5.11 million metric tons of sulphur dioxide were emitted into the air. Plainly, the accumulation of statistical scraps and tit-bits of this sort is almost wholly without value until the bits and pieces are given some sort of meaningful context; for the sociologist this means a context of structured social relationships. On the other hand, the same types of 'facts' can acquire a dangerous meaningfulness of their own, precluding awareness of unstated realities which the information masks. Thus, it is well known that the population of the UK is ageing dramatically; successive censuses reveal a steady and rapid increase in both the number and proportion of the elderly in the population. We had 5.7 million people over the age of 65 in 1941 (in a total population of 48 million) and an estimated 9.6 million in 1975 (in a total population of 56 million). Figures such as these point powerfully to the growing importance (and cost) of the social problem of dependency in old age. The trouble is that they tend to point too powerfully, suggesting that the social problem springs simply from biological characteristics (the infirmity of the old) and demographic changes (increases in life-expectancy and decreases in the birth rate). What is obscured is that the problem of dependency in old age is also *socially* created — by the family as a domestic institution, retirement as an economic institution and pensions as a political institution; in each case the particular sorts of institutions we have constructed help in turn to construct the problem of the elderly.

The problem of applying sociology to information of this sort about UK society therefore becomes primarily a problem of placing such information in its proper context of social relations and social structure. That is what this book tries to do. We have taken three of the most fundamental concerns of sociology — the division of labour, urbanism and inequality — and, from the available evidence, tried to develop an analysis of contemporary UK society. The result is something less than a portrait of a whole society; although it does perhaps confirm that in making these three themes central to their analysis of industrial societies, classical sociologists were forging an intellectual perspective of considerable and continuing explanatory power. Work, community and inequality provide a framework within which effective sense can still be made of the structures and experiences of an industrial society, and it is hoped that the studies in this book will do just that. Perforce, many matters of 'obvious' importance are wholly or largely ignored as a result of this treatment. To some extent this is because our approach necessarily cuts across some of the more conventional categories of social description. Thus, although we have no chapter devoted directly to the family, Hilary Wainwright's analysis of the various domestic, cultural and economic divisions of labour affecting women, and Paul Corrigan's study of the deprivations imposed on one-parent families, between them say a great deal about the nature and effects of British family life. Similarly, we pay no direct attention to education; but although this involves some real loss in that the excellent work that has been done on social interaction within the process of education is neglected, the other main theme of the sociology of education, the role of education in distributing children to adult roles and thereby perpetuating society as a system of inequalities is a theme of virtually every chapter. More generally, although there are indeed some topics — religion, leisure, the monarchy — which are totally over-looked, we have, through this narrowing of focus, sought to give a sociological account of the UK *as a society*, a social system, even if we have not given an account of everybody in it or of the whole range of activities and experiences it contains.

The position we have taken is then that the application of sociology to the understanding of UK society — or any other society — is essentially a critical exercise involving the re-working of commonsense knowledge, facts and evidence from the viewpoint of a distinct intellectual perspective. It is a position well summarized by Tom Burns in his now famous lecture on 'Sociological Explanation'. Having examined a series of major examples of sociological work and shown how their success in every case lay in their ability to unmask everyday stereotypes about the social world, he concludes:

> In this last instance, as in all the others, sociology defines itself as a critical activity. The purpose of sociology is to achieve an understanding of social behaviour and social institutions which is different from that current among the people through whose conduct the institutions exist; an understanding that is not merely different but new and better. The practice of sociology is criticism. It exists to criticise claims about the value of achievement and to question assumptions about the meaning of conduct. It is the business of sociologists to conduct a critical debate with the public about its equipment of social institutions.[6]

Straightforward, thorough, descriptive reporting is an important element in this debate; it establishes the appropriate basis for discussion. Burns cites the impact of the *Our Towns* study of the condition of children evacuated from city slums in 1940 as an example: 'The astonishing feature of the *Our Towns* report . . . was not the squalor and unseemliness of the children but the blank ignorance of all other sections of society about them and the circumstances of urban life which had pro-duced them'. After its publication the formation of social policy in health, housing and education simply had to proceed on a new basis. Some of the more recent findings about work, wealth and poverty discussed later in this book have had a very similar influence. But good descriptive reporting is only one of the essential ingredients of the debate between sociology and society. The other is a strategic understanding of what the descriptions could mean, a larger conception of how the institutions and behaviour being described relate to behaviour, institutions and experience in the rest of society. Such a perspective is implicit in our decision to concentrate the analysis of UK society in this book within the framework of in-equality, urbanism and the division of labour.

The intellectual history of sociology is indissolubly tied to the material history of industrialization. And the immediate experience of the transition to industrialism has almost invariably been one in which life seems to be dominated by a dramatic explosion of the division of labour, a transformation of old patterns of inequality and rapid and extensive if not ubiquitous urbanization. It would have been odd indeed if these phenomena and the peculiar problems of social integration, progress and values which they posed had not become the substantive core of a social science concerned above all to understand the nature of industrial society. What we find in the best sociology, whether in the writings of Marx, Durkheim and Weber or in the more modern writings of Bell, Sennett or Castells, is a sustained attempt to relate these phenomena of industrialization to one another and to grasp the underlying realities of structure and process from which they spring. Such works are only secondarily a matter of record or description; the distribution of persons to occupations, the scale and pace of urbanization, hierarchies of stratification and rates of social mobility are the distinctive phenomena to which sociological analysis refers. But the analysis itself is primarily concerned with the inter-relationships of such phenomena, not with their incidence. It is in the ways they act on one another that the division of labour, inequality and urbanism reveals and constitutes the peculiar social structure and dynamics of industrial societies. And it is towards an understanding of that interaction that sociology, pure or applied, consistently moves.

Attempts to isolate any one of these dimensions of industrialization from the others have, almost without exception, proved disastrous — most conspicuously in the efforts of Louis Wirth and his successors to develop a sociology of the urban community without reference to the contexts of inequality and the social division of labour in which cities exist. Emile Durkheim, whom I would regard as having done more than any other single writer to give modern sociology its special intellectual character, came close to a similar sterility in his own pioneering analysis of the division of labour. Only at the very end of *The Division of Labour in Society* does Durkheim actually place the division of labour *in* society, recognizing that the specialization of functions, the logical implications of which he had so brilliantly unravelled in the body of his book, also occurred in settings constructed historically in terms of the power of some social groups and the powerlessness of others.[7] Nevertheless, he does recognize this 'forcing' of the division of labour; and so concludes in the end that the actual working out of the ambiguous tendencies of the division of labour in any industrial society — tendencies towards both individual rationality and social meaninglessness, towards both cohesion and division in society — will have to be left as an open empirical question for the sociologist to resolve. And its resolution will be in part a matter of understanding the ways in which the history of the division of labour is contained within the history of social inequality and in turn acts on it. It is to the resolution of this sort of question that the following chapters by Richard Brown and Anthony Giddens and Philip Stanworth are especially addressed.

Marx and Weber were more sensitive than Durkheim to the interdependence of inequality and the division of labour; and also more aware of the ways in which the typical social forms of industrial society such as the city were expressions of that interdependence. Yet there is a surprising consensus among all three of the most eminent founding fathers of sociology on the nature of the sociological task. From the point of view of the individual the rise of industrial capitalism created a world which is simultaneously a world of emancipated self-interest, rational personal action, and collective irrationality, chaos and constraint. The moral absurdity of the situation of the individual is to be understood, perhaps even transcended, through social analysis of the bonds between the division of labour and the structure of inequality. Experiences of personal life — suicide, poverty, religion, the city or whatever form of experience might be in question — are to be explained by their location within that relationship.

This is a strong doctrine and it immediately indicates the second great danger that faces any attempt to unite sociology and social description in an effective, applied social analysis. The first danger is that of taking the findings of descriptive enquiries too much on trust, of allowing the data to speak for themselves. The second is that of allowing the wisdom or at least the logic of sociological theory to speak for *itself*, brutally imposing what inferentially must be on whatever commonsense appears to have observed. Applied sociology has to negotiate a passage between these two hazards and it can do so only by taking both social facts and sociological analysis quite seriously. It is in other words a matter of balance: of constantly looking at 'the evidence' from the point of view of theory, and of constantly looking at 'theory' from the point of view of the evidence. On each side of the balance perhaps the most important and valuable question the sociologist can ask is simply 'so what?'. It is this sort of balance that the various chapters of this book seek to maintain, a balance that is at once fragile, sceptical and constructive.

FROM FACTS TO ANALYSIS: THE PROBLEM OF AGE

Two examples will perhaps help to make clear just how difficult this type of balance is to achieve. Let us take first a field of social enquiry in which evidence has tended to dominate theory — the study of age; and then a field in which theory has tended to dominate evidence — the study of urban communities. In both cases the challenge to the applied sociologist is to use the apparently weaker element to subvert the apparent authority of the stronger.

Demographic data, basic information about rates of birth, marriage, death and migration, are commonly treated as one of the 'hardest' types of evidence available to the social scientist. At the same time it is well known that predictions and projections based on demographic data are, of all types of social prediction, the ones most likely to go wrong. The fact that in the late 1970s Britain is experiencing a so called 'crisis of teacher-training' — that is to say we are training far more teachers than government is willing to pay to teach — is a direct result of the official belief that the high marriage and birth rates of the early 1960s were themselves social facts which could be treated as a given and continuing basis for social policy. The belief that information about fertility in 1960 could provide a basis for knowing what sort of families people would have in the 1970s is the immediate cause of the prospect of unemployment that faces so many student teachers in 1978. Yet there is a sense in which demographers never learn. In the early 1960s we were told with complete confidence that the population of the United Kingdom would increase towards a figure of 66 millions by the end of the century. Today, in the 1976 edition of *Social Trends*, we are told no less confidently that the probable population of the United Kingdom in the year 2001 is a mere 59 million. Seven million people more or less have been demographically written off. Yet the basic datum on which both projections are based is the same; it is the number of women of child-bearing age already or prospectively in the population at the moment when the projection is made; coupled with the assumption that these women will behave in exactly the same way as their immediate predecessors. On the basis of this information and on this assumption the demographer concludes that the child-bearing behaviour of tomorrow's adults can be extrapolated in a law-like manner from his knowledge of the child-bearing behaviour of the adults of the immediate past.[8]

The belief that the incidence of a given type of behaviour at a given moment in time constitutes a social fact of general significance is here given a rigidity and force of a quite remarkable nature. As a result the history of demography is a history of endlessly revised projections. And yet, despite the fact that generation after generation of parents have spectacularly failed to behave in the way demographers expected them to behave, demography continues to flourish. Instead of abandoning the whole business of demographic projection and recognizing that family size, to say nothing of family relationships, are too susceptible to changing social pressures and personal choices to be treated as social facts in this simplistic way, the demographer tends simply to produce a new projection offered with all the authority of the one that has just been discredited.

Demography thus provides an exceptionally clear example of the way in which social description falls short of social analysis. Contemporary demographic facts about the UK would include the following. First, the births that have already occurred, together with our existing ability to prolong life, will mean that there will be very many fewer children of compulsory school age in the 1980s than there have been in the recent past, that there will be a short-term increase in the demand for higher education followed by a decline from the late 1980s to the end of the century, that there will be a quite rapid increase in the population of working age during the next decade and that there will be a considerable increase in the numbers of very old people between the ages of 75 and 85. Second, and only a little more speculatively, one could suggest that these changes will in turn entail a number of further changes; for example, a quite dramatic increase in the number of one-person households; since at present about three-quarters of such households; consist of single elderly people. The current projection is that the 3.5 million one-person households in the country in 1970 will have increased to 5.5 million by 1990. And thirdly it might not be unreasonable to argue that certain well-established trends in patterns of marriage and divorce will continue along broadly the same lines to the end of the century. Thus, both marriage and divorce have been becoming more popular and it is not implausible to suppose that both trends will persist. Between 1931 and 1973 the ratio of married people in Great Britain rose from 56 per cent to 67 per cent of the adult population. In 1931 only 25 per cent of women from 20 to 24 years old were married; but in 1973 the ratio was 58 per cent. At the same time there were 121,000 divorces in England and Wales in 1975, over three times as many as ten years earlier; and there were 116,000 re-marriages — marriages which were not the first marriage for one or both partners. Taken together such figures point to the strong probability of there being an increasing number of children living in families which do not consist of both their natural parents.

But what does all this tell us about the family as a social institution in UK society, or more specifically about the social significance of age and the social organization of the life-cycle? How can we make the leap from demographic data to sociological understanding? A slightly closer look at the problem might be helpful. Demography was after all one of the earliest social sciences. It took shape against the background of an essentially pre-industrial social order — in England, for example, between 1660 and 1720. Its methods tended to reflect the social realities of such social orders; realities in which rates of marriage, fertility and mortality were all relatively fixed from generation to generation and in which trends in any of the three matured slowly over very long periods of time and in a more or less invariable manner. Plagues, wars and famines apart, demographic data did look like social facts in pre-industrial societies. In the more 'ideal-typical' versions of such societies, biological age and inherited social identity were the cardinal sources of social organization, status and hierarchy. To know a person's kin and age was to know almost everything of social importance about him. The 'natural' phases of the life-cycle provided a stable basis for the social division of labour, power, privilege and identity. By contrast the extent to which age and kin control an individual's social destiny and status (or even reliably indicate them) in advanced industrial societies is remarkably slight. Of course people are still assigned to age-specific roles, such as childhood, adolescence and old age, in relatively inflexible ways; and the social organization of the life-cycle is still an important dimension of social organization as a whole. But for all the excitement about 'youth culture' and the 'generation gap' in the last two decades the striking thing about industrial societies is how little, comparatively speaking, age determines.

The same is increasingly true of the other basic elements of demographic enquiry. The law-like constraints of the life-cycle and of biological inheritance that are experienced in pre-industrial societies are being progressively relaxed in other areas too. The technologies of birth control and the politics of divorce and women's liberation have freed people from subjection to the social 'facts' of marriage and fertility rates. Medicine, and institutional and social care, are progressively making even the facts of mortality variable. Death was of course the beginning of demography. It was the predictability of death by gender, age, occupation and medical history that permitted the formation and profitability of life-insurance organization. And it was from this basis that demography as a predictive, statistical social science sprang. By undermining the certainties on which demography was constructed advanced industrialism makes the understanding of the life-cycle sociologically problematic in a way it has not been for a long time. As the predictions began to be falsified the need for an independent analysis of the social meaning of the data became steadily more evident. The demographic profile of contemporary UK society is easy to draw and not especially controversial. What is controversial is the meaning of that profile for social change and social policy.

One would begin by conceding that UK society is indeed becoming an older society. In 1900 the median age of our population was 24; today it is 34; by the end of the century we are told that it will be 38. Of all demographic projections those concerning mortality are the least unreliable since the normal tendency of medicine to extend life, and the normal propensity of human beings to avoid death, are about as reliable as any social data can be. To put it more directly; given a falling birth rate since the early 1960s and greater longevity among the old, the proportion of retired and dependent persons in the population as a whole has to increase. *Social Trends* expresses it rather opaquely as an increase in the 'upper quartile' of the age distribution of the population from 40 per cent in 1901 to 50 per cent in 1971. Another way of putting it is to note that there were 2.4 million people over the age of retirement in 1901, 5.7 million in 1941, 7.1 million in 1971 and the figure now projected for the year 2001 is 8.5 million. In other words Britain is an ageing society in quite a dramatic sense; with an overall population growth of 45 per cent since 1900 the number of people over the age of retirement has increased by 196 per cent. At the same time, although the number of people under the age of 16 has fractionally increased in absolute terms, it has declined as a proportion of the population as a whole. So that while the overall 'dependency' ratio — the proportion of the population that on grounds of age will have to be supported by others — may be said to have changed very little in the first three-quarters of this century (from 35 per cent to 38 per cent), its *constitution* has changed remarkably and in a way that gives us a new and acute social problem. At least it does for so long as we treat men over 65 and women over 60 as necessarily 'economically inactive'; but this again is a political not a demographic fact.

Unreliable as projections based on fertility rates and marriage rates are now recognized to be, the implications of our survival rate taken in conjunction with current levels of fertility are quite impressive. At present women are marrying younger (the average age of first marriage is now 23 as compared with 26 in 1900); as are men (25 now as compared with 27 in 1900) and, except in the professional middle classes, all married couples are having fewer children. Elizabeth Still has shown that graduates of higher education have now become the most prolific section of the population so far as child-bearing is concerned.[9] More generally the increasing popularity of marriage seems to be negatively related to family size. As marriage and parenthood both become increasingly matters of choice it seems that marriage is being chosen more frequently and parenthood less frequently. The current birth rate of 12.4 live births per 1,000 of the population is the lowest the country has had this century, compared with figures of 18 in 1961 and 29 in 1901. We do not know of course whether these trends will continue. It is difficult for example to know what allowance to make for the possible effects of future economic changes on people's attitudes to the 'value' of children. But for the moment we plainly have a population profile with a bulging forehead (of the elderly) and a receding chin (of the young) — a profile which, however sceptical one may be about the reliability of demographic projections, already has a serious message for policy-makers.

Yet here we hit upon a difficulty. Although demographic description indicates the existence of the social problem, it does not indicate its nature — if anything it misrepresents it. Demography encourages the interpretation of the problem of dependence in old age as a 'natural' hazard of the life-cycle and obscures the extent to which it is, rather, an effect of a particular social division of labour; and of particular relations of social inequality. The point is hardly new but it is one that almost always needs to be made when one attempts to move from this sort of descriptive evidence to an adequate understanding of the social relations of the family.

In Britain this point was made as long as eighty years ago by Seebohm Rowntree in his path-finding analyses of the social causes of poverty. In *Poverty: a Study of Town Life* Rowntree examined the relationship between poverty and the life-cycle and showed with devastating clarity that while the incidence of poverty was indeed strongly associated with particular phases of the life-cycle, its causes were to be found not in the life-cycle as such, but in the relationship between the social organization of age and an equally socially organized division of labour.[10] Anyone looking at Rowntree's chart (Figure 0.1), where the life-cycle is expressed as a series of age-specific waves of poverty and affluence, can see that the periodic reductions of well-being which he identified are a consequence not of biological facts alone, but of the relationship between the life-cyle and the labour market. In that relationship it is the structure of the labour market which has to be regarded as the variable element and therefore as the proper target of social policy. What was needed was not just old age pensions but a change in the relationship between the family and the economy. In his discussion of poverty in the UK Paul Corrigan suggests that the problem is not so very different today.

Demographic data, then, like other descriptive evidence, tell us something about the location and scale of our social problems. But they cannot on their own tell us why those problems exist or what should properly be done about them. To move from description to analysis some *theoretical* bridge has to be built between the evidence and its possible meaning. However reluctantly, Rowntree was forced to

Poverty and the Life Cycle

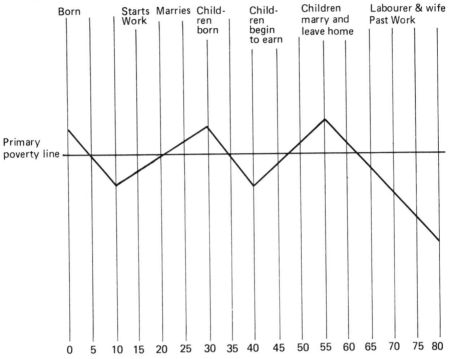

Figure 0.1   Poverty and the Life Cycle
Source: adapted from B. Seebohm Rowntree, *Poverty: a Study of Town Life* (London 1910)

conclude that this bridge was constituted by the wage economy. Looking at similar data today we must be at least as determined to resist the suggestion that the dependency of the old is merely a function of age. Of course old people do become crippled by arthritis and other disabilities, the biological process of ageing does take its toll. But we also institutionalize age and this is a socially variable matter. In many primitive societies age is institutionalized on the basis of authority; in modern UK society it is institutionalized on the basis of dependency. The social description of age masks the extent to which we have *created* age as a certain sort of social relationship. Perhaps at the present time in the UK the real 'problem' of old age is not that of dependency and disability at all, but that of retirement. It is important to remember that only a minute proportion of the elderly are in residential care – for example 7 per cent of those over 75 in 1960 – and there is some evidence that the figure is if anything falling. But they all face the issue of being old in a society where the social division of labour makes being old a form of redundancy. As Phillipson puts it in a recent analysis of the social creation of retirement:

One of the major innovations to have occurred in the twentieth century has been the emergence of retirement as a major part of the life-cycle. In addition the character of the retirement period has changed, and continues to change at a dramatic pace. From a point where it seemed merely a short stage (particularly for men) before death, there is now evolving a multi-staged period at least part of which, for increasing numbers, may mark a real measure of choice and scope to pursue diverse social activities. The evolution of ideas about the retirement stage in the life-cycle has developed in a hesitant manner, reflecting both ambiguities in social attitudes toward old age and competing economic and social priorities — these producing tension in the relationship between the work and post-work spheres and in the latter's cultural and social legitimation.[11]

He goes on to trace the particularly close connection in that evolution between the social position and treatment of the elderly and fluctuations in the supply and demand for labour in the wage economy as a whole. Against this background the problem of the elderly disappears and is replaced by the problem of the relationship of all age-groups to one another within an encompassing division of labour. Social policy for its part, having just begun to shift its attention from the idea of institutional care to that of domiciliary care, is now called upon to make a further move away from the idea of concentrating 'care' on a particular age group; and towards that of protecting and enhancing the family as a setting for relationships of reciprocity across the life-cycle as a whole. For despite the many suggestions in the demographic data which might be thought to point towards a weakening of family life, one of the plainest and firmest findings of more intensive sociological research is that the family in fact remains the strongest and most highly valued basis for social attachment UK society possesses.[12] Sociologically, the tough resilience of family relationships is not surprising; it follows from the discipline's earliest and most fundamental insights into the nature of solidarity, reciprocity and attachment. Had our discussion of the problem of old age in the contemporary UK started from the works of Durkheim, or Simmel, LePlay or Malinowski rather than from the latest census data the descriptive evidence would not have presented us with the relatively isolated problem of old age; but with the much more analytically fruitful question of the extent to which family relationships in the general setting of an advanced industrial society can survive as a basis for practical solidarity and attachment between individuals. That is in itself a controversial question, but at least it is a question which recognizes the social context of social problems.

Thus the first hazard of applied sociology is that of taking the fruits of social description too much on trust; and its first task is to reinterpret social description from the point of view of sociological theory. Nevertheless the second task is to pay proper respect to the findings of descriptive enquiries; and the second great hazard is that of allowing the logic of sociological theory to overwhelm the hard evidence of commonsense. This hazard has been particularly acute in sociological discussions of community.

FROM ANALYSIS TO FACTS: THE PROBLEM OF COMMUNITY

The apparent weakening of the family indicated in many descriptive studies is as nothing compared to the loss of community predicted by the whole tradition of sociological theory. Because sociology came into being as an attempt to apprehend the nature and dynamics of the transition to industrialism, it tended to identify the emergent industrial world in terms of a series of stark polarities, or contrasts-of-type, between pre-industrial and industrial societies. The most characteristic of these centred on the idea of community. Virtually without exception the pioneers of sociology understood industrialization to involve a disintegration of the bonds of community. Community became, as Robert Nisbet puts it 'the most fundamental and far-reaching of sociology's unit ideas'.[13] The term referred not only to attachments grounded in locality but, much more generally, to an inclusive moral cohesion believed to have characterized pre-industrial society. As Nisbet remarks again: 'the word . . . encompassed all forms of relationship which are characterized by a high degree of personal intimacy, emotional depth, moral commitment, social cohesion and continuity in time. Community is founded on man conceived in his wholeness rather than in one or another of the roles, taken separately, that he may hold in a social order'. Since the essential nature of industrial society involved an explosion of the division of labour which splintered people's lives into separated roles, industrialization logically threatened community. The theme is endlessly reiterated, becoming one of the commonplaces of sociological wisdom. The loss of community was associated especially with the growth of industrial cities which were contrasted not just with the past, but with the countryside as well. It is in the early urban sociology of Simmel and Wirth that these ideas are most directly presented. But this theme was not the sole preserve of sociologists. It was Benjamin Disraeli who gave it one of its crispest statements:

> There is no community in England; there is aggregation, but aggregation under circumstances which make it rather a dissociating than a uniting principle . . .
> In great cities men are brought together by the desire of gain. They are not in a state of co-operation but of isolation, as to the making of fortunes; and for the rest they are careless of neighbours. Christianity teaches us to love our neighbour as ourself; modern society acknowledges no neighbour.[14]

Ruth Glass has suggested that this tendency to contrast urban present and rural past in terms of community, and to the disadvantage of urban present, is a peculiar tendency of British intellectuals. While there is some truth in this, it is also the case that this particular contrast pervades the whole of sociology, European and American as much as British. A representative passage from Louis Wirth may speak for the whole sociological tradition, both in its assertion of the loss of community and in its belief in the vital importance of the city as a distinctive social form of industrial society.

> The multiplication of persons in a state of interaction under conditions which make their contact as full personalities impossible produces that segmentalization of human relationships which has sometimes been seized upon by students of the mental life of the cities as an explanation for the 'schizoid' character of urban personality . . . . Characteristically, urbanites meet one another in highly segmental roles. They are, to be sure, dependent upon more people for the satisfactions of their life-needs than are rural people and thus are associated with a greater number of organised groups, but they are less dependent upon particular persons, and their dependence upon others is confined to a highly fractionalized aspect of the other's round of activity. This is essentially what is meant by saying that the city is characterized by secondary rather than primary contacts. The contacts of the city may indeed be face to face but they are nevertheless impersonal, superficial, transitory and segmental. The reserve, the indifference and the blasé outlook which urbanites manifest in their relationships may thus be regarded as devices for immunizing themselves against the personal claims and expectations of others.[15]

The most remarkable thing about the body of doctrine and inference which such a passage represents is that it is so deeply rooted in the logic of sociological analysis that it has successfully resisted modification, despite a glaring absence of confirmatory evidence and the uncomfortable presence of a good deal of evidence pointing in a contrary direction. To begin with the analysis as a whole can not be fully validated as we lack thorough empirical studies of the supposed pre-industrial 'baseline' from which the loss of community is believed to have developed. We simply don't know what community in eighteenth-century England was like and it is unlikely that we shall ever be able to gain such knowledge. For the most part early sociologists treated the presence of strong communities in pre-industrial societies as axiomatic; and subsequent advocates of the loss of community thesis have been increasingly constrained to do the same. More disturbingly, quite a large number of descriptive studies of contemporary industrial societies, including the UK, have suggested that the various elements of community are in fact quite strongly present in such societies, even in their most highly urbanized areas.[16] The paradox of the sociology of community is the coexistence of a body of theory which constantly predicts the collapse of community and of a body of empirical studies which finds community alive and well.

In practice the problem is not quite as clear cut as that, nor is the difficulty all on one side. Nevertheless, if we take one theme from the field of community studies as an example, that of neighbouring, we can see that this is a field where applied sociology has been quite severely hampered by the general predominance of theory over description. In line with the tendency of community theory as a whole, the prediction emerging from sociological analysis about neighbouring has been that it, too, will be eroded with the development of industrialism. For Wirth again 'the bonds . . . of neighbourliness . . . are likely to be absent or, at best, relatively weak' in urban industrial milieux. And in a comprehensive and perceptive review of the whole literature on neighbouring, Suzanne Keller was able to condense conventional wisdom into a number of quite sharply focused propositions explaining why attachment and interaction among neighbours must be expected to be less important and less intense in the typical settings of industrial societies (cities) than in the typical settings of pre-industrial societies (villages). From this point of view the UK is one of the most 'industrial' of nations. Its population density, 601 people per square mile, is one of the highest in the world; and that population is predominantly urban. The ratio of those living in urban areas to those living in the countryside is about $3\frac{1}{2}$.1, with approximately a third of the population living in seven great conurbations. Keller summarises the analysis as follows:

1. As crises diminish in number and kind, where, that is, self-sufficiency increases, neighbour relations will diminish in strength and significance.
2. As new forms of social control arise, the significance of neighbouring as a means of social control will recede in importance.
3. Where neighbouring is a segmental activity in an open system rather than an integral part of a closed system, it will be a highly variable and unpredictable phenomenon.
4. Since all three conditions are more true of urban than of pre- or suburban areas, neighbouring should diminish in extent, significance and stability in cities.[17]

More recently and in very much the same spirit, Key has claimed to have shown that 'there is a negative relationship between the size of the community in which people reside and the frequency with which they participate in social relationships involving other people residing in portions of the community contiguous to their residence.'[18]

One difficulty with this sort of argument is that a large number of empirical studies have documented the existence of intensive and extensive neighbourliness in highly urbanized areas; the best known in this country being the work of Young and Wilmott in Bethnal Green.[19] A further difficulty is that even when the effects predicted for urban industrial societies *are* observed it is not at all clear that the effects that occur *in* cities or in industrial societies are in fact caused *by* cities or by industrialism. The implicit causal relation asserted in the theory of community has proved extraordinarily difficult to demonstrate explicitly. That is one reason why modern urban sociology, represented in this book by Brian Elliott's chapter, has increasingly moved away from the idea of the city as a distinct social entity, found in the work of Simmel and Wirth, towards a type of analysis in which cities are treated merely as settings in which the characteristic relationships of some larger social structure and some more inclusive division of labour work themselves out. It is a move away from urban sociology towards the political economy of towns. Alternatively, one could say that it is an attempt to place the analysis of urbanism within the broader sociological analysis of the division of labour and social inequality; instead of allowing it to remain a seemingly independent and isolated branch of the discipline.

But to return to community and to neighbouring. The concept of community for its part is slowly being evicted from British sociology; not because there is agreement on the empirical collapse of community; but rather because the term has come to be used so variously and different relationships, identified as those of community, have been discovered in so many different contexts that the word itself has become almost devoid of precise meaning. In particular there has been a determined effort to detach the study of social relationships from the study of spatial relationships — two themes which are hopelessly jumbled together in the traditional idea of community. The problem of solidarity is, recent authors have suggested, one that should be separated, as a matter of principle, from the problem of the effects of spatial arrangements on social relationships. As Pahl says in an important article developing this theme: 'any attempt to tie particular patterns of social relationships to specific geographical milieux is a singularly fruitless exercise'.[20] And Stacey, in a parallel argument about the 'myth of community studies', concludes that 'our concern as sociologists is with social relationships; a consideration of the social attributes of individuals living in a particular geographic area is therefore not sociology, although it may well be an essential preliminary to sociological analysis'.[21] In sum, there is now a prevailing scepticism about the possibility of studying spatial relationships sociologically; and a resulting insistence that insofar as the concept of community implicitly prejudges the nature of such relationships it should be expelled from the dictionary of sociology.

Where does that leave the study of neighbouring in contemporary industrial society? Obviously, unlike the concept of community, the concept of neighbouring *must* have spatial connotations: neighbours are defined as people who live close to each other. So the sociological problem about neighbours has to be one that includes a question about the effects on social relationships of different ways of living close to others. More generally, the issue is to determine what type of social and/or spatial circumstances are associated with what types of relationships between neighbours.

And here again such evidence as there is tends to belie the predictions of sociological theory. Two findings emerge especially strongly from the whole body of research. One concerns prevailing social norms about neighbourliness; the other involves the conditions under which members of our society are likely to be 'good' neighbours. So far as the norms of neighbourliness are concerned it seems clear that neighbourliness is very widely understood, in both town and country, and for that matter in both present and past, as a three-dimensional relationship composed of friendliness, helpfulness and distance.[22] Ideally, normatively, a neighbour is someone who is agreeable when casually encountered, there when you want them in an emergency and yet who does not 'live in your pocket'; who, while being both friendly and helpful, also respects your privacy. Not only is this norm widely diffused in contemporary UK society, but the circumstances under which such a norm can actually be realized in relationships between neighbours are also widely understood.

Thus, although the urban-rural contrast does not stand up to scrutiny, it seems that the nature of the locale in which people live does affect patterns of neighbouring in some quite definite ways. For example, the social homogeneity of a neighbourhood and the average length of residence of its inhabitants are both factors which seem to vary positively with the intensity and extensiveness of neighbouring.[23] There are also well-established social class variations; characterized by Keller as 'working class solidarity, middle class selectivity and suburban sociability'.[24] But these are typically much finer, subtler and more complex than the familiar generalizations would suggest. For example, one of the most recent English studies reports 'no clear dichotomy' in either behaviour or attitudes to neighbouring between classes but, within this 'general similarity of response', notes that working class people tend to 'see' their neighbours more often, and that the street is a more common meeting place for them than for middle class people — a difference which would seem to spring from variations in built-form, mobility and occupation rather than from class as such.[25] More generally, class differences in neighbouring would appear to be rooted in the ways in which the meaning of class is bound up with and affected by (for example) mobility, income, kinship, age, residential arrangements, social service provision, occupational patterns; in other words more specific influences operating within the worlds of class. A typical instance is the finding of one study that while working class people express rather more positive attitudes about the desirability of contact with neighbours than middle class people, this difference is not reflected in any degree of greater neighbouring activity. The authors explain this absence of variation by pointing out that the working class people in their study *did* have a great deal more to do with their relations than the middle class people.[26] For practical purposes kinship replaced neighbouring in the functions through which strong relationships with neighbours might have been constructed. Similar observations could be made about the relationship between neighbouring and built-form, mobility, stages in the life-cycle and numerous other factors. What emerges consistently throughout is that neighbourliness is a social relationship facilitated or impeded by a wide array of social-structural influences but determined by none of them. Disraeli was wrong: modern society *does* acknowledge neighbours. And the social analysis of neighbouring is slowly moving away from the sweeping application of deterministic social theory towards the detailed empirical rediscovery of the conditions under which it does so.

Applied sociology is, therefore, a dialogue between social theory and social description. In the chapters that follow we attempt to develop such a dialogue about

UK society seen from the point of view of three of the most crucial and distinctive concerns of sociological analysis. We have not tried to take the further step, often also thought of as applied sociology, of deriving proposals for policy from our analysis, but will be satisfied if the sort of analysis we offer here enables the discussion of policy to proceed in a more perceptive context of interpretation. To adapt a famous observation: philosophers have sought to change the world; the task, however, is to interpret it.

Notes to Introduction

1   A. Sillitoe, *Britain in Figures* (Penguin edn. 1971).
2   HMSO, *Social Trends* (1971–6).
3   A. H. Halsey (ed.), *Trends in British Society since 1900* (London 1972).
4   A. Cherns (ed.), *Sociotechnics* (London 1976).
5   B. Hindess, *The Use of Official Statistics in Sociology* (London 1973).
6   T. Burns, 'Sociological Explanation', *British Journal of Sociology,* Vol. 18 (1967).
7   E. Durkheim, *The Division of Labour in Society* (London 1933), esp. Bk. 3.
8   P. Abrams, 'Age and Generation' in P. Barker (ed.), *A Sociological Portrait* (Penguin edn. 1972).
9   E. Still, 'The Fashion for Families', *New Society* (8.6.1967.).
10 B. Seebohm Rowntree, *Poverty: a Study of Town Life* (London 1910).
11 C. Phillipson, *The Emergence of Retirement,* Working Papers in Sociology, No. 14, University of Durham (1977).
12 See, especially, E. Shanas and G. Streib, *Social Structure and the Family*, Wiley, 1965.
13 R. Nisbet, *The Sociological Tradition* (London 1966), p. 47.
14 R. Nisbet, *op. cit.*
15 L. Wirth, 'Urbanism as a Way of Life', *American Journal of Sociology,* Vol. 44 (1938).
16 See, especially, C. Bell and H. Newby, *Community Studies* (London 1971).
17 S. Keller, *The Urban Neighbourhood* (New York 1968).
18 W. H. Key, 'Urbanism and Neighbouring', *Sociological Quarterly* (1965), p. 384.
19 M. Young and P. Wilmott, *Family and Kinship in East London,* (London 1957).
20 R. E. Pahl, 'The Rural-Urban Continuum', *Sociological Ruralis,* Vol. 6 (1966).
21 M. Stacey, 'The Myth of Community Studies', *British Journal of Sociology,* Vol. 20 (1969).
22 F. Robinson and P. Abrams, *What We Know About the Neighbours*, Rowntree Research Unit, University of Durham (1977).
23 See especially, H. Gans, *The Levittowners* (Penguin edn. 1967) and 'Urbanism and Suburbanism as Ways of Life' in R. Pahl (ed.), *Readings in Urban Sociology* (Oxford, 1968); also P. Wilmott, *The Evolution of a Community,* (London 1963).
24 S. Keller, *op. cit.*
25 Kingston Polytechnic, *The Buxton Report* (1976).
26 *Ibid.*

1

Social Change in the City: Structure and Process

INTRODUCTION

In this chapter we are concerned with cities in Britain — with recent changes in their social and spatial arrangements and with their relationships to social, economic and political processes in the wider society. In attempting any overview of urban developments in the post-war period it has to be admitted right from the start that the specifically sociological literature is sparse and typically rather narrow and atheoretical in character. In this country we have generally shown remarkably little curiosity about the sociology of our cities. Perhaps it is as Peter Hall and his colleagues suggest: 'The British are so conscious of being an urban nation that they treat the fact as self-evident; it does not occur to them to question it or to ask themselves what they mean by it.'[1]

Our 'urbanity' is something we can take for granted. After all, for the past seventy-five years this has been a thoroughly urbanized society, at least in the sense that the vast majority of the population has lived in urban centres. By 1901 77 per cent of the people in England and Wales were city-dwellers and that figure grew only marginally to the 80.8 per cent recorded in the 1951 census. Since then the proportion has declined and by 1971 was down to 78.3 per cent, reflecting both the voluntary and the contrived dispersal of fractions of the urban population. It is customary too to argue that we are urbanized in a more radical sense; that today the city is everywhere, its influence penetrating every corner of the country, its culture and institutions destroying the last signs of any real contrast between urban and rural.

It is partly for these reasons that we find so little sociological interest in the city. After all, in a totally urbanized society the context of human institutions and social processes is easily treated as constant and unproblematic. Even among the few sociologists who have devoted time and energy to the examination of urban phenomena there are misgivings about identifying patterns of behaviour or belief as specifically urban and this shows up in the frequent attempts to resist the usual institutionalization of their specialist concerns in an 'urban' sociology.[2] There is considerable sympathy with Max Weber's message that the city is dead.[3] It is dead because everywhere it has lost its autonomy and become subservient to the nation state. The city is dead because modes of action, patterns of thought and economic and social relationships which developed within it and once were distinctive, have now been diffused through almost the entire population.

But we must note too that the poverty of sociological enquiry about the city reflects the general development of the discipline in Britain. Until the 1960s sociology barely existed in this country. Anthropology was well-established in a few centres as a more acceptable and respectable enterprise and under its auspices some curiosity about the exotic tribes inhabiting our largely urban environments did develop. Interest in the early attempts to clear the slums and in the problems of those who were resettled in the peripheral housing estates had begun before the war[4] and the 'community studies' style of investigation flourished in the 1950s as students, trained principally in the structural functionalist traditions of social anthropology, set out to describe and analyse a series of local social systems.[5] Valuable as these pioneering efforts were they could not conceal the fact that sociology was still a puny infant struggling for a toehold in the universities and colleges; it was a long way from providing a large body of systematic knowledge relevant to the major social changes which were being engineered in that period immediately after the war. The Labour Government came to power in 1945 committed to a radical restructuring of British society. As part of this commitment, and drawing upon ideas which had been debated for more than a decade, it put in hand measures designed not simply to repair bomb damage but to reshape our urban environments in a fundamental way. Most of the ideas found their expression in the Town and Country Planning Act of 1947.

The lack of a mature sociology with established traditions of theory and research ensured that most of the problems of the cities were perceived and analysed in terms which were almost entirely *physical.* The schemes for redevelopment, renewal and the attendant movement of people, were conceived and executed with a minimum of concern about the social problems which they might generate for those whose lives would be immediately involved. The effects of that 1947 Act are immensely important. As a nation we engaged in the creation of new towns, we expanded smaller urban centres, cleared slums and rebuilt central areas and spent millions of pounds on huge public housing schemes. We conducted what were really massive social experiments, but we did remarkably little to monitor them, to assess their impact on the people concerned. Planning took shape — and has remained — as an enterprise engaged above all with the *physical* environment. The criticism and appraisal of urban life was, and is, conducted in terms which are primarily physical not social. At the point of its real development planning looked not to the social sciences but to those disciplines which traditionally manipulated the built environment: architecture and engineering.[6] Of course there were those who saw their task in a broader framework and attempted to relate their spatial preoccupations to the likely social consequences. Many of them cast around for a body of writing which would enable them to link their work to the needs and aspirations of those whose lives they would affect, but in their quest for an adequate sociology they were disappointed. Instead they found Lewis Mumford.[7] Admirable though his work is in many ways its continued influence on British planners, even into the 1960s, is an indictment of our indigenous sociology.

The creation of the post-war legislation was really the product of several distinct and sometimes conflicting interests. On the one hand there was the deeply entrenched concern with the growth of the cities. In the 1920s and 1930s there certainly had been very considerable growth, especially in the major towns and cities. London's population, for instance, grew from six million to eight million between 1919 and 1939, and, much more importantly, it expanded its land area almost five times.[8] The extension of road and rail networks, the government subsidies to developers and builders,[9] produced a rapid expansion of the major urban areas and these developments excited some ancient fears about the growth of the city. There can be no doubt that post-war legislation reflected this fear; the urban sprawl had to be contained, the countryside preserved. Thus a principal aim of planning was deeply conservative, seeking to prevent change, defending the interests of rural landowners and giving expression to the old mistrust of the city. But planning was not all negative. Alongside the conservatives, indeed allied with them at least for a while, we find advocates of more radical change. Men like Abercrombie and Osborn saw planning as an instrument for a more equitable distribution of resources, as a way of really ameliorating the lot of those condemned for years to live in squalor. Their claim to represent a more radical vision resides principally in their willingness to establish a high degree of public control of land and its development. The problems of cities could not be solved nor many of the difficulties of the new garden cities averted unless the free market in land was curtailed and public ownership established. Thus two very different views came together, each representing separate interests and seeking solutions to different problems but united, at least for a while, in their determination to see the machinery of rational planning set up. The alliance, however, was fragile and as the real import of the 1947 legislation was appreciated by those who owned land or who hoped to benefit from land development, it was shattered. By 1958, under a Tory government, the public control envisaged by the Act was largely removed.[10] By the mid-fifties planning in Britain was firmly established as a conservative force, its enthusiasm for containing urban growth an obvious representation of the interests of the counties and its engagement with social issues centred on the desire to produce harmonious, consensual 'communities'. Again the practical goals of establishing 'balanced' communities and carefully contrived 'neighbourhood units' drew support from diverse quarters. As the first study of a New Town[11] revealed, the Right wing could construe 'balancing' the community, that is, providing a broad social mix, as a scheme which would ensure community leadership by the middle class; for naïve socialists the idea had appeal as a move in the destruction of class barriers.

The period since 1945 is one of very considerable change in our urban environment. It is a period in which the determination to ensure a real extension of citizenship rights influenced the physical structure of our cities, just as it created the complex of institutions and fiscal measures which we call the welfare state. The last thirty years are the years of a novel and massive intervention by the state and by local authorities in the organization of space. But they are also years of unattained hopes and unredeemed promises. In the sphere of planning, as elsewhere, the euphoria of the immediate post-war period and the confidence that radical policies could produce a new egalitarianism gave way to scepticism and disillusion.

URBAN STRUCTURE

One of the most fundamental changes in the structure of our cities since the war can be found by looking at the housing market. In 1947 only 26 per cent of households in Britain owned their own homes, a few, 13 per cent, had council houses and flats but the majority, 61 per cent, rented from private landlords. The pattern in which only a minority owned housing was long established and although it is impossible to get accurate statistics it is likely that around the beginning of this century about 90 per cent of all households lived in accommodation rented from private landlords. During the twenties and thirties there took place an extraordinary burst of building activity along the major transportation routes into all the major cities. With government subsidies to railway companies and builders enormous areas of suburban housing were constructed, and many clerks and artisans and others of comparatively modest means became house owners.[12] At the same time local authorities began to attack the problem of the slums and the more general problems of housing the poor, and embarked on ambitious programmes of public housing. After 1945 these trends continued until by 1972 almost half of all households in the UK were living in owner-occupied houses; the local authorities and New Town corporations provided accommodation for one-third and the private landlords' share was reduced to a mere 17 per cent.

David Eversley's figures (see table 1.1) show in more detail just how the decline in the number of private landlords has taken place. The pattern is remarkably consistent and specific items of legislation, like the 1957 Rent Act passed by the Tory government and intended to make private rental a more attractive proposition, appear to have had little effect.

The reasons for the restructuring of the housing market are not hard to find. They relate principally to three things. First, the changing aspirations of a great many families and individuals. The pre-war, speculatively built estates had demonstrated that with a reasonable income and tolerable job security an artisan or a clerical worker really could own his own house. When the Tories came to power in 1951 they sought to extend private ownership and in a generally favourable economic climate were able to sustain and encourage the development of the private house

TABLE 1.1

Estimates of percentage distribution of dwellings and households in private tenure, 1947–73

	Area	Dwellings or households	Owner-occupied	Rented from local authority or New Town	Rented privately	Other tenures
1947	GB	hh	26	13	61	*
1950	GB	dw	29	18	45	3
1951	GB	dw	29	18	45	6
1958	England	hh	39	20	40	*
1960	GB	dw	42	27	26	6
1961	GB	dw	43	27	25	5
1961	GB	hh	41	26	28	6
1962	GB	dw	44	27	24	6
1962	England	hh	43	21	36	*
1964	GB	dw	46	28	21	5
1964	E & W	hh	46	26	28	*
1965	GB	dw	47	28	20	5
1966	GB	dw	47	29	19	5
1966	GB	hh	45	28	21	5
1969	GB	dw	49	30	16	5
1971	GB	hh	49	31	15	5
1971	E & W	hh	48	28	21	3
1972	GB	dw	51	31	13	5
1971	GB	dw	50	31	14	5
1972	UK	hh	47	33	17	3
1973	GB	dw	52	31	17	*

E & W – England and Wales   * included in 'rented privately'.
Source: D. Eversley, 'Landlords' Slow Goodbye' in *New Society* (16 Jan. 1975)

market. The Labour Party, which traditionally had put great stress on the necessity of more public housing to provide for the poor, by 1964 had become sharply sensitive to the changing ambitions and interests of a large and growing group of house-owners. By the 1970s the 'property-owning democracy' was an idea supported by all the major political parties. Thus the number of private landlords declined because economic and social conditions made possible the formation of many small households able to acquire a mortgage and the benefits of owner-occupation.[13]

Secondly, though, the pressure on landlords came from the public sector. If Labour has come to accept a part of a traditional Tory commitment to private ownership, the Tories for their part could not avoid the fact that support for local authority housing was a necessary and sizeable responsibility. Although encouragement was given by the Heath government (1970—4) for the sale of council houses there was no serious challenge to the principle of public housing. Indeed under Tory governments the renewal of slum clearance programmes in the fifties and the encouragement of ambitious programmes of urban redevelopment in the sixties ensured that local authorities would supplant many private landlords and even dispossess a good many owner-occupiers.

Thirdly, there is the economics of the landlord system. Ever since 1915 there have been controls on rent levels and on the conditions of eviction, and over the years these have made most forms of private rental economically unattractive. In 1972 the Family Expenditure Survey showed that 17 per cent of all privately un-furnished rents were beneath £40 per annum, and that a further 34 per cent were between £40 and £80 each year; and there is no doubt that in some areas, Scotland for instance, the structure of rents would produce even higher percentages in these low-rent categories.[14] The effects of rent levels coupled with the almost annual changes in legislation affecting a landlord's rights and responsibilities have meant that many are anxious to sell their property at the earliest opportunity and as Eversley observes: 'The rising price of even old property, the improvement grant obtainable on a very large scale after 1969 with no ties as to the future tenure of the premises, and the accelerated processes which created more small households with relatively high purchasing power, all played a role.'[15]

However, it looks as though the decline of the private landlord has been slowing down. In part this may be due to the fact that some landlords are choosing to change from unfurnished rentals — say on the death of a tenant enjoying a controlled tenancy — to furnished rentals for students or young couples which offer much higher returns and until very recently, much easier prospects of repossession.

One disturbing aspect of the changes in this sector of the market is the fact that the decline in the number of privately-rented dwellings is not matched by a comparable decline in the number of households or persons living in them. As Eversley points out, between 1961 and 1971 privately-rented dwellings in England and Wales fell by 40 per cent, households by only 22 per cent and the number of persons by 23 per cent.[16] And all in the sector of the housing market known to contain much property in the worst physical condition. In 1971 no less than 51.8 per cent of the unfit dwellings in England and Wales were rented from private individuals. Much of this housing is found in the old, declining districts near the city centres, often much of it has been transmitted by inheritance to owners who take no interest but leave all management to agents or lawyers to whom it is frequently more troublesome than profitable.[17]

The pressure on this kind of housing is enormous, for the demand for cheap

TABLE 1.2

Stock of buildings: change and tenure, UK

Thousands

	1951–60	1961–5	1966–70	1971	1972	1973	1974
Stock of dwellings – at end of period							
Owner-occupied	6,967	8,243	9,567	9,809	10,095	10,356	10,536
Rented from local authorities or New Town corporations	4,400	5,023	5,848	5,975	6,030	6,089	6,228
Rented from private owners Other tenures	4,306 927	3,589 946	3,768	3,673	3,549	3,436	3,331
Total	16,600	17,801	19,183	19,457	19,674	19,881	20,095
Annual Averages							
Annual net gain + or loss –:							
Total	+234	+240	+276	+242	+217	+207	+214

By nature of change:							
New construction –							
Public sector	+189	+145	+196	+168	+130	+113	+134
Local authorities	+169	+131	+174	+141	+111	+94	+109
New Town authorities	+9	+7	+11	+13	+10	+9	+12
housing associations	+4	+2	+6	+11	+8	+9	+10
government departments	+7	+5	+5	+3	+2	+2	+3
Private sector	+104	+195	+200	+196	+201	+191	+144
Other gains	+10	+8	+5	+8	+10	+12	+12
Slum clearance	-51	-79	-92	-99	-92	-85	-59
Other losses	-18	-27	-33	-31	-32	-24	-17
By tenure:							
Owner-occupied	+277	+255	+265	+242	+286	+261	+180
Rented from local authorities or New Town corporations	+187	+124	+165	+127	+55	+59	+139
Rented from private owners	-214	-143⎫	-154	-127	-124	-113	-105
Other tenures	-16	+4⎭					

Source: Department of the Environment, *Social Trends* (1975)

accommodation close to the heart of the city grows as more students attend colleges and universities, more young people move in search of jobs or are moved by their firms, as immigrant groups press into the central areas to find a niche in both the housing and the occupational systems, and as old folk wish to maintain households separate from their children. And in the foreseeable future the problems will get worse because the building of new housing will not take place at such a rate that the rules of eligibility will be changed. Students and young mobile people will still find many ahead of them in the housing queue. At the same time the cost of purchase has already moved ahead at such a pace that there has been a noticeable decline in the proportion of the population able to contemplate house-buying.

Tables 1.2 and 1.3 provide a description of the general housing stock and the changing distribution between the three main sectors. From table 1.2 the rapid development of private sector building is apparent. In 1951–60 there were far more new houses constructed by public authorities than by speculative builders, but by 1961–5 the private companies had almost doubled their annual average output and at no point from 1965–74 does the figure for local authority building surpass them, though comparison of annual gains by tenure for 1973 and 1974 reveals a very marked decline in the private sector and a dramatic increase in the public sector.

Of course, there exist considerable variations in the housing stock across the country and table 1.3 details some of the most important. Owner-occupation, as one would expect, is highest in the South East and the Outer Metropolitan Area and lowest in the North and in Scotland. Conversely, local authority housing makes up more than half of Scotland's entire housing stock and 40 per cent of that in the northern region. The high proportion of privately-rented housing in London is very noticeable and underlines the importance of looking behind the national statistics before concluding that such housing is now of little significance. The figures on the age of housing stock again point the contrast which exists in the London region, with the Greater London area having 39 per cent of its stock in the form of pre-1918 housing and only 30 per cent built since the war, whereas in the rest of the region more than half of the stock is post-war.

During the last decade, particularly in the big cities and especially in London, we have seen some of the more undesirable effects of a booming market in land and property. Throughout the sixties the demand for office space was high and the supply considerably restricted by the local planning authorities and by government determination to contain the growth of office work in central London. The moratorium on office development introduced by the Labour Minister, George Brown, in 1964 had the effect of forcing up prices in a dramatic way and in the past decade central and local government attempts to control office development have generally exerted a squeeze on the supply of office accommodation and contributed to the soaring prices. A Counter Information Services report[18] provided some comparative figures for 1972. First-class office space commanded annual rentals of £10 per square foot in the City, £8.50 in the West End. This compared with £8.00 for Paris, £4.00 for New York and £2.50 for Brussels. By 1974 firms were paying over £25 per square foot in London. In the late sixties property offered rich pickings for investors and while most of the activity was concentrated in the speculative development of office and commercial property the effects were clearly felt in the housing market. Banks and insurance companies and those administering pension funds, as well as hosts of smaller investors, found in property dealings quicker and larger profits than they could get from investment in manufacturing. Property development became really

TABLE 1.3

Stock of dwellings: by region, December 1974

| | Number of dwellings (millions) | | | Tenure of dwellings (percentages) | | | Age of dwellings (percentages) | | | |
| | | | | | Rented from | | | | | |
	In metropolitan counties	Elsewhere	Total	Owner occupied	Local authority	Private owner	Pre-1891	1891 to 1918	1919 to 1944	Post-1944
Standard regions										
Northern	0.44	0.70	1.14	44	40	16	15	17	22	46
Yorks. & Humberside	1.24	0.55	1.79	52	32	16	17	17	24	42
Midlands	—	1.35	1.35	55	28	17	18	14	22	46
Anglia	—	0.66	0.66	55	26	19	25	9	17	49
SE	2.63	3.47	6.10	54	26	20	17	15	26	42
Greater London	2.63	—	2.63	46	28	26	30	9	31	30
Rest of region	—	3.47	3.47	60	24	16	15	11	22	52
SW	—	1.55	1.55	61	22	17	24	12	19	45
W Midlands	0.95	0.85	1.80	54	33	13	14	13	26	47
NW	1.54	0.83	2.37	57	29	14	20	16	24	40
England	6.80	9.96	16.76	54	29	17	18	15	24	43
Wales	—	1.00	1.00	58	28	14	25	20	15	40
Scotland	0.57	1.30	1.87	33	54	13	15	18	19	48
Great Britain	7.37	12.26	19.63	52	31	17	18	15	23	44
N Ireland	—	0.47	0.47	48	37	15	13	21	16	50
United Kingdom	7.37	12.73	20.10	52	31	17	33		23	44

Source: *Social Trends* (1975)

big business and in 1974 companies like Land Securities Investment Trust had a capitalization of £166.3 millions, Metropolitan Estate and Property Company had £108.3 millions, St Martin's Property commanded nearly £88 million and the Hammerson Group more than £40 million.

One of the most notorious property companies and one which had large investments in domestic property was the Freshwater Group owned by William Stern. In their book Ambrose and Colenutt provide a good description of the practice of remortgaging which demonstrates the willingness of banks to advance money to speculative developers and illustrates clearly the margins of profit which a skilful entrepreneur could obtain:

> The company bought a shop and residential block in North London at a cost of £72,000. Freshwater obtained a £55,000 mortgage and found the extra £17,000 itself. The rents of the shops and flats were immediately pushed up so that yearly rental rose from £5,480 to £9,026, which in turn meant that the capital value of the block rose sharply. Three years after purchase the property was revalued at £115,000 and the company took a new mortgage on it, this time of £76,000. This was enough to repay the original mortgage and leave a surplus of £21,000. Thus, after three years the company had paid back its first mortgage, had got back all its own investment plus a bonus of £4,000, and on top of all that had taken £27,000 in rent. It also held the property as an enormously valuable asset.[19]

The effect of this kind of activity on the private house market was rapid inflation and an exacerbation of the housing problem. Table 1.4 tells some of the story.

Average house prices more than doubled between 1969 and 1973 and have continued to rise, but building societies advanced lower proportions of the purchase price leaving prospective buyers with sizeable capital sums to find. While borrowers' income rose considerably between 1969 and 1973 the ratio of house price to income, and advance to income, gave some indication of the growing financial burden which

TABLE 1.4

Building Societies: Dwelling prices, mortgage advances and incomes of borrowers, UK						
	1969	1970	1971	1972	1973	1974
Average price (£)						
All dwellings	4,640	4,975	5,632	7,374	9,942	10,990
New dwellings	4,736	5,051	5,609	6,988	9,683	11,114
Other dwellings	4,598	4,946	5,640	7,518	10,943	10,950
Average advance (£)	3,297	3,591	4,104	5,195	6,181	6,568
As a percentage of average price	71.1	72.2	72.9	70.5	62.2	59.8
Average recorded income of borrowers (£)	1,760	1,928	2,187	2,474	2,923	3,411
Ratio of price to income	2.64	2.58	2.58	2.98	3.40	3.22
Ratio of advance to income	1.87	1.86	1.88	2.10	2.11	1.93
Percentages of mortgages which are						
Option mortgages	6.1	6.5	8.7	20.6	19.3	16.9
To previous non-owner-occupiers	63.0	61.0	60.4	57.9	51.9	50.8

Source: *Social Trends* (1975)

TABLE 1.5

Housing subsidies and tax relief on mortgages, UK

	1960–1	1969–70	1970–1	1971–2	1972–3
Housing subsidies					
Government contribution (£ million) towards					
Conversion or improvement of existing dwellings					
By local authorities[1]	0.4	3.5	4.6	7.4	9.5
By private owners	2.9	12.9	14.6	17.7	25.5
Provision of permanent dwellings[2]	78.6	162.2	203.2[3]	239.6	276.0
Local authority rate fund contribution to housing revenue account (£ million)	32.9	102.5	97.6	79.6	60.7[4]
Average contribution per dwelling (£)					
Government contributions towards permanent dwellings	19	29	35	41	46
Local authority rate fund contribution	8	20	18	15	11
Tax relief on mortgages[5]					
Total benefit to house mortgagors (£ million)	–	235	300	340	390
Average benefit to house mortgagors (£)[6]	–	50	61	79	78

Notes:

1 Including the Scottish Special Housing Association and New Town authorities
2 Contributions under all subsidy legislation including subsidies to the New Town Commission, development corporations and certain housing associations, including the SSHA, and grants towards its deficits on housing revenue account
3 Not including £4.2 million in respect of grants for remedial works to multi-storey flats
4 Excluding £69 million rent rebate subsidy and £13 million rent allowance subsidy
5 Subsidy under the option mortgage scheme amounted to £28 million in 1972–73
6 Calculated by reference to owner-occupiers in receipt of tax relief on mortgage interest. If the average were calculated by reference to all owner-occupiers, including those not in receipt of tax relief, the figures would be: 1969–70 £25; 1970–1 £32; 1971–2 £35; 1972–3 £39.

Source: *Social Trends* (1974)

the inflation in prices created in this period and this is underlined by the steady decline in the percentage of mortgages going to first-time buyers. A corollary of the high prices and high interest rates is that the subsidy given to owner-occupiers in the form of tax relief increases considerably. In 1969–70 the benefit to mortgagors was £235 million; by 1972–3 it had reached £390 million and that in individual terms represents a subsidy of £50 per mortgagor in 1960–70 and £78 at the later date.

Since 1973 there is evidence that the inflationary pressures have eased and indeed in London and the South where the highest average prices were reached (£13,223 and £12,954 respectively in that year) there has been some slight decline, but in all other regions the pressure has continued, with Scotland's price rise (from £7,706 in 1973 to £9,247 in 1974) being easily the sharpest.

With very steep increases in purchase prices on the one hand and the marked decline in the rate of new construction in the public sector (as table 1.2 shows), the pressure on the already tight private rental market has grown alarmingly and the clearest evidence of the difficulties is found in the numbers of homeless families. Shelter, the housing organization, estimated that on 31 December 1973 there were 3,332 families in London living in temporary accommodation for the homeless. In England and Wales as a whole 30,586 people were housed in this way. In March 1973, 7,152 children were in care due to family homelessness or unsatisfactory home conditions. The proximate causes of homelessness are well known;[20] by far the largest number of applications for temporary accommodation list 'Action by Landlord' as the reason. Department of Health and Social Security statistics show plainly that of 13,790 applications in the Greater London area in 1973 more than 5,000 arose because landlords had secured Court Orders or (more commonly) had evicted the applicants in some other way.

The 1974 Rent Act, which was designed in part to give security of tenure to those in furnished accommodation, will not lead to any major improvement, for while it undoubtedly helps those confronted by unscrupulous landlords it does nothing to increase the overall supply of housing. Indeed, it is already being suggested that those with property to rent are currently not putting it on the market, because they fear that the provisions of the Act will not allow them to repossess the flats or houses at some point in the future. Thus the stock of rented accommodation is being reduced. It is also claimed that in inner city areas, especially in London, some property owners are avoiding the provisions of the Act by upgrading their property to the point where its rateable value takes it outside the statutory controls, and are then renting at extremely high levels to large companies or to a small population of very wealthy tenants. More commonly, it is claimed, landlords are turning their flats and houses into 'bed and breakfast' establishments. And some of them actually benefit from homelessness, for in the inner boroughs local councils have been forced to make increasing use of 'bed and breakfast' accommodation as shelter for the homeless!

There is no doubt that it is the inner city areas that have attracted most attention, not only from sociologists but from a host of other academics and from pressure groups and politicians. That is hardly surprising since it is the inner city which provides a good many of the most urgent problems and which affords an arena for some of the sharpest clashes of interest. The tensions between commercial and residential interests are most marked in the old areas close to the heart of the city, the arguments between public and private authorities are most strident here and it is here too that the established and immigrant populations confront each other most directly.

Traditionally, much of the academic and political concern with inner areas focused on the inadequacies of housing. The 'slum problem', the subject of debate and legislation from the mid-nineteenth century on, has been seen principally as a problem of decaying tenements and villas in the inner city. Although special Acts of Parliament gave to the Scottish cities (whose problems were perhaps the most acute) as early as the 1860s the power to undertake slum clearance programmes, the problem was not really tackled in a thoroughgoing way until the Housing Act of 1930. From the passsing of that Act until the outbreak of World War II there was considerable progress in attacking the old problem of the slums. Under that legislation government had for the first time provided an incentive in the form of per capita subsidies for those rehoused; this spurred local authorities to an unprecedented level of activity. In 1939, the year that war broke out, 90,000[21] houses were demolished: we have never again reached that figure. During the war that legislation was suspended and afterwards Aneurin Bevan kept the suspension order in force, for the first priority was not the removal of slums but the creation of new housing to replace that damaged by war. It was not until 1953 that the government, by then a Tory administration, turned its attention to slum clearance again. Thus, there was a long pause in the campaign against Britain's worst housing. The suspension of activities which might improve the conditions of those living in the most unsanitary conditions was justified in terms of the scarcity of resources and the pressing need to provide shelter for those with no home of their own at all, but in effect it represented a return to a situation in which the hopes of the worst-housed lay in the process known as 'filtering up'. Before the 1930 Housing Act it was assumed that if the housing stock were sufficiently increased then there would be a general movement of families into progressively better housing and thus the need to treat slum property directly would be reduced. The legislation of 1930 was specific recognition that such a process did not work and now in the post-war years the lesson was to be learned again. Our capacity to create new housing or to improve basically sound but rather decrepit property has never matched the demand for decent housing. The fact that more people marry and marry younger, that old people live longer and more frequently maintain a separate household, the mobility of young unmarrieds seeking work and education, all these factors increase the demand for housing, and in the heightened competition those living in the worst conditions found the notion of 'filtering up' a hollow hope.

In the late fifties and sixties the rate of slum clearance grew, indeed it was already growing before there was the change in government policy. By 1961 a rate of 60,000 demolitions per year was reached and that rate remained remarkably constant until the Labour government spurred local authorities to greater action in the late sixties. The level of activity has since declined from 70,000 in 1971 to 63,600 in 1973.

Over the years the attack on unfit housing has altered its character. If we trace the patterns over thirty years it is obvious that less and less clearance involves individual houses and more and more relates to sizeable areas which are designated for demolition. And it is clear too that the enthusiasm for policies of large-scale clearance soon brought vigorous protests and complaints from inhabitants of designated areas and from a growing number of environmental pressure groups. Clearance – or 'urban renewal' as it has been called – has often had sorry effects on those who inhabited the old working-class districts of the inner city. Much has been written about the destruction of a 'community' and a good deal of it romanticises working-class life, but it remains true that the bulldozers have destroyed much more than bricks and mortar. Some of the areas razed have had populations which were stable over many years, even over generations, and this stability, along with proximity and poverty, had produced in those who lived there a strong sense of attachment to the place and more importantly to the social networks of which they were a part. The 'mutuality of the oppressed', in Raymond Williams' phrase, gave rise to patterns of support and reciprocal aid, to local institutions like pubs, pawnshops and parlour stores geared to the economic circumstances of their clienteles and to moral orders rooted in the experience of poverty. Life was hard and insecure but it was made supportable by social and moral frameworks which were shared and by sanctions, codes and controls which were exercised by those who had to live by them.

The fragility of these social orders has been described many times in the literature on 'urban renewal'.[22] The breaking of familial bonds as young families were given priority over older people and childless couples and moved out to new housing estates, the stranding of the aged in progressively deserted, decrepit areas where shops, cinemas and places of employment were shut down, all this has been reported many times. So too have the problems of adjustment facing those who arrived at the new housing schemes deprived of those social ties which had traditionally offered some protection against irregular employment or low pay. For many the experience of indisputably better standards of housing has been accompanied by loneliness, continuing poverty and a new powerlessness and dependency. All too often the 'housing problem' has been tackled in isolation, and tower blocks and terraces have been built with little reference to employment prospects, to shopping or recreational requirements;[23] and on estates which number their inhabitants by the tens of thousands the salient codes and rules are not rooted in the lives of the people: they are bureaucratic rules imposed by distant authorities but reaching into the minutiae of everyday life. It is in this sense that writers like Goodman[24] have seen the clearances leading, not to improvement or liberation, but to a new repression. The indictments of housing policy, and in particular the criticisms of separating housing from general economic and industrial policy, show a wearisome similarity, from the earliest studies of pre-war housing estates[25] to the most recent official report on the inner areas of Liverpool, Birmingham and London.[26] The failure to integrate the policies of the Department of the Environment with those of the Department of Health and Social Security, the Home Office, the Department of Education and Science and the Ministries of Industry and Employment, has produced the bleak suburban estates with their many pockets of deprivation as well as the accelerating decay of the inner city itself. As studies both here and in other countries, especially America,[27] began to count the social as well as the economic cost, as critics revealed that it was frequently the relatively wealthy rather than the relatively poor, the incomers rather than the old inhabitants, who benefited from many of these programmes, so the emphasis of government policy changed. The 1964 Housing Act put the stress on improvement rather than demolition. Local authorities could establish areas for improvement in districts where a majority of the dwellings lacked basic amenities; landlords could be compelled to improve the standard of their property and municipalities were to encourage upgrading of housing through the use of grants. The effects of this legislation have so far been disappointing. The use of grants, for instance, has had only a marginal effect upon the quality of the housing stock.

Criticism of massive redevelopment schemes may have given some local authorities pause for thought; it probably encouraged a number to establish more sensible and sensitive measures for rehousing displaced populations, but it certainly did not halt the march of 'comprehensive' planning. Particularly in the last ten years local authorities have extended their activities in the housing field and in the name of redevelopment have undertaken the demolition of a good deal of housing not classified as slum property. In London, for instance, an unpublished GLC survey showed that 'between 1967 and 1971 some 91,300 houses were destroyed in Greater London — one in ten of all the houses in the city. And of these, no fewer than 54,000, or 59 per cent, had been reported in the 1967 Housing Condition Survey as being in "good" or "fair" condition.'[28]

In fact the justification for massive redevelopment schemes has shifted. No longer is it a matter of clearing obvious 'slums', instead the attack is now on the so-called 'twilight' areas within which many basically sound though rundown houses exist. The declared purpose of municipal activity is the provision of more and better housing, and in pursuit of this worthy aim a borough like Camden spent £45 million between 1965 and 1973. In doing so it has produced very few schemes in which there is a net increase in the housing stock. Indeed if we count the losses in 'bed spaces' over the years which the development process takes, then the action of the borough has led to an enormous net loss. It is not too much to claim that municipal efforts have contributed significantly to the 'housing stress' in the inner city areas, for under the 1957 Housing Act the council does not have to accept responsibility for rehousing all those who are displaced. In Camden it is estimated that only 54 per cent were rehoused — the rest had to find their own accommodation. Inevitably many must have squeezed into already overcrowded areas in this and adjacent boroughs.

The problem of the inner city areas has been compounded of many elements over the past two or three decades; of awful slums and milder forms of dilapidation in the housing stock; of private individuals and institutions unable or unwilling to rehabitate or rebuild; of public authorities pressing forward with sometimes ill-considered and destructive schemes. But it is made up too of changes in demographic patterns, of shifts of occupational structure and processes of differential migration.

POVERTY AND SOCIAL STRUCTURE

Most discussions of changes in the inner city begin by pointing to the evident decline in population in many districts. Thus, the Inner Areas Studies report[29] shows how in Liverpool the population of the inner area was approximately 300,000 in 1971, but forty years earlier the same area had housed 725,000; and that in the Small Heath district of Birmingham the population fell from 50,000 to around 32,000 between 1951 and 1976. At the same time it is evident that in the inner areas of many major cities there are concentrations of deprivation, neighbourhoods where many are unemployed or impoverished, where overcrowding is rife, housing conditions deplorable and educational provision inadequate. With the example of American cities before them this has led some commentators to argue that just as the outward migration of the relatively wealthy has left a poor black population to inhabit the inner areas there, so similar patterns of migration and changes in occupational structure have turned British inner cities into traps for the poor. Thus, Pahl[30] suggests that the general shift towards a service economy can be seen in the spatial organization of the city. As the professional and technical occupations grow, and with them the opportunities for highly-paid work, so also there develops a series of menial, unskilled jobs supporting these new activities. Within the city there are areal concentrations of these professional and technical occupations and whereas the professionals themselves are able to afford to live well away from their centrally-situated offices, those on whom they depend are less well-placed. For them the limitations of money dictate that they live near their work and this means struggling for a place in the areas of greatest housing stress. Following Harvey's suggestion[31] that there are unforeseen redistributions of real income taking place in the city, Pahl argues that we may be witnessing processes of pauperization as a result of the entrapment of these low-paid service workers in areas where housing costs are extremely high and public resources frequently thinly distributed.

The suspicion that processes like these could be in train persuaded other researchers to look more precisely at the issues and Lomas[32] examines the suggestion that there is real concentration of the low-paid, unskilled workers in the central areas. Although the available data are far from perfect he is able to show that at least in London the less-skilled workers are not becoming increasingly segregated from the rest of society and concentrated in the inner city. Many semi- and unskilled workers are to be found in areas a long way from the city core — which is not surprising when one considers the policies of industrial and residential location which have been pursued since the 1930s.

Dividing Greater London into four rings, Lomas is able to show that in 1966 the unskilled and semi-skilled were not heavily concentrated in the inner city area. It is true that within the inner districts the unskilled made up a higher proportion of the occupied population than in other districts but the differences are not very large, nor

TABLE 1.6

The less-skilled male workers in London, 1966

Males	Central Area	Inner London	Middle Ring	Outer London	Greater London
Numbers in specified socio-economic groups					
Personal service	11,290	10,240	9,410	11,130	42,070
Semi-skilled	19,820	74,820	100,620	117,730	312,990
Unskilled	16,410	62,250	62,350	55,630	196,640
Distribution of each SEG between zones					
Personal service	26.8	24.3	22.4	26.4	100.0
Semi-skilled	6.3	23.9	32.1	37.6	100.0
Unskilled	8.3	31.6	31.7	28.3	100.0
Each SEG as proportion of all workers					
Personal service	5.2	2.1	1.4	1.0	1.7
Semi-skilled	9.2	15.5	14.4	10.9	12.7
Unskilled	7.6	12.9	8.9	5.2	8.0
(Sub-total)	(22.0)	(30.5)	(24.7)	(17.1)	(22.4)
All economically active	216,170	481,980	695,960	1,074,190	2,468,300

Source: *10 per cent Sample Census* (1966); G. Lomas, 'Labour and Life in London', in D. Donnison and D. Eversley, *London: Urban Patterns, Problems and Policies*

is the proportion itself (12.9) very substantial. Lomas' data refer to 1966 but in a more recent study Hamnett[33] compares the patterns for 1961, 1966 and 1971 and his analysis of this Census material for those years corroborates Lomas' conclusion. It seems then that one of the fears expressed in the Strategic Plan for the South East is not really justified: the expansion of service industry does not appear to trap large numbers of low-skilled workers in the inner city. The very high concentrations of unskilled employees remain in those districts associated with traditional manufacturing and warehousing, by no means all in the central areas of the city.

Lomas also challenged the idea that the central area contains an inordinately high concentration of low-paid workers, a fear voiced in the Greater London Development Plan as well as the Strategic Plan for the South East and echoed in Pahl's essay.

The data from the New Earnings Survey and the 1966 Census do not support the suspicion, nor do Hamnett's findings encourage this belief. It is true that some of the occupations picked out by Pahl as representative of the changes taking place — messengers, clerks and catering and hotel workers — *are* associated with the central area, but as a fraction of all low-paid workers they are not really significant. Overall, low pay is not markedly biased towards the inner city districts.

TABLE 1.7

The lowest paid male occupations

Area of residence of workers	Labourers	Clerks	15 Others	Total
Numbers				
Central Area	11,680	20,710	28,120	60,510
Inner London	43,510	42,430	88,630	174,630
Middle Ring	47,100	72,460	94,420	213,980
Outer London	45,030	120,010	113,360	278,400
Greater London	147,320	255,670	324,530	727,520
Percentages				
Central Area	7.9	8.1	8.7	8.3
Inner London	29.5	16.6	27.3	24.0
Middle Ring	32.0	28.3	29.1	29.4
Outer London	30.6	47.0	34.9	38.3
Greater London	100.0	100.0	100.0	100.0

Note:

The seventeen occupations in which over 35 per cent of all male workers earn less than £20 week (gross) are included. The residential distribution of male workers in these occupations is calculated from the 1966 Census of Population. The occupations are as follows: Caretaker, office-keeper (83.6 per cent); shop salesman, assistant (72.3 per cent); routine clerk (71.2 per cent); cleaner (69.6 per cent); storekeeper warehouseman (65.1 per cent) goods porter (64.6 per cent); guard watchman (39.7 per cent); labourer (56.3 per cent); roundsman, retail sales (54.3 per cent); male nurse (53.0 per cent); chef, cook (51.7 per cent); postman, male sorter (50.7 per cent); messenger (50.7 per cent); packer, bottler, canner (49.8 per cent); bus conductor (37.7 per cent); painter and decorator (35.3 per cent)

Sources: *New Earnings Survey* (1968); *Census of Population* (1966). G. Lomas, 'Labour and Life in London', in D. Donnison and D. Eversley, *London: Urban Patterns, Problems and Policies*

Most of those who have commented on this 'pauperization' thesis have linked their remarks about the concentration of poverty in the inner city to assessments of the economic position of coloured immigrants and Lomas' data do indeed show that there is a marked concentration of black immigrants in the less-skilled jobs and that they are concentrated in areas of housing stress near the city centre. To talk of black 'ghettos' is hardly warranted since black households would make up a majority of residents only in very small areas; the situation is not yet analagous to that in many major American cities, but there most certainly is a spatial representation of the life chances of black immigrants. It is also true that among the black population, and especially among the young men, unemployment is noticeably higher than for the population of London as a whole. Even in periods when the demand for labour is high, as in the mid-sixties, the central areas did contain enclaves of high unemployment and among immigrant groups the geographical concentration of unemployment was easily seen. Lomas[34] shows that more than half the West Indian unemployed, for example, were found in just six Employment Exchange areas.

The suggestion that the inner city areas are characterized by progressive impoverishment cannot then be accepted as a valid generalization about London. Nor will it hold for other cities. This is not to deny that within the inner districts there *are* pockets of poverty and misery, but as the statistical analyses by the Department of the Environment[35] and by city authorities themselves[36] reveal, the problems are not *exclusively* inner city problems. Overcrowding, unemployment, poor health, low levels of education – these and many other 'problems' exist in peripheral as well as central areas. There is some danger that in the current wave of enquiry and policy-making the issues will be treated too narrowly, the problems tackled on too localized a scale, that the inner city will receive 'aid' or special treatment while decaying suburban areas and ageing public housing areas, often on the city fringe, will be ignored. The fact is, the problems of the inner city cannot be divorced from policies for housing, employment, education and welfare which operate for the city as a whole.

GENTRIFICATION

In sharp contrast to the 'impoverishment' thesis discussed above there is another view of important changes in the social composition of inner city areas in which it is claimed that the most remarkable trend is the growth in the proportion of those in high-status occupations living in the inner districts. Ruth Glass described the process whereby those of lower economic status were displaced by the relatively wealthy managers and professionals as 'gentrification' and a number of recent studies, in very different ways, provide corroboration of her general observation. Hamnett,[37] for instance, shows that between 1966 and 1971 the percentage of managers and professionals in inner London increased by nearly 6 per cent and he argued that over the decade 1961–71 the figures show quite clearly an upward shift in the socio-economic composition of the inner districts. In part this is explained by general shifts in occupational structure, with the emergence of more and more professional, scientific and technical occupations and the reduction in less-skilled jobs, and this makes intelligible the fact that accompanying the growth of these occupations in the centre there is also a sizeable 'export' of professional and managerial workers to outer areas of the metropolis. And one must recognize that behind the very noticeable percentage increase of these groups there lies the large overall loss in the economically active population of inner London as a whole. Nevertheless, 'gentrification' describes a real and important change in these areas. In order to explain it we need to consider some broad features of city development over the past thirty years or so.

The planning legislation since 1945 has contained and shaped the patterns of urban growth and prevented many of the most unsightly ribbon developments and manifestations of urban sprawl which marked earlier phases of city growth. However, the process of suburbanization has not been halted and around most of our towns new housing areas have opened up to meet the demands of the rising population and the increasing rate of household formation. Small towns in the neighbourhood of the cities have been surrounded by large estates of speculatively built housing while villages and hamlets many miles from urban centres have accommodated smaller, more 'select' developments, or have found many of their existing buildings occupied by townsmen.[38] As in North America, the move out of the city has been selective, consisting for the most part of the relatively wealthy and young. But the search for a better, freer residential environment has brought its own problems. The advantages of suburban living have to be weighed against the difficulties and expenses of commuting and as the roads and railways have become more congested, as public transport has declined in the face of the increasing use of private cars, so the balance sheet has been reappraised. For some middle-class families the city areas once again have begun to look attractive.

At the same time the city fathers have lamented the loss of middle income-earners. They have bemoaned the inability to tax those commuters who take advantage of the cities' facilities but do not contribute to their upkeep; they have worried over the cultural and economic life of a city deprived of those whose budgets and tastes keep theatres, concert halls and specialist associations and shops alive. In consequence they have been interested in encouraging the relatively wealthy to stay and have even sought to promote the return of some who joined the suburban exodus. Their efforts in this direction have been assisted by the emergence of well-organized pressure groups concerned with 'conservation', 'preservation' and 'environmental protection', for these lobbies have been sharp in their condemnation of many of the large redevelopment schemes and passionate in their advocacy of 'rehabilitation'. Typically, their prime interests are cultural or aesthetic. A building in a street should be preserved because it is a good example of a specific cultural or historical development but from time to time the argument comes down to simple economics: it would be cheaper to restore and renovate than to destroy and rebuild. Occasionally the aesthetes ally themselves with those whose concern is principally with the social effects of large-scale urban renewal, whose interests lie in the preservation of communities or who defend the rights of the relatively poor to stay in the central areas rather than be 'decanted' to peripheral housing schemes. With such diverse support it is small wonder that by the late 1960s rehabilitation became fashionable and central government policy, through systems of grants and loans, encouraged the upgrading of whole areas. The effects were not entirely as expected.

Property dealers were quick to see the potential for profit and there soon sprang up a flourishing trade in houses which had been improved and modernized by the property agents or were sold as suitable for such a grant-aided facelift by an enterprising owner. Buildings with the slightest pretensions to architectural merit or interest became 'houses of character' to be disposed of to middle-class buyers. With a little capital, a grant for rewiring, replumbing and structural repairs, many Victorian houses could be upgraded and provide better accommodation than that offered by the average new houses. The government hoped that the financial assistance provided through the local authorities would benefit principally the owner-occupiers or owners of rented property and that out of their individual efforts would come a real improvement in the quality of the housing stock. All too often, though, it was the property speculator who saw the opportunities and who made a profit from the public purse and it was not the existing tenants who benefited from the renovation of property but typically a much wealthier person who became the new tenant or new owner. The 1969 legislation encouraged the 'gentrification' process.

In its general form, though, the process whereby the relatively wealthy ousted the relatively poor from some of the inner city districts had been going on for several years. The Milner Holland Committee[39] provided one of the earliest accounts of what can happen when developers decide that an area is ripe for rehabilitation. Pressures would be put on sitting tenants or owner-occupiers to move or to sell. Financial inducements might be followed by threats and harassment and when these succeeded the flats and houses could be sold or renovated, their prices or rents being raised to levels which only the comparatively rich could afford. In this way the social composition of apartment blocks, streets and whole areas has been changed.

A study by Ferris[40] offers an excellent description of the conflict between the middle-class incomers and the existing, largely working-class population in one area. He documents and analyses the confrontations between the organizations formed to represent the divergent interests of the two groups and their difference of opinion about planning proposals for the area. The wealthier, better-educated group was able to mobilize opinion and exert pressure through the judicious use of expertise and the scheme which they favoured was the one eventually implemented by the council. Gentrification then can be seen not only as the supplanting of one social group by another but the extension of the interests and influence of the more powerful 'incomers' throughout the area. In pressing for environmental changes consistent with their life-style and incomes they ensure that the incursions of the relatively wealthy will continue, their claim to the territory will be consolidated.

A report which contains more information about the gentrification process is that provided by Counter Information Services[41] in which the unintended consequences of the legislation designed to encourage the improvement of owner-occupied and privately rented properties are traced out. The 1969 legislation rapidly turned into a massive tax subsidy for property companies. 'In Hammersmith, for years a rundown working class area, the council has paid out £950,000 in improvement grants, and property developers have received £700,000 of it. Between 1971 and 1972 landlords and developers in Kensington and Chelsea received almost 70 per cent of the grants, in Hammersmith 67 per cent and in Westminster 64 per cent.'[42]

North Kensington and districts which were 'improved' by property companies have changed from 'low rent' to 'high rent' areas. Cheap 'flats' have become luxury 'apartments' and rents of less than £5 a week (in 1972) have multiplied by a factor of 3, 4 or 5. The profits from such ventures have been enormous. 'Properly done, conversions are the next best thing to counterfeiting money' said the London Property Letter and there can be no doubt that prior to the current economic recession the extraordinary sums to be made in this way by developers and speculators provided much of the force for the wild inflationary spiral in house prices in the early 1970s. The effect has been to reduce even further the prospects of decent housing for the poorer sectors of the population in the central city area.

But gentrification is also a product of municipal housing programmes. With the encouragement of central government and under pressure from the conservationist lobbies, the local authorities began their own schemes of restoration and renovation and there is no doubt that buildings in many inner city districts have benefited from these 'facelift' schemes. But rehabilitation rather than redevelopment did not invariably lead to benefits for the inhabitants. In many cases it still meant that poor families with little prospect of council housing or owner-occupation were forced into already overcrowded low-rent areas or at best were rehoused in public housing estates, typically far from the central city areas with their familiar social and economic relations and institutions. Edinburgh provides an example of just such a process. Its famous Royal Mile has been subject to a good deal of restoration and some rebuilding which in recent years has produced good housing, vastly better than much of the squalid property which was there. But for those who once lived in the street rehabilitation has brought a flat in a suburban housing estate, while a noticeably wealthier population has moved into this desirably central location. Initially rents in the refurbished properties were determined by a system of competitive bidding among those who wished to live in such historic surroundings and although owned by the municipality, accommodation here was treated quite separately from the rest of the public housing stock. The Royal Mile is a tourist attraction, its buildings and its inhabitants are seen by almost every visitor. The 'improvement' in its character has meant not just expensive restoration and rebuilding but a consciously engineered change in its population. It has effectively been 'gentrified'.

RACE AND THE INNER CITY

No account of changes in the inner city can ignore the issue of race. The appearance of coloured communities in major cities like London, Birmingham and Glasgow has been used by politicians to create a good deal of alarm and to raise the spectre of violent confrontations between black and white on the pattern established in many of the northern cities of the USA. The growth of the immigrant population has been rapid. In 1961 there were fewer than 300,000 coloured people settled in Britain, by 1974 the figure was 1,744,000.[43] However, the rate of growth has recently been checked, partly by legislation restricting the flow of new immigrants and partly by a reduction in the rate of natural increase among those already settled here. Between 1966 and 1974 the coloured population grew from 2.1 per cent to 3.2 per cent of the total population but the concern with those from the so-called New Commonwealth was stimulated less by this overall growth than by the emergence of areas with sizeable concentrations of Asian and West Indian migrants. Some districts have become publicly identified with particular ethnic groups. In London, for instance, Southall is an 'Asian' area, while Brixton has for many years been identified with the West Indian community.

The forces which make for these concentrations of coloured population are not difficult to establish. Many migrants arrive with relatively few skills and little capital. They look for work and for housing in areas where industries provide a demand for unskilled labour and where housing is relatively cheap and accessible. In the first instance at least they lack the money to buy private houses and their recent arrival makes them ineligible for council housing. At the same time there are positive inducements to live close to fellow-countrymen or at least other newcomers. Coping with the problems of employment or housing is easier when shared with others in a similar situation and it is good to hear familiar accents, to share some common assumptions or specific religions or social values. It is true too that the newcomers, especially if they are black, face hostility from the indigenous population and this too creates pressure for spatial segregation.

The emergence of visible immigrant communities and the political storms over immigration policy have led to a number of sociological studies over the past decade. Out of these have come not only a more precise description and analysis of the problems faced by the migrants, but also a series of general propositions about the structuring of relationships in the city. Most writers have concluded that the immigrant populations do not face or create any really new problems in employment or housing; they reveal the fundamental weaknesses in our system for allocating or distributing resources.[44] Prejudice and discrimination exist of course, but they will not stand as the most important elements in any explanation of the position of black immigrants in the markets for jobs or houses.

One writer who has been consistently interested in the problems of race in the city is Rex and from his original study, conducted with Robert Moore, there emerged a good discussion of the factors creating segregation and also a general theory with which to comprehend the physical and social structuring of the city.

In their study of the Sparkbrook area of Birmingham Rex and Moore[45] looked at the classic situation of a somewhat rundown central city area offering a variety of relatively cheap housing, which was being 'invaded' by immigrants. In their work these authors tried to provide an analysis which focused not simply upon racial antagonisms but upon the interests generated by occupancy, ownership, or specific kinds of housing, and the ways in which these interests often crossed rather than ran parallel to the boundaries of ethnicity. In a subsequent article Rex developed some of these ideas and produced a theory of 'housing classes',[46] in which he depicted a class struggle over the use of housing as the central process in the city. Spatial segregation then was a function of differential access to particular sectors of the housing market. The city was represented as a system within which conflicts revolved principally around the different interests generated by the varieties of ownership and tenure. The outright owner of a desirable house in the suburbs had quite different interests from the tenant of a purpose-built council house; the mortgage-paying owner-occupier had different interests from the tenant of a slum property held by the municipality or by private landlords; and the lodging-house owners who had converted large Edwardian or Victorian villas to multiple occupancy had interests different from their lodgers. In the specific situation of Sparkbrook it was possible to show how the diverse 'classes' (and of course not all of the seven housing classes identified by Rex were represented there) developed patterns of antipathy and antagonism, allegiance and coalition.

The idea of housing classes sharpened awareness of some of the fundamental economic constraints under which the groups concerned, and especially the immigrants, were forced to operate. Rex provided a good analysis of the reasons why some immigrants appeared in such districts as the owners of large properties which they divided and sub-let, commonly though not invariably, to other immigrants. The immigrant was often effectively excluded by the rules of eligibility from the public housing stock. As a newcomer he could not meet the residency requirements and consequently could not even be put on the waiting-list of some local authorities.

At best he would rank low in the points system operated by those who were willing to give him a place in the queue. At the same time he was commonly excluded from the market for private housing, being judged a poor risk by cautious building societies. So all that was left was the shrinking sector of privately-rented flats and rooms, commonly expensive, mostly providing poor accommodation in run-down districts of the city, or the purchase of a large property financed by a high-interest loan from a moneylender. If the rates of repayment for the latter were exceedingly high, at least the house was large enough to split up and sub-let and that way the debt could be managed. Other writers have provided corroborative evidence on this, some of them exploring more fully the role of building society managers and estate agents. What Rex does is to give us a model of the city as a system in which the life chances of individuals are shaped not only by their positions in the labour market but also by their relationship to housing as a scarce resource. Within the city there is a pervasive struggle over housing; individuals and groups are differently located in the market or the allocative system for housing. Their chances in the competition for housing reflect the economic resources which they bring to the market or the standing which they enjoy as the bureaucratic order of eligibility. The housing which they occupy and their prospects for future accommodation generate specific interests — class interests according to Rex. To analyse the situation of the immigrants and their relations with the indigenous population it is not enough to conceive of the issues in terms of racial prejudice or discrimination. What we need is a comprehensive treatment of the city as a system for the creation, distribution and consumption of resources like housing, education and medicine. Rex provides a starting-point. His scheme has, of course, attracted a good deal of criticism; the most stringent came from Roy Haddon in an interesting, if rather inaccessible, article in which, apart from taking Rex to task on a number of issues, he also underlines and amplifies an argument which has attracted a good deal of discussion in the general urban literature. In stressing the constraints which immigrants face Haddon insists that we must pay particular attention to the 'means of access' and 'rules of eligibility' which govern housing. Thus in looking at the experience of immigrant groups it is essential to observe the ways in which they negotiate these 'means' and 'rules'. In their search for housing immigrants are faced with a series of individuals whose decisions crucially affect their prospects. The route to owner-occupation is guarded by estate agents and building society managers, eligibility for public housing is assessed by public servants in the municipal housing departments and allocation to particular estates influenced by housing inspectors and social workers as well as the staff of the housing manager. Thus in both the public and the private sector there are important 'gatekeepers' who play, as Pahl[47] has frequently argued, an important part in the management of the urban system. The career contingencies of immigrants in the housing market depend very much upon the decisions of those whom Lipsky has called the 'street level bureaucrats'[48]. Haddon concentrates on the 'means of access' and 'rules of eligibility' governing public housing in London, highlighting the fact that the recent migrant finds himself with low priority on the general waiting-list. He is, after all, a newcomer and even if he is able to register for public housing he may not be deemed 'eligible' until he has fulfilled residential qualifications — most commonly five years' residence in Greater London, the last year having been in the borough to which application is made. And matters are made worse if the points system weighs heavily in favour of long residence in this area. As far as re-housing from redevelopment areas is concerned — a second 'means of access' — it appears that the areas most commonly treated to comprehensive redevelopment are typically long-established ones whose population is well-entrenched and contains few immigrants. Furthermore, legislation concerning rehousing from redevelopment areas confers a good deal of discretion on the part of local authorities, with the result that those who are sub-tenants, furnished tenants and lodgers are frequently not provided with alternative accommodation. A good many immigrants thus find this route into public housing closed off. If they turn to the private market they encounter there a variety of discriminating practices over the raising of mortgages, or the 'steering' of buyers towards 'suitable' areas so that the houses which are acquired tend to be concentrated in the older, often central areas of towns. Nonetheless, for some immigrant groups, Asians for instance, the propensity to own is quite high and following Thernstrom's work[49] it is tempting to see the acquisition of property on even this petty scale as a kind of social mobility. Certainly the ownership of domestic property, if accomplished in the way described earlier, does mean that some immigrants find themselves playing the role of small businessmen. The property-owner becomes a landlord and under certain circumstances, even in a market as relatively tightly controlled as ours, that can be profitable. Owning a few rooms requires little initial capital but like the ownership of restaurants or shops it does enable some immigrants to occupy familiar and relatively lucrative roles, Thus, the acquisition of petty property and the enactment of the role of small businessmen may be seen as a kind of accommodation to the host society.[50]

If rental is the only solution then there are strong pressures inducing immigrants to concentrate in 'zones of transition', in the way Rex has suggested, and to rent furnished accommodation in owner-occupied housing. The immigrant is heavily dependent on personal connections both in order to find housing and also to accommodate himself to the new society. The search for housing frequently involves the quest for, or the maintenance of, a 'primary community',[51] a small network of social relations linking those with whom the immigrant can share basic beliefs, can recount common experiences or cherish similar hopes. But taking privately rented accommodation frequently brings problems, not least problems of insecurity and forced mobility. Until the most recent legislation tenants in furnished rooms had little security of tenure. For the immigrant, whose best hope of decent housing lay in the public sector, this was doubly disadvantageous, for the process of mobility frequently took him across administrative boundaries, often reducing his eligibility for local authority housing.

Overall, the picture that emerges from recent studies is one which highlights the difficulties of dispersal and the likelihood of increasing concentrations of blacks, both immigrants and native-born, in the twilight areas of our cities. Davies and Newton[52] in their study of Birmingham have shown how processes of selective immigration are producing areas of greater homogeneity. Between 1961 and 1966 coloured immigrants replaced Irish families in a number of the city's older areas, the largest increase in the numbers of coloured people occurring in those areas where there were already the most sizeable coloured communities. Thus the pattern of Irish and coloured immigrants living together in the same districts appears to be giving way to more sharply segregated arrangements. The Irish face relatively little resistance to their dispersal from the inner city. (Peach[53] for instance, was able to show that in Birmingham there were no enumeration districts without some Irish population but more than 50 per cent of that city's enumeration districts contained no West Indians.) Living for the most part in towns with decreasing populations, in urban areas of net outward migration, in districts with the highest proportion of rented (and typically poor) housing, in areas with very high population densities and with large proportions of young people, and in the twilight zones where educational provision and job opportunities are restricted, the coloured communities are not likely to disperse rapidly. Most individuals, at least in the short run, will lack the economic resources to buy property other than that found in, or adjacent to, these 'zones of transition' and municipal policies are unlikely to lead to any sizeable relocation of these populations.

In many major urban centres the black communities are consolidating themselves, establishing new and distinctive institutional and organizational frameworks or setting their own cultural imprint upon existing ones. Places of entertainment, of worship, shops and businesses, are increasingly created, run and owned by immigrants and this can be a source of pride and strength. But it can also help develop a sharply differentiated, encapsulated world and a progressive alienation from a white society at best indifferent and commonly hostile to the immigrants. The racial murders in Greenford and Southall in 1974 and 1975 and the 'Carnival' riots in August 1976 and 1977 reveal something of the tension which exists in many areas, and the anger and indignation evident in a publication like *Race Today* reflect the sentiments of black citizens who are well-informed about inequalities in housing and in jobs. To talk of 'black ghettos' in British cities may be alarmist, but to ignore the forces making for greater spatial and moral divisions would be complacent.

SOCIAL SEGREGATION

So far we have been concerned largely with the processes that shape the inner city but we need to look too at the changing social and spatial arrangements in a wider perspective. For many years the patterns of land use, and their development and alteration, have attracted the attention of sociologists, geographers and economists. Burgess's concentric zone model, Hoyt's sectoral development theory, Harris and Ulman and their Multiple Nucleii Scheme, these and many other attempts to describe and analyse the physical structure of cities continue to sustain academic debate.

In recent years a number of projects very firmly located in this tradition of urban ecology have been completed in Britain and they cast light upon processes of residential segregation in particular towns.

Perhaps the best study in this genre is that made by Robson.[54] He provides an excellent discussion of the development of urban ecology and then proceeds to examine the changing patterns of land-use in Sunderland in an attempt to understand the forces which have given this town its present shape and to assess the usefulness of the traditional ecological models. What he finds is that both of the major models are relevant, the northern part of the town showing the concentric circle pattern with low-value housing (he bases much of his analysis on rateable values) lying close to the river and to the industrial areas and rings of higher value property developing as one moves out from the centre. To the south the structure is wedge-shaped, with four distinct areas easily distinguished by their differing average rateable values and by their corresponding proximity to industry or open space. However, as has been observed in many studies, the sectoral development does have superimposed upon it some elements of concentric patterning. In this case the author shows how the distribution of sub-divided housing forms a zone common to both northern and southern areas and particularly to the south 'forms a broad girdle encircling the Central Business District.' Tracing the land-use patterns in 1850, 1892 and 1963, Robson is able to show how the highly-rated sector grew up along the original line of development, demonstrating the importance (which Hoyt stressed) of major lines of communication in shaping the distribution of housing for the relatively wealthy. The historical analysis also confirmed that the highly-rented sector first formed very close to the commercial and business areas and that its subsequent development greatly influenced the overall pattern of residential areas in Sunderland.

Robson's is a nice examination of the interplay of centrifugal and centripetal forces – the 'repulsion' of industrial districts and the 'attraction' of the central business areas – in determining residential patterns, and the importance of earlier geography in shaping the present outlines of the city. But, as he points out, the value of the traditional ecological models is today greatly limited because so much of the city's residential structure is now planned and undertaken by public and not private agencies.

A number of other studies in this mould have been summarized by Johnston[55] and it is clear that urban residential patterns in Britain do not conform to the major American models. Quite apart from the provision of public housing (and the scale of this, particularly in the Scottish cities, is often very large) there is the imposition of extensive planning controls which affect the zoning of industry, the siting of recreational developments and the location of shopping areas. Thus any contemporary analysis must recognize the existence of powerful political rather than economic mechanisms for determining land use.

An account of London's social ecology was provided by Westergaard in his contribution to *London: Aspects of Change.*[56] Using data from the 1951 and 1961 censuses he showed how selective migration had produced a series of concentric rings in which the status of residents increased with distance from the centre. But, as ever, the pattern was by no means perfect. The rings which were clearly developed to the south of the Thames were broken in the east and west, with long arms of working-class housing extending from the East End out beyond the boundary of the connurbation, and from the West End high-status accommodation stretching into the north-western suburbs.

Westergaard also provides data on journeys to work, on housing patterns, the structure of employment and the demographic profiles of various areas. This latter form of analysis, which may well be seen as a basic element in any sociological examination of the city, is found only rarely in contemporary work. It requires little imagination to see that variations or changes in demographic structure must have quite profound effects upon the patterns of neighbourhood life, the development of institutions and the forms of social organization. Westergaard's account does not link the demographic structure to specific social patterns but it does offer a useful description of the broad alignments of age and sex groupings which we find in particular districts. In the Central and West End areas the age structure is markedly different from that in the city as a whole, with very high proportions of young adults and very small proportions of children. These areas provide work, educational and recreational opportunities, but they do not offer suitable homes for people later in their lives. In the middle-ring suburbs the relatively low fertility and mortality of the middle-class inhabitants produces a demographic profile characterized by a small number of children and a large number of elderly people. By contrast, the outer suburbs, and particularly the areas of large public housing schemes, typically have very high proportions of children and young married adults and few in any other category. Surprisingly little sociological attention has been directed to the social implications of differences in age structure and the marked generational imbalances that exist, yet these affect the social and moral order of urban areas. The framing of social codes, the patterning of social behaviour, the operation of social control, all are vitally affected by basic demography.[57]

Some of the earliest studies of public housing in Britain did note the problems which stemmed from the distorted demography of the burgeoning council estates and the depleted areas of London's East End.[58] Both the young couples on new estates and the older generation left behind in the city had to find in neighbours and friends the support which otherwise would have come from kin. For the young it was difficult, for the old sometimes impossible, as the stories of long-unnoticed deaths and awful loneliness confirm. All too often the elderly have been stranded in areas whose population decline and demographic imbalance brought a reduction in employment, recreation and sociability. On the other hand, the council estates, although their population structures change over time, continue in their early years to have marked excesses of children and later of adolescents. In such areas the maintenance of informal social controls is seriously inhibited simply by the lack of older people whose presence, whose utilization of public space, whose scrutiny of youthful activities, establishes an elementary constraint.[59] The vandalism, neglect and petty crime evident in many public housing areas must be seen, at least in part, as the product of this elementary failure in informal social control. In some areas attempts have been made to produce more 'balanced' population structures on housing estates, but it remains administratively convenient, publicly justifiable and economical to create estates which are almost exclusively for the young and to pay little attention to the social consequences of these policies.

The ecology of London has continued to be of interest and Young and Willmott[60] have produced a new description of the patterns of class segregation in the metropolis. Their work suggests that instead of the usual concentric zones, the class pattern formed the shape of a cross and this is represented in fig. 1.1 where the shaded areas are districts in which 76 per cent or more of the employed men are found in social classes other than the Registrar General's class I and II. Conversely, the 'less working-class districts' are those with 25 per cent or more in classes I and II. The cross in which working people are concentrated runs east to west along the Thames Valley, north along the river Lea and to the south it follows rather roughly the valley of the river Wandle. The pattern is explained largely in terms of the location of industry, commerce and docking. Using the census data for 1951 and 1966 the authors argue that 'a process of differential migration was taking place. Higher-class people became relatively more concentrated in the central residential district, the suburban quarters and the Outer Metropolitan Area. Working-class people, especially the less skilled, became more concentrated in the cross. Thus economic and social trends in the London Region were, if anything, reinforcing its class geography.'[61]

The figures in table 1.8 reveal that the suburban quarters and the Outer Metropolitan Area had relatively large gains in Classes I and II but the cross gained less than average. On the other hand, the decreases in the proportion of Classes IV and V were smaller in the cross than in the centre and the OMA. The quarters seem to have acquired a higher-than-average proportion of the higher classes but to have lost less than the average of the partly skilled and unskilled.

Figure 1.1   Social Class in Greater London, 1966
Source: P. Willmott and M. Young, *The Symmetrical Family* (London 1973)

Willmott and Young argue that the basic pattern of class segregation was determined by geography and the growth of industry and communications but that this
has in recent years been reinforced, the degree of separation heightened, by processes
of differential migration. The effects of the increasing segregation of classes on
opportunities, living standards or patterns of social relations are not clearly established, but the authors conclude with the 'opinion' that increasing class concentration
is 'probably more harmful than beneficial and therefore that policy should seek to
check it.'[62]

Even more recently a study of Edinburgh's urban structure has produced some
very interesting findings which in many respects run parallel to those of Young and
Willmott.[63] Using the 1966 census data, Richardson and his colleagues assess the
degree of class segregation in the city by means of Duncan and his 'index of dis-
similarity'. The index expresses the percentage of one social class which would have
to change homes in order to be distributed among the enumeration districts in the
city in exactly the same proportions as another class. Regrouping the Registrar
General's seventeen socio-economic groups into six classes; (i) professional workers,
(ii) employers and managers, (iii) non-manual workers, (iv) foremen, skilled manual

TABLE 1.8

Summary of changes in social class of occupied and retired men in main types of district in London Metropolitan Region, 1951 and 1966

	Percentages					
(a) Distributions	1951			1966		
	I and II	III	IV and V	I and II	III	IV and V
Central residential district	29	45	31	36	39	25
Cross	13	54	33	16	54	30
Quarters	26	53	21	32	50	18
Outer Metropolitan Area	20	50	30	27	49	24
(b) Changes 1951–66	I and II	III	IV and V			
Central residential district	+7	−1	−6			
Cross	+3	No change	−3			
Quarters	+6	−3	−3			
Outer Metropolitan Area	+7	−1	−6			
London Metropolitan Region	+6	−1	−5			

Source: *The Symmetrical Family* (London 1973)

and own-account workers, (v) personal service workers, semi-skilled manual workers and agricultural workers (vi) unskilled manual workers, the authors show that Edinburgh is very highly segregated. Comparison with the figures for other cities which have been studied in this way make that plain. If we take the indices between the highest and the lowest class in Edinburgh the figure is 71 compared with 54 in Chicago, 46 in Oxford, 44 in Oslo and 53 in the Outer Metropolitan Area of Kent.[64] Using another measure, the 'index of segregation' which measures the degree to which each social class is contained within relatively homogeneous areas, the researchers were able to demonstrate that the upper and lower ends of the social hierarchy are very highly segregated. Again, the statistics show this kind of separation to be more marked in Edinburgh than in other urban areas on which we have comparative data.

Richardson and his colleagues also provide a map outlining the class differences between enumeration districts. The technique employed is essentially similar to that used by Moser and Scott.[65] Districts are categorized according to the proportion of their populations in the top two socio-economic groups (as defined in the 1966 census).

The pattern which emerges confirms the high degree of spatial segregation and the general shape is rather like that found by Willmott and Young in London. The most solidly working-class areas have developed around the port of Leith or on low ground which, in providing water or transportation routes, has attracted industry. The high-class areas are concentrated in the west and north-west and are well insulated from the effects of industry. The map has a powerfully 'sectoral' as opposed to a 'zonal' character and this in part reflects the interesting fact that many of the inner suburbs have not declined as the zonal theory implies, but have largely retained their social character and continued to attract families of relatively high

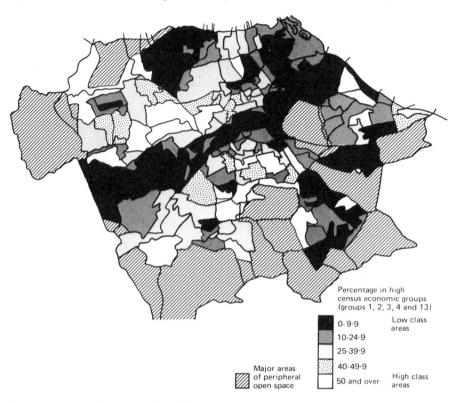

Figure 1.2   Social Segregation in Edinburgh
Source: H. Richardson, J. Vipond and R. Furbey, *Housing and Urban Spatial Structure* (London 1975)

socio-economic status. The analysis of house-purchase patterns over time shows how many of the inner areas have proved more, not less, attractive in recent years to some of Edinburgh's wealthier citizens. Like London, Edinburgh is marked by sharp differences in the class composition of its various districts and this research, using a wider array of techniques and sources of data, demonstrates even more clearly that the patterns of spatial segregation are becoming more, not less, marked.

In all the accounts of spatial structure it is very obvious that the historical development of a town, and in particular the growth of middle-class or wealthy residential areas and the opening up of transport routes, are extremely influential factors. A writer who has provided a good account of the importance of transport around London is Pollins[66] and his discussion reveals the extent to which the railway companies were constrained by political as well as economic factors. In the nineteenth century the companies did not rush to provide cheap fares for working men; they were pressured into doing so by governments. Often the provision of cheap workmen's tickets was the price they paid for demolishing rows of housing in the heart of the city, but the effect of these fare concessions on the spatial structure is seen to this day in those extensive 'arms' of working-class housing which stretch out along the old rail routes.

Workmen's trains thus had a considerable influence in developing the socio-geographical pattern of Greater London. There is plenty of evidence that working-class suburban settlement — due largely to workmen's fares on the railways — tended to be avoided by middle-class people. Thus, whereas the Walthamstow area was deficient of middle-class people, the new districts on another Great Eastern Railway Line — to Ongar — were almost entirely settled by middle-class people because, in the nineteenth century, there were no workmen's trains or workmen's fares on this line.[67]

At a later period the railway companies formed a deliberate policy which may be seen as a reaction to the political constraints under which they had been forced to operate. In the early years of this century they encouraged the creation of middle-class areas at some distance from the city. Conveying these commuters over fifteen or twenty miles was not only profitable but 'some companies argued that it was about time something was done for the middle class instead of concentrating on the working class all the time.'[68]

In related ways the history of tramcar, horse, bus and underground forms of transport all reveal the extent to which the organization of space in and around the city reflected not simply the working out of economic processes but also the effects of deliberate political decisions. Since the Second World War of course it has been roads rather than railways that have been at the centre of transport policy-making. It has been the growth of roads and the ownership of private cars which have facilitated the growth of the post-war suburbs and the even wider dispersion to dormitory villages on the urban fringe. The construction of ring-roads and urban motorways has cut swathes through the housing areas of many cities, and brought in its wake protest and confrontation between public authorities and citizens, accentuated spatial divisions between the classes and produced frequent demonstrations of the powerlessness of the relatively poor.

In general the literature on urban ecology underlines the processes maintaining and even heightening the segregation of different classes and status groups in Britain. It has long been the policy of planners to strive for 'balanced' communities but their efforts to provide a mixture of occupational groups have typically enjoyed short-run success at best. Even in the New Towns, where the range of occupational status is typically rather narrow, the planned social mix breaks down fairly quickly and many from the wealthier or more prestigious groups relocate themselves beyond the town in the rural but still accessible villages.[69] There are many factors which help to explain the persistence or growth of segregation. The creation of a large council estate is obviously one, for the provision of public housing helps sift and separate the relatively poor. In the private sector the growth of large building companies with their standardized housing, carefully graded in sophistication and price and often constructed in large, homogeneous estates encourages another process of segregation. Both public and private developments take place in a context of 'rational' planning with its insistence on the sharp definition of functions and usage of space, and this philosophy has frequently meant the destruction or re-organization of areas of economic and social diversity. And as education has become more important in terms of social mobility, as it has become more extensively provided and controlled by the state, so the attractions of a 'good' school have become more powerful and those who can afford to do so have moved into the appropriate catchment areas. The mechanism may change but space remains an important means of expressing and maintaining the boundaries of class and status.

These traditional studies of spatial structure still have value in providing basic descriptions of ecological arrangements and they hint at some of the processes which are involved in the social organization of space, but in recent years they have rightly come in for a good deal of criticism. It is indisputably true, as Castells, Harvey and other Marxists[70] have claimed, that urban sociology has traditionally been an awkward assemblage of disparate studies — lacking any real theoretical coherence. Many who do not share their general perspective would agree with these writers that such fragmentary atheoretical researches have made sociological studies of urban phenomena peripheral to the main strands of argument and interest within the discipline. Contemporary Marxian writing attempts to remedy that by insisting that we cannot understand the social and spatial development of urban areas unless we locate them in their proper economic and political context. Thus, to analyse what is going on in present-day western cities we must recognize that they are the product of, and are set in, specifically capitalist societies.

From the chaos of the conventional urban sociology we can rescue two broad lines of analysis, the first concerned with the 'production of space' and a second dealing with 'collective consumption'.[71] The utilization of space in the city then reflects the development of capitalism, the division of labour within it and the emergence of increasingly specialized agencies dealing with production, consumption, exchange and management. The shape of the city, the patterns of rebuilding, reflect the growing importance of financial and commercial institutions in a modern economy; old central city areas of working-class housing are frequently taken over and replaced by office blocks and shopping precincts.[72] Space in the city is a scarce, expensive commodity squabbled over by diverse interests. As such its disposition is a matter of intense political activity and it is this which leads Castells to argue that in studying the distribution of resources like housing, educational and medical services, in exploring 'collective consumption', we must develop a sociology of planning. Increasingly the state and the municipalities manage space, and planners and bureaucrats act in ways which typically (in this view) favour the interests of capital. Analysis of the processes whereby collective resources are managed must lie at the heart of any sociological interest in the city.

It is plain that many of the interests which Marxian writers wish to sustain and develop are shared by those whose intellectual debt is to Weber or Durkheim but the Marxists can legitimately claim that theirs is easily the most comprehensive and integrated conceptual scheme within which the current problems of the city may be explored.

CONCLUSIONS

In the last thirty years British cities have undergone major changes, many of which have contributed to an indisputable improvement in the lives and conditions of the mass of the people. Much of the worst housing has been demolished and other property upgraded, the state and the municipalities have accepted responsibility for housing the poorer, weaker sections of the community and the establishment of planning controls and building standards have ensured that, at least in terms of basic amenities, British housing compares very favourably with that in any continental countries.

But the task is by no means complete, for there remain awful pockets of poverty and deprivation. In areas like Clydeside the problems are extensive and deeply entrenched. The analysis of census data made in an unpublished report of the Department of the Environment[73] revealed the concentration of problems of unemployment, overcrowding and inadequate housing in Scottish cities and particularly in the Glasgow region. Examining the data on overcrowding and un-employment the report comments:

> Clydeside accounts for 29 per cent of enumeration districts in Great Britain in the worst 15 per cent on both indicators; at the 1 per cent level, Clydeside accounts for as much as 90 per cent of the enumeration districts in the worst 15 per cent on both indicators . . . This pattern is repeated for every combination of indicators tested, reinforcing the conclusion that when deprivation is measured at small-area level, Scotland and Clydeside have more of it than anywhere else; it is more severe there, and there is more of it in the same place.[74]

There is little doubt that in the future we shall need to establish massive programmes of aid to those pockets of deprivation in cities and regions where the measures of the past three decades have not been sufficiently comprehensive or inter-related to produce the economic regeneration which is required. The housing and employment problems are clearly beyond the capacities of local governments to tackle.

Even where the planners have been successful, their advances in providing better physical environments have to be set against less progressive changes of a social and political kind. Planning has meant the creation of bureaucracies for the management of change, it has meant the establishment of technical experts, of formally qualified controllers of almost all aspects of our environments. These rational procedures which have helped destroy the ugliness and squalor of the slums, which have reduced pollution, or have provided good houses and schools and areas of recreation, have also become oppressive. The apparatus of planning and management of urban resources is easily seen as alien and threatening, the rules and procedures established in the name of equity have a logic which all too often is impenetrable to the average citizen. Those most immediately dependent on the local authority bureaucrats, those who live in council property, find themselves hedged about by a plethora of rules and regulations, rules which they did not help to make and which they will have little part in changing. They find themselves, too, confronting a monolithic authority whose demands in terms of rents and rules are generally irresistible and whose responsiveness to local demands is frequently sluggish. The effect is to produce in domestic life a new kind of alienation. And it is not only those so directly influenced by the councils that we need consider, for the bureaucratic management of the environment and of urban resources touches most people. It typically re-inforces the sense of powerlessness, the remoteness from authority. Among the poor, dependent upon bureaucratic allocation for financial support as well as for housing, the effect is to reduce the citizen to the role of spectator. Matters which affect his life in the most immediate way are subject to control by others.[75] His prospects are negotiated for him by bureaucrats while he looks on, largely powerless to influence the decision-making. Democracy and bureaucracy are, at once, intimately linked and inevitably in opposition to one another. It is not conceivable that in a complex industrial society democracy could operate without bureaucracies but in the recent history of our cities the extensiveness of bureaucratic control has pro-duced in many a sense of social and political impotence.

Ironically, this has been brought about as a direct result of governments' determination to guarantee to individuals certain rights: rights to minimal levels of support and to minimal shares in the collective wealth of society. Since the war the nature of British capitalism has changed as competitive markets have given way to oligopolistic structures and the increasingly extensive allocative systems. The emergence of these allocative systems is based upon, and reinforces, a fundamental change in the nature of capitalism's central institution — private property. As C. B. Macpherson[76] has pointed out, the narrow materialistic conception of property as the right to *exclude* others from the benefit or use of something has given way to a much broader (and much older) view in which property is a right to the means of life and livelihood, and, indeed, there is reappearing the idea that 'a man has a property not just in the material means of life but in his life itself, in the realization of all his active potentialities.'[77]

National and local governments are increasingly being forced to respond to the demands of individuals for a share in the means of life and livelihood. Neither the 'right to work' nor the right to a 'minimum income' is yet firmly established but the right to the necessities of life, to food and to shelter *are* conceded and as governments acknowledge those rights so the traditional view of property is modified. What matters now is *access* to the means of life and livelihood: to housing and schools and opportunities for employment. More and more property is collective property and consequently much of the contemporary political conflict in the city is about access to this property and to a say in its control. The actions of rent-strikers, of squatters and the many forms of community action can be seen in this light. Pressing the claims of an ethnic minority for access to housing or other resources, challenging the right of councils to change specific patterns of land-use or to raise rent levels — these and many other sporadic protests are commonly focused upon, and serve to assert, the new sense of property. The changes are unlikely to amount to a dramatic, nationwide confrontation, for this is a quiet revolution. It will almost certainly take place as Macpherson says 'by a conjuncture of partial breakdowns of the political order and partial breakthroughs of public consciousness.'[78] The cities, and particularly the big cities, will provide the locus of this process.

Notes to Chapter 1

1   P.Hall, H.Gracey, R.Drewitt and R.Thomas, *The Containment of Urban England* (London 1973), p. 59.
2   See, for example, M.Castells, 'Y-a-t-il une sociologie urbaine?', *Sociologie du Travail*, No. 1 (1968).
3   M.Weber, *The City*, trans. D.Martindale and G.Neuwirth (New York 1958).
4   See R.Durant, *Watling: A Survey of Social Life on a New Housing Estate* (London 1959).
5   See, for example, L.Kuper, *Living in Towns* (London 1953); N.Dennis, F.Henriques and C.Slaughter, *Coal is Our Life* (London 1957); J.M.Mogey *Family and Neighbourhood: two studies in Oxford* (Oxford 1956); C.D.Mitchell, T.Lupton, M.Hodges and C.Smith, *Neighbourhood and Community* (Liverpool 1954).
6   On the effects of this process see M.Broady, *Planning for People* (London 1968).
7   Among Lewis Mumford's most influential writings are *The Culture of Cities* (London 1938); *City Development* (London 1946); and *The City in History* (London 1961).
8   P.Hall et al, p. 83.
9   See A.Jackson, *Semi-Detached London* (London 1973).
10 R.Glass, 'The Evaluation of Planning; some sociological considerations' *International Social Science Journal* Vol. XI, 3(1959) reprinted in A.Faludi (ed.), *A Reader in Planning Theory* (Oxford 1973), p. 51.
11 H.Orlans, *Stevenage: a sociological portrait of a New Town* (London 1952).
12 See A.Jackson, *op. cit.*
13 For discussion of the processes making for higher rates of household formation see J.B.Cullingworth, *Housing Needs and Planning Policy* (London 1960).
14 See J.B.Cullingworth, *Owner Occupation in Scotland and in England and Wales: A Comparative Study* (London 1969).
15 D.Eversley, 'Landlords' Slow Goodbye', *New Society* (15 January 1975).
16 *Ibid.*
17 A good deal of evidence on this is emerging in an ongoing study in Edinburgh. See B.Elliott and D.McCrone, 'Landlords in Edinburgh: some preliminary findings', *Sociological Review* Vol. 23, 3(1975).
18 Counter Information Services, *The Recurrent Crisis of London: anti-report on the property developers* (London 1973).
19 P.Ambrose and B.Colenutt, *The Property Machine* (Penguin edn. 1975), p. 45. See too O.Marriott, *The Property Boom* (London 1967).
20 See, for instance, J.Greve and D.Page, *Homelessness in London* (Edinburgh 1971).

21   J.English and P.Norman, 'One Hundred Years of Slum Clearance in England and Wales — Policies and Programmes 1868 to 1970', *Discussion Papers in Social Research*, No. 1 (University of Glasgow 1974).

22   There is a sizeable literature on programmes of redevelopment and renewal. In the United States one of the earliest and best assessments of these policies is H.Gans, *The Urban Villagers* (New York 1962). See, too, essays in his *People and Plans* (Penguin edn. 1972). Recent studies in Britain include N.Dennis, *People and Planning* (London 1970) and D.Muchnick, 'Urban Renewal in Liverpool: A Study of the Politics of Redevelopment', *Occasional Papers on Social Administration*, 33(London 1970).

23   Criticism of the earliest council schemes led in the 1940s and 1950s to an enthusiasm among planners and architects for the 'neighbourhood unit' idea in which populations and amenities would be related in such a way as to produce not just convenience but a positive sense of 'community'. The fact that in the surge of redevelopment in the 1960s so little attention was paid to these matters may be seen in part as a reaction to the perceived naivete of the neighbourhood unit idea.

24   R.Goodman, *After the Planners* (Pelican edn. 1972).

25   See R.Durant, *op. cit.*

26   Department of the Environment, *Inner Area Studies* (HMSO 1977).

27   J.O.Wilson, *Urban Renewal* (Cambridge, Mass. 1966); J.Jacobs, *The Death and Life of Great American Cities* (London 1962); N.Dennis, *People and Planning*; H.Gans, *The Urban Villagers*.

28   C.Booker and B.Gray, 'The Great Bulldozer Blunder', in the *Observer* (7 December 1975).

29   Department of the Environment, *Inner Areas Studies.*

30   R.Pahl, 'Poverty and the Urban System' in M.Chisholm and A.Manners, *Spatial Policy Problems of the British Economy* (Cambridge 1971).

31   D.Harvey, *Social Justice in the City* (London 1973).

32   G.Lomas, 'Life and Labour in London' in D.Donnison and D.Eversley, *London—Urban Patterns, Problems and Policies* (London 1973): a study sponsored by the Centre for Environmental Studies.

33   C.Hamnett, 'Social Change and Social Segregation in Inner London 1961—71', *Urban Studies*, Vol. 13, 3(1976).

34   G.Lomas, 'Life and Labour in London'.

35   Department of the Environment, *Census Indicators of Urban Deprivation*, Working Note No. 6 (1975).

36   *Urban Trends*, City of Newcastle-upon-Tyne Household Survey (1975).

37   C.Hamnett, *op. cit.*

38   R.Pahl, *Urbs in Rure; The metropolitan fringe in Hertfordshire* (1965). London School of Economics and Political Science, Geographical Papers No. 2 is one of the few studies of the invasion of village by middle-class commuters.

39   Milner Holland, *Report of the Committee on Housing in Greater London*, Cmnd 2605 (HMSO 1965).

40   J.Ferris, *Participation in Urban Planning: The Barnsbury Case — a study of environmental improvement in London* (London 1972).

41   Counter Information Services, *op. cit.*

42   *Ibid.*

43   'The Coloured Population of Great Britain', Runnymede Trust, Occasional

Reprint (1976).

44   E. Burney, *Housing on Trial* (London 1967) makes this point very forcibly. The presence of the immigrant serves simply to *reveal* the inadequacies of our housing system.

45   J. Rex and R. Moore, *Race, Community and Conflict: a study of Sparkbrook* (London 1967).

46   J. Rex, 'The Sociology of a Zone of Transition' in R. Pahl *Readings in Urban Sociology* (Oxford 1969); for further developments of Rex's interest in these matters see his *Race, Colonialism and the City* (London 1973). The best critique is that by R. Haddon, 'The Location of West Indians in the London Housing Market' *The New Atlantis,* Vol. 2, No. 1 (1970). Part of this article, though not the critique of Rex, is reprinted in C. Lambert and D. Weir, *Cities in Modern Britain* (Fontana edn. 1975).

47   R. Pahl, 'Urban Social Theory and Research' *Centre for Environmental Studies, Working Paper No. 5* (1969), reprinted in his book *Whose City*, and other essays on Sociology and Planning (Harlow 1970), 2nd edn., in which he responds to criticism of the original formulation. A good critical appraisal is found in P. Norman, 'Managerialism: a review of recent work', in Centre for Environmental Studies, Conference Paper 14, *Proceedings of the Conference on Urban Change and Conflict* (1975).
      On the role of one particular kind of 'urban manager' see J. Ford, 'The Role of Building Society Managers in the Urban Stratification System: autonomy versus constraint', *Urban Studies* Vol. 12, 3(1975).

48   M. Lipsky, 'Toward a Theory of Street-Level Bureaucracy' in W. Hawley, Michael Lipsky et al., *Theoretical Perspectives on Urban Politics* (Englewood Cliffs, New Jersey 1976).

49   S. Thernstrom, *Poverty and Progress: social mobility in a nineteenth-century city* (Cambridge, Mass. 1974).

50   One of the few people currently exploring the role of the immigrant business-man is Howard Aldrich; H. Aldrich and S. Feit, 'Black Entrepreneurs in England' (mimeo 1975).

51   Rex, *op. cit.*

52   P. Davies and K. Newton, 'The Social Patterns of Immigrant Areas', *Race,* Vol. XIV, 1(1972).

53   C. Peach, *West Indian Migration to Britain* (Oxford 1968).

54   B. T. Robson, *Urban Analysis* (Cambridge 1969).

55   R. J. Johnston, *Urban Residential Patterns* (London 1971).

56   J. Westergaard, 'The Structure of Greater London', in Centre for Urban Studies (ed.) *London: aspects of change* (London 1964).

57   The point was made very frequently by Durkheim and reinforced by Halbwachs. In the United States the work of the neo-ecologists like Duncan and Schnore proceeds from a similar conviction.

58   The work of the Institute of Community Studies is very important in this context. See M. Young and P. Willmott, *Family and Kinship in East London* (London 1957); P. Willmott, *The Evolution of a Community* (London 1963).

59   For some discussion of these themes see J. Jacobs, *op. cit.,* and more recently O. Newman, *Defensible Space* (New York 1973).

60   P. Willmott and M. Young, 'Social Class and Geography' in Donnison and Eversley, *op. cit.* See too M. Young and P. Willmott *The Symmetrical Family:*

a study of work and leisure in the London Region (London 1973).

61   Willmott and Young, *op. cit.*, p. 191.
62   Willmott and Young, *op. cit.*, p. 212.
63   See H. Richardson, J. Vipond and R. Furbey, *Housing and Urban Spatial Structure: a case study* (Farnborough 1975).
64   *Ibid.* p. 158.
65   C. Moser and W. Scott, *British Towns: a statistical study of their economic and social differences* (Edinburgh 1961).
66   H. Pollins, 'Transport Lines and Social Divisions' in Centre for Urban Studies (ed.) *London: aspects of change.*
67   *Ibid.,* p. 44.
68   *Ibid.,* p. 45.
69   B. Heraud, 'Social Class in the New Towns', *Urban Studies*, Vol. 5 1(1968).
70   See the recent collection of essays edited by C. Pickvance, *Urban Sociology: Critical Essays* (London 1976) and among D. Harvey's work see 'The Political Economy of Urbanization in Advanced Capitalist Societies, The John Hopkins University Center for Metropolitan Planning (1975).
71   M. Castells, 'Theory and Ideology in Urban Sociology' in Pickvance, *op. cit.*
72   See the argument put forward by F. Lamarche in 'Property Development and the Economic Foundations of the Urban Question', in Pickvance, *op. cit.*
73   Department of the Environment, 'Census Indicators of Urban Deprivation, Working Note No. 6, (Febuary 1975).
74   *Ibid.,* p. 12.
75   S. Damer, 'Wine Alley: the sociology of a dreadful enclosure' *Sociological Review,* Vol. 22 No. 2 (May 1974) provides a discussion of some of the ways in which council tenants may be 'acted upon'.
76   C. B. Macpherson 'Capitalism and the Changing Concept of Property' in E. Kamenka and R. S. Neale, *Feudalism, Capitalism and Beyond* (London 1975).
77   *Ibid.,* p. 122.
78   *Ibid.,* p. 124.

2
Work

INTRODUCTION

'What does he do?' remains the most illuminating question to ask about someone met for the first time.[1] It is illuminating precisely because a man's or a woman's work, or the fact that they do not need to or cannot work, is indicative of so much else about their social situations and their likely life experiences. Even now when we enjoy a shorter working week and longer holidays than our forefathers, most adults in the United Kingdom probably spend between a fifth and a quarter of every year at work outside the home – nearly a third of their waking hours – and house –, and other, work consumes a varying amount of time in addition. This sort of quantitative importance, however, is not the only or even the main reason for considering work in the context of a discussion of UK society. Its significance for society and its members is much more complex, but before considering in a little more detail the possible areas of interest in work it will be helpful to distinguish (and make use of) some of the definitions which 'work' can be given.

Even a brief consideration of the writing on this subject will reveal a wide variety of approaches. There is no agreement among social scientists as to the definition and significance of 'work'. One source of difficulty lies in the fact that 'work' cannot be used unambiguously as referring to certain activities. In attempting to distinguish 'work' from 'leisure', for example, Parker has argued that it is necessary to use the two 'dimensions' of 'time' and 'activity' to provide an adequate definition of 'work' (and of 'leisure'). He has suggested, therefore, that 'work is an activity that is carried on under conditions in which there are normally demands with respect to time and place and in which effort is directed to the production of goods and services . . . work contributes something which others are willing to pay for (or for which others would have to be paid if one did not do it oneself) . . .'[2]

In contrast Jaques has stressed the psychological, decision-making, responsibility-taking characteristics of work. He has emphasized the need to get away from physical definitions – such as the reference to effort – and has defined 'psychological work' as 'the exercise of discretion within prescribed limits in order to reach a goal or objective'. This remains very broad, however, and he delimited one type of 'psychological work' by reference to the economic and social context in which it is performed; 'economic work' is 'all work whose designated goal is part of the social network connected with the creation and distribution of goods and services' – and thus excludes housework, do-it-yourself, and so on. 'Economic work' can be divided into 'entrepreneurial work' and 'contractual employment work', which 'does not carry the responsibility for setting goals or objectives', and this further distinction obviously implies an economic and social system with certain characteristics.[3]

Developing an approach based on Marx, Braverman also stressed the goal-directed nature of human work and the importance of where the power to set goals is located. 'Human work is conscious and purposive, while the work of animals is instinctual . . . at the end of every labour process, we get a result that already existed in the imagination of the labourer at its commencement'. But in the case of human work 'the unity of conception and execution may be dissolved' so that the ability of one individual to work ('his power to labour over an agreed period of time') may be sold to an employer. In the resulting 'labour process', however, the worker may not share his employer's goals, and so the employer has to try to exercise control in order to ensure that his purposes are realized, that the right quantity and quality of work is actually done in what, from the employer's point of view, is the appropriate period of time.[4]

Even these three examples indicate both certain common points of reference and important differences in understanding and emphasis. For our purposes *work* can perhaps best be regarded as a very general, all-embracing term, used to refer to all those physical and mental activities which are intended to transform natural materials into a more useful form, to improve human knowledge and understanding of the world, and/or to provide or distribute goods and services to others, in whatever context such activities are carried out. As such it obviously includes housework and many other activities carried out in what the performers would regard as 'non-work' time; and some concentration of the focus of attention is necessary if the discussion in this chapter is to be manageable.

Such a limitation is indicated by the conventional answer to the 'what does he/she do?' question; this would usually refer to a person's job or *occupation*, or — if they had no occupation — to the fact that they were retired, unemployed or in full-time education. An occupation is a socially structured and socially recognized set of work activities, the carrying out of which produces goods and/or services for which others would be willing to pay. It therefore implies both a place in the social division of labour — and in highly industrialized societies like our own this is very complex so that there are thousands of more or less distinct occupations — and a potential or actual place in the market for goods and services. The discussion which follows will indeed be almost entirely concerned with the nature and characteristics of the *occupational structure* of British society, which is considered more fully below, and it will pay little or no attention to certain other areas of work, like housework, which are undoubtedly of importance for a complete understanding of the economic and social system.

Except in the case of attempts at self-sufficiency, which can only be partially achieved in any highly industrialized society, the occupational work people do is rewarded by their receiving payment. They are therefore necessarily involved in exchange relations with others, and the nature of these relations is a crucial characteristic of their work-related social situation. Some may work as independent artisans or self-employed professionals whose relations with their customers or clients need not extend beyond the actual period of the exchange. For the majority in our sort of society, however, 'work' means employment — a continuing relationship with an employer carrying out such activities as he directs and under his control in return for a wage or salary. The *employment relationship* is therefore of central importance in a discussion of work in UK society and we shall consider it more fully in the section on the rewards and deprivations of work.

In recent years there has been some tendency among social scientists to pay less attention to work and to see it as less important for an understanding of highly industrialized societies. This may reflect the degree of technological mastery over the physical world which men apparently possess, so that in such societies problems of material want and scarcity can be seen — unjustifiably — as merely residual; it may reflect too the fact that rising standards of living have given many the opportunity to develop their interests and lives outside work in 'leisure' activities, at the same time as the repetitive and fragmented nature of much of the work which helps to make such standards of living possible reduces any intrinsic value work might have had for them; and indeed much work is often so opaque that it is not obvious even to those who do it, and still less to outside observers, exactly what part their occupation plays in the economic and social system as a whole.

Thus in some versions of 'post-industrial society' theory, for example, much greater emphasis is placed on the control and expansion of knowledge than on the control and expansion of production for an understanding of future developments.[5] Other social scientists have argued that work is no longer 'a central life interest' for most people, that it is merely something done in order to make enough money to 'live' properly in non-working hours, and in itself has no value and significance for them.[6] In some contributions to current debates about social stratification, too, an emphasis has been placed on cultural sources of deprivation or privilege, minimizing the significance of the possession or lack of material, and work-related, resources.[7]

For an understanding of our society and of the experiences of those who are members of it, I do not wish to claim that work has exactly the same significance as it had a century ago. There have of course been considerable changes, though by no means all in the same direction. Attempts to remove work from a central place in an analysis of modern society, however, are at best premature and probably entirely mistaken.

In the first place, work is important because without it there would be no human society. Whatever else it may now include, work also refers to those activities in a society which enable essential material needs to be met. For this reason it has central social and cultural significance in all societies. The ways in which work is organized, however, the social relations surrounding it, and the social meanings attributed to it can vary enormously both within and between societies. Indeed it may be helpful to consider work in a variety of ways: the occupational structure and the social relations of production are central elements of the social structure; they are also ones which provide varying opportunities and/or constraints to the individual members of a society; and work is a set of activities and social relations which are invested with important meaning and significance, both socially and individually.

In the case of the UK, for example, the development of a capitalist industrial society from the middle of the eighteenth century onwards meant far-reaching changes in the social organization of work and the social relations of production. The division of labour and the nature of work tasks were transformed as ownership of the means of production was concentrated in the hands of a few who employed, as 'free' wage labour, those who had formerly been more nearly economically independent workers. The subsequent growth in size and concentration of the ownership and control of units of production and administration, and their consequent bureaucratization, meant that more and more work was carried out within an employment relationship, in the company of others with similar tasks and in a similar situation, and where the control of the ultimate 'employer' was exercised through an extensive hierarchy of managers and supervisors.

As Weber more than perhaps anyone else has emphasized, the industrial revolution itself, and the subsequent developments in industrialized societies, were dependent on, and also embodied and reinforced, certain distinctive values relating to work.[8] These emphasized the intrinsic importance and value of work and the obligation of all to work hard and to the best of their ability; and the desirability of the rational organization of work, free of traditional and personal restraints, to attain given ends. Labour was to be regarded as a commodity to be bought and sold without regard to the character or needs of the labourer, and work was to be organized to maximize efficiency and productivity, not to provide interesting and rewarding tasks, or opportunities for participation or control by the workers. In the early years of the factory system of production much attention was devoted by employers to inculcating an appropriate work ethic and an acceptance of these values;[9] and powerful mechanisms of socialization and communication currently exist to ensure that obligations to work are internalized.[10]

Work therefore has meanings which are given to it by dominant groups in a society and which serve the interests of the powerful. To a greater or lesser extent these may be accepted and internalized by individual members of society, but they do not exhaust the possible meanings work may have for an individual, nor the range of 'subordinate' value systems which may co-exist in the same society. In a valuable discussion of the meaning of work, Fox has suggested that there are 'two great alternative meanings' for the individual: work as an activity of 'central importance to his personality development and life fulfilment' or as 'little more than a tiresome necessity in acquiring the resources for survival or for what he may define as the real living which he begins as work ends'.[11] The objective necessity of work for the survival of human society means that the second, instrumental, view of work must always have some part in the meaning of work for many if not all members of any society, but it may be seen as less important than work viewed as an end in itself, especially if we consider what individuals think ought to be the case rather than what is. Indeed, as Fox goes on to show, the latter type of meaning of work for the individual has a number of possible components.[12]

> First, then, it is clear that work provides the individual with opportunities to relate himself to society . . . . Work can serve for the individual as an organizing principle in the sense of gearing him into society and enabling him to view himself as making a useful contribution by providing goods and services . . .
>
> The second personal meaning we must note here is that work may serve sociability needs by providing the individual with opportunities for interaction with others. The workplace has always been, for some, a place to meet people, converse, and perhaps form friendships, as, for example, when married women previously tied to home and children welcome the chance to move into a wider world . . .
>
> Third, comes the role of work in enabling the individual to sustain status and self-respect. This has several aspects. 'The job is a key element in wider social status . . .' the loss of a job can bring a sense of humiliation and consequent withdrawal to avoid embarrassment . . .
>
> Next comes the significance of work in terms of personal identity . . . Jobs differ profoundly, of course, in what they offer along these dimensions, but even in the humblest activities prestige may attach to the worker who distinguishes himself in strength, dexterity, or whatever else is valued, and the recipient may derive meaning from this reputation.

The fifth possible meaning is more important for many people than it may at first seem. 'Work roles structure the passage of time . . .' The significance here is of work providing a routine that wards off boredom, structures one's life, passes the time, offers something to do . . .

This role of work merges with the next — the value of meaningful activity in helping to distract the individual from private worries, fears, disappointments, depression and emotional disturbance . . .

A seventh significant factor in work is its importance in providing scope for the satisfaction of 'achievement', usually defined in terms of a struggle towards high standards that are recognized as such by some valued group, large or small . . . jobs differ widely in what they offer along this dimension . . . achievement motivation in contemporary Western societies is considered to be particularly associated with middle-class values, opportunities and education . . .

Finally, it is a fact of observation that people derive meaning from a job situation in which the work itself is humble and repetitive or in some way disagreeable, trying, or dangerous, if they are conscious of contributing to some transcendent cause with which they feel able to identify . . . Sometimes the cause is embodied, more indirectly so far as lower participants are concerned, in an organization to which they feel proud to contribute . . .

It is obviously very difficult to explore on a large scale and in quantitative terms these eight ways in which work may be significant to an individual, but it is important to keep them in mind as possibilities when considering the more tangible, and often very restricted rewards, and costs, of working.

Work is important to an individual not just in ways of which he may be aware, however, but also because the work men do — their occupations — are the most important influences on the life chances of them and their families. When it comes to considering income, health, educational opportunity and achievement of children, liability to accident, to unemployment and redundancy, rates of infant and adult mortality and morbidity, and many other social characteristics, it is occupational categories which reveal the clearest patterns of difference. Indeed for this reason most discussions of 'social stratification' or 'social class' in contemporary Britain are based on occupational categories.[13] Such work-related inequalities of condition and opportunity exist even though those affected may not always be aware of them or may consider them unacceptable.

This is not to argue, of course, either that occupational categories are a satisfactory basis for discussion of 'social class' or that life chances are solely related to occupation. Occupational categories provide little help, for example, in distinguishing the 'owners of the means of production' from the non-owners, or the 'propertied' from those who lack property, which Marx and Weber in their rather different ways saw as the basic divisions in the class structure in capitalist societies.[14] There are, too, other powerful influences on life chances. There are considerable regional differences within Britain, though they may be accounted for partly by the different industrial and occupational composition of the various regions.[15] Those who have investigated housing markets have argued that housing 'classes' determined by their differential access to the means of accommodation do not correspond to occupationally-based classes, because of the allocation of public housing in terms of administrative rather than market criteria, and because of discrimination on the grounds of colour or ethnic origin.[16] Similarly, in studies of educational opportunity and achievement a number of factors, such as size of family, social origin of the mother, parental interest, and the nature of the school, which are not directly related to the occupation of the parents, can be influential on the outcomes of the educational process.[17] Nevertheless, it can be argued, I think, that these and similar factors are modifications of the central influence and importance of occupation.

In the following sections we shall pursue some of these concerns with work in more detail and attempt to describe and understand the current situation in Britain. We shall consider first of all the changing occupational structure of British society and the ways in which occupations can be classified to indicate similarities of social situation and life chances. Then we shall look at the costs and rewards of work, particularly for those in employment, including both the more obvious material rewards and the less tangible privileges and deprivations associated with various types of occupations. Finally, the question of the occupational opportunities open to different social groups must be considered to see how access to particular types of work and employment is structured. In this context aspects of the educational system and of the workings of the labour market will be seen to be of considerable importance.

THE CHANGING OCCUPATIONAL STRUCTURE

Highly industrialized societies are characterized by an extensive and complex division of labour. As even a brief look at the 'Situations Vacant' columns reveals, the variety of jobs which men and women do is extremely large. The most comprehensive indices of this are the lists of job titles used by census and other authorities in their coding of occupations for official statistics or other administrative purposes. For example, before the last four censuses a 'Classification of Occupations' was published which, in 1966, listed approximately 32,000 separate occupations, classified into 211 separate unit groups. Any attempt to describe the occupational structure of a society must therefore categorize and classify the variety of men's and women's work in some way. All forms of categorization are both arbitrary (to some extent at least) and likely to conceal as well as to reveal significant differences and similarities between occupations.[18] This can be partly overcome by considering a variety of approaches, and in this section we shall consider several types of classification, which can be roughly ranged along a continuum from the 'non-evaluative' (or less evaluative) to the 'more evaluative'.

By 'non-evaluative' I mean those sets of categories which refer, so far as this is ever possible, to objective characteristics of the job or occupation. The occupational structures of societies differ, for example, in terms of the distribution of the working population between different industries or economic sectors, that is groups of related industries. The working population can be differentiated too in terms of its members' economic status; slavery and other forms of unfree labour no longer exist in most industrialized societies, but there are significant differences in the social and economic situation of employers, the self-employed, employees, and unpaid family workers, and their relative proportions have changed over time. Thirdly, there is the possibility of grouping occupations in terms of the similarities in the type of work done, whatever may be the economic status of the persons concerned or their industrial location; in this case we can describe groups of occupations as 'manual or non-manual'; as 'clerical', 'technical', 'managerial', and 'professional'; and more evaluatively, as 'skilled' or 'unskilled'.[19]

'Evaluative' schemes pose rather more problems but can be much more revealing. They involve grouping and ranking occupations in terms of some judgment of their desirability, standing or prestige, judgments which are made either by the administrator or investigator, or by a sample of members of the population in question. As examples of the first type of evaluation we have the Registrar General's allocation of all occupations to one of five (or more recently six) 'social classes', based on 'general standing within the community of the occupation concerned', and to one of sixteen (sometimes seventeen) 'socio-economic groups' based on differences in status and skill. Because of the apparent arbitrariness of these categorizations some investigators have asked a sample of respondents to grade occupations, and have then attempted to create their own scales.

For our purposes the main advantage of evaluative schemes is that they may group occupations in a way which takes account of a number of their socially relevant concomitants — such as their level and type of rewards, their social standing, the education, training and skills needed, and so on. Although no set of occupational categories can be regarded as a straightforward division of the population into 'classes' as the sociologist would understand that term, schemes of occupational grading probably come closest to grouping together those with similar 'life chances'. They are therefore the best available basis for exploring the differential impact of work for men's and women's lives and social situations in our society.

It is not my intention to provide a detailed description and analysis of the changing occupational structure of Britain. Such accounts are already available and involve considering in detail the ways in which sources and classifications of data have changed over time.[20] But a brief historical background will be helpful in putting the subsequent discussion into perspective.

Occupational Classifications

During the past 130 years — the period for which detailed and moderately reliable statistics are available — not only has the absolute size of the economically active population grown as a result of the overall increase in population, from just under 7 million in 1841 to over 25 million in 1971, but the activity rate (roughly speaking the proportion of those old enough to work who are actually working) has also increased (tables 2.1 and 2.2). Whereas until 1921 this increase occurred for both men and women, since then the increased proportion of women in employment, and especially of married women, has more than compensated for the declining proportion of adult men who are working. In table 2.3 we can see that in recent years this decline has been due to the growing proportion of men who have been full-time students or retired, while it is the proportion of women classified as 'other persons' (mainly housewives) which has fallen very considerably, and has far more than offset the increased proportion of women students.

The industrial distribution of the labour force (including employers and workers on their own account) shows considerable change over the same period, and this reflects the continuing processes of industrialization (table 2.4). In 1851 22 per cent of the economically active population in Great Britain were engaged in agriculture, forestry and fishing; by 1911 this proportion had fallen to under 8 per cent; a further sixty years later, in 1971, the proportion was less than 2 per cent. In contrast the proportion in manufacturing industry (including gas, electricity and water) has remained fairly constant at 40 per cent, nearly 35 per cent and nearly 40 per cent in these same three years; and the major growth has occurred in the 'service industries'

TABLE 2.1

Economic activity, GB, 1841–1921

Thousands

	1841			1881			1921		
	Total	Males	Females	Total	Males	Females	Total	Males	Females
(i) Number occupied*	6,908	5,093	1,815	12,731	8,844	3,887	19,354	13,670	5,684
(ii) Number unoccupied*	6,973	1,604	5,369	9,345	1,778	7,567	13,985	2,002	11,983
Activity rate	50%	76%	25%	58%	83%	34%	58%	87%	31%
$\dfrac{\text{(i)}}{\text{(i)} + \text{(ii)}} \times 100$									
(iii) Total population	18,535	9,020	9,515	29,710	14,439	15,271	42,769	20,423	22,346

* The total occupied includes children aged under 10, whereas the total unoccupied does not. The figures for 1881 were calculated by assuming that all children in the 5–14 age group who were occupied were aged 10 and over

Sources: (i) and (ii) *British Labour Statistics: Historical Abstract 1886–1968* (HMSO 1971), table 102, p. 195
(iii) calculated from B. R. Mitchell and P. Deane, *Abstract of British Historical Statistics* (Cambridge 1962), p. 6

TABLE 2.2

Economic activity, GB, 1921–71

All ages over 15

Year	All Males and Females			All Males			All Females			Married Females		
	Number occupied/ economically active	Population	Activity rate[†]	Number occupied/ economically active	Population	Activity rate[†]	Number occupied/ economically active	Population	Activity rate[†]	Number occupied/ economically active	Population	Activity rate[†]
	Thousands	Thousands	Per cent	Thousands	Thousands	Per cent	Thousands	Thousands	Per cent	Thousands	Thousands	Per cent
1921	19,357	33,339	58.1	13,656	15,672	87.1	5,701	17,667	32.3	733	8,434	8.7
1931	21,055	34,662	60.7	14,790	16,341	90.5	6,265	18,320	34.2	953	9,492	10.0
1951	22,610	37,908	59.6	15,649	17,862	87.6	6,961	20,045	34.7	2,658	12,228	21.7
1961	23,810	39,360	60.5	16,071	18,677	86.0	7,740	20,683	37.4	3,886	13,070	29.7
1966	24,857	40,041	62.1	15,994	19,030	84.0	8,863	21,011	42.2	5,063	13,296	38.1
1971	25,103	41,048	61.2	15,917	19,560	81.4	9,186	21,488	42.7	5,799	13,729	42.2

† Activity rate is defined as the proportion of those occupied or economically active to the total population

Based on: Department of Employment Gazette, Census of Population

Source: Central Office of Information, Reference Pamphlet 139, *Occupations and Conditions of Work* (HMSO 1976), p. 42

TABLE 2.3

Economic activity, GB, 1951–71

Thousands (Males and Females "At April")

	Total				Males			Females		
	1951	1961	1966	1971[2]	1961	1966	1971[2]	1961	1966	1971[2]
Population aged 15 and over[1]	37,908	39,569	40,041	41,048	18,811	19,030	19,560	20,758	21,011	21,488
Economically active										
In employment										
Self-employed and employers	1,649	1,717	1,586		1,385	1,231		331	355	
Employees	20,486	21,622	22,583	23,797	14,363	14,344	15,058	7,259	8,239	8,739
Part-time workers[3] (incl. above)	831	2,066	3,121		174	373		1,892	2,748	
Out of employment										
Sick	475	297	216	296	216	133	192	81	82	104
Other		378	472	1,011	268	287	667	110	186	344
Total	22,610	24,014	24,857	25,103	16,232	15,994	15,917	7,782	8,863	9,186
Economically inactive										
Students	1,821	994	1,265	1,785	540	675	954	454	591	831
Retired	13,477	2,448	2,411	14,160	1,808	1,911	2,302	639	500	11,471
Other persons		12,113	11,508		230	450	387	11,883	11,058	
Total	15,298	15,555	15,184	15,945	2,578	3,036	3,643	12,976	12,148	12,302
As percentage of population aged 15 and over:										
Economically active	59.6	60.7	62.1	61.2	86.3	84.0	81.4	37.5	42.2	42.7
Students	4.8	2.5	3.2	4.3	2.9	3.5	4.9	2.2	2.8	3.9
Retired	35.6	6.2	6.0		9.6	10.0	11.8	3.1	2.4	
Other persons		30.6	28.7	34.5	1.2	2.4	2.0	57.2	52.6	53.4

1   The populations aged 15 and over were taken from the 100% results in 1951 and 1971 and from the 10% sample figures in 1961 and 1966. The 1966 figures do not include foreign visitors unless they had a place of work in Great Britain. No adjustment has been made either for bias in the 1961 figures or for possible under-enumeration in 1966

2   Final 1971 Census figures

3   The definition of part-time workers was changed for each census – see note in Appendix A

Based on: Census of Population reports

Source: *Social Trends*, No. 5 (HMSO 1974), p. 96

(but excluding building and construction – about 6 per cent of the labour force) which have grown in size almost without interruption – 29 per cent in 1851, 45 per cent in 1911 and nearly 51 per cent in 1971. None of the economic sectors so far mentioned includes 'mining and quarrying', which sits uncomfortably between the 'primary' and 'secondary' sectors, and in which employment reached a peak of over 7 per cent of the labour force in 1921 to decline to less than 4 per cent in 1951 (when there were still nearly 700,000 miners) and less than 2 per cent in 1971.

These overall figures conceal some important intra-sectoral changes. Within manufacturing, for example, more than 12 per cent of the occupied population were employed in the textile industries in 1841 and 8 per cent in clothing and footwear, and these proportions had only fallen slightly, to 8 per cent and 7 per cent respectively, by 1911; in 1971, however, textiles accounted for approximately $2\frac{1}{2}$ per cent of the occupied population and clothing and footwear for 2 per cent. In contrast the group of industries described in the 1911 categorization as 'metal manufacture, machines, implements, vehicles, precious metals, etc' has employed a greatly increasing proportion of the labour force – 6 per cent in 1841, $10\frac{1}{2}$ per cent in 1911 and about 19 per cent in 1971. Within the service sector, too, there have been changes of a similar magnitude: a marked decline in employment in private domestic and other services, from 19 per cent of the labour force in 1841 and over 14 per cent in 1911 to 8 per cent (in 'miscellaneous services') in 1971; and a steady growth of the proportion in commercial and financial activities and in public administration (see table 2.4).[21] Such changes in industrial distribution, allied to technological and organizational changes within industries, have had significant consequences for typical patterns of work experience and of social relations with fellow employees and with employers.

Thirdly, there have been changes in the economic status of those who are economically active (table 2.5). At all dates for which the relevant data are available, at least nine out of every ten members of the occupied population have been employees, but this status has become even more common during the past fifty years; the proportions of those who are employers or self-employed (working on their own account) have both declined to comprise 2.9 per cent and 4.5 per cent of the occupied population, respectively, in 1971.

Most interesting and relevant to our subsequent discussion are the changes in the occupational distribution of the labour force. Unfortunately the distinction between the industrial and occupational distributions of the labour force has only been embodied in census statistics since 1921, and classifications have been changed at intervals since then so that it is impossible to compile a continuous series of data classified on the same basis. It is, however, possible to suggest some of the more important changes which have taken place, and to indicate in a little more detail the ways in which certain occupations less affected by alterations in classification have grown or declined in importance.

A detailed and long-term consideration of what he termed 'the immense increase in the numbers of black-coated and professional workers' is possible, thanks to the work of G. D. H. Cole who described the changes between 1851 and 1951 as follows:[22]

Clerks and commercial travellers, who were grouped together, in 1851 numbered only 60,000: in the census of 1951 clerks, draughtsmen and typists added up to nearly two and a half millions. In 1851 the group included no women at all: in

TABLE 2.4

Industrial distribution of labour force, and employers and workers on own account, as percentage of whole, GB

Year	Total Labour Force (1841– 1951 excluding Women in Agriculture)	Primary Sector Agriculture, Forestry, Fishing	Mining & Quarrying	Secondary Sector Manufacturing inc. Electricity, Gas, Water	Building & Construction	Sub- total
	millions	percentages				
1841	6,7	23.1	3.1	36.6	5.8	45.5
1851	9,4	22.2	3.3	40.1	5.4	48.8
1861	10,6	19.0	3.7	39.8	5.5	49.0
1871	11,8	15.0	3.8	39.8	6.2	49.8
1881	12,8	12.3	4.1	39.5	6.7	50.3
1891	14,1	10.4	4.5	38.6	6.3	49.4
1901	15,4	8.7	5.9	32.9	8.0	46.8
1911	18,2	7.8	6.9	34.6	5.2	46.7
1921	19,4	6.7	7.3	38.7	4.1	50.1
1931	21,	5.7	6.1	35.0	5.4	46.5
1951	22,5	4.5	3.9	39.5	6.3	49.7
1961	24,8	2.6	3.3	41.0	6.6	50.9
1971	24,9	1.6	1.8	40.0	5.7	47.5

TABLE 2.4 continued

Year	Tertiary Sector Transport & Communication	Commerce & Finance	Professions & Entertainment	Armed Forces	Other Government Services	Private Domestic Service	Other Services	Sub-total
1841	3.0	5.7	2.9	0.7	0.4	19.1		31.8
1851	4.4	6.3	3.1	1.0	0.6	14.0		29.4
1861	4.8	7.1	3.2	1.3	0.8	15.2		32.4
1871	5.2	8.3	3.4	1.2	0.8	16.6		35.5
1881	5.9	9.2	3.8	1.0	0.9	16.6		37.4
1891	7.5	10.3	5.0	0.9	1.1	15.4		40.2
1901	9.3	11.0	4.4	1.1	1.4	14.3	2.0	43.5
1911	8.0	18.7		4.2		9.0	5.6	45.5
1921	8.1	13.2	3.7	1.6	4.8	7.0	4.5	42.9
1931	8.0	16.0	4.1	1.2	5.4	7.8	4.9	47.4
1951	7.8	14.2	7.0	3.4	4.6	2.3	6.8	46.1

Year	Transport & Communication	Distributive trades	Financial, Prof. & Scientific Services	Public Administration	Miscellaneous Services	Sub-total
1961	7.4	12.5	11.7	5.7	8.8	46.1
1971	7.1	11.7	17.6	6.4	8.1	50.9

Sources: 1841–1951: Colin Clark, *The Conditions of Economic Progress* (1957), pp. 510–20
1961–71: *Social Trends*, No. 5 (1974), p. 98

TABLE 2.5

Economic status of gainfully occupied population, GB, 1911–51/1961, 1971

	Employers/ Self-employed with employees		Own account/ Self-employed without employees		Employees		Status not distinguished		Thousands Total
		%		%		%		%	
1911	763	4.2	937	5.1	15,903	86.7	744	4.1	18,347
1921	735	3.8	1,207	6.2	17,391	90	–		19,333
1931	780	3.7	1,270	6.0	18,976	90.3	–		21,026
1951	501	2.2	1,147	5.1	20,866	92.7	–		22,514
1961	1,672	6.7%			23,101	93.3			24,773
1971	723	2.9	1,119	4.5	23,178	92.6			25,020

Source: adapted from G.G.C. Routh, *Occupation and Pay in Great Britain 1906–1960* (Cambridge 1965), pp. 4–5; and (1961 and 1971) from *British Labour Statistics Yearbook 1974* (London 1976), p. 227; and Office of Population Censuses and Surveys, *Census 1971*, Economic Activity, Part II (London 1975), pp. 51–6

1951 the females numbered 1,428,000, as against 1,030,000 males. Persons engaged in merchanting, shop-keeping and financial occupations numbered about 130,000 in 1851: the most nearly comparable group in 1931 (*sic*) accounted for 2,230,000. Education occupied about 100,000 teachers in 1851 and 356,000 in 1951. The services of government and local government (excluding clerks and professional workers) employed 75,000 in 1851: for 1951 the nearest comparable total is 333,000. The professions, excluding education, added up in 1851 to about 15,000: in 1951 they were well over a million. All these figures are very inexact, because of changes in classification; but I feel sure that the broad impression conveyed by them is correct.[23]

The development which Cole emphasized, the enormous absolute and relative increase in the numbers of non-manual workers, is indeed probably the most dramatic and important change in the occupational structure of Britain since the Industrial Revolution and the shift from agriculture to industry. As his account indicates it has a number of components. Of the greatest quantitative importance are the growth in employment in 'clerical' occupations and the expansion of (broadly) 'commercial' occupations; the work situations and social relations of the former have been described and analysed by a number of sociologists, but the latter rather less socially distinct grouping appears so far to have attracted less interest.[24]

A second important component of this shift into white-collar occupations is the growth of public employment, a phenomenon which has attracted a lot of public comment in recent years. As table 2.6 shows there has been a continuous growth in the absolute and relative numbers of national and local government employees since 1901, and in the last twenty-five years this has more than outweighed the declining numbers in the armed forces and in the nationalized industries, so that public-sector employment has continued to grow. Though these figures include many manual workers and professional employees, a large proportion are in clerical or administrative occupations.

An especially significant increase has been that of the professions because it is the occupations which have successfully established the claim to be 'professional' which have secured for their members the greatest control over conditions of work and autonomy on the job.[25] The attractions of 'professional' status mean that this label is more widely claimed than it is granted, and precise definitions of 'professional occupations' are impossible, but table 2.7 provides a clear general indication of the trend over the past century or so. In addition to the considerable absolute and relative increase in the numbers of 'professionals' there have been significant changes in the internal composition of this category of occupations: the traditional 'professions' — clergy, lawyers and doctors — are a much smaller proportion of the total, as also are teachers; the newer 'professions' based on science and technology have increased enormously and the former more or less clear demarcation between men's and women's 'professional' work has been somewhat eroded though not eliminated.

A more evaluative occupational classification is available from the work of Routh and of Bain which shows the main changes since 1911 (table 2.8). There has been a decline in the proportion of the occupied population who were manual workers from nearly 75 per cent to less than 60 per cent, and a corresponding increase in the proportion in non-manual and white-collar work from just over 25 per cent in 1911 to nearly 42 per cent in 1971. The relative decline in manual work has been visible in all three categories (skilled, semi-skilled and unskilled), though for unskilled manual workers the decline is greatest since 1921. The increasing proportions in white-collar work as clerks and professionals, and as managers and administrators, foremen and inspectors, are, of course, related to the industrial and occupational changes described above: the shift into the 'service sector' involves increasing white-collar employment; and the shift within manufacturing industry from traditional and more labour intensive industries, like textiles and clothing, to more technologically advanced and capital intensive ones, such as many branches of engineering, has been associated with the employment of an increasing proportion of administrative, technical and clerical workers. This growth of the 'administrative overhead' is one of the most striking changes in industry during the present century, and has been well documented by Melman, Bendix and others (see table 2.9). Indeed their work is a valuable reminder that the occupational trends so far discussed are not unique to Britain but have been paralleled in all highly industrialized societies.[26]

These three indices – the distribution in terms of industry, economic status, and occupation – indicate the broad long-term changes which have taken place in the occupational structure of Britain over the past century or more. Such sociographic and descriptive data do provide an important point of reference. The traditional area of work for most of the world's population during most of recorded history (work on the land) is of minor importance, statistically, in Britain, and has been for nearly a hundred years. Work for an increasing proportion of the population, indeed, no longer means manual labour – or even manual labour with the assistance of mechanical power – but the manipulation of symbolic materials in an office, or the processing, in some way or other, of people. Work for an increasing proportion is no longer concerned with the production or distribution of a material product, but with providing services. Even in manufacturing industry the heavy labour which was romanticized by the pre-Raphaelites, or captured more grimly and prosaically by many illustrators and engravers,[27] is less important, and work for many involves making a minute contribution to a possibly unknown product in mass production or process industry. The fascination of construction sites and men digging holes in the road is perhaps all the greater for its increasing rarity as a type of work.

One further change should also be emphasized: the very much greater size, in terms of numbers employed, of the establishments within which people work. Although very many small shops, offices and workshops remain – over 30,000 *firms* in manufacturing industry with ten or fewer employees were recorded in the UK in 1963 – the number of manufacturing *establishments* with 1,500 or more employees increased from 277 in 1930 to 669 in 1963.[28] As the construction of office blocks indicates, similar changes are taking place outside the manufacturing industry; this is reflected in table 2.10, which records enterprise rather than plant size.

There is evidence to suggest that size is the major determinant of important aspects of bureaucratization, and although the occupational consequences of such trends can vary, increase in clerical and administrative work is very probable.[29] Thus not only has the *content* of work changed but so has its *context*.

Status Rankings

The more evaluative classifications build on the type of occupational categories included in table 2.8 to produce rankings either of the whole occupied population, or of heads of households and their families, which reflect other social characteristics. The Registrar General's classification of Social Class has been in use, in one form or

TABLE 2.6

Public sector employment, GB, 1901–74

	1901		1950		1965		1974	
	No. in thousands	Percentage	No. in thousands	Percentage	No. in thousands	Percentage	No. in thousands	Percentage
Total working population	16,605	100	23,068	100	25,463	100	24,990	100
Total public sector	c. 958	5.8	5,597	24.3	5,975	23.5	6,843	27.4
Central government (civilians)	c. 160	1.0	1,102	4.8	1,370	5.4	1,724	6.9
Armed forces	c. 423	2.5	690	3.0	423	1.7	345	1.4
Local authorities	c. 375	2.3	1,422	6.2	2,154	8.5	2,844	11.4
Public corporations	n.a.	—	2,383	10.3	2,028	8.0	1,930	7.7

Sources: 1901 and 1950: M. Abramovitz and V. F. Eliasberg, *The Growth of Public Employment in Great Britain* (Princeton 1957), pp. 25, 107
1965 and 1974: *British Labour Statistics Yearbook*, 1974, p. 222;
British Labour Statistics; Historical Abstract, p. 223; and
Department of Employment Gazette, Vol. 82, 12(1974), p. 1161

TABLE 2.7

Number and percentage distribution of persons in 'professional' occupations, 1861–1957 and 1971

Profession	1861			1891		
	Male	Female	Total	Male	Female	Total
Religious	30,270 *97*	939	31,209 (11.4)	41,919 *83*	8,872	50,791 (11.0)
Legal	14,517 *100*	–	14,517 (5.5)	19,978 *100*		19,978 (4.5)
Medical	22,780 *100*	46	22,826 (8.7)	26,755 *98*	448	27,203 (6.1)
Nursing	– *0*	29,531	29,531 (11.1)	601 *1*	53,057	53,658 (12.0)
Medical Auxiliary	16,334 *97*	496	16,830 (6.3)	24,077 *92*	2,227	26,304 (5.9)
Teaching	32,755 *28*	83,120	115,875 (43.7)	54,220 *27*	146,375	200,595 (44.9)
Engineering	11,221 *100*	29	11,250 (4.6)	35,399 *99*	488	35,887 (8.0)
Scientific	579 *93*	42	621 (0.2)	1,920 *98*	42	1,962 (0.4)
Accounting	6,239 *99*	34	6,273 (2.4)	7,930 *99*	50	7,980 (1.8)
Literary	2,697 *94*	185	2,882 (1.1)	7,485 *90*	787	8,272 (1.8)
Librarian	445 *80*	113	558 (0.2)			
Officials of Associations				1,530 *77*	465	1,995 (0.4)
Social Welfare	702 *42*	985	1,687 (0.6)			
Artistic	9,952 *100*	911	10,863 (4.1)	9,250 *75*	3,032	12,282 (2.7)
Others n.e.c.	277 *100*	–	277 (0.1)			
TOTAL:-	148,768 *56*	116,431	265,199 (100)	231,064 *52*	215,843	446,907 (100)

Professional occupations
as a percentage of total
occupied population.

Note:
Figures in brackets in 'Total' columns show the distribution of each group of 'professional' occupations as a percentage of all occupations classified as 'professional'
Figures in italics in the 'Male' columns are the percentages of males in each group of 'professional' occupations.
Figures for 1971 are based on 10% sample and are for Great Britain.
The classification of occupations for the years 1861–1951 is based on the 1951 Census categories, and so far as possible these have been used in allocating occupations to categories in 1971. The details of the categories are as follows:

Religious	– clergymen, priests, ministers, itinerant preachers, monks, nuns
Legal	– judges, barristers, solicitors, notaries
Medical	– physicians, surgeons, radiologists, dentists, (veterinary surgeons – 1861–1951)
Nursing	– nurses, midwives, student nurses, nursery nurses
Medical	
Auxiliary	– pharmacists, physiotherapists, radiographers, opticians, chiropodists, etc

	England and Wales						*Great Britain*	
	1921			1951			1971	
Male	Female	Total	Male	Female	Total	Male	Female	Total
38,975 *76*	12,078	51,053 *(8.2)*	35,799 *70*	15,399	51,198 *(4.1)*	35,730 *87*	5,410	41,140 *(1.5)*
17,909 *100*	37	17,946 *(2.9)*	22,773 *97*	677	23,450 *(1.9)*	36,050 *94*	2,470	38,520 *(1.4)*
34,055 *96*	1,573	35,628 *(5.8)*	49,555 *87*	7,679	57,234 *(4.6)*	64,980 *81*	15,040	80,020 *(2.9)*
2,118 *2*	99,888	102,006 *(16.5)*	25,527 *11*	209,870	235,397 *(19.0)*	37,950 *9*	401,030	438,980 *(16.1)*
5,559 *46*	6,585	12,144 *(2.0)*	34,097 *56*	26,548	60,645 *(4.9)*	40,570 *50*	41,350	81,920 *(3.0)*
73,774 *27*	203,802	277,576 *(44.8)*	122,019 *39*	191,216	313,235 *(25.3)*	307,690 *45*	380,530	688,220 *(25.3)*
57,960 *100*	286	58,246 *(9.4)*	234,901 *94*	15,018	249,919 *(20.2)*	744,670 *93*	59,630	804,300 *(29.5)*
15,494 *90*	1,646	17,140 *(2.8)*	88,452 *81*	21,021	109,473 *(8.8)*	146,690 *73*	54,590	201,280 *(7.4)*
7,217 *99*	43	7,260 *(1.2)*	31,851 *98*	573	32,424 *(2.6)*	73,960 *97*	2,650	76,610 *(2.8)*
11,229 *85*	2,028	13,257 *(2.1)*	19,086 *80*	4,736	23,822 *(1.9)*	38,790 *75*	12,680	51,470 *(1.9)*
1,310 *61*	832	2,142 *(0.3)*	4,734 *32*	10,170	14,904 *(1.2)*	–	–	n.a.
4,524 *91*	470	4,994 *(0.8)*	6,699 *86*	1,105	7,804 *(0.7)*	7,240 *91*	700	7,940 *(0.3)*
1,222 *40*	1,863	3,085 *(0.5)*	9,418 *43*	12,733	22,151 *(1.8)*	21,550 *35*	39,690	61,240 *(2.2)*
8,134 *66*	4,184	12,318 *(1.7)*	12,084 *73*	4,464	16,548 *(1.3)*	27,040 *63*	16,070	43,110 *(1.6)*
3,016 *72*	1,150	4,166 *(0.7)*	17,202 *90*	1,848	19,050 *(1.5)*	69,120 *64*	38,100	107,220 *(3.9)*
282,496 *46*	336,465	618,961 *(100)*	714,197 *58*	523,057	1,237,254 *(100)*	1,652,030 *61*	1,069,940	2,721,970 *(100)*
		3.6%			6%			10.9%

Engineering	– civil, electrical, mechanical, chemical and gas, and mining engineers; surveyors, architects, town, planners, naval architects, industrial designers, draughtsmen, technologists, technical and related workers
Scientific	– chemists, metallurgists, physicists, biologists, statisticians, laboratory assistants, etc
Literary	– authors, journalists, editors, etc
Officials	– officials of trade or professional associations
Artistic	– painters, sculptors, etc

Sources: 1861–1951: M. J. Woolgar, 'The growth of the clergy as a profession in England and Wales' (unpublished P. D. Thesis, University of Leicester, 1960), p. 41
1971: Office of Population Censuses and Surveys, *Census 1971*, Economic Activity Part II, pp. 51–6

TABLE 2.8

The occupied population of Great Britain by major occupational groups, 1911–71

Occupational groups	Number of persons in major occupational groups 1911–71 (thousands)						
	1911	1921	1931	1951	1961	1966	1971
1 Employers and Proprietors	1,232	1,318	1,407	1,117	1,140	832	622
2 White-collar workers	3,433	4,094	4,841	6,948	8,479	9,461	10,405
(a) Managers and administrators	631	704	770	1,245	1,270	1,514	2,085
(b) Higher professionals	184	196	240	435	718	829	928
(c) Lower professionals and technicians	560	679	728	1,059	1,418	1,604	1,880
(d) Foremen and inspectors	237	279	323	590	681	736	736
(e) Clerks	832	1,256	1,404	2,341	2,994	3,262	3,412
(f) Salesmen and shop assistants	989	980	1,376	1,278	1,398	1,516	1,364
3 Manual workers	13,685	13,920	14,776	14,450	14,021	14,393	13,343
(a) Skilled	5,608	5,572	5,618	5,617	5,981	5,857	
(b) Semi-skilled	6,310	5,608	6,044	6,124	6,004	6,437	
(c) Unskilled	1,767	2,740	3,114	2,709	2,037	2,099	
4 Total occupied population	18,350	19,332	21,024	22,515	23,639	24,686	24,370

Note: In the 1966 sample census and the 1971 census the employer and managerial status categories given are 'self-employed with and without employers' and 'managers'. In contrast with 1961 this distinguishes employers from managers but it does not distinguish the self-employed (without employees), which are included in the groups according to the nature of their occupations, from the employers and proprietors. People of both employer and self-employed status are included in the employer and the proprietor occupations and in the higher and lower professional groups in the table so that no division of the 'self-employed with and without employers' was necessary. For the other groups in the table, however, the 'self-employed with and without employees' were divided into employers and self-employed according to the 1951 ratio of employers to self-employed in these groups. The 'employers' were then added to the 'employers and proprietors' group and the 'self-employed' added to their appropriate groups (skilled, semi-skilled, etc).

Sources: G.S. Bain, R. Bacon and R. Pimlott, 'The Labour Force' in A.H. Halsey (ed.), *Trends in British Society since 1900* (London 1972), p. 113; and R. Price and G.S. Bain, 'Union Growth Revisited: 1948–1974 in Perspective', *British Journal of Industrial Relations*, vol. 14, No. 3 (November 1976), p. 346. There are slight differences in the 1961 figures between these two sources; the more recent figures have been taken

TABLE 2.8 continued

	Major occupational groups as a percentage of total occupied population 1911–71 (percentages)							Growth indices of major occupational groups, 1911–71 (1911 = 100)						
	1911	1921	1931	1951	1961	1966	1971	1911	1921	1931	1951	1961	1966	1971
1 Employers and Proprietors	6.7	6.8	6.7	5.0	4.8	3.4	2.6	100	107	114	91	93	68	50
2 White-collar workers	18.7	21.2	23.0	30.9	35.9	38.3	42.7	100	119	141	202	247	276	303
(a) Managers and administrators	3.4	3.6	3.7	5.5	5.4	6.1	8.6	100	112	122	197	201	240	330
(b) Higher professionals	1.0	1.0	1.1	1.9	3.0	3.4	3.8	100	107	130	236	390	451	504
(c) Lower professionals and technicians	3.1	3.5	3.5	4.7	6.0	6.5	7.7	100	121	130	189	253	286	336
(d) Foremen and inspectors	1.3	1.4	1.5	2.6	2.9	3.0	3.0	100	118	136	249	287	311	311
(e) Clerks	4.5	6.5	6.7	10.4	12.7	13.2	14.0	100	151	169	281	360	392	410
(f) Salesmen and shop assistants	5.4	5.1	6.5	5.7	5.9	6.1	5.6	100	99	139	129	141	153	138
3 Manual workers	74.6	72.0	70.3	64.2	59.3	58.3	54.7	100	102	108	106	102	105	98
(a) Skilled	30.5	28.8	26.7	24.9	25.3	23.7		100	99	100	100	107	104	
(b) Semi-skilled	34.4	29.0	28.7	27.2	25.4	26.1		100	89	96	97	95	102	
(c) Unskilled	9.6	14.2	14.8	12.0	8.6	8.5		100	155	176	153	115	119	
4 Total occupied population	100.0	100.0	100.0	100.0	100.0	100.0	100.0	100	105	115	123	129	135	133

This table is largely based on G. S. Bain, *The Growth of White-Collar Unionism* (Oxford 1970); Guy Routh, *Occupation and Pay in Great Britain* (Cambridge 1965), and the Census of Population of England and Wales and Scotland for the various years. For a discussion of the way in which the original table was constructed see Bain op. cit., pp. 189–90.

TABLE 2.9

The growth of the administrative overhead, GB

In industry			Thousands
	Administrative employees	Production employees	A/P (per cent)
1907	408	4,755	8.6
1924	627	4,708	13.0
1930	589	4,286	13.7
1935	676	4,482	15.0
1948(a)	1,126	5,651	20.0
Manufacturing industry			
1948(b)	1,293	6,743	19.2
1958	1,938	7,194	26.9
1968	2,259	6,502	34.7
1974	2,068	5,596	37.0

Sources: 1907–48(a): R. Bendix, *Work and Authority in Industry* (Chichester 1956), p. 214
1948(b)–68: *British Labour Statistics, Historical Abstract* (HMSO 1971), pp. 236–9, 276–7
1974: *British Labour Statistics Year Book, 1974* (HMSO 1976), p. 185

another, since 1911. Originally introduced to show variations in infant mortality rates (that most sensitive indicator of standards of living), it has been used to identify a whole range of social differences in British society. The six categories (treating the third as two separate categories) currently in use are:[30]

    I Professional, etc., occupations (including doctors, lawyers, chemists, and clergymen)

    II Intermediate occupations (including most managerial and senior administrative occupations, e.g. sales managers, authors, MPs, colliery managers, personnel managers, senior government officials, school teachers, farmers, physiotherapists, and nurses)

    III Skilled occupations

        (N) Non-manual (including typists, clerical workers, sales workers, sales representatives, and shop assistants)

        (M) Manual (including cooks, railway guards, plasterers, bricklayers, foremen packers, and foremen in the engineering and allied trades)

    IV Partly-skilled occupations (including barmen, bus conductors, canteen assistants, and telephone operators [but not supervisors who are III N])

    V Unskilled occupations (including office cleaners and stevedores [but not foremen who are III M], lorry drivers' mates, and labourers)

The distribution of the population of Great Britain, in terms of these categories, is shown in tables 2.11 and 2.12. These tables are comparable with the occupational distribution in table 2.8 in terms of the proportions classified in non-manual and manual work, but differ from it in so far as a much larger proportion of the occupied population are shown as skilled manual workers (Social Class III M). It also demonstrates that there are considerable differences in the 'Social Class' distributions of men and women; this means that there are many households in which

TABLE 2.10

The size of UK enterprises

UK enterprises with over 200 employees in the UK

ANALYSIS BY INDUSTRY AND NUMBER OF EMPLOYEES

Standard Industrial Classification order	Sector	No. of UK employees							Total
		201–500	501–1,000	1,001–2,000	2,001–5,000	5,001–10,000	Over 10,000	Total over 2,000	
		Number of enterprises (of which controlled from overseas)							
I–III	Food, drink and tobacco	21(3)	30(7)	28(4)	20(4)	9(3)	22(1)	51(8)	130(22)
IV–V	Petroleum products etc. and chemicals etc.	34(18)	31(19)	24(11)	21(9)	8(3)	7(1)	36(13)	125(61)
VI–XII	Metal manufacturing, engineering, shipbuilding, vehicles	55(17)	140(30)	138(31)	125(34)	45(9)	48(10)	218(53)	551(131)
XIII–XV	Textiles and clothing	11(1)	44(4)	44(2)	37(3)	8(–)	10(–)	55(3)	154(10)
XVI–XIX	Other manufacturing	32(5)	78(5)	62(8)	57(7)	35(1)	17(3)	109(11)	281(29)
XX and XXII	Construction, transport and communications	32(2)	44(3)	55(2)	40(1)	16(–)	11(–)	67(1)	198(8)
XXIII	Wholesale and retail distribution	43(10)	65(4)	55(7)	59(5)	17(1)	22(3)	98(9)	261(30)
XXIV	Insurance, banking, finance and business services	124(19)	73(6)	37(1)	32(1)	18(–)	11(–)	61(1)	295(27)
XXVI	Miscellaneous services	17(6)	21(6)	18(4)	22(1)	12(–)	9(–)	43(1)	99(17)
	TOTAL	369(81)	526(84)	461(70)	413(65)	168(17)	157(18)	738(100)	2,094(335)

Note: See text of the Report (paragraph 3) for definitions and methodology
Source: *Report of the Committee of Inquiry on Industrial Democracy* (Bullock Report), Cmnd 6706 (HMSO 1977), p. 5

Work

TABLE 2.11

Social class composition of people aged 15 and over, for various groups, GB, 1971

	Men only			Women only			Men and women aged 15 & over		
				Married		Single widowed and divorced			
	Economically active	Retired	Economically active and retired	Own¹ class	Husbands² class	Own³ class	Own occupation of economically active and retired	Head of family	Chief economic supporter
	(1)	(2)	(3)	(4)	(5)	(6)	(7)	(8)	(9)
Percentage in each Social Class:									
I	5.2	3.0	5.0	0.9	5.3	1.2	3.6	5.1	4.9
II	17.8	19.1	18.0	16.2	19.8	19.2	17.8	20.0	19.8
III N	11.9	12.1	11.9	35.4	11.3	41.2	21.1	11.9	14.2
III M	39.0	34.2	38.5	10.0	39.0	10.8	28.4	37.9	34.8
IV	17.8	20.3	18.1	28.2	17.5	22.7	20.9	18.0	18.6
V	8.3	11.2	8.6	9.4	7.1	4.9	8.2	7.3	7.7
Total classified (= 100%)	15,368	1,911	17,279	5,697	12,365	3,834	26,809	13,150	15,907
Total⁴ unclassified	516	323	909	1,101	471	1,549	3,488	694	1,374
Total in Great Britain	15,884	2,304	18,188	6,797	12,835	5,383	30,367	13,844	17,281

Notes:
1 Economically active and retired married women by own social class.
2 Married women enumerated with their husband by the social class of husband including both the economically active and retired, and those economically active.
3 Economically active and retired single, widowed, and divorced women.
4 Unclassified persons: those for whom no occupation or inadequate information was reported in the Census. A large proportion of this group were out of work, retired, or inactive at Census date.
Based on: Census of Population, 1971, Economic Activity Tables
Source: *Social Trends*, No. 6 (HMSO 1975) p. 11

TABLE 2.12

Married couples both economically active, GB, 1971

								Percentages
	Social Class of husband							
	I	II	III N	III M	IV	V	NC	Total (thousands)
Social Class of wife:								
I	6	2	–	–	–	–	1	44
II	31	34	15	9	8	5	12	806
III N	46	40	51	32	25	19	29	1,868
III M	3	4	7	12	11	10	7	502
IV	9	13	19	32	36	37	26	1,443
V	2	2	5	11	14	22	10	518
Not classified	4	4	3	4	4	6	16	232
Total (= 100%) (thousands)	242	1,031	647	2,111	955	339	92	5,414

Based on: *Census of Population, (1971); Classification: Own Social Class*
Source: *Social Trends*, No. 6 (HMSO 1975), pp. 11, 12

husband and wife are in a different 'Social Class' if this is categorized on the basis of their own work. Indeed this situation is the more common, and in a considerable number of cases the wife has the 'higher' 'Social Class' ranking. Such differences necessitate some reservations about attempting to relate work to other social characteristics, when this is done on the assumption that households can be classified in terms of the husband's occupation. The distinction between Social Class I and II is also somewhat arbitrary; all major professional occupations are classed as I, but even higher administrative and managerial occupations are classed as II.

More recently the Census authorities have devised a separate classification of Socio-Economic Groups, with the intention of forming categories of people with similar 'social, cultural and recreational standards' and of producing a larger number of more sharply defined groups. The categories used, and the relationship between them and the Social Class categories can be seen in tables 2.13 and 2.14. Although there are important areas of overlap, the separation of workers in agriculture from other workers, and the use of employment status as a differentiating factor, make the relationship a fairly complex one.

In the General Household Survey the Office of Population Censuses and Surveys has collapsed the sixteen Socio-Economic Groups into six ranked groupings which, it should be noted, are roughly comparable to the Registrar General's Social Classes. These groupings are used for the tabulation of some data to be presented below:[31]

General Household Survey Socio-Economic Groups	Corresponding SEGs	Examples
1 Professional	3, 4	Doctors, lawyers, chemists, clergymen
2 Employers and managers	1, 2, 13	Sales managers, MPs, colliery managers, personnel managers, senior government officials, farmers

TABLE 2.13

Social class by socio-economic group of chief economic supporter of household, GB, 1971

Percentages

Socio-economic group:	I	II	Social Class III N	III M	IV	V	NC
Employers and managers (large establishments)		21	—				
Employers and managers (small establishments)		35	2	3	1	—	
Professional – self-employed	18						
Professional – employees	82						
Intermediate non-manual		30	6				
Junior non-manual			88				
Personal service		—	2	1	11		
Foreman – manual				11	8		
Skilled manual				77			
Semi-skilled manual					70		
Unskilled manual						97	
Own account (non-professional)		6	2	6	3		
Farmers – employers, managers		5					
Farmers – own account		4					
Agricultural				—	7	3	
Not adequately described							100
Total[1] (= 100%) (thousands)	762	3,145	2,245	5,500	2,965	1,205	1,338

Note: [1] There are some differences from the 10% sample results due to sampling error.
Based on *Census of Population, 1971. 1% sample; Classification: Occupation of the chief economic supporter of the household*
Source: *Social Trends* No. 6 (HMSO 1975), p. 32

TABLE 2.14

Socio-economic group by social class of chief economic supporter of household, GB, 1971

Percentages

Socio-economic group:	Social Class							Total[1] (= 100%) (thousands)
	I	II	III N	III M	IV	V	NC	
Employers and managers (large establishments)		97	–	3				681
Employers and managers (small establishments)		80	4	14	2		–	1,366
Professional – self-employed	100							137
Professional – employees	100							625
Intermediate non-manual		88	12					1,069
Junior non-manual		1	85		15			2,306
Personal service			10	22	67			363
Foreman – manual				100				613
Skilled manual				100				4,247
Semi-skilled manual					100			2,077
Unskilled manual						100		1,167
Own account (non-professional)		25	8	50	12	5		686
Farmers – employers, managers		100						146
Farmers – own account		100						131
Agricultural				7	93			209
Not adequately described							100	1,338

Note: [1] There are some differences from the 10% sample results due to sampling error.
Based on *Census of Population, 1971. 1% sample; Classification: Occupation of the chief economic supporter of the household*
Source: *Social Trends*, No. 6 (HMSO 1975), p. 32

General Household Survey Socio-Economic Groups	Corresponding SEGs	Examples
3 Intermediate and junior non-manual	5, 6	Teachers, nurses, physiotherapists, sales representatives, clerical workers, typists, telephone operators, shop assistants
4 Skilled manual (including foremen and supervisors) including own account non-professionals	8, 9, 12, 14	Railway guards, foremen packers, foremen in engineering and allied trades, bricklayers
5 Semi-skilled manual and personal service	7, 10, 15	Cooks, canteen assistants, barmen, bus conductors
6 Unskilled manual	11	Lorry drivers' mates, labourers, stevedores, office cleaners.

In devising these classifications of 'Social Class' and 'Socio-Economic Groupings' the Census Office were using evaluative criteria to determine into which category any particular occupation was to be placed. The bases of the classifications were not exclusively or even mainly economic, but represented a synthesis of mostly implicit criteria, such as the skill of the occupation and the education and/or training required for it, but also including — in the case of 'Social Class' at least — an assessment of how members of society in general regarded the occupation, how they would rank it as compared with others. These assessments were, in a sense, second-hand and represented 'what the investigators thought other people would think' of an occupation. Such procedures obviously have severe limitations and as has been mentioned already this has led sociologists to attempt to develop occupational prestige rankings which are empirically based on the views expressed by samples of the population. In Britain the Hall-Jones scale, developed initially to measure social mobility, has been used in some form in a number of social surveys and community studies.[32] Such occupational rankings might be thought preferable to the official categories, but their use in any discussion such as this one is both impractical and more problematic than might at first be thought. It is impractical because the official and national statistics have not been tabulated in these terms, and cannot be so retabulated; and more problematic because of the ambiguities about precisely what respondents are doing when they grade occupations. Are they assessing prestige, strictly defined as symbolic advantages and power, or are they evaluating jobs as more or less desirable in terms of a range of considerations?[33] Thus while acknowledging the limitations of official classifications of occupations our subsequent analysis will depend very heavily on them. For discovering broad differences in the costs and rewards of work — to which we now turn — they are probably adequate.

THE REWARDS AND DEPRIVATIONS OF WORK

As we have seen, 'work' for most people in Britain means work as an employee. In the majority of cases, therefore, the nature of the employment contract is a crucial analytical point of reference in considering the rewards and deprivations arising from work. Before considering it in more detail, however, we need to discuss briefly whether the conditions and experience of work for those not dependent on an employer are likely to be very different from those of comparable employees.

Self-employment

Those who run their own business and employ others, or who are self-employed, comprised less than 8 per cent of the occupied population in 1971. In terms of their industrial distribution they were numerically important only in agriculture, forestry and fishing (approximately 63 per cent of all occupied), in construction (approximately 26 per cent), in the distributive trades (approximately 18 per cent) and in 'miscellaneous services' (approximately 19 per cent).[34] In contrast, of all those working in manufacturing industry as a whole, only about $1\frac{1}{2}$ per cent were employers or self-employed. The occupational distribution of employers and the self-employed presents a similar picture — they outnumber employees in the same occupations only in a very few cases — farmers, builders, shopkeepers, certain professional groups (lawyers, clergymen, dentists and chiropodists) and certain service occupations (watch repairers, shoe repairers, publicans, hotel keepers and restaurateurs); and it is only in these and a few similar occupations that this category of workers is at all numerous in absolute terms.[35]

The sense of autonomy, of working for oneself, of running one's own business, is both the main differentiating characteristic of self-employment and the main attraction for those who aspire to such economic independence. In most cases the types of tasks which have to be performed — and the conditions under which they are performed — and the other rewards and deprivations of working are largely the same. For many people in our society, the importance of autonomy and independence as an ideal should not, however, be underestimated. Among architects, for example, this aspect of work is especially important because of the aesthetic elements in their job:

> The architects seemed to regard it as axiomatic that, given their interest in and concern for designing buildings, and since, by their reckoning, this is an artistic activity, then by virtue of the sorts of attitudes about artistic activities current in this sort of society, *they must be as free as possible from any sort of interference or restriction . . .*
>
> Because of the value architects attach to design autonomy they tended to evaluate types of architectural work in terms of the opportunities they provided for the employment of their design skills. It was generally considered that the self-employed principal of a private practice had the best chance of doing the kind of work that the architects in the sample aspired to.[36] [Italics in the original]

Similarly, economic independence and running one's own business have been stressed as the main attractions of being a small shopkeeper, and the distinctive characteristic of what is perhaps the most numerous type of small businessman:

> The most important single characteristic of the small shopkeeper's work situation is surely his independence. The autonomy which he enjoys serves to distinguish him sharply from most other groups in the lower middle class. . . .
>
> The ability to control one's own working life is a classic feature of middle-class life-style and today few occupations share the apparent degree of freedom enjoyed by the keeper of a little shop. It is true that this freedom is being eroded but it remains a factor of crucial importance, for it is still the most cherished characteristic of the occupation. Given the economically precarious nature of shop-keeping, the statistics that indicate little change in the numbers of small

businesses must conceal the fact that there is a steady flow of new recruits to
fill the places vacated by those who have been forced out of business. . . .

If we attempt to generalize about the economic orientations of our sample,
it is this 'individualism' that emerges as the dominant theme. Shopkeepers prize
'independence': they feel that if a man is his own master, then success or failure
depend directly upon his own efforts and energies. In an ideal world, hard work
will bring its own rewards.[37]

Farming is a special case and the experience of work for working farmers, smallholders *and* farm labourers is probably distinct from that of employers and employees
in most other occupations, except perhaps in the case of the most highly capitalized
'modern' farms where factory-like methods have been adopted. The situation of the
farmer can of course vary enormously, depending on whether he is owner or tenant,
on the type of agriculture involved, and the number of employees he has, if any;
and his interpretation of this situation varies too in terms of his own orientation
which is likely to be strongly related to the reasons for entering farming in the first
place (family inheritance or tradition, the style of life, an investment, a means of
securing 'losses' to set against tax, and so on). Despite these sources of variation
among farmers it can be argued that working in agriculture as such, in any status,
with the special demands and rhythms of agricultural work, is the most distinctive
attribute. This may lead to a situation where the prime sense of identification is
with the industry as such rather than with the interest of the urban and industrial
majority, a feeling among farm labourers, for example, that they 'have more in
common with farmers than with workers in industry'.[38]

Economic independence as an employer or self-employed person can of course
also bring the benefit of high financial rewards, though it appears difficult to demonstrate this in quantitative terms.[39] (Only one of the fifty-two architects interviewed
by Salaman, however, gave 'inadequate level of pay' as a source of work dissatisfaction,[40] and professional occupations like lawyer and dentist are not noted for their
low levels of earnings.) For the smaller small businessman, however, economic
independence can be bought at a very high price, both in terms of a low income and
of very hard work over long hours and a great deal of worry and anxiety. In the case
of the Edinburgh small shopkeepers, for example, Bechhofer and Elliott reported that
in 1969 the average annual income, including any profits, was only about £100 more
than the average income of manual workers, and this was the result of working at
least an average of $10\frac{1}{2}$ hours per day (when the shop was open) and in many cases
on Sundays as well.[41] In addition there are the further deprivations of a considerable risk of business failure and loss of initial capital, of social isolation because of
the demands of running the shop, and of the need to call on the unpaid help of
other members of the family, so that 'if we compare the shopkeeper with the better-
paid manual workers it seems that the only real advantage or privilege that he enjoys
is that of independence. Certainly he has little real authority for he typically employs
very few staff and those mostly from his own family . . . Shop-keeping is an arduous
business'.[42]

The autonomy and independence gained from self-employment may attract small
businessmen, like shopkeepers and some of the other categories mentioned above,
and differentiate them from those who are employed, but in other respects their
conditions of work and employment are similar, or even rather worse. At the other
end of the scale, among directors of large companies, it can be argued that the situ-

ations and outlooks of the 'propertied' and economically independent and of the 'non-propertied', whose income derives primarily from employment, are very similar. In such situations all top executives, whether they have substantial ownership rights or not, can expect to have considerable autonomy on the job, and all can expect to receive substantial incomes. Thus Nichols has argued, for example, that one cannot regard non-propertied directors as being a distinct 'class' from propertied directors, especially if the normative and relational dimensions of class are taken into account. He has written: 'Once the hitherto manager has gained his directorship, bought his shares, and perhaps even sent his son to public school, then, in many important respects, he is indistinguishable from the propertied director.'[43]

Thus, although the self-employed are of numerical importance in a few sectors of the economy, and the ideal of economic independence and autonomy at work still has considerable symbolic importance more generally, this sub-category of the occupied population can be regarded as experiencing much the same deprivations and rewards from work as do those in the same occupations but working as employees; the only important difference is the one characteristic which distinguishes them — they are not subordinate to an employer. To be independent, to have autonomy at work, is important subjectively and objectively, as we shall see in discussing employment, but with few exceptions it is not associated with other differences from the general patterns of occupation-related characteristics.

The employment contract

For the great majority of the occupied population in the UK work is regulated primarily by a contract of employment, an agreement to an exchange between the employer and the employee. The nature of the agreement is, however, very complex, especially if it is seen as also being typically surrounded by a variety of obligations and expectations which may not be formally specified. At its simplest it represents the exchange of payment for labour power, and in certain pieceworking and sub-contracting situations may involve little more than that. In all other situations and thus for almost all employees, however, the exchange necessarily involves the employee entering into a continuing relationship with the employer, a relationship in which he is placed in a position of subordination. Giddens has written: 'What really distinguishes capitalism as a form of economic system is that labour (power) *itself* becomes a commodity, bought and sold on the market'.[44] In contrast to the case with other commodities, however, the exchange of labour power cannot be instantaneous; what the employer obtains is the employee's *capacity to work*, and to make effective use of this he has to control and direct the activities of the employee while he is in his employment. From the employee's point of view, therefore, work involves not only the deprivations which result from the expenditure of physical and mental energy but also those incurred by the loss of autonomy to the authority of the employer. How this authority is exercised, the sorts of controls and direction to which the employee is subject, these form part of the costs of working, though ones which it may be difficult to quantify.

For these reasons employment in capitalist societies like the UK must be regarded as involving an inherent coercive element. All those without sufficient wealth to provide for themselves without working are forced to sell their labour power to an employer in the labour market; and this necessarily involves entering a subordinate role in the employing organization, though the degree of subordination may vary considerably — some employees share in the exercise of authority. Control over the exercise and products of a man's labour are therefore lost. In return for his labour, of course, the employee receives the means of subsistence. In terms of conventional analyses there is disagreement as to what would constitute a 'fair' return for work, as wages and salaries are clearly not just the product of market forces and cannot be legitimated in those terms. In terms of a Marxist analysis, in contrast, there can never be a 'fair' wage or salary in a capitalist society as the employer appropriates the 'surplus value' which is created by the employee over and above that needed for his own maintenance and reproduction.[45]

Whether or not a Marxist analysis is accepted, many commentators accept the notion that employees in modern industrial societies suffer 'alienation'. They differ however in whether they see 'alienation' as inherent in the structure of work relations in capitalist and similar societies, or whether they see it as possible to modify or eliminate 'alienation' by appropriate changes in industrial organization and technology, but still within the same overall societal framework. Marx's original conception is well represented in the following passage:

> In what does this alienation of labour consist? First, that the work is *external* to the worker, that it is not part of his nature, that consequently he does not fulfil himself in his work but denies himself, has a feeling of misery, not of well-being, does not develop freely a physical and mental energy, but is physically exhausted and mentally debased. The worker therefore feels himself at home only during his leisure, whereas at work he feels homeless. His work is not voluntary but imposed, *forced labour*. It is not the satisfaction of a need, but only a *means* for satisfying other needs. Its alien character is clearly shown by the fact that as soon as there is no physical or other compulsion it is avoided like the plague. Finally, the alienated character of work for the worker appears in the fact that it is not his work but work for someone else, that in work he does not belong to himself but to another person.[46]

Such a conception of alienation contains, but should not be reduced to, reference to the psychological state of a particular actor or actors; it is more than a synonym for 'job dissatisfaction'. It encompasses as an essential element particular structural features of a society, whether or not the actors recognize them.[47]

This more wide-ranging view of 'alienation' implies two assertions: first, that something can be said in general about the nature of man and what he needs to realize his full potential, to be fully free; and secondly, that such needs cannot be met within the existing social arrangements of modern industrial society, particularly in its capitalist variants, but probably in most socialist ones also. Both these judgments have been challenged. Some writers have stressed the cultural determination and variability of what people want from their work so that it makes no sense, beyond a very trivial level, to talk of 'needs' or of 'man's essence'.[48] Other writers, operating with different conceptions of human needs or of man's nature, have argued for the possibility of meeting such needs or of realizing man's potential with only relatively minor changes to the organization and administration of work.[49] Thus considerations of work and the employment contract necessarily enter an area where there are basic philosophical disagreements which influence the conduct of research and the interpretations of its findings, and these should be borne in mind when considering the empirical evidence which is discussed below.

It is neither possible nor necessary to continue these debates here, but one implication of them for a discussion of the employment contract is that any consideration of the rewards and deprivations of work must be concerned with more than just the obvious financial rewards and should see subordination and loss of autonomy as a part of the costs of working which can also vary considerably between different work situations. Some would go further and stress that apparent sources of positive satisfaction in work are merely *relative* to the over-riding deprivations of work in our sort of society. This is the position taken by Baldamus. He has pointed to the open-ended nature of the employment contract – pay may be specified but the content and intensity of work is not, and often cannot be. The employer therefore has to exercise control over his employees to secure appropriate levels of effort. 'Effort', Baldamus suggests, should be conceptualized as the deprivations of 'impairment', 'tedium' and 'weariness' arising from the work realities of unpleasant and damaging physical conditions, repetitive tasks and coercive work routines, and partially offset by the relative satisfactions of 'inurement', 'traction' and 'contentment'. As such effort is both inherently subjective (only really known by those experiencing it) and empirically potentially unstable. Stability in the 'effort bargain', which determines the actual day-to-day working out of the relationship between pay and effort, is dependent on shared definitions of what constitutes a 'fair day's pay for a fair day's work', and these arise during socialization before entering work and more especially in the work place.[50]

Baldamus's analysis of the contract of employment is based on the case of the non-skilled worker who only has basic labour power to sell. Many employees, however, have skills, qualifications and/or experience to offer on the labour market, and/ or do work where they carry considerable responsibility for reaching decisions. Wages and salaries, therefore, must be seen in many cases as payments for skill or compensations for carrying responsibility. As with effort, both these qualities are hard to define precisely and are subject to negotiation in practice. In the case of skill this is reflected in the frequent disputes and negotiations about differentials and the apportionment of work which occur in industry and elsewhere. In the case of responsibility Jaques has argued that an element of discretion is a characteristic of all employment work, that it becomes increasingly important as one moves up the organizational hierarchy, and that it can be measured in terms of 'time span' and is the essential factor to which 'fair' levels of pay should be related. The first two points are widely accepted, but the degree of responsibility expected and the payment due for it are typically seen as matters for negotiation on the job, and are not regarded as something which can be objectively determined.[51]

The implications of the discussion in this section so far are that the employment contract necessarily involves elements of coercion and conflict; and that it contains inherent ambiguities or uncertainties over the contribution which the employer can legitimately expect from his employees. In turning to look at the rewards of work in detail we shall see that they too are far from straightforward.

As will be apparent from the above discussion, and as has been stressed by a number of writers, the relationship between employer and employee has central 'calculative' elements, though coercive and/or normative ones are normally also involved.[52] In our sort of society most labour is 'formally free', not legally coerced; and men work because they need to earn their means of subsistence and not primarily for idealistic reasons. The prime rewards for the employee are financial, and jobs are assessed in these terms. A comparison of relative advantages, even in these terms, however, is far from easy as earnings may include a number of components – basic pay, bonuses, overtime pay, shift allowances, and so on. Certainly basic wage rates and salary scales are not necessarily a good guide to the likely level of earnings at a particular point in time and in the working life of any individual do not necessarily reflect likely lifetime earnings, nor the opportunities within a particular occupation for promotion, or a career, leading to higher earnings in the future.

Though pay is the most important reward for work it is by no means the only one, and this further complicates consideration of occupational rewards. Many employees receive fringe benefits — holidays with pay, sick pay, pensions, subsidized meals, car allowances or the use of a company car, accommodation allowances or housing at reduced rent, the perks of expense account lunches or the possibility of buying company goods or services at reduced prices, and so on. Systematic information about all these benefits does not exist, but it is possible to consider some of them in detail and their relationship to occupational categories.

It is more difficult to take account of rewards which cannot even potentially be quantified and expressed in money terms, yet there are such rewards which can be of considerable importance in many occupations. Some of them have already been referred to in the introduction in the discussion of the possible meanings of work: status and prestige among one's fellows at work and elsewhere; the gratifications deriving from doing work which is intrinsically interesting or which is seen as socially valuable, or which provides opportunities for achievement or personal development. Some jobs are seen as attractive because they are convenient (reasonable hours, a short journey to work) or clean, safe or secure, though such 'attractions' are perhaps better seen as the absence of deprivations than as anything more positive.[53] All these less tangible rewards are normally encompassed within investigations of job satisfaction. Ideally such investigations recognize and try to take account of the variety of considerations which may enter into any overall synthesizing judgment about a job. It remains difficult, however, if not impossible without further information, to be sure of the meaning and significance of a general claim to be 'satisfied' or 'dissatisfied' with one's job, so that although we shall consider such evidence we must do so with caution. It must be remembered too that all such judgments are relative to the respondent's expectations and orientations; a work situation with apparently the same 'objective' characteristics may therefore be very differently evaluated by the same respondent at different times, or by different respondents at any one time.[54]

Finally, it is important to try to consider the degree of countervailing power typically possessed by an occupation which may enable workers to secure some control over their market and work situations, and so reduce their dependence on employers. In most cases such power derives from the collective organization of the relevant employees so that they can bargain with employers, and if necessary attempt to secure their aims by strikes or other forms of industrial action. The degree of organization in trade unions or professional associations is thus an important means by which the rewards from work may be increased and the deprivations contained. As has been stressed many times in the literature on trade unions, of course, this 'remedy' may prove as bad as — or worse than — the 'disease'; the occupational association may become oligarchically controlled and dominate the market and work situations of its members in as alien a way as did the employers.[55]

The basic deprivations of work have already been discussed — the physical and mental effort involved in working; the psychological costs of carrying responsibility; the costs in terms of effort and deferred gratifications involved in training and in acquiring skills and qualifications. It will be apparent that they are very difficult, and probably impossible, to quantify systematically across a whole range of occupations. Some general indications of varying demands for effort can be inferred from information about hours of work, the incidence of shift working, of payments by results, and so on, which we shall consider in conjunction with data on pay. Certain other sources of deprivation are rather less problematic. The physical and social conditions of work differ in their consequences for the health of the employee, so that occupations can be compared in terms of their accident rates, and the likely health and life expectancy of their members. Secondly, occupations, and industries, differ in terms of the degree of job security they offer, though recent experience has indicated that this may change unexpectedly over time; rates of unemployment, the availability of alternative vacancies, the incidence of redundancy, can all, in principle at least, be compared.

A final problem must be mentioned, though it will prove less important than might be thought at first. Many of the characteristics mentioned are incommensurable – they cannot be assessed on the same scale, so that it is impossible to say, for example, that so much extra pay compensates precisely for certain dangerous working conditions. In theory it could become very difficult to make anything but rather impressionistic comparisons between occupations; in practice it is less so because, as we shall see, rather than higher rewards of one sort compensating for absence of other sorts of reward, or for particularly severe deprivations, occupations tend to be generally favoured or deprived in terms of many if not all indices.

In considering the detailed evidence a variety of comparisons will be possible. In some cases particular occupations or industries can be considered; in others only general types of work – skilled manual, for example, or professional; and in others only the basic comparison between manual and non-manual occupations will be possible.

Pay and hours

The employment contract involves more than an exchange of work (or labour power) for pay, but the income they receive is the most important reward for most employees. We shall consider first the changes in relative earnings for the main occupational categories which have taken place during the present century, then go on to look at the most recent data for all employees in a little more detail, and finally discuss very briefly those at the two ends of the earnings continuum, the high- and the low-paid.

In the conclusion to his survey of changes in occupational structure and earnings in Great Britain between 1906 and 1960 Routh commented: 'The outstanding characteristic of the national pay structure is the rigidity of its relationships', and as the summaries of his findings in table 2.15 and 2.16 indicate, this is broadly true.[56] Professional, managerial and supervisory employees earned more than manual workers in 1913–14, and continued to earn more in 1960; men earned on average between 114 and 119 per cent of the average earnings for both men and women throughout the period, while the comparable range for women was consistently very much lower at between 58 and 66 per cent; skilled male manual workers (but not skilled women) consistently earned more than semi- and unskilled workers, whose percentages of average earnings were virtually the same in 1960 as they had been before the First World War.

Even so there have been some important changes over the period as a whole. In

TABLE 2.15

Average earnings, seven occupational classes, 1913–14, 1922–4, 1935–6, 1955–6 and 1960

	1913/14 £	1922/4 £	% of 1913/14	1935/6 £	% of 1922/4	1955/6 £	% of 1935/6	1960 £	% of 1955/6	% of 1913/14
Men										
1. Professional										
A. Higher	328	582	177	634	109	1,541	243	2,034	132	620
B. Lower	155	320	206	308	96	610	198	847	139	546
2B. Managers, etc.	200	480	240	440	92	1,480	336	1,850	125	925
3. Clerks	99	182	184	192	105	523	272	682	130	689
4. Foremen	113	268	237	273	102	784	287	1,015	129	898
Manual										
5. Skilled	99	180	181	195	108	622	319	796	128	804
6. Semi-skilled	69	126	183	134	106	469	350	581	124	842
7. Unskilled	63	128	203	129	101	435	337	535	123	849
Averages										
Current weights[1]	92	180	194	186	104	634	340	808	127	874
1911 weights	92	177	191	185	104	590	319	746	126	807
Women										
1. Professional										
A. Higher	..	..	..	..	..	(1,080)	..	(1,425)	(138)	..
B. Lower	89	214	240	211	99	438	208	606	138	680
2B. Managers, etc.	(80)[2]	160	..	(168)	105	800	(524)	1,000	125	(1,250)
3. Clerks	45	106	235	99	93	317	320	427	135	949
4. Forewomen	57	154	270	156	101	477	306	602	126	1,056
Manual										

5. Skilled	44	87	*198*	86	*99*	317	*369*	395	*125*	*898*
6. Semi-skilled	50	98	*196*	100	*102*	269	*270*	339	*126*	*678*
7. Unskilled	28	73	*261*	73	*100*	227	*280*	283	*125*	*1,000*
Averages										
Current weights[3]	50	103	*204*	104	*101*	319	*307*	436	*137*	*866*
1911 weights	50	103	*205*	104	*101*	307	*295*	402	*131*	*797*
Men and women weighted average[3]	80	157	*196*	162	*103*	531	*328*	683	*129*	*854*

Notes:
1 According to number of men or women in relevant class. 1959 : 1951 adjusted for changes in industrial distribution
2 Included in weighted average. Their exclusion lowers the average fractionally
3 According to proportions in occupational classes in nearest census year until 1935/6 and to proportions in total labour force, 1955 and 1960

Source: G. Routh, *Occupation and Pay in Great Britain 1906–60* (Cambridge 1965), pp. 104, 107

TABLE 2.16

Occupational class averages as percentages of the average for all occupational classes, men and women, 1913–14, 1922–4, 1935–6, 1955–6 and 1960

	1913/14 % of av.	1922/4 % of av.	1922/4 % of 1913/14	1935/6 % of av.	1935/6 % of 1922/4	1955/6 % of av.	1955/6 % of 1935/6	1960 % of av.	1960 % of 1955/6	1960 % of 1913/14
Men										
1. Professional										
A. Higher	410	372	91	392	105	290	74	298	103	73
B. Lower	194	204	105	190	93	115	60	124	108	64
2B. Managers, etc.	250	307	123	272	89	279	103	271	97	108
3. Clerks	124	116	94	119	103	98	82	100	102	81
4. Foremen	141	171	121	169	99	148	88	149	101	106
Manual										
5. Skilled	124	115	93	121	105	117	97	117	100	94
6. Semi-skilled	86	80	93	83	104	88	97	85	97	99
7. Unskilled	79	82	104	80	98	82	102	79	96	100
Men's average (current weights)	115	114	99	115	100	119	103	118	99	103
Mean deviation (per cent)	67	73		70		48		49		

Women									
1. Professional									
A. Higher	..	..	..	..	(203)	..	(209)	(102)	..
B. Lower	111	137	123	130	82	63	89	109	80
2B. Managers, etc.	(100)	102	(102)	104	151	145	146	97	(146)
3. Clerks	56	68	121	61	60	98	62	103	111
4. Forewomen	71	98	138	96	90	94	88	98	124
Manual									
5. Skilled	55	56	102	53	60	113	58	97	105
6. Semi-skilled	62	63	102	62	51	82	50	98	81
7. Unskilled	35	47	134	45	43	96	41	95	117
Women's average (current weights)[1]	63	66	105	64	58	91	64	110	102
Mean deviation (per cent)[1]	31	37		38	43		39		
Average men and women %	100	100	100	100	100		100		
£	80	157		162	531		683		

Note:

1 Excluding class 1A

Source: G. Routh, *Occupation and Pay in Great Britain 1906–60* (Cambridge, 1965), pp. 104, 107

the first place the degree of dispersion of male earnings, measured by the mean deviation, has declined considerably, and this is reflected, for example, in the fact that whereas in 1913–14 a 'higher professional' earned on average more than three times as much as a skilled manual worker (£328 and £90 p.a. respectively), in 1960 the differential had been reduced to $2\frac{1}{2}$ times (£2,034 and £796 p.a.). More striking perhaps is the decline in the relative position of male 'lower professionals' and 'clerks', the latter in particular receiving clearly lower earnings than male skilled manual workers in 1960, although the two categories had had almost identical average earnings until before the Second World War. Among women there were marked changes in the period from 1913–14 to 1922–4 when the non-manual groups and unskilled manual workers all improved their relative earnings considerably, but these advantages were reduced as a result of changes in subsequent years.

Routh attributed the relative stability of the pay structure to the very strongly held, even if intuitive, opinions wage and salary earners have about the appropriate, 'just', pay for their occupations, and the efforts they therefore undertake to maintain or restore differentials. The stability of the overall structure of earnings in the long-term is seen as the outcome of the 'almost constant state of change' which results from occupational groups' attempts to improve or regain their relative position in the pay hierarchy – attempts which have the effect of making any major restructuring very difficult.[57]

In 1976 there was also a clear general hierarchy of earnings (in terms of overall averages) which paralleled that reported by Routh for 1960 and earlier; the most highly paid category were male non-manual workers, followed by male manual workers, female non-manual workers and female manual workers (table 2.17). Indeed if the figures for juveniles are included the earnings hierarchy continues with boys under 18 and girls under 18, in that order, forming the two lowest paid categories (see fig. 2.1).[58] The differential between the average earnings of the two main categories of men is not very great, but on average women earn less than two-thirds as much as men (though not entirely because of low rates of pay). In fact in recent years this differential, and those between younger and adult workers, and between manual and non-manual workers, have all narrowed somewhat. Between April 1970 and April 1974 'in general the earnings of women increased relatively faster than those of men, the earnings of manual workers relatively faster than those of non-manual workers and the earnings of the lower paid relatively faster than those of the higher paid. Such changes in the overall dispersion of earnings have occurred steadily from year to year and have been noticeable in their effects.'[59]

Examination of the make-up of pay reveals further differences between the main categories. The differential in hourly rates of earnings between male manual and non-manual workers is markedly greater than the earnings difference (as it is to a much smaller extent for women), but the gap between the sexes narrows when hourly earnings are considered. This is because male manual workers work on average more than five hours a week longer than any other category, mostly but not entirely because of overtime; more than a quarter of all male workers worked more than 48 hours a week, while hardly any employees in the other groupings worked such long hours; and over half the male manual workers had their earnings augmented by overtime payments, as compared with fewer than a fifth in any other category. The other two sources of augmented earnings (and also, of course, of intensified demands for effort) – payment by results and shift payments – are also primarily of relevance

Full-time males and females whose pay was not affected by absence

Age groups as at 1.1.76	Weekly earnings (Lowest Decile / Median / Highest Decile)	Mean Weekly Earnings £	Nos. in each category	Per cent of Total %
Girls under 18	25·1 — 36	26·0	1,979	1·5
Boys under 18	18·5 — 26·5 — 38·7	28·1	2,316	1·8
18–20	27·6 — 41·4 — 62·1	43·5	5,049	3·9
Women manual workers, 18 and over	26 — 38·4 — 53·9	39·4	10,096	7·7
Women non-manual workers, 18 and over	28·8 — 44·2 — 76·4	48·8	25,903	19·8
Men manual workers, 21 and over	43·6 — 62·1 — 90·1	65·1	50,585	38·8
Men non-manual workers 21 and over	46·2 — 73·9 — 123·7	81·6	34,575	26·5
			130,503	100

Weekly earnings axis (£): 10 20 30 40 50 60 70 80 90 100 110 120

Figure 2.1   Distribution of Gross Weekly Earnings, April 1976

Source: Department of Employment, *New Earnings Survey 1976*, Part E, Analyses by Region and Age Group (HMSO 1977), pp. 32, 34

TABLE 2.17

The earnings and hours of work of male and female employees, in full-time employment, manual and non-manual, GB

	Full-time men aged 21 and over				
	Manual	% of all	Non-manual	% of all	All
Employees whose pay was not affected by absence					
Average gross weekly earnings	£65.1	90.6	81.6	113.6	71.8 100
of which: overtime payments	8.7		2.3		6.1
PBR etc payments	5.2		1.8		3.8
Shift etc premium payments	2.1		0.5		1.4
Distribution of average gross weekly earnings.					
10 per cent earned less than	43.6		46.2		44.5
50 per cent earned less than	62.1		73.9		65.8
10 per cent earned more than	90.1		123.7		104.9
Average gross hourly earnings,	p. 143.7	86.2	210.6	126	166.8 100
excluding overtime	p. 141.0		210.6		166.6
Average weekly hours,	45.3	106.0	38.5	90.2	42.7 100
of which overtime hours	5.4		1.3		3.8
Distribution of hours – percentage of employees –					
36 hours or less	1.5		23.9		10.1
36–40 hours	40.4		58.6		47.4
40–48 hours	31.8		12.3		24.3
more than 48 hours	26.3		5.2		18.2
Employees who received overtime payments					
percentage of employees	54.5		17.4		39.4
average payment per week	16.0		13.4		15.5
average overtime hours per week	9.7		6.6		9.2
Employees who received PBR etc payments					
percentage of employees	37.9		7.6		25.6
average payment per week	13.8		23.1		14.9
Employees who received shift etc payments					
percentage of employees	23.2		5.7		16.1
average payment per week	8.9		8.0		8.8

Full-time women aged 18 and over						April 1976
Manual		Non-manual		All		% of men
	% of all		% of all			
39.4	85.3	48.8	105.6	46.2	100	64.3
1.0		0.4		0.6		
3.7		0.2		1.2		
0.8		0.3		0.4		
26.0		28.8		28.0		
38.4		44.2		42.4		
53.9		76.4		70.3		
100.7	82.1	132.0	107.6	122.6	100	73.5
100.2		131.8		122.4		
39.3	105.4	36.5	97.9	37.3	100	87.4
0.8		0.3		0.4		
19.2		36.4		31.5		
66.1		58.9		61.0		
11.7		4.1		6.3		
3.0		0.6		1.2		
14.3		8.5		10.2		
7.0		5.2		5.9		
5.6		3.3		4.3		
31.0		3.2		11.0		
11.9		7.4		11.0		
11.2		8.6		9.3		
6.8		3.8		4.8		

Source: Department of Employment, *New Earnings Survey 1976*, Part A, Report and Key Results (HMSO 1976); table 1, p. A5

for manual workers, though in this case a substantial proportion of women workers are involved as well, especially in working under incentive payment schemes.

Thus male manual workers work longer hours, and possibly under more intense demands for effort, to receive lower pay on average than male non-manual workers; and the same is true, but to a markedly lesser extent for female employees. The difference between men's and women's earnings on the other hand is primarily a question of lower hourly rates of pay for women, but in the case of manual workers the effect of this is increased by the absence, for most women, of any overtime or shift payments.

The aggregate figures so far discussed conceal the great range of different levels and patterns of earnings received by specific occupational groupings. In the case of non-manual employees it is possible to compare both meaningful general categories ('professional', 'managerial', etc.) and certain specific occupations (see tables 2.18 and 2.19). It is again possible to observe the way in which relative advantages tend to reinforce each other, rather than compensate for disadvantages: in the case of both men and women the more highly paid non-manual occupations work slightly shorter hours (though presumably schoolteachers would claim that the figures in the tables take no account of work done outside school hours), and with few exceptions are less likely to be involved in working overtime, shifts and under payment by results. In the case of all the categories men earn more than women in the same occupational grouping; in cases where equal pay has been operative for some years, for example teaching, this is presumably due to the fact that male teachers are on average older, and more likely to occupy posts of responsibility. Men in each case also work slightly longer hours, and are more likely to receive pay for overtime and payment by results (except managerial employees). The pattern of shift-working is less clear-cut, presumably because certain predominantly female occupations, such as nursing, are heavily involved in shift-work.

It is important to note that the non-manual category includes some substantial groupings of employees who are relatively low paid by any standard; clerical workers and, even more so, those involved in selling, both men and women, earn less than the average for all occupations. In the case of sales assistants the average level of earnings is nearly as low as that for the lowest 10 per cent of all employees (one conventional definition of the low paid). On the other hand the financial rewards of a 'professional' occupation are clear, relative to those of other non-manual employees of the same sex, and this is the case for men in managerial occupations (and would be even more clearly the case if the more highly paid employees in 'general management' were included in the published tables).

The patterns but not the levels of hours and earnings for manual employees are similar in many respects (table 2.20). For both men and women there are considerable differences in earnings between occupations at the top and the bottom of the hierarchy. Whatever their occupational category, however, men on average are clearly in an advantageous position compared with even the most highly paid women, and this is so whether gross, net or hourly earnings are considered. Relatively few men in any occupational category earned less than £40 per week in 1976, while this was the case in many categories of women's employment. Men on average work longer hours and consequently receive overtime pay and in many cases shift pay. The distribution of payment by results is less clearly differentiated. In cases where the same occupational titles can be compared (inspectors and testers, repetitive assemblers, packers, etc. and storekeepers) women earn on average about two-thirds as much as men in each case, though the proportion is increased to nearly three-quarters in the case of the lower paid categories when overtime, payment by results and shift pay are excluded. Occupational categories specific to women (e.g. cleaners, sewing machinists, kitchen hands) are even less well paid.

Considering male manual workers in more detail it can be seen that in a number of cases the relatively high gross earnings represent compensation for conditions of work likely to cause deprivation. Most face-trained coal miners receive shift pay (and nearly half overtime too); overtime obviously contributes substantially to the earnings of heavy goods drivers; nearly three-quarters of workers in the building industry (bricklayers, mates and labourers) receive incentive payments. This has two results: the differential between the gross earnings of the most highly paid and the least highly paid occupations tends to be increased; and the occupational hierarchy in terms of gross pay is not the same as that in terms of earnings excluding pay for overtime and so on. Unfortunately the available figures are not presented in terms of the main divisions into skilled, semi-skilled and unskilled workers, but in general it is clear from the representative selection of occupations in table 2.20 that the most highly paid are all skilled workers and the least well paid are unskilled.

The data reported in the New Earnings Survey from which tables 2.17–2.20 are derived do not permit very much to be said about those with very high earnings from employment, but they can be augmented from the work of the Royal Commission on the Distribution of Incomes and Wealth, though for a slightly earlier period. The Commission estimated that about 65,000 individuals in the UK had incomes from employment (including self-employment) of £10,000 or more in 1974–5, about 0.3 per cent of the recipients of total employment incomes at all levels; and if the distribution between the sexes parallels that for the previous year, almost all of them were men.[60] (£10,000 represents about £192 per week; in 1975 the New Earnings Survey reported average gross weekly earnings in Great Britain of £60.8 for men and £37.4 for women).[61] Those with incomes from employment of £10,000 or more in 1974–5 probably represented about 30 per cent of all income units (married couples or single persons) with incomes of this size. As tables 2.21 and 2.22 show, in 1974 they were to be found primarily in manufacturing industry, and in insurance, banking, finance, etc., with substantial numbers also in the distributive trades. Occupationally the most important categories were general management (55 per cent of those earning £10,000 or more a year), and 'professional and related occupations supporting management and administration' (e.g. including lawyers, company secretaries, accountants, personnel managers, marketing and advertising managers, administrative civil servants and local government officers, and so on). These tables do not include any of those with high incomes from self-employment, and this may lead to an underestimate of the number concerned with cultural and sporting activities.[62]

Unlike the case with high pay the earnings data considered above do provide an indication of the extent and patterns of the distribution of low pay. If £40 per week is taken as the relevant criterion,[63] almost all the occupations listed in tables 2.18–2.20 include a proportion receiving earnings as low as this, though among men that proportion is greater than 10 per cent only among some unskilled manual workers (labourers and storekeepers), and in the 'selling' category among non-manual workers. In the same terms more than half of female manual workers and nearly as many or more of the women in the 'managerial', 'clerical' and 'selling' categories of non-manual workers are low paid.

TABLE 2.18

The earnings and hours of work of male employees, in full-time employment, in selected non-manual occupations, GB, April 1976

Full-time men aged 21 and over

Employees whose pay was not affected by absence	Average gross weekly earnings	Average earnings less overtime, PBR & shift premium pay	Percentage earning under £40 p.w.	over £100 p.w.
	£	£	%	%
Professional & related supporting management and administration	93.8	90.8	2.5	34.8
e.g. Accountants	86.5	84.6	7.0	29.2
Professional & related in education, welfare & health	91.3	89.5	2.4	35.3
e.g. Secondary Teachers	90.3	90.1	0.4	36.1
Professional & related in science, engineering, technology, etc.	86.5	82.8	1.5	26.3
e.g. Engineers – electrical & electronic	98.5	94.1	0.0	31.7
Draughtsmen – engineering	71.3	67.2	0.9	5.5
Laboratory technicians (Scientific, medical)	68.5	63.9	2.8	9.4
Managerial (excluding general management)	80.4	76.1	4.4	21.6
Clerical & related	62.4	55.8	6.2	4.2
e.g. General clerks & clerks n.i.e.	57.3	53.3	8.5	2.6
Selling	63.9	51.5	13.5	7.3
e.g. Salesmen, shop assistants, shelf fillers	48.9	40.6	34.6	2.6
All non-manual	81.6	77.0	4.6	22.5
All occupations	71.8	60.4	5.2	12.3

Sources: Department of Employment, *New Earnings Survey 1976* Part A (HMSO 1976), table 8, pp. 14–16; Part D (HMSO 1977), table 99, pp. 31–3.

Average hourly earnings, excl. overtime	Average weekly hours	of which overtime	Percentage of employees who received		Shift etc premium pay
			overtime pay	PBR etc pay	
pence			%	%	%
249.8	37.5	0.6	10.0	4.6	1.7
234.2	37.0	0.5	12.3	2.7	0.4
272.4	33.2	0.7	6.8	1.2	6.8
327.1	27.7	0.0	1.9	0.1	0.4
221.0	38.7	1.2	18.3	4.2	4.7
255.0	38.6	1.2	20.5	2.6	8.3
182.1	38.9	1.7	29.6	4.3	0.9
174.2	38.8	1.4	20.4	3.9	10.1
205.2	39.9	1.2	15.6	9.1	5.5
154.6	40.0	2.7	35.1	5.1	18.7
147.1	38.6	1.7	27.0	6.8	4.5
157.0	40.0	1.4	12.7	40.0	6.7
118.1	40.9	0.9	16.7	33.0	6.6
210.6	38.5	1.3	17.4	7.6	5.7
166.6	42.7	3.8	39.4	25.6	16.1

TABLE 2.19

The earnings and hours of work of female employees, in full-time employment, in selected non-manual occupations, GB, April 1976

Full-time Women aged 18 and over

Employees whose pay was not affected by absence	Average gross weekly earnings	Average earnings less overtime, PBR & shift premium pay	Percentage under £40 p.w.	Earning over £100 p.w.
	£	£	%	%
Professional & related supporting management and administration	66.9	66.0	14.2	n.a.
Professional & related in education, welfare & health	65.5	64.0	12.3	n.a.
e.g. Secondary Teachers	78.8	78.6	0.7	n.a.
Professional & related in science, engineering, technology, etc.	55.9	54.7	19.8	n.a.
e.g. Engineers – electrical & electronic	–	–	–	–
Draughtsmen – engineering	–	–	–	–
Laboratory technicians (scientific, medical)	50.0	48.8	23.0	n.a.
Managerial (excluding general management)	46.4	44.8	44.0	n.a.
Clerical & related	43.0	42.2	44.0	n.a.
e.g. General clerks & clerks n.i.e.	43.1	42.5	41.4	n.a.
Selling	31.8	30.6	86.6	n.a.
e.g. Salesmen, shop assistants, shelf fillers	29.8	29.0	93.1	n.a.
All non-manual	48.8	47.8	38.2	n.a.
All occupations	46.2	43.9	43.2	n.a.

Sources: Department of Employment, *New Earnings Survey 1976*, Part A (HMSO 1976), table 9, p. 7; Part D (HMSO 1977), table 100, p. 34

Average hourly earnings, excl. overtime	Average weekly hours	of which overtime	Percentage of employees who received		Shift etc. premium pay
			overtime pay	PBR etc pay	
pence			%	%	%
181.4	36.8	0.3	7.3	2.2	2.7
187.7	34.3	0.2	4.5	0.8	23.8
284.7	27.6	0.0	1.3	0.0	0.4
146.8	37.6	0.3	7.4	2.3	4.9
—	—	—	—	—	—
—	—	—	—	—	—
130.9	37.7	0.4	7.3	2.0	6.9
120.8	38.9	0.5	8.8	9.9	5.6
116.6	36.8	0.3	10.5	3.1	2.4
117.1	36.8	0.2	9.5	2.7	1.1
81.6	38.6	0.3	6.4	10.1	11.6
77.3	38.6	0.2	5.9	8.2	12.8
131.8	36.5	0.3	8.5	3.2	8.6
122.4	37.3	0.4	10.2	11.0	9.3

TABLE 2.20

The earnings and hours of work of male and female employees, in selected manual occupations, GB, April 1976

Employees whose pay was not affected by absence	Average gross weekly earnings	Average earnings less overtime, PBR & shift premium pay	Percentage earning under £40 p.w.	Average hourly earnings, excl. overtime
Full-time men aged 21 & over	£	£	%	pence
Face-trained coal miners	80.7	65.8	0.0	190.7
Foreman (engin. machining)	76.3	64.2	0.8	171.8
Electrician (instal. & mainten. plant)	76.0	56.4	0.5	159.4
Maintenance fitter (non-elec.)	72.9	54.8	1.0	152.7
Inspector & tester (metal & elec.)	69.1	56.6	1.0	156.5
Heavy goods driver (over 3 tons)	67.5	46.0	3.0	127.5
Bricklayers	65.8	46.0	1.4	148.8
Carpenters & joiners (build & maint.)	63.6	47.9	1.8	143.3
Repetitive assemblers (metal & elec.)	62.7	49.2	3.5	143.7
Packers, bottlers, canners, etc.	59.3	44.0	8.9	127.9
Craftsmen's mates, building labourers n.i.e.	57.8	41.2	6.8	126.9
General labourers (incl. engin. & shipbuilding)	56.3	42.8	13.3	120.9
Storekeepers, etc.	54.7	44.4	14.5	120.8
All manual occupations	65.1	49.1	5.6	141.0
All occupations	71.8	60.4	5.2	166.6
Full-time women aged 18 & over				
Inspectors & testers (metal & elec.)	46.0	41.9	19.0	115.6
Repetitive assemblers (metal & elec.)	42.8	36.0	36.6	107.1
Packers, bottlers, canners, etc.	39.2	35.0	56.5	98.3
Storekeepers, etc.	38.8	36.6	58.4	98.3
Other cleaners	37.2	34.1	62.2	96.7
Sewing machinists (textiles)	34.9	22.9	73.6	90.8
Kitchen hands	34.1	32.1	80.1	91.4
All manual occupations	39.4	34.0	56.0	100.2
All occupations	46.2	43.9	43.2	122.4

Source: Department of Employment, *New Earnings Survey 1976*, Part A (HMSO 1976), tables 8 and 9, pp. 14–17; Part B (HMSO 1977), tables 99 and 100, pp. 31–34

Average weekly hours	of which overtime	Percentage of employees who receive overtime pay	PBR etc pay	Shift etc premium pay
		%	%	%
40.7	4.1	47.3	2.5	84.2
43.6	4.0	53.0	17.3	15.4
46.0	6.6	62.4	35.4	26.5
46.1	6.6	64.8	31.2	30.0
43.3	3.7	48.3	28.3	19.9
51.1	10.3	76.8	42.9	10.6
43.9	3.5	44.6	64.3	7.7
44.1	3.7	49.2	57.2	2.3
43.0	3.2	41.3	40.5	17.4
45.4	5.6	59.4	34.1	27.5
45.5	5.0	56.0	67.5	5.1
45.3	5.4	56.2	43.4	21.3
44.2	4.5	52.1	27.9	11.9
45.3	5.4	54.5	37.9	23.3
42.7	3.8	39.4	25.6	16.1
39.6	0.3	10.5	40.0	7.6
39.9	0.6	12.2	55.9	2.4
39.6	0.7	14.9	30.3	12.1
39.4	0.5	10.4	24.3	1.0
38.7	1.0	13.8	19.9	18.8
38.5	0.3	7.1	51.7	1.8
37.1	0.6	9.9	16.9	12.0
39.3	0.8	14.3	31.0	11.2
37.3	0.4	10.2	11.0	9.3

TABLE 2.21

Industrial distribution of employees with higher earnings, GB, April 1974

The distribution between broad industrial groupings of full-time adult men employees earning £8,000 and over

Income unit: adult men employees

Industry[1]	Range of earnings			
	£8,000 and under £10,000	£10,000 and under £12,000	£12,000 and over	Total and percentage
Agriculture, forestry, fishing, mining and quarrying	3	1	–	4 (1%)
Manufacturing Industry	67	23	21	111 (29%)
Construction	4	–	3	7 (2%)
Gas, electricity and water	1	4	–	5 (1%)
Transport and communication	17	5	4	26 (7%)
Distributive trades	26	7	7	40 (10%)
Insurance, banking, finance and business services	51	18	28	97 (26%)
Professional and scientific services	33	4	4	41 (11%)
Miscellaneous services	4	6	4	14 (4%)
Public administration	29	3	2	34 (9%)
Total (all industries)	235	71	73	379 (100%)

Note:
1   Standard Industrial Classification, 1968
Based on: NES (the NES does not include the self-employed)

Source: Royal Commission on the Distribution of Incomes and Wealth, *Report No. 3, Higher Incomes from Employment*, Cmnd 6383 (HMSO 1976), pp. 34, 35

This indication that low pay is particularly a question of low pay for women can be further reinforced. On the basis of data for 1975, for example, it has been calculated that 5 out of the total of 175 manual and non-manual occupations for men separately enumerated in the New Earnings Survey had median earnings below £40 a week (general farm hands, barmen, agricultural machinery operators, managers of independent shops, gardeners and groundsmen); the comparable figures for women were 37 out of 48.[64]

Because of the multiplicity of separate occupations and the vagaries of the categories used, the industrial distribution of the low-paid is perhaps more instructive. As tables 2.23 and 2.24 show agriculture had the largest proportion of men earning less than £40 per week in 1975, but the largest numbers of low paid male workers were in 'miscellaneous services' and distribution; these two industries also contained the largest number of low-paid women workers (using £25 per week or less as the criterion).

A review of a wider range of evidence than the New Earnings Survey statistics has concluded that the low-paid are disproportionately composed not only of women, but also of those at the two ends of the age continuum (under 21 and over 50), the unskilled, those with ill-health, and immigrants.[65] Like the industrial and occupational distributions these characteristics remain relatively constant over time. The

TABLE 2.22

Occupational distribution of employees with higher earnings, GB, April 1974

The distribution between broad occupational groupings of full-time adult men employees earning £8,000 and over

Income unit: adult men employees

Occupational group	Range of earnings			
	£8,000 and under £10,000	£10,000 and under £12,000	£12,000 and over	Total and percentage
Managerial (general management)	82	35	44	161 (43%)
Professional and related supporting management and administration	62	18	20	100 (26%)
Professional and related in education, welfare and health	19	3	2	24 (6%)
Literary, artistic and sports	2	2	1	5 (1%)
Professional and related in science, engineering and technology	29	4	1	34 (9%)
Managerial (excluding general management)	23	2	2	27 (7%)
Selling	9	6	2	17 (5%)
Others	9	1	1	11 (3%)
Total (all occupations)	235	71	73	379 (100%)

Based on: NES (The NES does not include the self-employed)

Source: Royal Commission on the Distribution of Incomes and Wealth, *Report No. 3, Higher Incomes from Employment,* Cmnd 6383 (HMSO 1976), pp. 34, 35

actual individuals who are low-paid, however, appear to change quite rapidly. In a study of individuals whose pay was recorded in the New Earnings Surveys between 1970 and 1974,

> 21.4 per cent of manual men were in the lowest paid tenth in at least one of the five surveys but only 2.9 per cent were in this tenth in all these surveys. Of those who were in the lowest paid tenth in 1970 but not in 1971, almost half were in the lowest paid tenth in one of the subsequent three surveys. This confirms a considerable two-way movement across the boundary of the lowest tenth; and of those who are in the lowest tenth at one particular time, less than one-third are in the lowest tenth every time.[66]

Even though some of those excluded from one or two of the surveys may have been unemployed or sick, the comparison revealed a considerable degree of change of individual position even though the general distribution of earnings did not change very much.

It is possible to summarize the above discussion of pay and hours by making a number of simplified summary statements: the evidence is that non-manual employees earn more than manual employees, even though they work shorter hours; men earn more than women; adults more than juveniles; and the skilled/qualified more than the unskilled/unqualified. We can add that when manual workers (and especially men)

TABLE 2.23

Industrial distribution of low-paid men, April 1975

	Percentage of full-time manual workers earning below £40	Percentage of all low-paid men (manual and non-manual) employed in each industry below £40
Agriculture	54.1	6.1
Miscellaneous services	42.0	11.9
Distribution	39.2	15.3
Clothing and footwear	36.2	1.4
Insurance and banking	32.0	4.9
Public administration	29.4	9.3
Professional and scientific services	29.0	8.2
Textiles	23.2	3.2

Based on: New Earnings Survey, 1975

Source: C. Pond and S. Winyard, 'A profile of the low paid' in F. Field (ed.), *Are Low Wages Inevitable?* (Nottingham 1976), pp. 27, 28

TABLE 2.24

Industrial distribution of low-paid women, April 1975

	Percentage of full-time manual workers earning below £40 in each industry		Percentage of all women earning below £25 employed in industry
Distribution	96.3	Distribution	29.0
Clothing and footwear	90.3	Miscellaneous Services	18.4
Chemicals and allied industries	90.1	Prof. and scientific services	12.2
Other manufacturing	89.7	Ins. and Banking	7.2
Textiles	88.8	Clothing and footwear	7.1
Miscellaneous services	88.5	Textiles	4.2
Paper, printing and publishing	85.2	Food, drink and tobacco	3.1
Other metal goods	84.8	Other metal goods	2.1
All industries and services	82.9		

Based on: *New Earnings Survey,* 1975

Source: C. Pond and S. Winyard, 'A profile of the low paid' in F. Field (ed.), *Are Low Wages Inevitable?* (Nottingham 1976), pp. 27, 28

receive high earnings it is often associated with overtime, payment by results, and/or shift working. In addition, if lifetime earnings are considered the advantages of the non-manual worker are further increased; though their average earnings are lower than those of manual workers until the late twenties (or younger for women), their earnings peak is not reached until the 40—49 age group, whereas manual workers reach their maximum earnings at a younger age and decline more rapidly.[67] Non-manual workers have the advantages, with reference to lifetime earnings, of increments and greater opportunities for promotion; manual workers suffer the disadvantages of declining physical strength and fitness, and thus declining ability in later years to increase their pay by working overtime or earning high bonus rates.

The explanations of these differences are too complex to be fully explored here.[68] Part of the higher earnings for skilled and/or qualified workers is compensation for the occupational costs (in terms of earnings foregone and/or the cost of education and training) which they have incurred in gaining those skills and qualifications. The differences also reflect the differential distribution of (inherited) abilities, and the differential distribution of the opportunities to improve and exploit such abilities, to acquire others and to gain qualifications, as between families, and more generally classes and regions. The labour market does not operate in terms of perfect competition and this contributes further to the pattern of inequalities: some occupations (especially professions and skilled trades) restrict entry and so increase the price of their labour; entry to many of the more skilled and responsible jobs is also restricted because they are filled internally from within an organization; and workers may lack the information or the means to be spatially mobile for better paying jobs. Earnings are also affected by the outcomes of bargaining between employers and employees; this is likely to be affected by considerations of customary differentials (as Routh emphasized), but even more so by the power exercised by organized groups of employees in trade unions or professional associations. As we shall see, the industries and occupations characterized by low levels of earnings are typically also ones which are poorly organized.

What does not appear to be the case, however, is that low levels of pay are to any marked and general extent compensated for by other sorts of benefits. Indeed, as we shall see in the next section, the other rewards of work are distributed similarly to pay itself.

'Fringe Benefits' and other Rewards from Work

In addition to a wage or salary almost all employees now receive additional 'benefits' from their work. Many of these have a real or notional money value, but others are more intangible. We will briefly review the distribution of these rewards, and then consider the 'costs' of work and the nature of the overall pattern which available information reveals.

The most comprehensive attempt to ascertain the position with regard to fringe benefits and other conditions of employment is probably that of Wedderburn and Craig who in 1968 surveyed a random sample of establishments in manufacturing industry with 100 or more employees and received replies from nearly 450 of them.[69] Their findings show that in all the cases they investigated manual workers were less well-placed than non-manual workers; and where there were significant differences in the conditions between types of non-manual workers, senior and middle management had superior conditions of employment to those of foremen, clerical workers and technicians (table 2.25). Thus, for example, operatives were less likely to receive sick pay, or pensions, or fifteen days or more holiday a year (or a choice of holiday dates), or time off with pay for domestic reasons; and they were more stringently regulated and sanctioned with regard to lateness, absence, and notice of dismissal. A minority of establishments had the same conditions for all grades of employee; others treated

TABLE 2.25

Terms and conditions of employment (percentage of establishments where the condition applies)

Selected conditions of employment	Operatives	Foremen	Clerical workers	Technicians	Management	
					Middle	Senior
Formal sick pay scheme available	46	65	63	65	63	63
Sick pay provided for more than 3 months	49	58	55	57	65	67
Coverage by formal pension scheme	67	94	90	94	96	95
Pension calculated as fixed amount per year of service	48	18	16	14	13	12
Holidays, excluding public holidays, of 15 days or more a year	38	71	74	77	84	88
Choice of time at which holidays taken	35	54	76	76	84	88
Time off with pay for domestic reasons	29	84	84	86	92	93
Period of notice of dismissal in excess of statutory requirements	13	29	26	29	53	61
Clocking on to record attendance	92	33	24	29	2	4
Pay deduction as penalty for lateness	90	20	8	11	1	–
Warning followed by dismissal for frequent absence without leave	94	86	94	92	74	67

Based on: Craig, *Men in Manufacturing Industry*

Source: D. Wedderburn and C. Craig, 'Relative Deprivation in Work', in D. Wedderburn (ed.), *Poverty, Inequality and Class Structure* (Cambridge 1974), pp. 144, 146

TABLE 2.26

Summary of the degree of uniformity of treatment of different occupational groups

	Percentage of establishments where the condition of employment is the		
	Same for all grades	Least favourable for operatives: Same for non-manual grades	Least favourable for operatives and differences between non-manual grades[2]
Sick pay schemes	16	49	27
Pension schemes	31	52	10
Holidays	19	27	41
Canteen facilities[1]	42	11	33
Penalties for lateness	6	52	33
Penalties for bad time keeping	17	23	50

Notes:
1 'Least favourable' in this context means 'separate'. No data was available to judge the quality of the canteen.
2 Some establishments could not be fitted into these three categories and have been omitted.

Based on: Craig, *Men in Manufacturing Industry*
Source: D. Wedderburn and C. Craig, 'Relative Deprivation in Work', in D. Wedderburn (ed.), *Poverty, Inequality and Class Structure* (Cambridge 1974), pp. 144, 146

operatives less favourably than non-manual grades; and quite a substantial number had differences between non-manual grades too (table 2.26).

A more recent survey by the British Institute of Management, published in 1976, showed that 'more British companies are removing the fringe benefit differentials between white and blue collars but there is still a long way to go. In a sample of 328 companies, larger and probably more progressive than the average, they found that 25 per cent have introduced single status for all employees . . .' The trend was towards a reduction in differentials, but 'nevertheless all aspects of discrimination against manual workers remain common.'[70] This general picture of less favourable conditions of employment for manual workers, and to a lesser extent for junior non-manual workers, can be reinforced by considering those conditions of employment where recent relatively comprehensive data are available.

Holidays with Pay In 1951 national collective agreements or statutory orders under Wages Councils Acts provided that two-thirds of manual workers affected by such agreements would receive two weeks paid holiday a year (not counting public holidays), while 28 per cent received only one week; twenty-three years later, in 1974, the equivalent agreements provided all except 2 per cent of manual workers with at least three weeks paid holiday a year, and 28 per cent with four weeks or more.[71]

The provision of paid holidays is therefore now much more widespread than it used to be. Nevertheless there remain important differences in holiday entitlement for different categories of employee (table 2.27). Fewer than 1 per cent of men and

1½ per cent of women receive no holidays with pay at all; indeed over 90 per cent of them get three weeks or more each year. However, although in some occupations (printing, coalmining, dockwork) four weeks holiday or more is common or even universal, manual workers typically still receive shorter holidays than non-manual workers. 60 per cent of non-manual workers are entitled to four weeks or longer each year, but this is the case for fewer than 24 per cent of manual workers.

Among non-manual workers, however, there are striking differences in holiday entitlement. For example, more than half the men and three-quarters of the women employed in 'selling' occupations receive three weeks or shorter holidays each year — much worse provision than for manual workers. In contrast half the male and nearly a third of the female clerical workers had four weeks holiday or more, rather more than the proportions for manual workers; and among male employees in professional and related occupations two-thirds or more had four weeks holiday or longer each year.

Even more striking is the differential between men and women. Although the holiday entitlements of female employees also vary widely as between different

TABLE 2.27

Distribution of annual holiday entitlements (excluding the seven public holidays), by occupational category, GB, April 1974

Full-time men, aged 21 or over and
Full-time women, aged 18 or over (in brackets)

Occupational category	Percentage of employees with annual holiday entitlements of				
	Under 3 weeks	3 weeks	Over 3 under 4	4 weeks	Over 4 weeks
Managerial (general management)	5.3	26.9	4.3	45.0	18.4
Professional & related supporting management & administration	1.7 (1.7)	20.2 (29.7)	11.0 (17.3)	32.2 (26.3)	34.9 (24.9)
Professional & related in education, welfare & health	2.6 (2.5)	4.5 (7.8)	4.2 (4.9)	10.9 (11.6)	77.9 (73.2)
Professional & related in science, engineering technology, etc.	1.5 (3.9)	13.5 (32.2)	13.0 (20.0)	31.4 (30.4)	40.6 (13.6)
Managerial (excl. general management)	4.6 (9.3)	33.6 (51.6)	10.9 (11.7)	29.2 (15.4)	21.8 (12.0)
Clerical & related	2.2 (6.0)	21.3 (39.1)	23.0 (22.7)	29.3 (22.3)	24.0 (10.0)
Selling	8.1 (15.3)	49.8 (64.7)	16.1 (9.3)	19.9 (9.3)	6.1 (1.5)
All non-manual	3.0 (6.1)	22.4 (34.8)	14.2 (17.1)	27.5 (18.9)	32.9 (23.2)
All manual	5.9 (9.2)	39.7 (39.9)	31.3 (38.8)	13.2 (8.9)	10.1 (3.3)
All occupations	4.9 (7.1)	33.6 (36.7)	25.3 (24.9)	18.2 (15.3)	18.1 (16.1)

Based on: *New Earnings Survey, 1974*
Source: *British Labour Statistics Year-book, 1974* (HMSO 1976), pp. 63–6

occupational categories, paralleling the differences for men, in every case the women's position is worse than that of the comparable category of men. It is particularly ironic that those who conventionally carry the heavier burden of domestic and child-care duties should receive shorter holidays.

Sick Pay: Although details of the provision are not available, *The General Household Survey* found that just over 70 per cent of both men and women full-time employees were covered by sick pay arrangements of some sort in 1972. As table 2.28 shows, however, there were important differences between 'socio-economic groups' in the extent of this provision. 85 per cent or more of those in the non-manual categories were covered, but only just over half of the manual workers, with the unskilled (unusually) being apparently slightly better provided for than the skilled.

Pension Schemes: In this case, too, details of the provision are not given, but in contrast to the situation regarding sick pay far more men than women employees were covered by a private pension scheme run by their employers (54.9 per cent as compared with 33.5 per cent).[73] The occupational distribution is not available but in general those employed in industries with a large element of public ownership (public administration, defence; mining; gas, electricity and water; transport and communications) were more likely to be covered by pension schemes. Indeed there is a strong correlation between the industrial distribution of sick pay schemes and of occupational pension schemes.[74]

Job Satisfaction: Jobs vary widely in many other ways than those so far discussed. The content of the work may be varied and intrinsically interesting or repetitive and boring; its mastery may demand long periods of training, or it may be picked up in a

TABLE 2.28

Full-time employees covered by sick pay arrangements run by their employers, by socio-economic group, GB

Arranged in decreasing order of the proportion who get paid when sick

Socio-economic group	Get paid when sick	Do not get paid when sick	BASE (= 100%)
	%	%	
Professional workers – employees	99.6	0.4	285
Managers (large establishments)	98.4	1.6	500
Intermediate non-manual	96.1	3.9	544
Managers (small establishments)	94.1	5.9	353
Junior non-manual	89.5	10.5	2,115
Foremen and supervisors	85.3	14.7	434
Agricultural workers	69.2	30.8	104
Personal service workers	69.1	30.9	272
Unskilled manual	54.9	45.1	415
Skilled manual	51.6	48.4	2,701
Semi-skilled manual	50.2	49.8	1,538
Farmers (managers) No.	[10]	[NIL]	10

Source: Office of Population Censuses and Surveys, *The General Household Survey* 1972 (HMSO 1975), p. 142

few hours; there may be opportunities to exercise discretion and take responsibility, or work activities may be minutely controlled and all significant decisions taken by others; the job may offer possibilities for self-development, leading perhaps to promotion to a more demanding and better-paid position, or it may offer nothing but the prospects of carrying out the same easily-learnt tasks for the rest of a working life. Whether the more desirable of these sets of characteristics are seen as positive rewards or merely relative satisfactions, they certainly contribute significantly to the experience of work of those in different occupations.

Unfortunately it is very difficult to assess a wide range of jobs in these terms, though attempts, more or less successful, have been made in the context of studies of particular workplaces or occupation.[75] An alternative is to try to obtain a summary measure of people's experience of their work through questions on job satisfaction, but this too presents certain difficulties. First of all there appears to be a tendency for a very high proportion of respondents to express satisfaction with their job, however unrewarding it may appear to be, and this may reflect the feeling that to admit dissatisfaction is to admit personal failure. Secondly, the source of satisfaction with a job, and the meaning it has for the respondent, may vary very considerably between respondents, but this will not be apparent unless more and more searching questions are asked. Thirdly, satisfaction is always relative to expectations so that an expression of satisfaction or dissatisfaction may tell us more about the respondent's aspirations and orientation than about his or her work. Indeed job satisfaction studies can be regarded as providing a notable example of the limited horizons and standards of comparison of those in objectively deprived situations, of the tendency for aspirations to become tailored to experience so that what appears to the respondent as inescapable (in this case, say, a dead-end job) may be helped in fact to become so.[76]

The results of job satisfaction questions are not entirely useless, however, especially if the variations within the respondent group are studied rather than the overall level of satisfaction. Thus *The General Household Survey* reported a slight decline in the overall (high) level of job satisfaction between 1971 and 1972 which they tentatively explained in terms of rising unemployment and consequently declining opportunities to move to a 'better' job. In both years, indeed, there was a close association between expressions of job dissatisfaction and the intention to change job, and there was also a close association between dissatisfaction and absence from work.[77] Further, there are variations in the degree of job satisfaction reported, which paralleled those found in other studies.[78] Though the percentage differences are not large, the 'very satisfied' were more commonly female than male, middle-aged than young, married (and especially widowed) than single, part-time than full-time, with a year or more of service with the same employer rather than less than twelve months in the same job. Occupationally (in terms of socio-economic groups) the findings also reflected those of the other studies in that in general non-manual workers were more satisfied than manual workers. There were exceptions, however, such as the very high levels of satisfaction of agricultural and personal service workers and the relatively low levels of satisfaction of professional employees, and presumably these reflect the differing expectations of these workers (table 2.29).

Absence: It is now notorious that opinions expressed in attitude surveys may be a poor predictor of behaviour, and in this connection data on absence from work provide an interesting check on expressions of satisfaction or dissatisfaction with a job. Absence statistics are of course also difficult to interpret because they include both 'voluntary' and 'involuntary' absences and the conventional categories of reasons for absence cannot really be taken to reflect that distinction. Nevertheless in aggregate absence statistics can be regarded as an approximate index of general levels of 'morale' – in this context implying identification with the purposes of the employing organization.

There are clear differences in the levels of absence – whatever the reason – between senior non-manual workers (professional employees, managers, intermediate non-manual workers) and manual workers, with the other occupational categories coming in between (table 2.30). As the absences by reason of illness or accident indicate, this is partly a reflection of the inferior health and safety situation of manual employees, but it can be taken more generally as providing further support for the argument that the work of non-manual workers, and especially of those with the more skilled and responsible positions, is more attractive and rewarding than that of manual workers.

Labour turnover statistics are another conventional index of 'satisfaction' or 'morale', although, like absence data, they are always susceptible to a variety of explanations and interpretations. Between 1970 and 1974, however, non-manual male workers had consistently better rates of job stability than manual workers (i.e. more had been with the same employer for twelve months or longer);[79] this can perhaps be taken as an indication of greater satisfaction with their current job, though it also reflects alternative job opportunities in the labour market, the costs of moving to them, and so on. The differences between manual and non-manual female workers were smaller, but in this case manual workers consistently showed the greater stability.

The Costs of Work

As we have seen, some of the most important rewards which can be derived from work (especially those which are inherent in the job itself) are not easily reported and compared. This difficulty is even greater when the attempt is made to compare the deprivations associated with different types of work – to look, as it were, at the 'effort' involved in the employer/employee bargain. The total 'costs' of working to the employee cannot be properly assessed, but important aspects can be compared by considering some of the disadvantages associated with particular occupations or occupational groupings. We have already considered hours of work, including overtime and shift work, and the intensity of effort demanded in so far as this is transmitted through payment by results schemes; and we will now discuss occupational differences in security of employment as it is reflected in unemployment data, and the costs of work in terms of accidents and ill health.

Unemployment: The worker who sells his labour power in the market is dependent for his income on the existence of employers who wish to purchase his ability to work. In the early stages of industrialization this generally resulted in a very one-sided relationship, and periods of unemployment, due to cyclical changes in demand or to structural changes in the economy, which meant that particular workers were no longer required, were the common experience of many men and women. Trade union organization and action, and state intervention, have limited the extent to which employers can hire and fire at will, and state action in particular has reduced the financial hardship associated with redundancy and unemployment.[80] Nevertheless, the insecurity associated with particular types of occupation, the likelihood

TABLE 2.29

Job satisfaction: working persons aged 15 or over by socio-economic group by degree of job satisfaction, GB

Arranged in decreasing order of proportion who are very satisfied

Socio-economic group		Degree of job satisfaction					BASE (= 100%)	Average (mean) score	Average (mean) score 1971
		Very satisfied	Fairly satisfied	Neither satisfied nor dissatisfied	Rather dissatisfied	Very dissatisfied			
	Score	5	4	3	2	1			
Professional workers – self-employed	No.	[57]	[25]	[1]	[5]	[2]	90	4.4	4.7
Agricultural workers	%	59.6	32.2	4.8	2.1	1.4	146	4.5	4.5
Employers and managers in large establishments	%	57.5	34.1	4.3	2.8	1.2	563	4.4	4.5
Personal service workers	%	56.9	33.2	6.3	2.1	1.5	805	4.4	4.5
Employers and managers in small establishments	%	53.7	34.4	6.0	3.3	2.7	736	4.3	4.4

Farmers – self-employed	No.	[27]	[15]	[7]	[NIL]	[2]	51	4.3	4.3
Farmers – managers	No.	[43]	[31]	[3]	[4]	[1]	82	4.4	4.2
Intermediate non-manual workers	%	50.8	38.1	5.4	4.5	1.2	1,164	4.3	4.4
Foremen and supervisors	%	49.8	41.9	4.1	2.9	1.4	442	4.4	4.3
Junior non-manual workers	%	47.5	39.2	7.4	4.0	1.8	3,187	4.3	4.4
Unskilled manual workers	%	45.5	38.8	9.9	2.9	3.0	902	4.2	4.4
Non-professional self-employed	%	45.5	35.2	15.2	3.1	1.0	415	4.2	4.3
Professional workers – employees	%	41.1	45.0	7.2	5.7	1.0	387	4.2	4.2
Semi-skilled manual workers	%	38.9	45.1	8.6	3.9	3.5	1,838	4.2	4.3
Skilled manual workers	%	36.7	46.0	8.7	5.4	3.2	2,848	4.1	4.2

Source: Office of Population Censuses and Surveys, *The General Household Survey 1972* (HMSO 1975) p. 129

TABLE 2.30

Absence from work, GB

Working persons aged 15 or over by socio-economic group
Percentage in each group absent from work in the reference week, subdivided by reasons for absence

Socio-economic group	Reasons for absence from work			All reasons	BASE (= 100%) all persons working
	Own illness/accident	strike/short time/lay-off	Personal or other reasons		
Professional workers – employees	1.7	–	0.4	2.1	408
Employers/managers in small establishments	3.1	–	0.7	3.8	795
Employers/managers in large establishments	3.3	–	0.6	3.9	604
Intermediate non-manual	3.9	0.1	0.3	4.3	1,200
Foremen and supervisors	2.6	2.1	0.6	5.3	459
Junior non-manual	4.4	0.2	1.6	6.2	3,307
Agricultural workers	3.2	0.6	2.5	6.3	154
Personal service workers	4.2	0.8	2.0	7.0	829
Non-professional self-employed	3.9	1.8	1.6	7.3	431
Unskilled manual	6.1	1.1	1.8	9.0	940
Skilled manual	7.2	2.7	1.3	11.2	3,030
Semi-skilled manual	7.7	3.0	1.9	12.6	1,927
Total	5.2	1.4	1.5	8.1	14,322
Total 1971	5.0	0.7	1.2	6.9	15,325

Note: Self-employed professional workers, and farmers (managers and self-employed) have been omitted from this table because the numbers included in the Survey are too small for reliable results

Source: Office of Population Censuses and Surveys, *The General Household Survey 1972* (HMSO 1975), p. 137

of unemployment and the chances of obtaining another job, vary considerably for different types of employee, and for many of them are one of the deprivations associated with their occupation.

For most of the first two and a half decades after the Second World War unemployment rates in Great Britain remained at less than 3 per cent of all employees (never more than 450,000 men and women) — in marked contrast to the inter-war period — though they were considerably higher in Northern Ireland throughout this period, and a little higher in some other regions. Since about 1970 the rate has increased and by the beginning of 1977 nearly 6 per cent of employees were out of work, a total of 1.3 million people.[81] Indeed it is likely that this figure represents an under-estimate as it is based on those registered as unemployed and *The General Household Survey,* among other enquiries, has demonstrated that a proportion (probably a fifth to a quarter) of those unemployed — especially married women — do not register.[82]

The likelihood of unemployment varies considerably with age and is greatest for those at the two extremes of the age range, especially those under 25 and those over 60. Its likelihood also varies considerably with occupation, although this is more difficult to establish. However, as table 2.31 indicates, in 1975 the chances of unemployment, for both men and women, were considerably greater for a manual

TABLE 2.31

Unemployment: Occupational distribution, GB

Occupational category	Approx. percentage of all employees in category*	Number unemployed March 1975	Percentage of total number unemployed
Men			
Managerial & professional	23	39,611	6.4
Clerical & related	9	60,357	9.7
Other non-manual	6	15,150	2.4
Craft & similar occupations		89,931	14.5
General labourers		269,213	43.4
Other manual		146,304	23.6
All manual	62	505,448	81.5
Total	100	620,566	100.0
Women			
Managerial & professional	21	9,199	7.4
Clerical & related	41	38,908	31.5
Other non-manual	6	14,645	11.8
Craft & similar occupations		3,351	2.7
General labourers		28,518	23.1
Other manual		29,065	23.5
All manual	32	60,934	49.3
Total	100	123,686	100.0

* Note: These figures have been calculated from the 'Number in the Sample' figures provided in the *New Earnings Survey 1975.* They must be regarded as rough approximations only. The distributions of employees, working population, etc, in terms of this occupational breakdown does not appear to be available

Source: *Department of Employment Gazette,* Vol. 85 No. 4 (April 1977), p. 403; *New Earnings Survey 1975* Part D HMSO 1976, pp. 4–6

worker than for a non-manual worker; managerial and professional workers had much less likelihood of being unemployed than clerical and other non-manual workers; and among manual workers it is safe to say, in the light of the figures in the table, that the unskilled were the most likely to be unemployed, and the skilled workers the least likely, even though precise breakdowns are not available. Since 1975 unemployment has increased considerably for both men and women, but the proportions in each occupational category have changed very little.

The impact of unemployment on the individual concerned varies greatly in relation to the length of the period out of work. Over the eleven years 1964—74 inclusive when the numbers unemployed ranged from just over 250,000 to just over 800,000 between a sixth and a quarter (17 to 25 per cent) of those unemployed were out of work for two weeks or less, while between 29 per cent and 38 per cent were unemployed for six months or more, more than half of whom, in most years, were out of work for over a year. As might be expected the proportion of the long-term unemployed tended to increase when overall levels of unemployment increased.[83] It is likely that these figures under-estimate the impact of unemployment for some workers, who are confined to the 'secondary' labour market and experience a succession of short jobs and short periods of unemployment.[84]

The occupational incidence of both unemployment and the chances of getting another job can be assessed by comparing the unemployment and vacancies figures. These data (table 2.32) have to be treated with considerable caution; as we have seen, many unemployed women in particular do not register (and some, especially older, men may register as unemployed even though they do not really want or expect to get a job); and even though the Department of Employment has attempted with some success to extend the coverage of its placement activities, many vacancies, especially for managerial, professional and clerical workers, are not notified, and the excess of unemployed over vacancies for these categories does not necessarily reflect the true situation. The figures are for the whole country, and given the regional imbalance in unemployment many of the vacancies are of course in areas with low unemployment levels.

It is noticeable, however, that in the case of both men and women, the excess of unemployed over vacancies in the 'miscellaneous' manual workers category (which includes many of the unskilled) is far greater than it is in those categories, such as the processing, etc. of metal and electrical goods, which include many skilled workers. The same is true to a lesser extent for men in construction, mining, transport and related occupations, which also include relatively smaller proportions of skilled workers. Thus, as might be expected, the indications are that the chances of obtaining work for those who are unemployed are much smaller for the unskilled men than for the skilled; and the same appears to be the case for men in the less skilled, clerical and related, non-manual occupations.

Accidents and Ill-health: The costs of work in terms of its effects on physical and mental health are manifested in a variety of ways. Some occupations are obviously dangerous so that the risk of a severe or fatal accident is high; some occupations involve working in conditions which have a less immediately obvious, longer-term effect on health, perhaps in time giving rise to a disabling disease, such as pneumoconiosis among miners; all occupations, however, can be regarded as influencing, for better or worse, the health of those engaged in them so that morbidity and mortality statistics provide a good indication of their relative cost to the employee, of the degree to which, in a literal sense, they affect his or her life chances.

In 1974 there were 256,930 accidents notified to the Factory Inspectorate, the lowest figure for any year since 1964.[85] They included 479 fatalities, and were classified by the Inspectorate as comprising 44,660 Group 1 accidents (severe and fatal accidents unambiguously the direct result of an accident at work); 66,240 Group 2 accidents (involving admission to hospital for in-patient treatment or absence from work for more than 28 days, but including a proportion, 'particularly strains and sprains where there is legitimate doubt about whether they were caused by a truly accidental happening at work'); and 146,020 Group 3 accidents (the remainder — all of which caused someone to be off work for at least three days, the criterion for a notifiable accident).[86] However, these figures only cover accidents in factories, the construction industry and in docks and inland warehouses, as other accidents were reported to different inspectorates administering different Acts. The full figures for fatal accidents between 1971 and 1974 are shown in table 2.33, where it is apparent that workers in mining, on the railways and in shipping are particularly subject to the risk of such accidents. Even these figures, however, have been criticized as not fully revealing the extent to which those at work are liable to hazards likely to lead to loss of life or of health, and the following 'realistic annual figures' have been suggested:[87]

killed at work or dying from injuries	2,000
killed by recognized industrial diseases	1,000
injured or off work with industrial disease	
for at least three days	nearly 1,000,000
injured — needing first aid	10,000,000

The figures in the table do indicate, however, that the liability to accident at work is unequally distributed. For example, it has been estimated that the Factories Acts cover about $8\frac{1}{2}$ million people, the Mines and Quarries Acts about 345,000, and the Offices, Shops and Railway Premises Act about 8 million;[88] the average annual number of fatal accidents in each category during 1971—4 were respectively 519 (approx. 6 per 100,000), 89 (approx. 26 per 100,000) and 23 (approx. 0.3 per 100,000). These industrial differences also occur within the manufacturing industry category, as table 2.34 indicates.

The occupational distribution of accident liability is much harder to estimate, although as the differences between the incidence rates for factories, mining and offices suggest, non-manual workers are much less likely to be involved than manual workers. The best indication is probably provided by more general statistics relating to mortality and to the incidence of particular diseases and disabilities, though it is impossible to separate clearly the direct effects of work from the more general effects of different levels and patterns of living. However, as table 2.35 shows, not only are there clear and persistent differences in the life chances of the different 'social classes', but the relative differences are in fact widening not narrowing. (Expectations of life have, of course, improved for all classes during this period.) Commenting on these and other figures Preston has argued that some, but not all, the differences between 'classes' can be attributed to causes of death specific to certain occupations; and he has argued against the possibility that poor health determines social class rather than the opposite.[89]

The more detailed occupational breakdown provided in tables 2.36 and 2.37 shows that there are important differences in life chances, and in the risks of suffering

TABLE 2.32

Unemployment and vacancies – occupational distribution, UK, September 1974

Thousands

Occupational category	Men			Women		
	Unemployed (a)	Vacancies unfilled (b)	Approx. ratio a/b	Unemployed (a)	Vacancies unfilled (b)	Approx. ratio a/b
Managerial (general management)	1,3	0,1	13.0	–	–	–
Professional & related supporting management & admin.	7,9	5,7	1.4	1,4	0,07	20.0
Professional & related in education, welfare, health	4,1	2,6	1.6	4,9	7,5	0.7
Literary, artistic & sports	4,9	0,4	12.3	1,9	0,2	9.5
Professional & related in science, engineering, etc.	9,0	9,9	0.9	0,8	0,1	8.0
Managerial (excl. general management)	10,0	4,0	2.5	0,7	0,6	1.2
Clerical & related	59,7	13,9	4.3	35,5	29,2	1.2
Selling	10,7	9,3	1.2	10,2	9,1	1.1

Security & protective service	2,5	5,4	0.5	0,06	0,5	0.1
Catering, cleaning etc.	11,0	14,5	0.8	14,2	35,8	0.4
Farming, fishing, etc.	6,2	2,4	2.6	0,7	0,4	1.8
Materials processing (excl. metal)	4,7	5,2	0.9	1,3	3,3	0.4
Making & repairing (excl. metal & electrical)	10,6	11,6	0.9	2,6	13,4	0.2
Processing, making, repairing, etc. (metal & electrical)	42,6	53,5	0.8	0,7	3,9	0.2
Painting, repetitive assembly, etc.	10,3	8,6	1.2	4,0	9,9	0.4
Construction, mining, etc.	35,4	8,0	4.4	–	–	–
Transport, etc.	39,2	17,7	2.2	0,9	1,0	0.9
Miscellaneous	253,9	16,7	15.2	30,6	7,3	4.2
TOTAL	524,3	189,4	2.8	110,4	122,0	0.9

Note: The figures in this table must be treated with considerable caution. Not all those who are unemployed register as such with the Department of Employment; by no means all vacancies are notified to the Department's offices; and the size of the discrepancies between registered unemployed and those 'really' out of work and seeking employment, and between notified vacancies and 'real' vacancies varies considerably as between the sexes and the different occupational categories

Source: *British Labour Statistics Yearbook, 1974* (HMSO, 1976), pp. 273, 277, 309, 313

TABLE 2.33

Numbers of fatal industrial accidents, 1971–4, UK

	Processes covered by Factories Act				Workers covered by other Acts										Total persons killed (columns (5) and (15))
	Factory processes	Construction processes[1]	Docks, wharves, quays, and inland warehouses	Total (columns (2)–(4))	Explosives Act	Mines producing coal	Mines of stratified ironstone, oil shale, or fireclay	Miscellaneous mines	Quarries Acts[2]	Railways	Shipping[3]	Commercial aviation[4]	Offices, Shops, and Railway Premises Act	Total (columns (6)–(14))	
(1)	(2)	(3)	(4)	(5)	(6)	(7)	(8)	(9)	(10)	(11)	(12)	(13)	(14)	(15)	(16)
1971	304	202	32	538	7	72	1	6	20	58	42	9	35	250	788
1972	270	196	17	483	4	64	–	7	16	48	106	8	23	276	759
1973	296	233	29	558	6	80	–	8	14	48	51	9	15	231	789
1974	301	167	30	498	3	48	–	2	17	38	101	4	20	233	731

Notes: For statistical purposes, each fatality is recorded as one accident
(Northern Ireland legislation covering industrial accidents closely follows that of Great Britain, although the title of individual Acts and the date of introduction may vary.)
1 Includes works of engineering construction.
2 Includes accidents in open cast coal sites.
3 Deaths in vessels registered in the United Kingdom.
4 Employees of UK corporations and other UK air transport operators, or commercial aviation concerns killed in the United Kingdom. Includes only deaths in accidents in this country and engaged on air transport flights or other flights for reward.

Source: Department of Employment, *British Labour Statistics Yearbook, 1974* (HMSO 1976), p. 335

TABLE 2.34

Numbers of fatal accidents, and incidence rates of fatal accidents and severe injuries, in manufacturing and construction industries, GB, 1971–4

Industry Order (Standard Industrial Classification 1968)	SIC Order Number	1971			1972			1973			1974		
		Fatal accidents	Incidence rates[1]		Fatal accidents	Incidence rates[1]		Fatal accidents	Incidence rates[1]		Fatal accidents	Incidence rates[1]	
			Fatal accidents	Severe injuries[2]		Fatal accidents	Severe injuries[2]		Fatal accidents	Severe injuries[2]		Fatal accidents	Severe injuries[2]
Food, drink and tobacco	III	25	4.0	690	16	2.6	630	16	2.7	710	24	3.7	560
Coal and petroleum products	IV	2	5.6	460	3	9.1	450	5	15.7	930	3	9.7	590
Chemicals and allied industries	V	22	7.9	490	14	5.2	600	19	6.8	600	46	16.2	660
Metal manufacture	VI	58	13.9	1,160	46	11.9	1,010	67	17.2	930	53	14.0	1,120
Mechanical engineering	VII	24	3.1	710	27	3.9	660	24	3.4	580	20	2.8	660
Instrument engineering	VIII	1	1.0	250	—	—	200	1	1.0	280	1	1.0	270
Electrical engineering	IX	7	1.2	330	4	0.7	320	4	0.7	360	3	0.5	280
Shipbuilding and marine engineering	X	18	11.9	810	24	16.5	870	19	13.4	830	15	10.3	860
Vehicles	XI	13	2.3	520	13	2.3	470	13	2.3	410	10	1.8	440
Metal goods not elsewhere specified	XII	16	3.4	640	7	1.6	690	19	4.1	720	16	3.4	640
Textiles	XIII	20	3.9	510	6	1.2	530	8	1.7	560	19	4.0	420
Leather, leather goods, and fur	XIV	2	4.7	340	1	2.5	330	1	2.5	380	1	2.6	540
Clothing and footwear	XV	—	—	130	1	0.2	120	3	0.8	100	2	0.5	110
Bricks, pottery, glass, cement, etc.	XVI	18	7.1	840	22	9.0	870	16	6.4	790	16	6.4	660
Timber, furniture etc.	XVII	9	3.9	800	9	3.9	860	7	2.8	620	14	6.1	850
Paper, printing and publishing	XVIII	10	2.3	460	13	3.1	510	4	1.0	510	8	8.3	500
Other manufacturing industries	XIX	6	2.3	580	8	3.2	560	10	3.7	460	3	1.1	430
Total, manufacturing industries		251	4.1	590	214	3.6	580	236	3.9	550	254	4.2	550
Construction	XX	201	19.2	750	190	18.3	800	231	21.1	700	166	15.7	740

Notes: This table relates only to accidents covered by the Factories Act

An accident occurring in a place subject to the Factories Act is notifiable to the Factory Inspectorate if it causes either loss of life or disables an employed person for more than three days from earning full wages from the work on which he was employed. For statistical purposes each injury or fatality is recorded as one accident

1 Annual incidence rates per 100,000 persons at risk

2 Data on severe injuries are obtained by a 5 per cent random sample enquiry into accidents notified under the Factories Act

Source: Department of Employment, *British Labour Statistics Yearbook, 1974* (HMSO 1976), p. 335

TABLE 2.35

Standardized mortality ratios, adult males under 65 years of age, England and Wales

			Social class		
	I	II	III	V	VI
Period	Professional, etc	Intermediate non-manual	Skilled manual routine non-manual	Semi-skilled manual	Unskilled manual
1930–2	90	94	97	102	111
1949–53	86	92	101	104	118
1959–63	76	81	100	103	143

Source: Open University, *Inequality within Nations, Health and Inequality*(Milton Keynes 1976), p. 23. Based on B. Preston, 'Statistics of Inequality' *Sociological Review*, Vol. 22, No.2, 1974, pp. 103–17, and using Registrar General, *Decennial Supplement, England and Wales*, 1961, *Occupational Mortality Tables* (HMSO 1971)

TABLE 2.36

Mortality ratios for different occupational categories, England and Wales

Occupational category	Deaths from all causes	Tuberculosis	Lung cancer	Bronchitis
Coalface miners	180	294	140	293
Construction riggers	142	138	152	149
Engineering labourers	139	169	151	217
Furnacemen	108	106	168	151
Fishermen	144	171	188	148
Textile process workers	133	111	116	161
Dockers	136	180	171	220
Kitchen hands	130	410	88	168
Mine managers	66	18	56	33
Contracting managers	50	33	66	21
Engineering managers	70	17	68	25
Personnel managers	67	40	44	64
Cabinet ministers, MPs	75	29	69	28
Judges, solicitors	76	33	40	24
Clergymen	62	9	17	17
Teachers	60	23	34	23

Note: 100 = the mortality rate for all classes/occupations; figures greater than 100 mean that there are above average chances of death, and vice versa

Based on: Registrar General's figures, no date given

Source: P. Kinnersley, *The Hazards of Work: how to fight them* (London 1973), pp. 9, 147

from a disabling illness like bronchitis, as between different types of manual workers. It is noticeable, however, that with one exception (the likelihood of dying from lung cancer among kitchen hands) the mortality ratios for all the manual occupations listed in table 2.36 are considerably higher than those for any of the non-manual occupations. Indeed all male non-manual workers have a much smaller than average likelihood of dying from tuberculosis or bronchitis, and a somewhat smaller likelihood of dying from cancer, while the risks for unskilled manual workers are considerably greater than average.[90]

TABLE 2.37

The incidence of bronchitis, England and Wales

Occupational category	Inception rate (attacks per 100 men)
Miners and quarrymen	7.24
Labourers	5.59
Drivers	4.96
Foundry workers	4.71
Transport	4.11
Construction	4.10
Engineering	3.8
Service: office	3.79
Service: food & drink	3.46
Woodworkers	3.27
Farmers	2.25
Sales	2.11
Professional	1.89
All occupations	3.69

Based on: an unspecified National Insurance Survey
Source: P. Kinnersley, *The Hazards of Work: how to fight them* (London 1973), pp. 9, 147

More systematic data about the occupational distribution of ill-health is available from *The General Household Survey* (table 2.38). As can be seen, in the case of both 'chronic' and 'acute' sickness there is a clear 'class gradient' with those in professional and managerial occupations having rates considerably less than average and those in manual occupations having rates above average, and in the case of many unskilled manual workers very considerably above average. These figures cover all persons and not just those who are employed, and the rates do vary considerably with age; the 'class gradient' however remains when those of working age are considered separately.[91] The rates of absence from work due to illness and injury among those who are employed are shown in table 2.39 (though unfortunately married women are categorized in terms of their husband's occupation). As in the case of the data for all persons there is a clear differentiation according to socio-economic group in both absence rates and the number of working days lost each year due to illness and injury; non-manual workers in general have less absence for these reasons than manual workers, and professional workers least of all; and among manual workers the incidence and severity of absence increase as levels of skill decrease, with male unskilled manual workers being markedly more likely to be absent because of illness or injury than any other category.

The picture revealed by the data considered in this whole section is a complex one, and it is made more complex by the differences between the categories which different organizations use to classify their statistics. Nonetheless a clear overall pattern can be discerned. In terms of almost all the criteria considered — pay, hours, fringe benefits, job satisfaction, job security, health — the non-manual worker is more highly rewarded and suffers fewer deprivations than the manual worker; and men are better placed than women. Within these overall categories certain further differences are apparent. Among non-manual employees it is particularly those in professional occupations who appear to have the most favourable conditions

TABLE 2.38

'Chronic' and 'acute' ill-health, England and Wales, 1972

Persons by sex and socio-economic group: observed rates as percentage of expected rates

Socio-economic group	'Chronic sickness' Limiting long-standing illness			'Acute sickness' Restricted activity in a two week reference period			Observed rates of consulting a GP (NHS) in 2 week period		
	Total	Males	Females	Total	Males	Females	Total	Males	Females
Professional	72	74	69	87	87	88	95	93	98
Employers & managers	76	78	75	89	91	87	93	98	89
Intermediate & junior non-manual	85	86	85	96	93	97	98	93	101
Skilled manual & own account non-professional	104	103	105	101	101	100	103	99	107
Semi-skilled manual & personal service	119	120	119	111	111	110	107	118	101
Unskilled manual	134	156	118	133	151	118	116	140	100
Rates per 1,000 reporting for all persons	120.8	114.9		80.3	75.5	84.7	113.3	96.6	129.0
Average no. of restricted activity days per person per year:				16.1	15.0	17.0			
Average no. of consultations per person per year:							3.8	3.3	4.2

Note: In tables 2.38 and 2.39 all individuals aged 15 or over, including students but excluding married women whose husbands were in the household, have been classified according to their present job, or most recent if retired or unemployed. Married women whose husbands were in the household have been classified according to their husband's group. Children under 15 have been classified according to their father's occupation; if the father was not in the household the mother's occupation has been used; if the mother was not in the household then the occupation of the HOH has been used. Students, the never worked, and inadequately described occupations have not been shown separately in the tables; they are however included in the rates for all persons

Source: Office of Population Censuses and Surveys, *The General Household Survey 1972* (HMSO 1975), pp. 198–227

of employment (except perhaps with regard to the chances of earning the very highest salaries where top managerial positions have the advantage); and certain non-manual occupations – 'clerical' and 'selling' – have a balance of rewards and

TABLE 2.39

Absence from work due to illness, England and Wales

Working persons aged 15 or over by sex and socio-economic group
(a) Rates per 1,000 reporting absence from work due to illness or injury in a 2-week reference
    period
(b) Average number of work-days lost per person per year

Socio-economic group	(a)						(b)		
	TOTAL		Males		Females		TOTAL	Males	Females
		BASE (= 1,000)		BASE (= 1,000)		BASE (= 1,000)			
Professional	21.2	(567)	19.3[1]	(414)	26.1[1]	(153)	3.1	3.0[1]	3.4[1]
Employers and managers	39.2	(1,682)	39.9	(1,129)	38.0	(553)	6.2	6.8	4.9
Intermediate and junior non-manual	48.3	(3,147)	39.9	(1,528)	56.2	(1,619)	6.0	5.3	6.5
Skilled manual (incl. foremen and supervisors) and own account non-professional	56.3	(4,689)	57.0	(3,208)	54.7	(1,481)	9.4	10.0	8.3
Semi-skilled manual and personal service	67.6	(2,101)	75.0	(1,200)	57.7	(901)	10.5	12.8	7.4
Unskilled manual	98.9	(637)	122.0	(410)	57.3	(227)	17.6	22.6	8.5
TOTAL	54.5	(12,823)	55.3	(7,889)	53.1	(4,934)	8.4	9.3	7.0

Note:
1   Based on 10 or fewer observations

Source: Office of Population Censuses and Surveys, *The General Household Survey 1972*,
(HMSO 1975), p. 207

deprivations which overlaps that of the more skilled manual workers. Among manual
workers there are several respects — chances of unemployment and health conditions, for example — in which the unskilled are clearly considerably more deprived
than the skilled and semi-skilled. Thus a clear class gradient remains, and the indications are that it is not changing very rapidly.

One final occupational characteristic must now be considered: the extent to which
different categories of employee are organized in trade unions or professional and
other associations, and therefore have a real opportunity to exercise some control,
collectively, over their terms and conditions of employment. Since official statistics
were first kept, in 1892, trade union membership has grown from 1,576,000 (just
over 11 per cent of the labour force) to 11¾ million (nearly 50 per cent of the labour
force).[92] These figures include the membership of all associations which are known
to include in their objects that of negotiating with employers with a view to regulat-
ing the wages and working conditions of their members. They therefore include,
quite rightly, the members of some 'professional associations'. Other professional

and occupational associations may not be trade unions in the terms of this definition, but their activities, such as awarding qualifications and laying down codes of practice and scales of fees, may well benefit the market and work situations of their members, but it will not be possible to consider them further here.[93]

The patterns of union growth as between men and women employees, and non-manual and manual workers, are shown in tables 2.40 and 2.41. Since 1948 union density for all employees has grown from 45.2 per cent to nearly 50 per cent, but these overall figures conceal certain conflicting trends. Total union membership among manual workers has grown very little, but because the total number of manual workers in the labour force has declined this represents a slight increase in union density, an increase which is especially marked among women manual workers. The union membership of white-collar workers has more than doubled in the post-war period, but because the number of white-collar workers has grown enormously, union density among non-manual workers has not increased at a very much faster rate than among manual workers. The current situation is that male manual workers are the most densely unionized (64.7 per cent), followed by male white-collar workers (44.5 per cent), female manual workers (42.1 per cent) and female white-collar workers (22.6 per cent).

The density of union membership also varies considerably between industries and industrial sectors, and with size of establishment (tables 2.42 and 2.43). The public sector is the most densely organized; manufacturing industry has above average union membership for manual workers; but white-collar workers in manufacturing industry, and employees in the primary sector, and especially in private sector services are very weakly organized. The primary sector includes agriculture, and the last grouping includes distribution and miscellaneous services which, as we have seen, contain large numbers of low-paid workers. The more detailed figures of membership by industry show that in 1974 unionization was virtually complete in mining, in the

TABLE 2.40

The growth of white-collar and manual unionism, UK, 1948–74

| | Union membership (000s) | | | | % Increase | |
	1948	1964	1970	1974	1948–74	1970–4
White collar	1,964	2,684	3,592	4,263	+117.1	+18.7
Manual	7,398	7,534	7,587	7,491	+0.1	−1.3
	Union density (%)				Increase	
	1948	1964	1970	1974	1948–74	1970–4
White collar	30.2	29.6	35.2	39.4	+9.2	+4.2
Manual	50.7	52.9	56.0	57.9	+7.2	+1.9

Source: R. Price and G. S. Bain, 'Union Growth Revisited: 1948–74 in perspective', *British Journal of Industrial Relations*, Vol. 14, No. 3, Nov. 1976, p. 347. The basic force figures used here are those reported in table 5 in the original article. The only source of information on the development of the white-collar and manual groups over time is the Census of Population: consequently, white-collar and manual figures for non Census years have been derived by interpolation. White-collar and manual employment in 1974 was estimated from 1971 Census data, together with the occupational labour force projections developed by the Department of Employment: see *The Changing Structure of the Labour Force*, London: Unit for Manpower Studies, Department of Employment, 1975, mimeographed. For details of the classification of union membership between white collar and manual categories, see the source article, Appendix A

TABLE 2.41

Unionization by sex and major occupational group, UK, 1948–74

Union membership (000s)

	Male				% Increase		Female				% Increase	
	1948	1964	1970	1974	1948–74	1970–4	1948	1964	1970	1974	1948–74	1970–4
White collar	1,267	1,681	2,143	2,593	+104.7	+21.0	697	1,003	1,447	1,629	+133.7	+12.6
Manual	6,410	6,329	6,123	5,972	−6.8	−2.5	988	1,206	1,364	1,561	+58.0	+14.4
Total	7,677	8,010	8,266	8,565	+11.6	+3.6	1,685	2,209	2,811	3,190	+89.3	+13.5

Union density (%)

	Male				Increase		Female				Increase	
	1948	1964	1970	1974	1948–74	1970–4	1948	1964	1970	1974	1948–74	1970–4
White collar	33.8	33.4	40.0	44.5	+10.7	+4.5	25.4	24.9	30.7	32.6	+7.2	+1.9
Manual	59.5	60.0	63.3	64.7	+5.2	+1.4	26.0	32.6	35.2	42.1	+16.1	+6.9
Total	52.9	51.4	55.0	56.9	+4.0	+1.9	25.7	28.6	32.7	36.7	+11.0	+4.0

Source: R. Price and G. S. Bain, 'Union Growth Revisited: 1948–74 in perspective', *British Journal of Industrial Relations*, Vol. 14, No. 3, Nov. 1976, p. 349. The basic labour force data used here are those reported in table 6 in the original article. They were sub-divided into male and female categories using the proportions of these categories in the white-collar and manual occupational groups at the nearest Census. The resultant labour force and density figures must therefore be regarded as approximations only. For details of the classification of the union membership data, see the source article, Appendix A

TABLE 2.42

Union membership and density by industry, UK, 1948 and 1974

Industry[1]	1948			1974		
	Labour force (000s)	Union membership[2] (000s)	Density (%)	Labour force (000s)	Union membership[2] (000s)	Density (%)
Agriculture and forestry	785.9	215.7	27.4	415.5	92.3	22.2
Fishing	37.7	14.9	39.6	12.2	7.4	60.5
Coal mining	802.7	675.3	84.1	314.0	302.1	96.2
Other mining	81.4	37.0	45.5	50.6	26.2	51.8
Food and drink	597.4	227.4	38.1}	783.9	401.1	51.2
Tobacco	49.1	26.1	53.1}			
Chemicals	426.8	127.3	29.8	483.6	247.4	51.2
Metals and engineering	3,676.1	1,837.5	50.0	4,118.0	2,862.7	69.4
Cotton and man-made fibres	395.2	276.6	70.0}	596.7	243.8	40.9
Other textiles	533.3	180.4	33.8}			
Leather	79.0	24.7	31.2	44.0	20.5	46.6
Clothing	429.1	145.5	33.9	345.8	207.7	60.0
Footwear	139.5	92.8	66.6	87.1	68.8	79.0
Bricks and building materials	172.2	70.1	40.8	171.9	69.4	40.4
Pottery	75.3	31.3	41.5	60.5	56.8	93.8
Glass	68.1	28.2	41.3	74.5	58.5	78.5
Wood and furniture	279.8	122.0	43.6	289.6	102.0	35.2
Paper, printing, and publishing	455.5	264.1	58.0	596.1	426.6	71.6
Rubber	97.9	48.5	49.6	127.2	71.1	55.9
Construction	1,353.7	613.2	45.3	1,428.8	388.1	27.2
Gas, electricity, and water	322.9	218.3	67.6	352.3	324.0	92.0
Railways	694.9	612.1	88.1	224.0	217.0	96.9
Road transport	490.6	295.0[3]	60.1[3]	468.3	445.4[3]	95.1[3]
Sea transport	120.8	108.0	89.3	90.6	90.3	99.6

Port and inland water transport	155.7	123.2	79.1	81.5	77.2	94.7
Air transport	32.1	13.0	40.5	79.8	74.7	93.6
Post office and telecommunications	353.2	283.4	80.2	509.7	448.1	87.9
Distribution	2,167.9	325.3	15.0	2,810.1	321.8	11.4
Insurance, banking, and finance	425.9	137.1	32.2	680.5	305.1	44.8
Entertainment and media services	238.4	95.7	40.1	189.6	123.0	64.9
Health	525.9	204.6	38.9	1,175.2	715.8	60.9
Hotels and catering	708.1	n.a.	—	824.2	42.5	5.2
Other professional services	276.8	n.a.	—	470.2	17.6	3.7
Education and local government	1,280.5	792.2	61.9	2,752.4	2,356.0	85.6
National government	724.1	480.6	66.4	623.7	564.5	90.5

Notes:
1   The following industries are not included in this table: miscellaneous transport services, other manufacturing (less rubber), business services (property owning, advertising and market research, other business services, central offices not allocable elsewhere), other miscellaneous services (betting and gambling, hairdressing and manicure, laundries, dry cleaning, motor repairers, distributors, garages and filling stations, repair of boots and shoes, and other services). Union density in this heterogeneous group of industries was less than 3 per cent in 1974: total employment was 2.4 million

2   For more detailed information on the compilation of these data, see Appendix A in the source article

3   These figures are substantially overstated since it has not been possible to disaggregate the membership of the Commerical Trade Group of the Transport and General Workers' Union into those employed by haulage firms and those employed by manufacturing concerns. Union membership among the latter group should be classified to the relevant manufacturing industry

Source: R. Price and G. S. Bain, 'Union Growth Revisited: 1948–74 in Perspective', British Journal of Industrial Relations, Vol. 14, No. 3 (Nov. 1976), pp. 342–3. Labour force data for 1948 are based on those published in 'The Employed Population, 1948–52', Ministry of Labour Gazette, LXI, February 1953, pp. 39–42; for 1974 they are taken from 'Employees in Employment in the United Kingdom at June 1974', Department of Employment Gazette, LXXXIII. July 1975, pp. 647–49, with the addition of unemployment from Industrial Analysis of the Unemployed at June 10, 1974', Department of Employment Gazette, LXXXII, July 1974, pp. 632–35

public utilities, in the transport industries and in national and local government, and very high, especially among manual workers, in most manufacturing industry, ranging from 35 per cent of all workers in wood and furniture to nearly 94 per cent in pottery. In most, but not all cases, union density has increased since 1948. In contrast the service industries show a very much more uneven pattern, with in some cases negligible union membership.

TABLE 2.43

Union membership and density by sector, UK, 1974

Sector[4]	Labour force (000s)	Union membership (000s)	Density (%)
Public sector[1]	6,112.6	5,079.4	83.1
Manufacturing	7,778.9	4,836.4	62.2
Manual	5,678.6	4,164.2	73.3
White collar[2]	2,100.3	672.2	32.0
Agriculture, forestry, and fishing	427.7	99.7	23.3
Private sector services[3]	6,689.3	810.0	12.1

Notes:
1. Comprises national government; local government; education; health service; Post Office; telecommunications; air transport; port and inland water transport; railways; gas, electricity, and water; and coal mining. The nationalised steel industry is included in manufacturing
2. The white collar labour force for manufacturing was calculated by applying the white-collar proportion of total manufacturing employment, as shown in 'Administrative, Technical and Clerical Workers in Manufacturing Industries', *Department of Employment Gazette,* LXXXIII, February 1975, p. 125, to the aggregate manufacturing figure derived from table 2.42. The white collar category is defined to include: managers, superintendents, and works foremen; research, development, technical, and design employees; draughtsmen, tracers, travellers, and office employees
3. Comprises professional services; hotels and catering; entertainment and media services; insurance, banking, and finance; distribution; business services; and miscellaneous services (hairdressing, laundries, dry cleaning, motor repairers, boot and shoe repair, and betting and gambling)
4. The following industries are not covered by the four sectors identified here: road transport, sea transport, construction, other mining, and miscellaneous manufacturing. Total employment in these industries amounted to 2.3 million in 1973; for details of their density levels in that year (except for miscellaneous manufacturing) see table 2.40

Source: R. Price and G. S. Bain 'Union Growth Revisited: 1948–74 in Perspective', *British Journal of Industrial Relations,* Vol. 14, No. 3 (Nov. 1976) p. 342

One structural characteristic which affects the industry figures is size of establishment. Price and Bain have argued that 'the available evidence suggests that establishment size is a virtual determinant of unionization'; and that 'the influence of establishment size is almost certainly a major reason for the low density levels . . . in construction, agriculture, and private sector services, which are all dominated by small undertakings'.[94] As we have seen, the average size of establishments has increased over the years which is one factor contributing to the overall growth of unionization.

The question of whether unions can really affect their members' levels of earnings, or whether market forces operate more or less regardless of union organization, has aroused a good deal of controversy among economists.[95] It may well be that certain structural characteristics of employment in the low-paid industries give rise to both levels of earnings and low union membership density; similarly, structural conditions may lie behind the low levels of unionization, and the poor levels of pay for women, who are in any case relatively heavily concentrated in the low-paid industries; what can be said, however, is that in addition to their low pay and poor conditions of employment workers in these industries also lack the organizational means to take collective action to improve their situation.

OCCUPATIONAL ALLOCATION – CHOICE AND CONSTRAINT

Thus far we have examined the changing occupational structure of Britain and the pattern of deprivations and rewards associated with particular types of work. We have seen that the distribution of work-related rewards and deprivations is such that a fairly clear hierarchy of occupations emerges, in which certain categories of employment offer relatively high pay and good conditions for doing work which must be regarded as less depriving than that for which lower levels of pay and fewer other benefits are received. This hierarchy is not clear-cut, and the ranking of any particular occupational grouping might vary a little depending on which character-istics were most emphasized. Nevertheless there is undoubtedly a systematic pattern of work-related inequalities.

The differentials which exist can be assessed in a variety of ways and according to a variety of criteria. For some they may seem entirely justified, as providing incentives for achievement and/or rewards for the exercise of skill or the carrying of responsibility.[96] For others they may seem unjustified, whether or nor they act as such incentives, in terms of basic beliefs and values about human equality. One important consideration, however, which is likely to affect most people's evaluation of these inequalities, is the nature of the allocation process which deter-mines how particular positions in the structure of occupations are filled. Is the process of occupational allocation more or less random; or meritocratic, with allocation in terms of abilities or achievement? Is there equal opportunity to be unequal; or is the process one which is structured to favour those who are initially privileged in terms of family of origin, or some other criterion? Discussion of these questions necessitates a brief consideration of the patterns of social mobility, and of the ways in which the educational system and the operation of the labour market tend to channel particular categories of people into particular types of work.

Social Mobility

Social mobility studies investigate the relationship between the social status (pri-marily based on occupation) of children and their parents. Until recently the most comprehensive source of information about social mobility in Britain was derived from studies carried out by Glass and his colleagues in the late 1940s.[97] On the basis, in particular, of the evidence from a large-scale survey, it has been argued that there was a relatively high degree of self-recruitment in Britain, especially at the two ends of the social scale, that most mobility was fairly short-range, and that the middle of the occupational hierarchy was characterized by a 'buffer zone' so that movement either way over the fundamental line of cleavage between manual and non-manual occupations, although not infrequent, would tend to be short-range.[98]

The Glass study, and arguments derived from it, have come under severe criticism, and more recent work has demonstrated that the situation is not as clear-cut as this.

Data for England and Wales, and for Scotland, show that there is still a considerable measure of self-recruitment, especially at the two ends of the occupational scale, and that in particular a large proportion of manual workers are the sons of manual workers – about 70 per cent in England and Wales, and over 75 per cent in Scotland (tables 2.44, 2.45 and 2.46). On the other hand the upper socio-economic groupings have recruited a substantial proportion from manual worker origins. This upward mobility is a consequence of the growth in the numbers in professional, administrative and managerial occupations which we have already noted, but the fact that such positions have been filled in substantial though by no means equal proportions by manual as well as non-manual workers' sons certainly undermines any notion of a 'buffer zone', or of the relative closure of the upper occupational status groups.[99]

In past discussions of social mobility it has been assumed that the main mechanism for upward mobility in recent decades has been the educational system. The professionalization of occupations and the growing size and bureaucratization of organizations, it was argued, led to the recruitment of employees on the basis of formal qualifications; and the expansion of educational opportunities with the introduction of secondary education for all after the Second World War, and the subsequent growth of higher education, enabled at least some of those with ability from less privileged backgrounds to obtain the necessary qualifications for a high-status job. At the same time it was argued that whereas in the past able individuals from humble origins had been able to improve their position by building up their own business or working their way up from the shop or office floor even without formal qualifications, these opportunities had been severely diminished by the same processes of professionalization and bureaucratization which favoured mobility through the educational system.[100] In fact in the recent study of social mobility in England and Wales it was found that a substantial proportion of those who were upwardly mobile (and indeed of those who maintained the occupational status of their family) had had experience of lower status work at an earlier stage in their work history; they had obtained their present situation at least in part by gaining advances during their working life. In addition analysis of different cohorts in the sample showed that those born more recently had, as expected, had apparently greater chances of direct entry into upper status groups (presumably through educational channels), but these increased chances were not 'counterbalanced' by a decline in the likelihood of upward mobility through 'work-life' advance.[101]

Thus data on social mobility can provide some indication of the overall dimensions of occupational allocation in Great Britain, but leave a number of questions for further exploration. Occupational allocation for men is neither completely random nor completely determined by the occupational status of the father; it is therefore important to see how the mechanisms of allocation both provide opportunities (within limits) and confer advantages on those already privileged. The point of initial entry into the labour market strongly influences subsequent job opportunities, especially but not only in those occupations, like skilled manual work and many professions, where formal qualifications are essential prerequisites; and educational achievement is likely to influence the range of opportunities available. It is therefore important to examine the links across generations between education and occupation. On the other hand changes of occupation during the course of a working life are still possible and frequent, and so the structure and operation of labour markets are also of relevance.

TABLE 2.44

Social mobility, England and Wales, 1972

| Father's[1] class | Class composition by class of father[1] at respondent's age 14 | | | | | | | | |
| | Respondent's class (1972) percentage[2] by column | | | | | | | | |
	I	II	III	IV	V	VI	VII	N	%
I	25.3 (24.2)	12.4 (12.0)	9.6 (9.1)	6.7 (6.0)	3.2 (3.0)	2.0 (1.8)	2.4 (2.0)	680 (688)	7.9 (7.3)
II	13.1 (12.5)	12.2 (11.8)	8.0 (7.6)	4.8 (4.4)	5.2 (4.9)	3.1 (2.9)	2.5 (2.2)	547 (554)	6.4 (5.9)
III	10.4 (10.0)	10.4 (10.0)	10.8 (10.2)	7.4 (6.1)	8.7 (8.2)	5.7 (5.4)	6.0 (5.3)	687 (694)	8.0 (7.3)
IV	10.1 (13.0)	12.2 (13.9)	9.8 (12.2)	27.2 (36.5)	8.6 (10.6)	7.1 (9.5)	7.7 (12.4)	886 (1,329)	10.3 (14.1)
V	12.5 (12.0)	14.0 (13.5)	13.2 (12.5)	12.1 (9.4)	16.6 (15.6)	12.2 (11.4)	9.6 (8.6)	1,072 (1,082)	12.5 (11.5)
VI	16.4 (15.7)	21.7 (21.0)	26.1 (24.8)	24.0 (19.2)	31.1 (29.2)	41.8 (39.1)	35.2 (30.5)	2,577 (2,594)	30.0 (27.5)
VII	12.1 (12.6)	17.1 (17.8)	22.6 (23.6)	17.8 (18.5)	26.7 (28.5)	28.0 (29.9)	36.6 (38.9)	2,126 (2,493)	24.8 (26.4)
N	1,230 (1,285)	1,050 (1,087)	827 (870)	687 (887)	1,026 (1,091)	1,883 (2,015)	1,872 (2,199)	8,575 (9,434)	
%	14.3 (13.6)	12.2 (11.5)	9.6 (9.2)	8.0 (9.4)	12.0 (11.6)	22.0 (21.3)	21.8 (23.3)		

Notes:
1. Or other 'head of household' (see text).
2. Bracketed figures are those produced if farmers (category 11) and smallholders (category 24) are allocated to Class IV and agriculture workers (category 31) to Class VII.

England and Wales the Classes are defined as follows:

I Higher-grade professionals, administrators; managers in large establishments; large proprietors
II Lower-grade professionals; higher-grade technicians; lower-grade administrators; managers in small establishments; supervisors of non-manual employees
III Routine non-manual (clerical) employees; sales personnel; other rank and file service workers
IV Small proprietors; self-employed artisans; non-professional 'own account' workers
V Lower-grade technicians; supervisors over manual workers
VI Skilled manual wage-workers
VII Semi- and un-skilled manual wage-workers

Source: J.H. Goldthorpe and C. Llewellyn, 'Class mobility in modern Britain', *Sociology*, Vol. 11, No. 2, p. 262

TABLE 2.45

Social mobility, England and Wales, 1972

Father's[1] class	Class distribution of respondents by class of father[1] at respondent's age 14								
					Respondent's class (1972) percentage[2] by row				
	I	II	III	IV	V	VI	VII	N	%
I	45.7 (45.2)	19.1 (18.9)	11.6 (11.5)	6.8 (7.7)	4.9 (4.8)	5.4 (5.4)	6.5 (6.5)	680 (688)	7.9 (7.3)
II	29.4 (29.1)	23.3 (23.1)	12.1 (11.9)	6.0 (7.0)	9.7 (9.6)	10.8 (10.6)	8.6 (8.7)	547 (554)	6.4 (5.9)
III	18.6 (18.4)	15.9 (15.7)	13.0 (12.8)	7.4 (7.8)	13.0 (12.8)	15.7 (15.6)	16.4 (16.9)	687 (694)	8.0 (7.3)
IV	14.0 (12.6)	14.4 (11.4)	9.1 (8.0)	21.1 (24.4)	9.9 (8.7)	15.7 (14.4)	16.3 (20.5)	886 (1,329)	10.3 (14.1)
V	14.4 (14.2)	13.7 (13.6)	10.2 (10.1)	7.7 (7.7)	15.9 (15.7)	21.4 (21.2)	16.8 (17.6)	1,072 (1,082)	12.5 (11.5)
VI	7.8 (7.8)	8.8 (8.8)	8.4 (8.3)	6.4 (6.6)	12.4 (12.3)	30.6 (30.4)	25.6 (25.9)	2,577 (2,594)	30.0 (27.5)
VII	7.1 (6.5)	8.5 (7.8)	8.8 (8.2)	5.7 (6.6)	12.9 (12.5)	24.8 (24.1)	32.2 (34.3)	2,126 (2,493)	24.8 (24.6)
N	1,230 (1,285)	1,050 (1,087)	827 (870)	687 (887)	1,026 (1,091)	1,883 (2,015)	1,872 (2,199)	8,575 (9,434)	
%	14.3 (13.6)	12.2 (11.5)	9.6 (9.2)	8.0 (9.4)	12.0 (11.6)	22.0 (21.3)	21.8 (23.3)		

Notes:
1. See note (1), Table 2.44
2. See note (2), Table 2.44

England and Wales the Classes are defined as follows:

I   Higher-grade professionals, administrators; managers in large establishments; large proprietors

II   Lower-grade professionals; higher-grade technicians; lower-grade administrators; managers in small establishments; supervisors of non-manual employees

III   Routine non-manual (clerical) employees; sales personnel; other rank and file service workers

IV   Small proprietors; self-employed artisans; non-professional 'own account' workers

V   Lower-grade technicians; supervisors over manual workers

VI   Skilled manual wage-workers

VII   Semi- and un-skilled manual wage-workers

Source: J.H.Goldthorpe and C.Llewellyn, 'Class mobility in modern Britain', *Sociology*, Vol. 11, No. 2, p. 267

TABLE 2.46

Social mobility, Scotland, 1975

		Mobility Table for 1975 Respondent's Current Occupation and 'Father's' Occupation when Respondent was 14 years old Inflow							
		1	2	3	4	5	6	7	Total
Father's	1	23.3	10.3	2.8	10.9	1.5	1.6	1.8	6.2
occupational	2	19.6	28.0	9.6	16.9	5.6	8.0	5.3	12.2
category	3	13.8	13.8	18.8	9.7	9.7	12.2	11.4	12.8
when R	4	7.5	5.1	2.5	5.6	2.2	1.6	1.7	3.3
was 14	5	16.5	18.6	26.7	23.6	42.6	29.5	32.9	28.7
	6	9.3	13.4	20.3	17.6	20.6	28.6	23.0	19.9
	7	10.0	10.9	19.3	15.7	17.7	18.6	23.9	16.9
		100.0	100.0	100.0	100.0	100.0	100.0	100.0	
Total		11.8	14.8	13.9	5.7	20.2	19.3	14.2	100.0

Notes:

Scotland the socio-economic categories are defined as follows:

1 Professionals, proprietors and managers of large organizations, and senior supervisory staff
2 Semi-professionals, higher technicians, proprietors and managers of small organizations (including farmers)
3 Supervisors of manual workers, self-employed artisans, and lower technicians
4 Routine non-manual workers
5 Skilled manual workers
6 Semi-skilled manual workers
7 Unskilled manual workers

Source: G.Payne, C.Ford, and C.Robertson, 'Changes in Occupational Mobility in Scotland, *The Scottish Journal of Sociology,* Vol. 1, No. 1 (Nov. 1976), p. 70

Education and Occupation

The General Household Survey provides us with some relatively recent information about the relationship between education and occupation. This enables us to establish some fairly clear links within and between the generations.

First, the occupational category (in terms of socio-economic group) of adults is related to their school/college experience (tables 2.47 and 2.48).[102] Over three-quarters of all manual workers attended non-selective schools. Among non-manual workers there are two distinct patterns: those in the 'professional' and 'intermediate' categories have typically either had experience of further or higher education (about half of the 'professionals' and a third of the 'intermediates') or had attended a selective school. This sort of educational advantage is much less frequent for 'employers and managers' and 'junior non-manual employees', very many of whom have attended non-selective schools.

Secondly, the same pattern of differences is reflected in table 2.49, which shows, for men, the relationship between age, educational qualifications and occupational category. Almost all those in professional occupations have some formal qualifications, and nearly three-quarters are classified as 'higher educational' — though it is

TABLE 2.47

Socio-economic group by type of school or college last attended full-time (males), England and Wales

Males aged 15 or over not in full-time or part-time education

Type of school or college last attended	Own Socio-economic Group									
	Pro-fessional	Employers and managers	Intermediate non-manual	Junior non-manual	Skilled manual and own account non-professional	Semi-skilled manual and personal service	Unskilled manual	TOTAL in labour force (incl. Armed Forces)	Others	TOTAL
	%	%	%	%	%	%	%	%	%	%
Elementary/primary school[1]	4.8	24.1	16.2	29.5	38.6	42.3	41.1	32.8	76.0	39.9
Central/intermediate/higher grade school	3.1	4.8	3.4	5.9	3.7	2.9	4.0	3.9	3.6	3.9
Secondary modern school	5.4	14.5	13.3	20.3	35.6	32.8	34.4	27.3	1.8	23.1
Comprehensive school	1.3	1.4	0.7	3.5	2.1	2.8	3.1	2.2	0.4	1.9
Technical school	6.1	4.0	2.8	4.0	2.5	1.0	1.3	2.8	1.0	2.5
Grammar school	19.9	22.3	21.2	20.2	5.9	5.2	1.5	11.4	5.9	10.5
Independent or direct grant school	6.1	8.3	3.6	4.3	1.2	0.9	0.2	2.9	2.9	2.9
Foreign or other (incl. special) school	1.0	3.3	2.6	2.9	5.0	8.4	11.8	5.1	3.5	4.9
College of further education[2] or college of education	15.1	9.5	22.0	7.7	4.6	3.1	2.3	6.9	1.9	6.1
University	25.6	5.3	11.5	1.0	0.2	NIL	NIL	3.0	2.0	2.8
Foreign or other college	11.5	2.5	2.6	0.7	0.6	0.7	0.2	1.6	1.0	1.5
BASE (= 100%)	391	1,117	495	932	3,157	1,233	474	7,913	1,566	9,479

Notes:
1. Including all-age schools, orphanages, and those who never went to school
2. Including technical and commercial colleges, colleges of art/music/drama/domestic science, polytechnics, etc
Source: Office of Population Censuses and Surveys, *The General Household Survey 1972* (HMSO 1975), p. 159

interesting that the proportion in the latter category is slightly smaller for the younger age groups. The proportion of intermediate non-manual workers with educational qualifications increases in the younger age groups. On the other hand, educational qualifications, particularly 'higher' qualifications, are much less common among employers and managers and junior non-manual workers, though in both cases, and especially for the latter category, the younger the employee the more likely he is to have some educational qualification. This trend is strongly marked too for skilled manual workers, over half of whom in the youngest age group have some form of qualification, and in this respect they are clearly distinguished from non-skilled manual workers. The overall pattern for women appears similar, but the numbers included in the *Survey* are too small for comparisons to be made in the same detail.[103]

Thirdly, data on earnings confirm the same picture. Table 2.50 shows both that those with educational qualifications tend to earn more, and that for those with qualifications, in contrast to those without, earnings tend to increase with age.

Thus in the past educational experience and qualifications have certainly influenced life chances, even though there are also substantial minorities who have attained higher status occupations, and higher earnings, without advantages gained from education; and it appears that education is becoming more important. Educational experience and qualifications, however, appear to have been more important in certain types of occupation than others, though in those managerial and skilled manual occupations where they were previously less important, the evidence suggests that they are becoming more so.

We have no means of knowing whether this pattern will continue into the future but it is likely to do so and thus occupational opportunities for future generations are likely to depend on current educational experience. The relationship between this and father's occupation is shown in table 2.51. The growing number of comprehensive schools makes the figures harder to interpret, but clearly non-manual workers' children are more likely than manual workers' children to receive pre-school education, to attend an independent or direct grant school, and at the secondary level to attend a selective state secondary school; and these advantages are particularly frequent in the case of the children of professional employees. The current relationship between school and subsequent education is shown in table 2.52. Well over half the boys and girls who attended independent and direct grant schools go on to further full-time education, many at degree level; and the same is true for half the girls and 40 per cent of the boys at selective state secondary schools. In contrast most of those leaving other types of schools go straight into employment. Such employment may of course offer training leading to a qualification, as for example is the case with apprenticeships. In 1974 a majority of boys, but a smaller proportion of girls, entered employment of this sort, the main reason for the difference being the much greater number of apprenticeships available for boys (table 2.53). Nearly a third of both sexes, however, entered manual employment which offered no training except perhaps a brief induction into the organization.

There is, therefore, a clear relationship between the past educational experience and qualifications of adults and their current occupations and earnings, and between current occupation (and earnings)[105] of parents and their ability to provide their children with educational opportunities which appear likely to give them the greatest chance of a more rewarding occupation in the future. In the case of attendance at fee-paying schools it is the parents' ability to pay which is decisive,

TABLE 2.48

Socio-economic group by type of school or college last attended full-time – females, England and Wales

Females aged 15 or over not in full-time or part-time education

Type of school or college last attended	Own Socio-economic Group								
	Professional & intermediate non-manual	Employers and managers	Junior non-manual	Skilled manual and own account non-professional	Semi-skilled manual and personal service	Unskilled manual	TOTAL in labour force (incl. Armed Forces)	Others	TOTAL
	%	%	%	%	%	%	%	%	%
Elementary/primary school[1]	10.7	31.2	22.1	42.6	45.7	64.3	33.3	51.4	43.2
Central/intermediate/ higher grade school	2.7	7.9	5.5	4.5	3.5	5.6	4.7	3.6	4.1
Secondary modern school	11.2	17.2	29.4	29.8	31.1	21.1	26.5	18.2	21.9
Comprehensive school	1.1	0.5	3.8	2.5	1.9	0.5	2.5	0.9	1.7
Technical school	0.9	NIL	2.1	1.0	0.8	NIL	1.2	1.1	1.1
Grammar school	14.4	12.6	15.8	8.2	5.8	2.7	10.9	7.9	9.2
Independent or direct grant school	3.4	5.1	3.9	1.7	1.1	0.4	2.6	4.5	3.6
Foreign or other (incl. special) school	6.2	3.7	3.0	3.0	6.5	4.7	4.5	4.6	4.6
College of further education[2] or college of education	35.7	17.7	13.3	4.7	2.9	0.4	11.2	6.2	8.5
University	7.8	1.9	0.3	0.6	0.1	NIL	1.2	0.6	0.9
Foreign or other college	5.9	2.3	0.8	1.5	0.6	0.2	1.5	1.0	1.2
BASE (= 100%)	561	215	1,862	403	1,391	445	4,879	5,946	10,825

Notes:

1   Including all-age schools, orphanages, and those who never went to school
2   Including technical and commercial colleges, colleges of art/music/drama/domestic science, polytechnics, etc

Source: Office of Population Censuses and Surveys, *The General Household Survey 1972* (HMSO 1975), p. 160

and this of course represents a major source of inequality of opportunity in British society, though one which affects only a minority of the population.[106] In the case of selective secondary schools and of educational qualifications, however, the ability and aspirations of the child are also of crucial importance, and our picture of the relationship between education and occupation needs to be completed with a brief discussion of the ways in which processes within the school tend to reinforce the advantages so far discussed.

These can be seen as of two sorts. On the one hand the educational system contains a series of selection and streaming mechanisms which function to constrict the academic and subsequent occupational opportunities of some children while maintaining or enlarging the choices for others. On the other hand, schools are also socializing agencies which influence very strongly the child's view of him or herself and his or her aspirations and ambitions. There are therefore both structural and cultural influences at work.

The discussion of selection and streaming has centred round the 11-plus exam and selective secondary schooling. With the growth of comprehensive schools selection at 11 is of declining importance, but many comprehensive schools stream children in terms of academic ability. The official assumption is that selection and streaming merely provide children with the education for which they are best fitted in terms of their abilities and aptitudes. A whole series of studies, however, has shown that the situation is not so simple. In the first place, such a process tends to act as a self-fulfilling prophecy — those labelled as 'able' do well, whereas those consigned to a lower stream come to accept that they are less able, and to achieve less than tests of ability would indicate as their potential.[107] Secondly, such selective processes tend to favour those from higher status backgrounds who are either more likely to 'pass' the selection tests because of greater verbal skills and/or are more likely to be placed in higher streams than their measured ability warrants because they possess other characteristics (appearance, behaviour, etc) which favourably impress the selectors. The net result is that among children of the same measured ability those from higher status backgrounds are more likely to 'do well' at school and to obtain educational qualifications. Such results were shown most clearly in the evidence published by the Robbins Committee on Higher Education and have also been reported by other enquiries.[108]

As socializing agencies the schools explicitly, and even more important, implicitly, prepare children for the occupations they are considered most likely to be able to enter. On the basis of research in Leicester, for example, Ashton has argued that schools both provide children with different opportunities and possibilities of reward, and give them experiences which lead to the development of 'different frames of reference that commit young people to certain types of occupation, and by providing them with different self-images and orientations to work enable them to adjust to their positions at work'.[109] He has suggested that three basic types of occupational opportunity can be distinguished: a 'middle-class career', based on an education in a grammar school or the higher streams of a comprehensive school and leading to non-manual employment, based on educational qualifications and with promotion prospects; a 'working class career' open to the more able children in the middle streams of a comprehensive school, or the top streams of a secondary modern school, and leading to a skilled manual occupation; and a 'careerless' occupation — unskilled manual work with no real prospects — open to those in the lower streams of secondary schools.

Educational qualifications

TABLE 2.49

Age and socio-economic group by highest qualification level attained* – males, GB

Males in the labour force and not in full-time education

				Own Socio-economic group			
Age	Pro-fessional	Employers and managers	Inter-mediate non-manual	Junior non-manual	Skilled manual and own account non-pro-fessional	Semi-skilled and unskilled manual and personal service	TOTAL in labour force (incl. Armed Forces)[2]
	% No.	%	% No.	%	%	%	%
20–29							
Higher education	68.7	15.5	45.8	13.8	3.8	1.0	13.4
Other qualifications	30.5	49.5	47.0	62.2	47.7	25.2	44.4
No qualifications	0.8	35.0	7.2	24.0	48.5	73.8	42.2
BASE (= 100%)	(128)	(194)	(166)	(275)	(784)	(393)	(1,952)
30–39							
Higher education	79.5	23.4	46.6	10.7	2.1	0.3	13.9
Other qualifications	17.1	47.3	38.2	45.3	36.4	17.4	34.5
No qualifications	3.4	29.3	15.2	44.0	61.5	82.3	51.6
BASE (= 100%)	(117)	(273)	(131)	(159)	(761)	(339)	(1,790)
40–49							
Higher education	81.7	18.8	41.5	2.9	1.2	NIL	11.3
Other qualifications	14.4	40.1	32.1	39.4	27.7	12.5	27.7
No qualifications	3.8	41.1	26.4	57.6	71.0	87.5	61.0
BASE (= 100%)	(104)	(314)	(106)	(170)	(732)	(319)	(1,743)
50–59							
Higher education	[51]	15.0	35.2	1.5	1.4	0.3	8.7
Other qualifications	[14]	36.2	30.5	32.7	25.9	11.6	25.6
No qualifications	[4]	48.8	34.3	65.8	72.7	88.1	65.6
BASE (= 100%)	(69)	(293)	(105)	(199)	(625)	(328)	(1,618)
60 or over							
Higher education	[21]	15.9	[16]	5.1	0.3	1.1	6.8
Other qualifications	[8]	31.8	[17]	20.5	23.1	11.7	20.2
No qualifications	[3]	52.2	[17]	74.4	76.6	87.2	72.9
BASE (= 100%)	(32)	(113)	(50)	(156)	(307)	(273)	(909)
ALL AGES[1]							
Higher education	73.5	17.7	40.8	6.7	1.9	0.5	10.5
Other qualifications	23.1	41.6	39.0	44.4	34.7	16.2	32.7
No qualifications	1.5	40.7	20.2	48.9	63.4	83.3	56.8
BASE (= 100%)	(443)	(1,162)	(552)	(1,032)	(3,464)	(1,820)	(8,586)

*Higher education = degrees, teaching qualifications, HNC/HMD, university diplomas and certificates, some nursing qualifications, etc

Other qualifications = 'A' level and 'O' level GCE, SCE, SUPE, SLC, ONC/OND, CSE, apprenticeship, etc

Notes:

1. Including those aged 15–19 (583) and age not known

2. Total in labour force may be less than the sum of the column totals owing to rounding of weighted figures for Scotland

Source: Office of Population Censuses and Surveys, *The General Household Survey 1972* (HMSO 1975), p. 168

TABLE 2.50

Median annual earnings* for levels of qualification, by age − males, GB

Males in full-time work[1]

Age		Highest qualification level attained				
		Degree or equivalent	Below-degree higher education	GCE 'A' or 'O' level or equivalent/CSE Grade 1	CSE other grades/ commercial/ apprenticeship	No qualifications
		£	£	£	£	£
15−19		²	²	600	490	570
	BASE			(119)	(115)	(288)
20−24		⎫		1,240	1,280	1,240
	BASE	⎪		(247)	(121)	(301)
		⎬ 1,720	1,670			
25−29		⎪ (101)	(128)	1,770	1,610	1,500
	BASE	⎭		(221)	(145)	(408)
30−39		3,000	2,210	1,940	1,800	1,580
	BASE	(95)	(130)	(257)	(219)	(813)
40−49		⎫		2,300	1,620	1,510
	BASE	⎬ over 3,000³	2,650	(172)	(184)	(943)
50−59		⎪ (153)	(129)	2,140	1,560	1,410
	BASE	⎭		(137)	(171)	(910)
60 or over		²	²	²	²	1,200
	BASE					(442)

* Median earnings derived by interpolation in earnings bands.

Notes:
1. Full-time = 31 hours or more per week (26 hours or more for teachers and lecturers)
2. Base too small for reliable estimates
3. £3,000 and over is the highest earnings band

Source: Office of Population Censuses and Surveys, *The General Household Survey 1972* (HMSO 1975), p. 174

These categories may well need elaboration and refinement in the light of further research, and they could not necessarily be applied identically to girls; other studies have also shown clearly, however, that most children have a very realistic assessment of their occupational opportunities, or lack of them. 'Anticipatory socialization' takes place at school and consequently the transition to work is often less stressful than might be expected. Of course, this is not true in circumstances such as high unemployment where there are insufficient jobs available of the types expected, or no jobs at all.[110] Recent official concern about the over-production of those with particular qualifications (e.g. teachers) and about unemployment among young

TABLE 2.51

Type of school attended by children aged under 15, by socio-economic group of father/head of

| | | Socio-economic Group | | |
Type of school	Pro-fessional	Employers and managers	Inter-mediate non-manual	Junior non-manual
	%	%	%	%
Under school age (under 5):[2]				
Not yet started	68.3	62.4	72.4	73.7
Day nursery/play group	18.0	25.5	17.0	18.9
Nursery school[3]	13.7	12.1	10.6	7.4
BASE (= 100%)	(139)	(330)	(170)	(243)
Primary schooling (5–10):[2]				
Primary school	91.4	94.3	98.1	98.8
Independent or direct grant school	8.6	5.7	1.9	1.2
BASE (= 100%)	(175)	(475)	(208)	(256)
Secondary schooling (11–14):[2]				
Secondary modern school	29.0	34.4	29.4	34.1
Comprehensive school	20.4	28.6	32.1	35.8
Grammar school	19.4	18.8	29.4	19.9
Direct grant or independent school	30.1	15.2	7.3	2.3
Other schools (incl. special)	1.1	2.9	1.8	7.9
BASE (= 100%)	(93)	(276)	(109)	(176)
ALL CHILDREN UNDER 15:				
Under school age	34.2	30.5	34.9	36.0
Primary schooling	43.0	43.9	42.7	37.9
Secondary schooling	22.8	25.5	22.4	26.1
TOTAL No.	407	1,081	487	675
%	5.4	14.3	6.4	8.9

Notes:
1. The SEG of the head of household (HOH) is taken where the father was not a member of the household
2. Where children were just outside the age group at the time of interview they have been allocated to the age group of the majority
3. Including primary and independent school for under 5s

Source: Office of Population Censuses and Surveys, *The General Household Survey 1972* (HMSO 1975), p. 157

household, England and Wales

of Father/HOH[1]

Skilled manual and own account non-professional	Semi-skilled manual and personal service	Unskilled manual	TOTAL in labour force (incl. Armed Forces)	Economically inactive	TOTAL
%	%	%	%	%	%
80.8	83.9	85.1	77.0	87.9	77.6
12.1	8.6	7.4	14.4	7.1	14.0
7.1	7.5	7.4	8.6	5.0	8.4
(1,013)	(397)	(121)	(2,445)	(140)	(2,585)
100	100	100	94.0	100	94.0
NIL	NIL	NIL	6.0	NIL	6.0
(1,242)	(427)	(145)	(2,978)	(178)	(3,156)
48.5	53.4	[42]	42.8	60.2	43.8
31.9	29.3	[26]	30.6	23.3	30.2
12.3	8.8	[5]	15.0	8.7	14.6
1.4	NIL	[NIL]	5.7	1.0	5.5
5.9	8.4	[13]	5.9	6.8	5.9
(699)	(249)	(86)	(1,712)	(103)	(1,815)
34.3	37.0	34.4	34.3	33.2	34.2
42.0	39.8	41.2	41.7	42.3	41.8
23.7	23.2	24.4	24.0	24.5	24.0
2,954	1,073	352	7,135	421	7,556
39.1	14.2	4.7	94.4	5.6	100

TABLE 2.52

Destination of school leavers: by type of school, England and Wales, 1973–4

Percentages and numbers

	Universities	Colleges of Education	Polytechnics	Other full-time further education	Employment[1]	Total (= 100%) (numbers)
Boys (percentages):						
Grammar	21.3	2.5	7.1	8.8	60.3	34,370
Comprehensive	4.3	0.8	1.8	5.2	87.9	195,630
Modern	0.3	0.1	0.2	7.5	91.9	82,530
Other secondary	3.2	1.0	2.3	7.3	86.2	14,130
Direct grant	38.4	2.4	9.9	10.1	39.2	8,070
Independent	31.6	0.7	6.1	17.5	44.1	14,910
Girls (percentages):						
Grammar	14.0	11.6	4.1	20.0	50.3	36,150
Comprehensive	2.6	3.4	1.0	10.6	82.4	184,520
Modern	0.1	0.6	0.3	13.7	85.3	77,870
Other secondary	1.6	3.3	0.6	11.9	82.6	13,300
Direct grant	26.0	12.6	5.2	18.6	37.6	7,970
Independent	14.8	5.5	3.8	36.9	39.0	11,990

Note:
1　Includes those entering temporary employment, pending entry into full-time further education not later than September–October 1975, and those who left for other reasons and whose destinations were not known

Source: *Social Trends*, No. 7 (HMSO 1976), p. 90

TABLE 2.53

Number of young persons entering employment, by class of employment, GB, 1974

	Boys		Girls	
	000s	per cent	000s	per cent
Employment leading to recognized professional qualifications	3,5	1.3	4,2	1.8
Apprenticeship to skilled occupation	118,2	43.0	15,5	6.5
Employment-planned training, apart from induction training	47,0	17.1	41,0	17.2
Clerical employment	19,2	7.0	96,3	40.5
Other employment	86,9	31.6	80,7	33.9
Total	274,8	100	237,8	100

Source: Department of Employment *British Labour Statistics Yearbook 1974* (HMSO 1976), p. 225

people reflects acknowledgment of the possibly long-term disruptive consequences of this lack of fit between legitimate aspirations and actual employment possibilities.

The clearest accounts of the socializing influence of the school probably came from research which compares the experience of boys and girls. It has several times been reported that girls are less likely to take GCE 'A' levels even though they do as well at the 'O' level stage as boys, and are less likely to go on to university education when they have the same number of 'A' levels.[111] A series of studies has shown how before leaving school girls acquire a conception of themselves and of the opportunities open to them which, in occupational terms, is much narrower and less ambitious than that acquired by boys.[112] In one study which attempted to measure ambitiousness, for example, a clear hierarchy emerged, with grammar-school girls appearing as less ambitious even than secondary modern-school boys; grammar-school boys were the most ambitious, and secondary modern-school girls the least.[113]

The educational system, therefore, is far from strictly 'meritocratic' in its effects. Certain structural characteristics (such as fee-paying schools, early selection, streaming, and regional and other geographical inequalities in resources)[114] lead to a distribution of opportunities which on the whole favours those who come from the more economically privileged backgrounds; and the assumptions of teachers, administrators, parents and — as time goes on — increasingly the children themselves, about the academic potential and occupational opportunities of particular categories of children are a further constraint. As we have seen many from less privileged backgrounds do succeed in using educational opportunities to be upwardly occupationally mobile, but they have to overcome handicaps on the way which are sufficient to block those with less ability, less determination, or less luck. Thus by the time any individual enters employment the chances of a rewarding career are determined to a considerable extent; it remains to be seen in what ways the operation of the labour market modifies this picture.

The Labour Market

A great deal of work still needs to be done to provide an adequate sociology of the labour market for a society like ours in the UK, and no attempt will be made here to meet this need.[115] There are however several more or less widely accepted characteristics of the labour market which have a considerable influence on the ways in which jobs are allocated, and some of these can be briefly discussed.

In the first place it is important to recognize that the 'market' for labour is highly fragmented — industrially, occupationally and geographically. This fragmentation means that very different conditions of employment can coexist for virtually the same type of work in the same society. Comparisons between jobs, and the operation of market forces to equalize the balance of costs and rewards in different types of employment, are restricted by institutional factors such as strongly defended occupational boundaries. The growth of large-scale national and multi-national organizations, the spread of collective bargaining, the public discussion of incomes policy, and other developments like the growing influence of the mass media and improved means of communication, have reduced the extent to which particular labour markets can remain self-contained in this way, but a considerable degree of fragmentation remains.

The various, partially overlapping, markets for labour operate very differently. For some occupations and/or industrial sectors they tend to be very 'formal' and bureaucratic: posts are advertised in known and public ways and stated universalistic criteria are relevant for appointments and promotions. This is broadly true, for example, in education and in national and local government. For other types of work and/or industries, the labour market may operate much more 'informally' and unpredictably, with particularistic criteria like kinship links, religious affiliation, or membership of the right clubs, of relevance for getting a job. Recruitment has often been carried out in this way for managerial posts in many small and medium-sized organizations, for example, and for manual jobs on the docks or in parts of the construction industry.

A further type of division is that between internal and external labour markets. In large organizations many posts are filled from within, so that external recruitment is normally only necessary for the basic grades of (say) manual, clerical and managerial work. The allocation of the more senior and better-rewarded positions is confined to those who are already working in the organization. This has two important results: it creates a degree of 'employment dependence' for those employees who have been promoted to positions with rewards for length of service and the carrying of responsibility which they would lose if they moved to another employer;[116] and it means that those seeking work who are outside such organizations are often restricted to choosing between employers each of whom is recruiting at a basic grade with opportunities for subsequent advancement which are uncertain and imprecisely specified. In addition, in situations where the junior posts are filled only from those below a certain age and all other posts are filled by internal promotions whenever possible, early employment can obviously determine subsequent chances of rewarding work.

The fragmentation of labour markets generally, the existence of many areas of work where the criteria for recruitment or advancement are uncertain or unknown, lack of knowledge about jobs and employers, and the development of internal labour markets, all make it difficult for workers to pursue 'economically rational' strategies in seeking employment. There is a good deal of dispute over whether employees do have a clear set of objectives with regard to employment, but even if they do they are severely constrained in their pursuit of such goals.[117] In addition to the characteristics of labour markets and recruitment processes already mentioned, employees are also constrained from being 'economic men (or women)' and pursuing the most advantageous jobs available, by attachments to family and/or locality, the difficulty of combining mobility in the labour market with mobility in the housing market, and/or identification with an occupation which may be a central part of their self-image.

We have as yet no overall picture of the ways in which employers' strategies in recruiting workers and employees' strategies in seeking work inter-relate to produce a particular allocation of workers to jobs. One example of an attempt to produce an overall picture for the less-skilled manual and non-manual occupations is the discussion of 'dual labour markets'. The argument here is that increasingly the economy is providing two sorts of jobs for such non-skilled workers — jobs in the primary sector where higher earnings and fringe benefits are the rewards for stability and loyalty, and those in the secondary sector which are low-paid and insecure. In terms of the allocation of employment such a development, if it is occurring, is important because of the associated argument that certain types of worker (for example, women) and workers with a history of frequent job changes — voluntary or involuntary — will tend to be confined to the secondary sector. The job security and rewards of primary sector employees depend in part on the existence of the secondary sector to take up the variations in demand in the economy, so that this form of labour market segmentation is also a way of dividing the working class and reducing the likelihood of collective action to improve the position of the lower paid.[118]

Thus labour markets appear to operate in ways which limit the opportunities open to employees to improve their situation, and which mean that the point of entry into employment, and subsequent work experience, largely determine future opportunities. Certainly the labour market is far from being a mechanism which equalizes the costs and rewards of employment even for those with the same range of abilities and qualifications; nor does it appear to do very much, if anything, to redress the inequalities in occupational allocation which result from educational processes. British society is not closed, but nor is it completely open, and whatever other justifications may be offered for the existing pattern of work-related inequalities, they cannot be defended as being rewards to those who are successful in a competition in which all have equal chances.

CONCLUSION

The nature and consequences of the division of labour have always been major questions of interest to social scientists. For some, like Adam Smith, the increase in the division of labour was a fundamental cause of economic growth and the possibility of the greater welfare of mankind; for others, as in some of the writings of Marx, its virtual abolition appeared to be a pre-requisite for real human freedom. It is perhaps with the work of Durkheim, however, that analysis of the problems of the division of labour is most notably associated.[119] For Durkheim the central question was whether, and if so how, social cohesion and social solidarity could be maintained in societies with an increasingly complex division of labour. He argued very forcefully that organic solidarity, based on the interdependence of those who have differentiated functions, would and should develop. In his discussion of 'abnormal forms', however, he acknowledged three other possibilities: an 'anomic' form of the division of labour in which there was inadequate normative regulation of economic life for solidarity to develop; the 'forced' division of labour in which individuals were constrained to undertake certain tasks, there was no 'harmony between individual natures and social functions', and 'social inequalities' did not 'exactly express natural inequalities'; and the situation where there is too much specialization, 'each employee is not sufficiently occupied' and 'operations are carried on without any unity'.[120]

In this chapter we have been concerned with aspects of the division of labour in contemporary Britain, and in the light of the evidence which has been discussed would have to conclude that the situation resembles Durkheim's 'abnormal' forms more closely than his ideal type of organic solidarity. For very many in our society their role in the division of labour is one which is forced on them by the constraints of their upbringing, education and lack of opportunity in the labour market; there is no consensus as to the appropriate distribution of obligations and rewards as between different classes and categories of occupations, whose situations are so unequal; and there is not only a 'social' but also a 'detailed' division of labour, which Braverman for example regards as the special product of capitalist society,[121] which leaves the worker performing only a fragment of a whole task.

It can, indeed, be argued that both anomie and alienation characterize the division of labour in Britain: an absence of normative consensus leading to disorder, as for example in industrial relations; and persistent inequalities of condition and of opportunity which constrain individuals in unacceptable ways and make any attempt to establish normative agreement difficult if not impossible.[122] At the moment there are no agreed remedies for these problems, nor any immediate prospect of their solution. In discussions of industrial relations and incomes policy, of social policy generally and the plight of the low-paid, and of the desirability of new forms of work organization and of developments towards industrial democracy, for example, the nature of the division of labour is a central, though not always acknowledged, issue. An examination of work in UK society can only outline some of the main characteristics of the existing situation. As such it may provide a base from which policy issues can be discussed. Both value judgments as to what is desirable, and empirical research as to what could be possible, will be needed for any progress to be made. What seems an important first step, however, is to acknowledge both the importance of work in the lives of men and women, and the far from satisfactory nature of the work which most of them are currently expected to do.

Notes to Chapter 2

1   In this sentence, and subsequently in this chapter, the use of the male pronoun to refer to both men and women is for stylistic convenience only.

2   S.R.Parker, R.K.Brown, J.Child and M.A.Smith, *The Sociology of Industry* (London 1972), pp. 173—5; see also S.R.Parker, *The Future of Work and Leisure* (London 1971), pp. 18—32.

3   E.Jaques, *Equitable Payment* (Penguin edn. 1967), pp. 52—5; see also W.Brown and E.Jaques, *Glacier Project Papers* (London 1965), esp. chs 3 and 4.

4   H.Braverman, *Labor and Monopoly Capital* (New York 1974), pp. 46—58. For yet another, very perceptive, approach to work, see E.C.Hughes, *Men and their Work* (New York 1958).

5   Notably in D.Bell, *The Coming of Post-Industrial Society* (Penguin edn. 1976).

6   See R.Dubin, 'Industrial workers' worlds — a study of the 'central life interests' of industrial workers', *Social Problems,* Vol. 3 (January 1956); see also J.H.Goldthorpe et al., *The Affluent Worker — Industrial Attitudes and Behaviour* (Cambridge 1968), esp. chs 2 and 7.

7   Such an interpretation has been made of some of the work of B.Bernstein, for example, *Class, Codes and Control*, Vol. 1, (London 1971); and of the concern with cycles of transmitted deprivation, see, for example, K.Joseph, 'The Cycle of Deprivation' in E.Butterworth and R.Holman (eds), *Social Welfare in Modern Britain* (Fontana edn. 1975), pp. 387—93, and Community Development Projects, *Gilding the Ghetto* (London 1977).

8   M.Weber, *The Protestant Ethic and the Spirit of Capitalism* (London 1930); and *General Economic History* (New York 1961), esp. ch. 30.

9   R.Bendix, *Work and Authority in Industry* (New York, 1963), esp.chs 2 and 4; S.Pollard, *The Genesis of Modern Management* (London 1965), esp. ch. 5; E.P.Thompson, 'Time, work discipline and industrial capitalism', in *Past and Present,* Vol. 38, (1967), pp. 56—97.

10 See, for example, W.Baldamus, *Efficiency and Effort* (London 1961), esp. ch. 8; and R.Hyman and I.Brough, *Social Values and Industrial Relations* (Oxford 1975).

11 A.Fox, 'The meaning of work' in Open University, *Occupational Categories and Cultures 1, People and Work* (Milton Keynes 1976), pp. 9—59. See also, R.Williams, 'The Meanings of Work' in R.Fraser (ed.), *Work: twenty personal accounts* (Penguin edn. 1968), pp. 280—98.

12 A.Fox, *op. cit.*, pp. 38—42.

13 See, for example. I.Read, *Social Class Differences in Britain: a source book* (London 1977), p. 15: 'Social class is a grouping of people into categories

on the basis of occupation'. For an analysis based on a quite clearly different approach see J.Westergaard and H.Resler, *Class in a Capitalist Society* (London 1975).

14   See T.B.Bottomore and M.Rubel (eds), *Karl Marx – selected writings in sociology and social philosophy* (London 1956) pp. 178 et seq; H.H.Gerth and C.W.Mills, *From Max Weber* (London 1948), p. 182.

15   I.Reid, *op. cit.* pp. 65–70.

16   J.Rex and R.Moore, *Race, Community and Conflict* (Oxford 1967).

17   J.W.B.Douglas, *The Home and the School* (Panther edn. 1967); D.S.Byrne, W.Williamson and B.Fletcher, *The Poverty of Education* (London 1975).

18   In addition to the Classification of Occupations used by the Office of Population Censuses and Surveys, the Department of Employment have produced their own comprehensive occupational classification, CODOT, (*Classification of Occupations & Directory of Occupational Titles*, HMSO 1972) which has an index of 11,000 job titles; and the results of the *New Earnings Survey* are classified using the *List of Key Occupations for Statistical Purposes,* which arranges 400 entries in 18 main groups.

19   Some of the problems involved in using even these apparently straight-forward categories are discussed in G.S.Bain and R.Price, 'Who is a white-collar employee?' in *British Journal of Industrial Relations,* Vol. 10, No. 3 (1972), pp. 325–39; and P.Sadler, 'Sociological aspects of skill' in *British Journal of Industrial Relations,* Vol. 8, No. 1 (1970), pp. 22–31.

20   Department of Employment, *British Labour Statistics: Historical Abstract 1886–1968* (HMSO 1971); A.H.Halsey (ed.), *Trends in British Society since 1900* (London 1972), esp. pp. 97–128; D.C.Marsh, *The Changing Social Structure of England and Wales, 1871–1961* (London 1965), esp. pp. 1–164; G.G.C.Routh, *Occupation and Pay in Great Britain, 1906–1960* (Cambridge 1965); Ministry of Labour, *Occupational Changes 1951–61,* Manpower Studies No. 6 (HMSO 1967); R.Knight, 'Changes in the Occupational Structure of the Working Population', *Journal of the Royal Statistical Society,* Vol. 130, Part 3 (1967), pp. 408–22.

21   *British Labour Statistics: Historical Abstract* (London 1971), p. 195; *British Labour Statistics Yearbook, 1974* (London 1976), pp. 170–1.

22   G.D.H.Cole, *Studies in Class Structure* (London 1955), p. 51.

23   In percentage terms these increases noted by Cole were *approximately* as follows: clerks, etc from 0.6 per cent in 1851 to 10.9 per cent in 1951; merchanting etc. 1.4 per cent and 9.9 per cent; teachers 1 per cent and 1.6 per cent; government services 0.8 per cent and 1.5 per cent; and professional occupations 1.6 per cent and 6 per cent.

24   On clerical workers see especially, D.Lockwood, *The Blackcoated Worker* (London 1958); and also R.M.Blackburn, *Union Character and Social Class* (London 1967); E.Mumford and O.Banks, *The Computer and the Clerk* (London 1967).

25   See the discussion in T.J.Johnson, *Professions and Power* (London 1972); and in G.Esland, 'Professions and Professionalism' in Open University, *Politics of Work and Occupation, People and Work* (Milton Keynes 1976).

26   R.Bendix, *Work and Authority in Industry* (London 1956), esp. ch. 4; S.Melman, *Dynamic Factors in Industrial Productivity* (Oxford 1956).

27   See F.D.Klingender, *Art and the Industrial Revolution* (Paladin edn. 1968).

28   *British Labour Statistics: Historical Abstract,* p. 408.

29   See, for example, D.S.Pugh and D.J.Hickson, *Organizational Structure in its Context* (Farnborough 1976), esp. ch. 5.

30   *Social Trends,* No. 6 (HMSO 1975), p. 29.

31   *Social Trends* (HMSO 1975), p. 30.

32   J.Hall and D.C.Jones, 'The social grading of occupations' in *British Journal of Sociology,* Vol. 1, No. 1 (March 1950), pp. 31–55; D.Glass (ed.), *Social Mobility in Britain* (London 1954), esp. ch. 2.

33   See, for example, the discussion in J.H.Goldthorpe and K.Hope, 'Occuptional Grading and Occupational Prestige' in K.Hope (ed.), *The Analysis of Social Mobility – methods and approaches,* Oxford Studies in Social Mobility, Working Papers 1 (Oxford 1972).

34   *British Labour Statistics Yearbook, 1974,* p. 232.

35   *British Labour Statistics Yearbook, 1974,* pp. 228–30.

36   G.Salaman, *Community and Occupation* (Cambridge 1974), pp. 98–9.

37   F.Bechhofer and B.Elliott, 'An Approach to a Study of Small Shopkeepers and the Class Structure', *Archives Européennes de Sociologie,* Vol. 9 (1968), pp. 185–7; F.Bechhofer et al., 'Small Shopkeepers: matters of money and meaning', in *Sociological Review,* Vol. 22, No. 4 (1974), p. 478.

38   C.Bell and H.Newby, 'The Sources of Variation in Agricultural Workers' Images of Society', in M.Bulmer (ed.) *Working Class Images of Society* (London 1975), p. 96; see also C.Bell and H.Newby, 'Capitalist Farmers in the British Class Structure,' *Sociologia Ruralis,* Vols 1 and 2 (1974), pp. 86–107.

39   The New Earnings Survey, the main and most comprehensive current source of data on earned incomes, excludes all self-employed workers. For a discussion of sources of data on incomes see Royal Commission on the Distribution of Income and Wealth, *Report No. 1, Initial Report on the Standing Reference,* Cmnd 6171 (HMSO 1975), esp. Appendices F and H.

40   G.Salaman, *op. cit.,* p. 68.

41   F.Bechhofer et al, *op. cit.,* pp. 468, 473.

42   F.Bechhofer et al., 'The Petits Bourgeois in the Class Structure: the case of the small shopkeepers,' in F.Parkin (ed)., *The Social Analysis of Class Structure* (London 1974), p. 110.

43   T.Nichols, *Ownership, Control and Ideology* (London 1969), p. 131.

44   A.Giddens, *The Class Structure of the Advanced Societies* (London 1973), p. 84.

45   For further discussion see B.Wootton, *The Social Foundations of Wage Policy* (London 1955); J.E.King, *Labour Economics* (London 1972); R.Hyman and I.Brough, *Social Values and Industrial Relations* (Oxford 1975); and the references cited by King, and Hyman and Brough.

46   T.B.Bottomore and M.Rubel (eds), *Karl Marx – Selected Writings in Sociology and Social Philosophy* (London 1956), pp. 169–70, quoted from the Economic and Philosophical Manuscripts of 1844.

47   For further discussion see J.E.T.Eldridge, *Sociology and Industrial Life* (London 1971), esp. Part 3; S.Lukes, 'Alienation and Anomie' in P.Laslett and W.G.Runciman (eds), *Philosophy, Politics and Society* (Oxford 1967), pp. 134–56.

48   See, for example, J.H.Goldthorpe et al, *The Affluent Worker: industrial*

attitudes and behaviour (Cambridge 1967), pp. 178–80.

49   F.Herzberg et al, *The Motivation to Work* (Chichester 1959); C.Argyris, *Personality and Organization* (New York 1957); V.H.Vroom and E.L.Deci (eds), *Management and Motivation* (Penguin edn. 1970).

50   W. Baldamus, *Efficiency and Effort* (London 1961).

51   E.Jaques, *Equitable Payment* (Penguin edn. 1967); for a different conceptualisation, see T.Lupton and D.Gowler, *Selecting a Wage Payment System* (London 1969).

52   These concepts are discussed in A.Etzioni, *A Comparative Analysis of Complex Organization* (New York 1961); see also the important discussion in A.Fox, *Beyond Contract: Work, Power and Trust Relations* (London 1974); and the reservations in P.R.D.Corrigan, 'Feudal Relics or Capitalist Monuments' in *Sociology,* Vol. 11, 3, (Sept. 1977), pp. 435–63.

53   W.Baldamus, *Efficiency and Effort,* esp. Part 2; this view appears close to the notion of 'hygiene' factors developed by Herzberg.

54   For a selection of writings on this topic see M.Weir (ed.), *Job Satisfaction* (Fontana edn. 1976); and for a brief discussion of major approaches, P.Warr and T.Wall, *Work and Well-being* (Penguin edn. 1975).

55   An introduction to the literature on trade union government can be found in J.A.Banks, *Trade Unionism* (London 1974), esp. Part 3; see also, T.Lane, *The Union Makes Us Strong* (Arrow edn. 1974).

56   G.Routh, *Occupation and Pay in Great Britain 1906–60* (Cambridge 1965), p. 147.

57   Routh, *op. cit.,* p. 150.

58   F.Field (ed.), *Are Low Wages Inevitable?* (Nottingham 1976), pp. 23–4, 107.

59   *Department of Employment Gazette,* Vol. 85, No. 1 (January 1977), p. 20; F.Field, *op. cit.,* p. 106.

60   Royal Commission on the Distribution of Income and Wealth, *Report No. 3, Higher Incomes from Employment,* Cmnd 6383 (HMSO 1976), pp. 7–12.

61   Department of Employment, *New Earnings Survey 1975,* Part A (HMSO 1975), p. A5.

62   Royal Commission on the Distribution of Income and Wealth, *Report No. 3,* pp. 29–35.

63   This figure was suggested as the relevant one for 1975 data by Field, *op. cit.,* pp. 12–14; as a result of inflation it is, of course, low for 1976 data.

64   F.Field, *op. cit.,* pp. 25–6.

65   F.Field, *op. cit.,* esp. pp. 23–5, 32–4.

66   *Department of Employment Gazette,* Vol. 85, No. 1 (January 1977), pp. 22–3.

67   *New Earnings Survey 1976,* Part A (HMSO 1976), tables 10 and 11.

68   In addition to the works by Wootton, King, Hyman and Brough cited above (45), see especially A.B.Atkinson, *The Economics of Inequality* (Oxford 1975); Open University, 'Income and Inequality' in *Patterns of Inequality* (Milton Keynes 1976); and G.G.C.Routh, 'Interpretations of Pay Structure' in *International Journal of Social Economics,* Vol. 1, No. 1 (1974), pp. 13–39.

69   D.Wedderburn and C.Craig, 'Relative Deprivation in Work', in D.Wedderburn (ed.), *Poverty, Inequality and Class Structure* (Cambridge 1974) pp. 141–64;

details of the sample are reported in D.Wedderburn, 'The Conditions of Employment of Manual and Non-Manual Workers', in Social Science Research Council, Conference Proceedings, *Social Stratification and Industrial Relations,* mimeo (Cambridge 1969), p. 30.

70   E.Wigham, 'Industry still divided by the colour of the collar', *Times Business News* (9 March 1976); I am grateful to Philip Corrigan for this reference (and many others).

71   *British Labour Statistics Yearbook, 1974,* p. 125.

72   *The General Household Survey 1972,* p. 140.

73   *The General Household Survey 1972,* p. 141. Changes in legislation are likely to alter this situation.

74   *The General Household Survey 1972,* p. 140.

75   See for example, J.H.Goldthorpe et al, *The Affluent Worker*; D. Wedderburn and R.Crompton, *Workers' Attitudes and Technology,* (Cambridge 1972); H.Beynon and R.M.Blackburn, *Perceptions of Work: variations within a factory* (Cambridge 1972).

76   See R.Blauner, 'Work Satisfaction and Industrial Trends in Modern Society', in R.Bendix and S.M.Lipset (eds), *Class, Status and Power* (London 1966) pp. 473–87.

77   *The General Household Survey 1972,* pp. 126–30; 207.

78   S.R.Parker et al, *The Sociology of Industry* (London 1972), pp. 170–2; R.Blauner, *op. cit.* pp. 474–7.

79   *British Labour Statistics Yearbook, 1974,* p. 199.

80   For a recent summary of state intervention, see *Occupations and Conditions of Work,* Central Office of Information Reference Pamphlet 139 (HMSO 1976).

81   *Department of Employment Gazette,* Vol. 85, No. 4 (April 1977), p. 402.

82   *The General Household Survey 1972,* pp. 145–7.

83   *Occupations and Conditions of Work,* p. 48.

84   Such 'sub-employment' is discussed in an unpublished paper by G.M.Norris, 'Sub-employment in Sunderland'.

85   HM Chief Inspector of Factories, *Annual Report 1974,* Cmnd 6322 (HMSO 1975), pp. 80–2.

86   *Annual Report 1974,* p. 111.

87   P.Kinnersley, *The Hazards of Work* (London 1973), p. 13. See also T.Nichols and P.Armstrong, *Safety or Profit: industrial accidents and the conventional wisdom* (Bristol 1973).

88   P.Kinnersley, *op. cit.,* pp. 240–1.

89   B.Preston, 'Statistics of Inequality' in *Sociological Review,* Vol. 22, No. 1 (1974), pp. 103–18.

90   J.Parker, C.Rollett and K.Jones, 'Health', in A.H.Halsey (ed.), *Trends in British Society since 1900* (London 1972), p. 342.

91   *The General Household Survey 1972,* pp. 198, 204.

92   R.Price and G.S.Bain, 'Union Growth Revisited: 1948–1974 in perspective' in *British Journal of Industrial Relations,* Vol. 14, No. 3 (Nov. 1976), p. 340.

93   For an account of some of these associations see G.Millerson, *The Qualifying Associations* (London 1964).

94   Price and Bain, *op. cit.,* p. 348; see also G.S.Bain, *The Growth of White*

Collar Unionism (Oxford 1970).

95   See among others, J.E.King, *Labour Economics* (London 1972), esp.
      pp. 43–9; E.H.Phelps Brown, *The Economics of Labour* (New Haven,
      Conn. 1962), pp. 175–93; and several contributions to *British Journal of
      Industrial Relations*, Vol. 15, No. 2 (July 1977).

96   This type of argument is a central feature of the 'functionalist theory' of
      stratification; see R.Bendix and S.M Lipset (eds), *Class, Status and Power*
      (London 1967), pp. 47–96.

97   D.Glass (ed.), *Social Mobility in Britain* (London 1954).

98   See the discussion and further references in J.H.Goldthorpe and C.
      Llewellyn, 'Class Mobility in Modern Britain: three theses examined', in
      Sociology, Vol. 11, No. 2 (May 1977), pp. 257–87, and also G.Payne,
      G.Ford and C.Robertson, 'A Reappraisal of Social Mobility in Britain' in
      Sociology, Vol. 11, No. 2 (May 1977), pp. 289–310.

99   J.H.Goldthorpe and C.Llewellyn, *op. cit.;* G.Payne, G.Ford and C.
      Robertson, 'Changes in Occupational Mobility in Scotland', in *Scottish
      Journal of Sociology*, Vol. 1, No. 1 (Nov. 1976), pp. 57–79.

100   The evidence for both parts of this argument has been questioned; see
      D.J.Lee, 'Class Differentials in Educational Opportunity and Promotions
      from the Ranks' in *Sociology*, Vol. 2, No. 3 (Sept. 1968), pp. 293–312;
      E.Thorpe, 'The Taken-for-granted Reference: an empirical examination' in
      Sociology, Vol. 7, No. 3 (Sept. 1973), pp. 361–76; T.Noble, 'Intra-
      generational Mobility in Britain: a criticism of the counterbalance theory'
      in *Sociology*, Vol. 8, No. 3 (Sept. 1974), pp. 475–83.

101   Goldthorpe and Llewellyn, *op. cit.,* pp. 273–7.

102   The spread of comprehensive schools has, of course, led to the disappearance
      of the visible streaming which the tripartite structure of secondary schooling
      embodied, and tabulations such as those in tables 2.47 and 2.48 become more
      difficult to interpret. The variable patterns of streaming within comprehensive
      schools are (unfortunately for present purposes) not reflected in the statistics.

103   *The General Household Survey 1972*, p. 169.

104   *The General Household Survey 1972*, p. 171.

105   *The General Household Survey 1972*, p. 163.

106   See the data reported in J.Urry and J.Wakeford (eds), *Power in Britain*
      (London 1973); and P.Stanworth and A.Giddens (eds), *Elites and Power in
      British Society* (Cambridge 1974).

107   For example, J.W.B.Douglas, *The Home and the School* (London 1964);
      D.Hargreaves, *Social Relations in a Secondary School* (London 1967);
      C.Lacey, 'Some Sociological Concomitants of Academic Streaming in a
      Grammar School' in *British Journal of Sociology*, Vol. 13, No. 3 (1966),
      pp. 245–62.

108   Committee on Higher Education, *Report*, Cmnd 2154 (HMSO 1963), esp.
      pp. 48–61; J.W.B.Douglas, *The Home and the School: Study of ability and
      attainment in the Primary School* (London 1964); J.W.B.Douglas, J.M.Ross
      and H.R.Simpson, *All Our Future* (Panther edn. 1971); J. Westergaard and
      A.Little, 'The Trend of Class Differentials in Educational Opportunity in
      England and Wales', in *British Journal of Sociology*, Vol. 15, No. 4 (1964),
      pp. 301–16.

109   D.N.Ashton, 'The Transition from School to Work: notes on the development

of different frames of reference among young male workers', in G.Esland, G.Salaman and M.A.Speakman (eds), *People and Work* (Edinburgh 1975), p. 157.

110　　D.N.Ashton, 'From School to Work: some problems of adjustment experienced by young male workers', in P.Brannen (ed.), *Entering the World of Work: some sociological perspectives* (HMSO 1975). This volume contains useful reviews of approaches, problems and research in this field by the editor and by C.S.Smith, as well as reports of research; see also W.M. Williams (ed.), *Occupational Choice* (London 1974), and M.Carter, *Into Work* (Penguin edn. 1966).

111　　See, for example, Committee on Higher Education, *Report,* p. 59; *Social Trends,* No. 4 (HMSO 1973), pp. 147–9.

112　　M.P.Carter, *Education, Employment, and Leisure* (Oxford 1963); J.Maizels, *Adolescent Needs and the Transition from School to Work* (London 1970); S.Sharpe, *'Just Like a Girl'* (Penguin edn. 1976).

113　　T.Veness, *School Leavers* (London 1962), esp. pp. 94–5, 161–4; for some further discussion of these processes, see R.K.Brown, 'Women as Employees: some comments on research in industrial sociology', in D.L.Barker and S.Allen (eds),*Dependence and Exploitation in Work and Marriage* (Harlow 1976), pp. 21–46.

114　　D.S.Byrne, W.Williamson and B.Fletcher, *The Poverty of Education* (London 1975).

115　　For a discussion of the relevant problems and literature, see J.M.Cousins, *Values and Value in the Labour Market,* Working Papers in Sociology, No. 9 (University of Durham, n.d.).

116　　See M.Mann, *Workers on the Move* (Cambridge 1973).

117　　For further discussion of these questions, see R.K.Brown, 'Sources of Objectives in Work and Employment', in J.Child (ed.), *Man and Organization* (London 1973), pp. 17–38; and R.M.Blackburn and M.Mann, 'Constraint and Choice: Stratification and the Market for Unskilled Labour', British Sociological Association Conference Paper 1973.

118　　The notion of a dual labour market is discussed in R.D.Barron and G.M. Norris, 'Sexual Divisions and the Dual Labour Market' in D.L.Barker and S.Allen (eds.), *Dependence and Exploitation in Work and Marriage* (Harlow 1976), pp. 47–69; and more sceptically in N.Bosanquet and P.B.Doeringer, 'Is there a Dual Labour Market in Great Britain?' in the *Economic Journal* (June 1973), pp. 421–435.

119　　E.Durkheim, *The Division of Labour in Society* (New York 1964). See also the discussion in J.E.T.Eldridge, *Sociology and Industrial Life* (London 1971), pp. 73–91.

120　　E.Durkheim, *op. cit.* pp. 376–7, 389.

121　　H.Braverman, *Labor and Monopoly Capital* (New York 1974), esp. pp. 70–84.

122　　See the discussion in A.Fox and A.Flanders, 'The Reform of Collective Bargaining: from Donovan to Durkheim' in *British Journal of Industrial Relations,* Vol. 7, No. 2 (July 1969), pp. 151–80; and J.H.Goldthorpe, 'Social Inequality and Social Integration in Modern Britain' in D.Wedderburn (ed.), *Poverty, Inequality and Class Structure* (Cambridge 1974), pp. 217–38.

3

Women and the Division of Labour

If this book had been written seven or eight years ago it is unlikely that it would have contained a chapter on women. In the margins of sociology there has always been a place for the apparently disconnected 'survivals' of women's inequality in public life, but the generalized sexual division of labour has not been discussed. As a result, there has been no basis for analysing women as a distinct social group, that is, as part of a distinct pattern of social relations. The sociology of sex and gender has until recently been isolated and underdeveloped.[1] A recognition of the distinct social position of women has been forced on sociology by women's resistance to, and consequent exposure of, their subordination. This chapter is therefore one result of women themselves questioning structures which sociologists had taken for granted.

This absence in social theory reflected the apparent invisibility — until recently — of the sexual division of labour in everyday social experience. In an economy in which a person's capacity to work is bought and sold in exchange for a wage, labour which is performed on the basis of personal relations rather than on the basis of monetary exchange is not recognized as labour. Consequently women's work in caring for children and husbands does not appear as necessary labour; it appears as a natural part of family life. The domestic position of women and all that flows directly and indirectly from it does not therefore seem to be the result of social constraints, the product of a particular relationship between work as paid labour and the rearing of a family. Domesticity appears as an inherent part of being a woman. Within this implicit, spontaneous framework, domestic labour appears as a choice to which women are by nature drawn. It is quite conceivable that within this framework women occasionally make different choices and develop more masculine tendencies. Domesticity can then be discarded as a woman enters a male-dominated world, in which, barring a few anachronistic areas of male prejudice, she can be equal. In this way the inequalities facing women have appeared to be the inequalities they face when they enter the world of men; there has been no need to explain why this world is a 'man's world'!

Not only has the separation of domestic from wage-earning labour had this mystifying effect; it has also indirectly denied women that recognition as autonomous individuals which is necessary for inequality vis-à-vis other individuals to be noticeable. Women have seemed merely 'different' and 'complementary'. They have appeared as part of a male-defined social unit, the family. The basis for individuality, the condition for identifying inequalities, is thus veiled, like the sexual division of labour itself, by the exchange basis of all labour except domestic labour. Earning a wage, being *directly* part of exchange relations (a woman buys commodities, but she does so with her husband's wage) is a condition of social recognition as an independent individual. Women, outside, or partially outside, these relations, consequently appeared only as secondary parts of a 'man and wife' entity.

Why should this have lost its former credibility? A full answer will not be clear until the end of this chapter, where recent trends will be illustrated in detail. However the consequence of these trends stands out clearly: the naturalness of women's responsibility for domestic labour is now *experienced* as increasingly contradictory to her situation as a wage-earning worker. (Although this does not necessarily entail the two sets of *institutional arrangements* being obviously in conflict. See pp. 167–178 on the superficial harmony between these two spheres.) A consequence of this experience is that the way in which domestic labour is organized is now being subjected to a close practical and theoretical scrutiny. It is slowly and sometimes painfully being disentangled from the emotional relations which hitherto concealed its economic character. For the first time large numbers of married women are earning their own wages, not because of exceptional and temporary circumstances, as during the two World Wars, not on a sporadic pin-money basis, and not in conditions where extended families could lighten the domestic burden. In Britain the proportion of married women working grew from 10 per cent in 1931 to 22 per cent in 1951 and to 42 per cent in 1971.[2] Their capacity to work is sold to employers or to the state, and little of it is left to be given automatically, as an act of love and care, to cherishing husbands and children. Domestic labour has thus come to be regarded as *work*; the problem of how to reduce and how to re-organize domestic labour consequently faces every married woman, in differing degrees. And in the resulting process of evaluating all the partial and ad hoc alternatives, the personal, sex-based nature of this labour becomes increasingly apparent. It becomes a problem which concerns the social organization and the social division of labour. Furthermore, as women increasingly consider themselves to be individuals with a permanent future outside the home, they are demanding equality with other workers and are thereby questioning the assumptions of domesticity and dependence which lie behind the inequalities.

As these changes in the position of women come up against the sexual division of labour and reveal it as a set of fundamental *social* relations, so a greater theoretical understanding of women's inequality becomes possible, and new political demands are made. In order to highlight the significance of these changes this chapter will start by criticizing those definitions of women's inequality which do not recognize the underlying sexual division of labour. Secondly, there will be a descriptive analysis of all the various manifestations, dimensions and consequences of this division. Thirdly, the links between these and the present social organization of domestic labour will be identified and their historical development traced. In the course of this analysis, and more directly at the end, the tendencies which erode, modify or reinforce private domestic labour and the inequalities it produces or makes possible, will be examined in detail.

PUBLIC EQUALITY, PRIVATE DEPENDENCE

John Stuart Mill, in his time an advanced advocate of the emancipation of women, expressed the partial definition of sex inequality very clearly when he wrote on the division of labour within the family:

> When the support of the family depends not on property, but on earnings, the common arrangement, by which the man earns the income and the wife super-intends the domestic expenditure, seems to me in general the most suitable division of labour between two persons. If, in addition to the physical suffering of bearing children, and the whole responsibility of their care and education in the early years, the wife undertakes the careful and economical application of the husband's earnings to the general comfort of the family, she takes not only her fair share, but usually the larger share, of the bodily and mental exertion of their joint existence. If she undertakes any additional portion, it seldom relieves her from this, but only prevents her from performing it properly. The care which she is herself disabled from taking of the children and the household, nobody else takes; those of the children who do not die grow up as they best can, and the management of the household is likely to be so bad as even in point of economy to be a great drawback from the value of the wife's earnings. In an otherwise just state of things, it is not, therefore, I think, a desirable custom that the wife should contribute by her labour to the income of the family.[3]

The majority of suffragette supporters similarly took for granted women's role in the rearing of children and the organization of the home. Their argument was that this role did not give grounds for excluding women from the political and legal gains won for men in the development of parliamentary democracy; women's specific contribution to the life of the nation gave them every right to participate in the decisions concerning the government of the nation. It is therefore not sur-prising to find suffragette literature frequently combining the glorification of motherhood with demands for political equality. The problem of sexual equality was seen solely as a matter of political and legal rights. The presence of deeper inequalities, rooted in the nature of the family and in the sexual division under-pinning the family's relation to production, was scarcely perceived.[4]

Recent legislation, particularly the *Sex Discrimination Act* (1975) and the *Equal Pay Act* (1970), in certain respects represents the logical culmination of this tradi-tion. On the one hand these Acts extend the principle — although not the full reality[5] — of equal rights, from the political institutions which concerned the early campaigners to economic institutions. Their *intentions* stop at this. They do not directly challenge, or provide the conditions for reorganizing sex-based domestic labour. On the other hand, the *implications* of these primarily economic reforms are far more subversive to the economic position of women in the family than were the political demands and reforms of the nineteenth and early twentieth centuries. The provisions of these recent reforms accede to the principle of women being equal competitors in the labour market, with an equal right of access to training for this market; and to the principle of women being buyers, creditors and property-owners in their own right. The widespread acceptance and expectation of such equality, which tends to flow from the legitimacy bestowed by legislation, conflicts with the assumptions underlying domestic labour and the relations of dependence through which this labour is performed. To be an equal competitor in the labour market implies being free of all obligations and hindrances that interfere with selling one's capacity to work to the highest bidder. To be an individual consumer implies economic independence. By contrast, previous reforms concerning political equality were quite compatible with women's distinct and separate domestic labours. Women could be politically equal while remaining economically and socially dependent.

THE FACTS OF INEQUALITY

A description of the extent and nature of inequality in the labour market, in education and training, and in relation to the tax and social security system, will provide a basis on which to evaluate how far in practice the legislative extension of women's public rights will weaken the sexual division of labour.

Sociology of Class

Before considering the statistics available it is important to note the inability of most sociological analyses of inequality to identify, let alone understand, the relation of women to class. This weakness lies in the way that such analyses start from the relation of the *family* rather than of the *individual* to the productive process.[6] The arguments usually advanced to justify this are not descriptively false. They include the fact that it is the family which guarantees the continuity of social classes through generations and that a women's status and wealth are determined primarily by the class position of her husband. But this denies the possibility that the organization of the family and its relation to production might itself be a crucial determinant of the pattern of inequality within and across classes. This weakness is characteristic of sociologists who, in analysing class, limit themselves to documenting the extent of the divisions and inequalities rather than identifying the social relations involved in the productive process and the position of each class or sub-class within them.[7] The latter approach would consider the fact that it is the *individual* worker who enters the labour market an important distinguishing feature of a capitalist economy. Such a starting-point would then leave open, as an explicit problem for analysis, the question of how the organization of the family related to class divisions.

Women within Class Divisions

What then is the position of women within the class divisions of British capitalism? There is little to be said about sex inequalities as far as ownership of capital is concerned. Primarily for reasons of tax and inheritance women have an almost equal share in the ownership of wealth: they owned about 40 per cent of all private wealth in 1970. This property is rarely controlled by the woman: it is family property, invested by the husband. Sex inequality, I shall be arguing, is primarily a result of the sex division of labour among those who rely for their subsistence on their capacity to work rather than on their wealth; it is therefore not surprising that the manifestations of inequality are most apparent within the labour market.[8]

The starting-point for analysing this must be the entry, unprecedented in peacetime, of women into the labour market during the course of the post-war boom. Between 1881 and 1951 the percentage of women in the work force aged 15 and over was relatively stable, ranging between 25 per cent and 27 per cent, with higher fluctuations during the two World Wars. In the course of the 1950s the conditions of full employment and relatively high growth produced selected labour scarcities

TABLE 3.1

The increase in the number of women working outside the home, 1961, 1966, 1971

	Total			Males			Females		
	1961	1966	1971	1961	1966	1971	1961	1966	1971
As percentage of population aged 15 and over									
Economically active	60.7	62.1	61.1	86.3	84.0	81.5	37.5	42.2	42.6
Students	2.5	3.2	4.3	2.9	3.5	4.8	2.2	2.8	3.8
Retired	6.2	6.0	13.1	9.6	10.0	11.8	3.1	2.4	14.2
Housewives and other persons	30.6	28.7	21.6	1.2	2.4	1.9	57.2	52.6	39.4

Source: Office of Population Censuses and Surveys, *Census of Population Reports*

and drew back into the labour force — at lower levels of the job hierarchy — many of the women who after the war had been squeezed out and encouraged to return to domesticity.

The extent and speed of this process is illustrated in table 3.1.

Table 3.2 describes this growth in terms of the changing ratio of male to female employees:

TABLE 3.2

Population and labour force, GB, 1911–68, 1973–4

				Thousands	
				Percentage of total labour force	
		Labour force			
	Population	Male	Female	Male	Female
1911	40,831	12,927	5,424	70	30
1921	42,769	13,656	5,701	71	29
1931	44,795	14,790	6,265	70	30
1951	48,918	16,007	7,419	68	32
1968	53,781	16,322	8,936	65	35
1973	55,900	16,200	9,400	63	37
1974	56,000	15,700	9,400	60	40

Source: 1911–68 figures from G. A. Philips and R. T. Maddock, *The Growth of the British Economy* (London 1973); 1973–4 figures from Government Statistical Service, *UK in figures* (HMSO, June 1975)

The central feature to note about this rapid increase of women in employment is that it is the increase in married women working which has accounted for most of the increase. This is illustrated in table 3.3.

TABLE 3.3

Proportion of married women working

1911	10%
1931	10%
1951	22%
1971	42%
1974	49%

Source: *Social Trends* (HMSO 1972, 1974 and 1976).

Proportion of female employees married

1951	43%
1961	53%
1971	62%

Source: Department of Employment *Gazette*

Figure 3.1 shows the activity rates of women according to the number of their children.

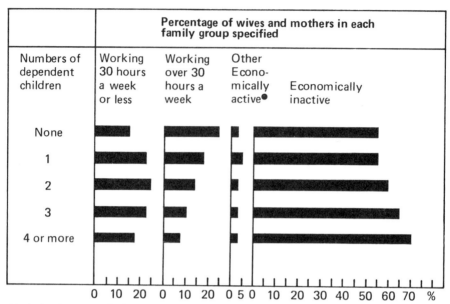

	Percentage of wives and mothers in each family group specified			
Numbers of dependent children	Working 30 hours a week or less	Working over 30 hours a week	Other Econo- mically active●	Economically inactive
None				
1				
2				
3				
4 or more				

0 10 20   0 10 20   0 5 0 10 20 30 40 50 60 70 %

●Includes those out of employment and those for whom working hours were not specified

Figure 3.1   Activity Rates of Women According to the Number of their Dependent Children
Source: 1971 *Census of Population*

A second central feature of the increase in women's employment is the high proportion of women entering part-time jobs. All the above figures include both part-time and full-time workers. The number of female part-time workers (working 30 hours or under a week) has increased both absolutely and as a proportion of all female workers. In 1951 13 per cent of all working women worked part-time, in 1965 17.8 per cent, in 1970 18.5 per cent, in 1973 20.6 per cent and in 1975 22.6 per cent. Table 3.4 shows the absolute increase and the comparison between female part-time workers and the very small numbers of male part-time workers:

TABLE 3.4

Numbers of male and female part-time workers, 1951, 1961, 1966, 1971

Year	Men	Women
1951	47,000	784,000
1961	172,900	1,882,000
1966	372,000	2,748,000
1971	572,000	3,152,000

Source: *Census of Population*, 1971

How far does this mass entry of married women into paid employment herald the end of a sexual division of labour?

Until the influence of the women's liberation movement began to spread and to focus attention on the position of women once they had entered the labour force, there was a rather over-optimistic tendency to consider that entry into the labour force was *itself* an indicator of increasing equality between men and women. The most developed sociological expression of this optimism lies behind some of the arguments of Young and Wilmott's *The Symmetrical Family*. At one point, in comparing with the past what they identify as the contemporary trend towards marital symmetry, they say: 'It was not a man's place to do women's work any more than the other way round. All that has now changed. Wives are working outside the home in what is much less of a man's world than it used to be.'[9] In fact, the evidence seems to indicate that the occupational sphere is no longer a man's world only in the minimal sense that women are also present. It remains a man's world in the more significant sense that, with few exceptions, women are still confined to a specific place within it, and, except at the professional level, the trends do not seem to be moving away from this segregation. The sexual division of labour has not been undermined at the same rate as women's entry into the labour force; in general, it has only been extended beyond the boundaries of the family. The statistics below must be examined, not merely as a verification of this fairly familiar point but also as clues to whether this problem is merely one of a time-lag, now to be speeded up by the Sex Discrimination Act; or whether the nature of women's involvement in the labour force has, under pressure, become moulded to fit the requirements imposed by the pre-existing division between domestic and wage-earning labour.

What features of women's position within the labour market would indicate whether there was a process of *accommodation* — albeit with important tensions and instabilities — or a process of *erosion* between the new mass presence of women in the paid labour force and the traditional division of labour? An erosion would tend to be the dominant process only if the cultural and material nature of women's paid labour overtly conflicted with the relations of private domestic labour. Here we will distinguish between, on the one hand, the relations of the job market itself and the question of whether these in themselves provide an impetus towards eliminating the sexual division of labour; and on the other hand, the ad hoc arrangements or direct challenges which women themselves create because of the new needs they experience. This distinction is necessary because it might well be that accommodation is the dominant process vis-à-vis the institutions of the job market and the state, while at the same time a process of resistance is developing precisely because of the deeper contradictions involved in this accommodation to the sexual division of labour.

What then are the cultural and material relations that underpin the present sex-based organization of domestic labour? Economic dependence and personal loyalty are the fundamental framework. Flowing from these are first, a relation of direct care and response to individual human needs: more specifically, care to meet the needs of children in their preparation for the division of labour; to ease the burdens of the paid worker and thereby guarantee his maximum work capacity, and finally, perhaps ultimately, care to preserve the family through periods of strain and stress. Also flowing from the basic relations of dependence and exclusive personal loyalty is the personal nature of domestic labour. Thirdly, specific power relations flow from the basic framework of domestic labour, under which women's control or shared control over social life is limited to the day-to-day problems of domestic labour.

How far has women's mass entry into paid labour involved women in direct conflict with their traditional role? The following two tables describe in a very

TABLE 3.5

The concentration of women in lower grade jobs within broad occupational bands, 1921, 1961 and 1966

	1921	1961	1966
Professional jobs	%	%	%
Per cent of all professional WOMEN in 'minor' professions	93	93	93
Per cent of all professional MEN in 'minor' professions	46	42	40
All non-manual (incl. professional) jobs			
Per cent of all non-manual WOMEN in routine grades	51	70	72
Per cent of all non-manual MEN in routine grades	38	40	40
All manual (incl. personal service) jobs			
Per cent of all manual WOMEN in non-skilled jobs	64	80	78
Per cent of all manual MEN in non-skilled jobs	47	45	39

Source: J. Westergaard and H. Resler, *Class in a Capitalist Society* (Penguin edn. 1976), p. 163

TABLE 3.6

Economically active females by socio-economic groupings, GB[1]

	(1) Females	(2) Total	Thousands (3) col. (1) as a % of col. (2)
Professional	87.5	886.9	9.9
Employers and managers	431.5	2,382.0	18.1
Intermediate and junior non-manual	4,418.9	7,201.0	61.4
Skilled manual[2]	800.5	6,980.0	11.5
Semi-skilled manual and personal service	2,344.9	4,780.1	49.1
Unskilled manual	667.1	1,888.7	35.3
Total	8,750.4	24,118.7	36.3

Notes:

1. Figures exclude members of armed forces or whose occupations were inadequately described
2. Includes foremen, supervisors, and own-account non-professionals

Source: 1971 *Census*, Economic Activity Tables, Part IV, table 29

general way the position of women within the job structure.

In order to examine in more detail what is implied, each possible clash will be looked at separately. First, what does women's job situation imply for the idea of direct personal care as an intrinsically female labour? Table 3.7 indicates that for a large number of women (the majority) their labour outside as well as within the home is characterized by an entrenched sexual bias: a bias which in turn is reflected in the fact that it is women, almost exclusively, who do the work that involves the direct servicing of people's immediate needs.

TABLE 3.7

Predominantly female occupations

	All persons	Thousands Women
90% or over female occupations		
Hand and machine sewers, embroiderers	238	230
Nurses	432	394
Maids, valets, etc.	443	428
Canteen assistants	304	293
Typists, secretaries, etc.	770	759
75% and under 90% female occupations		
Shop assistants	969	786
Charwomen, sweepers and cleaners	522	456
Kitchen hands	122	100
Office machine operators	177	153
Hairdressers, etc.	159	124
Telephone operators	107	89
60% and under 75% female occupations		
Clerks and cashiers	2,475	1,546
Waiters and waitresses	113	82
Primary and secondary teachers	496	318
Packers and labellers, etc.	183	121
Bartenders	103	73

Source: Annual Census of Employment (June 1974)

Table 3.8 illustrates the extreme concentration of women in those jobs — secretarial and clerical — where servicing others, primarily men, will in effect be the main task.

TABLE 3.8

Comparison between the percentage of male and female workers involved in the direct servicing of people's needs

May 1968	Male			Female		Thousands
	Total	Percentage of total male non-manual	Full-time	Part-time	Total	Percentage of total female non-manual
Managers	397	28.4	18	1	19	2.6
Scientists and technologists	92	6.6	3	–	3	0.4
Draughtsmen	105	7.5	1	–	1	0.2
Other technicians	183	13.1	14	–	14	2.0
Clerical and office staff	345	24.7	544	58	602	86.3
Other administrative, etc.	275	19.7	54	5	59	8.5
Total non-manual	1,397	100.0	634	64	698	100.0

Source: Memorandum submitted by the Department of Employment to the House of Lords Select Committee on the Anti-Discrimination Bill 1971–2

A similar situation prevails in the teaching profession. In spite of the fact that in January 1974 61.6 per cent of qualified teachers in all public sector and assisted schools in the UK were women, the higher the grade of teacher − that is the greater the administrative and intellectual content of the job − the smaller the number of women.

TABLE 3.9

Percentages of various grades of teachers who are women

Maintained primary and secondary schools, England and Wales

	Lowest Grade Scale 1 or equivalent	Highest Grade Scale 5 or equivalent
1965	77.0	20.0
1969	75.1	20.6
1974	71.7	n.a.

Source: Department of Education and Science, *Statistics of Education* 1974, Vol. 4 table 23; 1969, Vol. 4 table 21; 1965, Part II table 59

Figures for the medical profession reveal the same situation; the nearer a job is to the direct process of caring for people's immediate needs, the higher the concentration of women:

TABLE 3.10

Female hospital, medical and dental staff[1], England, September/October 1974

	(1) Female	(2) Total	(3) Col. (1) as a % of col. (2)
Hospital nursing staff[2]	269,145	301,849	89.2
Hospital medical staff[3]	4,407	27,576	16.0
General medical practitioners	2,975	21,531	13.8
Hospital medical consultants	894	10,603	8.4
General dental practitioners	1,020	11,023	9.3

Notes:

1. Total staff including part-time, honorary, etc staff
2. Includes registered, student, enrolled, pupil and other nursing staff
3. From consultant down to pre-registration house officers (plus a few other staff). Figures exclude 'paragraph 94' appointments − mainly GPs acting as part-time medical officers at convalescent homes, general practitioner, maternity hospitals or other hospitals, or carrying out occasional work in the Blood Transfusion Service

Source: *Health and Personal Social Services Statistics for England* (1975), tables 3.4, 3.13, 3.20, 3.28

The small proportion of skilled jobs held by the 38.8 per cent of women workers who are manual workers (see table 3.11) is a further illustration of the way in which the development and application of skills totally distinct from those connected with domestic labour is the exception to the norm. As the following figures indicate, it occurs either in trades where from the historical transition from home to factory production women have been long established as skilled workers, as in textiles, or in trades where their physical attributes (e.g. manual dexterity) are a significant advantage given the existing technology of the industry, as in instrument and electrical engineering.

TABLE 3.11

Female manual workers, by industry and social class

Industry	Percentage of total women full-time workers who are manual	Women as percentage of all workers in the category	
	1976	1971	
		Skilled	Unskilled
Food, drink and tobacco	62.8	18.1	30.7
Chemicals	46.3	9.1	29.6
Mechanical engineering	60.0	2.9	20.2
Instrument engineering	26.8	23.4	42.8
Electrical engineering	65.1	20.2	41.2
Vehicles	52.2	2.7	16.3
Textiles	81.5	43.7	31.8
Paper, printing, publishing	49.7	25.5	33.5
Transport and communication	20.3	1.2	14.1
Distributive trades	12.3	13.0	44.1

Sources: *New Earnings Survey,* (1976), tables 56, 57; 1971 Census *Economic Activity,* Part IV, table 33

Table 3.11 shows the static nature of the situation, and available information does not indicate any change. 1966 Census figures show that there has been a gradual decline in the proportion of skilled manual workers as a whole who are women, from 24 per cent in 1911 to 14.7 per cent in 1966, and a steady rise in the proportion of unskilled manual workers who are women (15.5 per cent in 1911, 27.5 per cent in 1966) and in the proportion of sales and shop assistants who are women (35.2 per cent in 1911 to 58.7 per cent in 1966). An analysis by the Manpower Research Unit of employment changes in forty less skilled occupations between 1961 and 1966 shows a proportionately far higher increase in the employment of women in these less skilled occupations compared with the increase of women's employment in all occupations. This is illustrated by table 3.12. It is interesting to note that this increase is greatest among women over 19, which might suggest that it is the increasing numbers of married women coming into employment who are tending to take the greatest proportion of unskilled jobs.

From these statistics it should be clear that the mass increase of women in paid labour has not involved the majority of women in forms of labour that clash with the cultural definitions of women's domestic identity. Women as a social group have not become separated sufficiently from domestic labour to break down the

TABLE 3.12

Percentage changes in employment, 1961–6

| | All occupations | | 40 less skilled occupations | |
	Male	Female	Male	Female
All ages	−0.9	+13.9	−0.9	+23.1
15–17	−8.5	−9.0	−10.6	−10.2
18–19	+28.0	+25.4	+17.6	+10.6

Source: Department of Employment *Gazette* (April 1969)

cultural image of masculinity and femininity which reflects and justifies the sexual division of labour, and so it is reproduced on the extended terrain of the labour market. So long as the trends towards domestic labour becoming 'sex neutral' remain so weak there will be little impetus to consider the present organization of domestic labour as historical rather than 'natural'. Yet this is a pre-condition for the conscious reorganization of domestic labour.

The extent of women's involvement in jobs through which they have, or share control over any form of social organization is similarly too minimal to clash with the characteristic impotence of domestic labour. The small areas where women do have some degree of control are those in which, as in domestic labour, they control the organization of children and other women. The situation in teaching is one of the best illustrations: table 3.13 shows the percentage of female heads of primary schools and mixed secondary schools over the last ten years.

TABLE 3.13

Women heads of schools, England and Wales

| | Per cent | |
	Primary %	Mixed secondary %
January 1975	42.2	6.3
January 1970	42.9	4.7
January 1966	47.3	2.6

Note: Excludes those teachers in nursery schools, special schools and immigrant centres
Sources: *Statistics of Education* (1975), Vol. 1, table 14; (1970), Vol. 1, table 13; (1966), Vol. 1, table 12

The absence of a clash between the conditions of women's paid work and the basic lack of power in their domestic situation is not merely an example of the way in which the sexual division of labour extends into the labour force. It is also a product of the inherent lack of democracy in the way in which the productive process is organized. Only a very small minority of men or women share in determining the organization of resources, machines, labour and culture. For the majority of men the family is the only situation which is not alien and outside the realm of their control. For an even greater number of women there is only a small area within the family which offers any possibility of control. The organizations which in theory are fighting for workers' control have not done much with regard to either their own structures or the demands they fight for, to transform the situation. Table 3.14 indicates the lack of concerted effort within workers' organizations to reverse the bias, inbuilt into the productive process, against women sharing power.

TABLE 3.14

Women's involvement with the unions

Union	Total membership	% Women	Full-time officials	Women
GMWU	853,353	28.8	162	4
T & G	1,638,686	13.6	600	1
Nat. Union of Public Employees	372,709	59.4	90	1
USDAW	329,890	51.8	150	3
NALGO	439,837	38.3	80	3
AUEW	1,294,944	11.1	200	1
CPSA (Civil Service)	184,935	66.0	17	0
Tailors and Garment Workers'	117,573	85.5	48	9
Clerical Workers'	125,541	53.2	44	2
Post Office Workers'	209,479	25.0	12	1

Source: TUC Statistics (1972)

The central pillar on which the sexual division of labour has previously rested is *material dependence* and this has turned personal relations between men and women into relations of power and subordination. Women's entry into paid labour has added to the joint income and occasionally this gives women more control over how the family wage is spent — although since the rapid increase in the rate of inflation there is probably little room for choice — but it has not altered the fundamental dependence. The majority of working women do not earn what the TUC has calculated to be a 'living wage':

TABLE 3.15

Average earnings of men and women[1], GB, 1973–6

Average hourly earnings (excluding the effect of overtime)

	April 1974 pence	April 1975 pence	April 1976 pence
Aged 18 and over			
Male	104.8	136.3	162.9
Female	70.6	98.3	122.4
Difference	34.2	38.0	40.5
Female earnings as a % of male earnings	67.4	72.1	75.1
Aged 21 and over			
Male	107.2	139.3	166.6
Female	73.2	101.8	127.2
Difference	34.0	37.5	39.4
Female earnings as a % of male earnings	68.3	73.1	76.4

continued

Average gross weekly earnings (including overtime pay)

	April 1973 £	April 1974 £	April 1975 £	April 1976 £
Aged 18 and over				
Male	41.1	46.6	59.5	70.2
Female	23.1	26.9	37.4	46.2
Difference	18.0	19.7	22.1	24.0
Female earnings as a				
% of male earnings	56.2	57.7	62.9	65.8
Aged 21 and over				
Male	41.9	47.7	60.8	71.8
Female	24.0	27.9	38.7	47.9
Difference	17.9	19.8	22.1	23.9
Female earnings as a				
% of male earnings	57.3	58.5	63.7	66.7

Note:

1. Full-time employees (both manual and non-manual) whose pay for the survey pay period was not affected by absence

Sources: *New Earnings Surveys* (1973, 1974, 1975, and 1976)

Before examining the reasons for this difference in earnings it is important to note that the averages used in table 3.15 conceal wide discrepancies, ranging from the chemical industry where women's rate was 96 per cent of men's rate, down to completely unorganized and relatively isolated groups of women, such as cinema employees, who receive only just over 60 per cent of men's average rate.

In spite of the 1970 Equal Pay Act, or rather because of all its loopholes, employers have a large repertoire of techniques that allow them to avoid significantly altering pay differentials. First, they can further consolidate the industrial apartheid between men and women by redefining men's jobs; for example, male shop assistants have been found to be described in company books as 'management trainees', so that comparison with female shop assistants is ruled out. The first report by the Office of Manpower Economics, published in 1972, gives further examples:

In one company, 80 per cent of employees were women engaged on work similar to that of men rated as semi-skilled; they were, however, paid a rate below that for unskilled men. The costs of meeting equal pay within the existing job and pay structure were considered by management to be prohibitive. With the acceptance of trade union representatives who are concerned about male un-employment in the area, it is therefore now separating men and women into distinct categories of jobs.

For example, the machine shop has had a female day shift and a male night shift; men are now being recruited for day work and women are being transferred to other departments. The more technical inspection jobs are being allotted to men and women are being transferred to simple inspection tasks; central packing is becoming a male area, line packing is reserved for women; work in the finishing and paint shops and in the stores is to be a male preserve; this also applies to sign-writing, even though many women are considered to be more skilful at this. White-collar jobs are to be graded into three grades: the lower one predominantly women, the middle one mixed and the upper one predominantly for men. As a result of this reorganization it is expected that by the end of 1972 very little of the work undertaken by women will be even broadly similar to that of men.[10]

For the majority of women anti-discrimination legislation has made little difference. It makes illegal all attempts to bar women explicitly from certain jobs. But the major proportion of job separation that renders the Equal Pay Act inadequate is not the result of explicit discrimination: employers do not need to tax their ingenuity when, as we have seen, women's position in the labour market is already firmly entrenched.

The following table from the OME 1972 Report, on the basis of a sample of 193 firms where women and men were employed together, indicates the extent to which the job hierarchy itself ensures that the majority of women fall through the safety net of equal pay.

TABLE 3.16

Percentage of women on work comparable to that of men

	Type of Work	
	Manual	Non-manual
90+%	None	None
50–89%	11%	5%
20–49%	5%	14%
1–19%	17%	17%
Nil	68%	64%
Number of companies	60	180

Source: OME Report (1972)

Job evaluation, which is not compulsory under the Act, does little either to over-come this lack of comparability, or to thwart employers who regrade techniques. In fact it can provide a pseudo-scientific rationalization for regrading. Service pay-ments are another way in which employers can ensure that men will earn more than women for the same or a similar job: large extra payments or bonuses for long unbroken service with the firm almost inevitably exclude the majority of the six and a half million working mothers in Britain who have stopped and restarted work at some point. Overtime and shift supplements provide another means of man-taining earnings differentials.

The situation facing those who work part time — over a quarter of all working women — is particularly bad:

TABLE 3.17

Average hourly earnings of workers, male and female, Oct. 1973–Oct. 1975

Average hourly earnings in pence	Oct. 1973	Oct. 1974	Oct. 1975
Full-time men	70.72	91.96	118.99
Youths and boys	56.84	73.44	97.78
Full-time women	55.83	74.89	98.71
Part-time women	52.11	70.58	93.21

Source: Department of Employment, *Gazette* (February 1976)

This use of women as a 'reserve pool of labour' is increasing as a proportion of all workers:

TABLE 3.18

Proportion of women working as reserve pools of labour, June 1971 and June 1974

	June 1971	June 1974
All males in employment	13,424,000	13,363,000
All females in employment	8,224,000	8,933,000
Part-time females in employment	2,757,000	3,421,000

Source: Annual Census of Employment (June 1974)

The State and Domestic Labour

Given the absence of any automatic tendency for women's paid employment to modify directly the assumptions and material relations justifying domestic labour, it is not surprising that neither the state nor employers have considered the need to reorganize domestic labour, nor has the union leadership attempted actively to fight for any reorganization. The present situation should be contrasted with the one period, the Second World War, when labour requirements did briefly conflict with the requirements of domestic labour. The government then encouraged local authorities to set up over one hundred new nurseries and in some areas subsidized restaurants in order to reduce the amount of time that women spent on housework so that they could become industrial workers. But this was not the beginning of any permanent change in the organization of housework. When the war ended and men returned from the armed forces in search of employment the majority of nurseries and all the subsidized restaurants were closed down. Between 1949 and 1970 the numbers of local authority day nurseries had declined from 903 to 435. Table 3.19 describes the situation in more detail:

TABLE 3.19

Children's services, England and Wales, 1961–73

	1951	1961	1966	1972	Thousands 1973
Maintained day nurseries – places	40	22	21	23	24
Registered (private) nurseries – places	10	18	75	296	335
Registered childminders – places	1	14	32	90	92
Nursery education – full-time	–	226	237	296	325
part-time	–	–	32	86	101

Source: *Social Trends* (1974), table 20, p. 87

Employers rarely feel any compulsion to fill this gap. Their use of women as a pool of flexible labour as distinct from a permanent part of the skilled or semi-skilled labour force *depends on* the existence of women's domestic obligations. Factory-based nurseries are rare.

Those aspects of welfare benefits that relate to women further consolidate the position of dependence that underlies domestic labour. Four areas of legislation — Supplementary Benefits, National Insurance, taxation, and student grants — are particularly important ways in which the state supports this dependence and discriminates against life-styles that attempt to achieve relationships based on material independence.

Supplementary Benefit regulations discriminate against women who are living with a man but who want to be financially independent. If a woman is married or if she is proved to be 'cohabiting' with a man, then she cannot make an independent claim for Supplementary Benefit. The man she is assumed to be dependent on has to claim for them both as a unit. They receive the rate for a married couple and this is significantly lower than the rate for two single people.[11]

The Supplementary Benefits handbook makes it clear that evidence which shows that the man is not financially supporting the woman is not accepted as conclusive evidence that they are not living as 'man and wife'. Other evidence, such as sharing accommodation, sharing the same bedroom, having a long-lasting relationship, can be sufficient to establish 'cohabitation' and therefore restriction to the married couple rate of benefit. Thus, the regulations are based on the assumption that a woman who is living with a man, or is married to him, should be supported by the man. The practical consequences of the regulations often have the effect of turning this value judgment into a reality. Women with children in particular are trapped within relationships of dependence by these regulations; on the one hand they cannot achieve a degree of independence by going out to work because of the lack of child care facilities, and on the other hand they cannot have the relationships that they choose without the continual threat of having their only source of independent income taken away.

National Insurance legislation also assumes that the married woman should be dependent on her husband's income. These assumptions have not significantly changed over the quarter of a century since William Beveridge recommended that the man should make contributions on behalf of himself and his wife as for a team. However, one innovation is that married women have the option of buying their own stamps; though this is not in fact an option for independence. In spite of the fact that a married woman who opts for her own stamps pays the same contribution as a single woman, she receives less than three-quarters the amount of Sickness and Unemployment Benefit paid to a single woman. For many women it is difficult even to achieve this token of independence since staying at home to look after her children does not entitle a woman to have stamps credited to her — it is not considered to be work; she has to pay for the stamps each week, even though looking after children makes her unable, under present conditions, to earn a wage. A woman who opts to buy her own stamps may find a further obstacle to independence when she reaches retirement age. Even if she has paid the full number of stamps for as long as thirty years she has still not contributed enough to draw a pension on her own insurance and she has to make do with a married woman's pension, which is significantly less than a single woman's.

The present taxation system financially favours those who are married as compared with those who are unmarried, whether the latter are sharing accommodation or living alone. In doing so it materially sustains the idea that the married woman performs the housework while the man is the main wage-earner. The married man receives an allowance which helps him to 'keep' his wife at home while compensating for the loss of her potential earnings. It is possible to be taxed as two single people but this is only financially beneficial for two people if their joint income is over £5,000; otherwise the married woman's income is treated as part of the husband's.

The philosophy of dependence prevails even in the student grants system. A woman student married to a non-student is assumed to be dependent on her husband; consequently she receives a lower grant than an unmarried student. This is not merely an economic calculation on the part of the state about the costs involved in joint living accommodation. The fact that this does not apply to male students married to working wives reveals the official assumption that for the woman marriage is a relationship of economic dependence.

These various aspects of the material and legislative reinforcement of marriage and woman's dependent position within it cannot be understood merely as survivals of Victorian morality. They must be seen in the context, described earlier in this chapter, of the crucial contribution of work done through the sexual division of labour within the family to the present economy. The comments of William Beveridge in recommending his plan for social security still underly the state's relation to the family, with only minor modifications to accommodate women's partial entry into paid work.

> In any measure of social policy in which regard is had to facts, the great majority of married women must be regarded as occupied on work which is vital though unpaid, without which their husbands could not do their paid work and without which the nation could not continue. In accord with the facts the Plan for Social Security treats married women as a special insurance class of occupied persons and treats man and wife as a team . . .
> The attitude of the housewife to gainful employment outside the home is not and should not be the same as that of the single woman. She has other duties . . . Taken as a whole the Plan for Social Security puts a premium on marriage in place of penalising it . . . In the next thirty years housewives as Mothers have vital work to do in ensuring the adequate continuance of the British race and of British ideals in the world . . .[12]

EXPLAINING THE SEXUAL DIVISION OF LABOUR

Its Continuation in each Generation

How does the sexual division of labour reproduce itself and what are its historical origins? The problem has four main aspects. First, the way in which family relations based on this division give men and women a sexual identity, an interpretation of their own biology around a sharp polarization between masculinity and femininity. Secondly, there is the way that the education system prepares the majority of women for the future job market on the assumption that 'homemaking' will be their primary obligation. Thirdly, there is the dependence of employers on a secondary labour market, a reserve force. Finally, there is no impetus for the state or for employers to concern themselves with domestic labour beyond ensuring that a sufficient supply of labour power reaches the market.

Starting from the pre-capitalist function of the family in producing labour power, state intervention in the organization of domestic labour has in the course of the development of modern capitalism in Britain been limited to complementing the private work of the wife and mother and to guaranteeing its efficiency. In this way the institutions in which social power and resources are concentrated are integrated into and dependent on the daily preservation of the sexual division of labour. The argument towards the end of this chapter will demonstrate that this process is not smooth, harmonious or stable; however the point in this section is that within the existing institutions of modern British capitalism the dominant tendency is to *reproduce* sexual divisions — even if these are in new forms with new ideologies; all erosions are therefore the product of counter-institutions and relationships which have to fight *against the grain* and mobilize alternative sources of power in order to survive.

Women's Conception of Themselves

When a girl joins the education system, when she becomes involved in a network of personal relations, when she gets a job, when she gets married and tries to combine her domestic obligations with her job outside the home, she is not simply the passive victim of an enforced division of labour. Women have absorbed, unconsciously and consciously, as part of their self-conceptions, a cultural interpretation of their biological distinctiveness as women. It is this which provides the basis for their active complicity in their own subordination. The processes whereby this complicity takes place have not yet been clearly understood. All that can be attempted here is a résumé of the argument so far. Until the middle fifties research on the formation of sexual identity was dominated by the debate over the relative importance of natural and social determinants of femininity and masculinity. Much of this debate centred around the seminal work of Margaret Mead[13] which analysed societies in which the characteristics normally associated with masculinity and femininity did not coincide in the 'normal' way with the biological division between the sexes. More recent research, within social psychology, for example the work of R.Hartley, H.A.Moss and L.Murphy,[14] has followed up Mead's stress on the social determination of masculinity and femininity with detailed studies of the possible mechanisms involved.

The question that is being investigated is how relationships within the family transmit the norms underpinning the sexual division of labour in such a way that the majority of girls slip unconsciously into them. In general the research summarized below does not pose the problem so explicitly. The most well known approach is that which points to the ways in which sex stereotypes are learned through the differential treatment of girls and boys right from babyhood. From a sample of American mothers H.A.Moss shows that there is a significant difference between the way in which mothers hold and cuddle sons compared with daughters; Ruth Hartley develops a typology of different treatment which includes manipulation (e.g. different forms of dress, different degrees of 'fuss'), canalization (e.g. being encouraged to play with different types of toys), verbal appellation (e.g. being praised and punished for different sorts of behaviour) and activity exposure (e.g. suggestions for different chores or forms of play); Lois Murphy shows evidence of mothers giving boys far more autonomy than girls. And there are many other studies that examine further aspects of differential treatment through which the little boy or girl learns what is expected from him, or her: what it means to be male or female.

These processes of learning through differential treatment are certainly important. The powerlessness of the child makes him or her their helpless victim. But there are a number of weaknesses in the accounts of these processes in so far as they attempt to provide theories on the formation of sexual identity *solely* in terms of this learning process.

In part, this is a consequence of failing to examine the effect of the mother's general social position on the way in which the mother/child relationship transmits the sexual division of labour. Certain links between the division of labour, specifically the general social context of the mother/child relationship, and the emotional content of family relations are fairly obvious. The mother's separateness from, or weak connection with, social life and her consequent lack of autonomy, means that she tends to seek her own fulfilment, her own identity, through her child — and her husband. The father, on the other hand, relates to the child as an autonomous individual with a consequent distance from the child's character and needs. This affects fundamentally the nature of the child's *emotional* relationship with each of the two parents. And it is primarily through this relationship that a child initially develops its sense of identity and therefore its responses to the division of labour. By failing to take full account of emotions in the formation of self-identity, studies based on learning theory do not come to grips with the deeply-rooted nature of sexual identity. To explain sexual identity in terms of social learning is like explaining objects that are attached to each other without identifying the glue. The nature of the emotional relations within the family provides the glue through which the learning process sticks and has significance. This can be illustrated by looking at the process of socialization in reverse, that is the process of self-conscious change in, and reconstruction of, a woman's social identity. The idea of the gradual learning of a social role by association and models tends to imply that once that role is consciously rejected all aspects of the identity that went with it can equally consciously be stipped off. It does not account for the persistence of unconscious but powerful processes producing feelings and emotions highly conducive to passivity and subservience, however consciously some of the subordinate roles have been rejected.

The slowness, until recently, with which women have come to challenge in practice their place as unpaid labour in the home and as low-paid labour in the factory, is partly a result of the way that domestic labour is unconsciously intertwined with emotions and feelings. Housework appears as a labour of love, an expression of care and concern. Questioning this labour would seem to imply the undermining of a woman's emotional relationships. The attitude can only be changed if emotions and feelings are separated from the requirements of housework. Only then will the economic function of housework become clear and the need to organize it on a non-sex basis become a possibility. The 'unlearning' of roles has rarely proved to be sufficient. Understanding the initial formation of these emotions rather than merely how models and norms are learnt is therefore central to understanding how women themselves reproduce the relations of their oppression.

Freud has probably come nearest to identifying the structures which produce the child's early emotional relations, although he certainly does not relate them to women's position in the division of labour. Freudians explain the formation of the female identity in terms of the way in which the initial emotional attachment that all infants have towards their mother, in the present structure of the nuclear family, must necessarily change for cultural reasons as the child grows up. The relationships involved in this change are described as the Oedipus complex. In the case of the girl this involves the culturally enforced repression of her desire for her mother and the culturally induced transfer of her sexual attention to her father. This transfer involves a repression, or rather a transformation, of her unconscious desire for a penis into a socially acceptable form, that is into the desire for a husband and a baby. In the course of this transfer the girl, who like the boy has a combination of passive and active impulses, brings to the fore her passive impulses, her impulses to live through others, and represses her active impulses to control and participate in the outside world. By this process her female identity at a conscious and, perhaps more important, unconscious, level is formed.

Of course there are complexities in this theory that cannot be discussed now. Although Freud may be an important starting-point for solving the problem of how women become mentally prepared for their social destiny he does not provide the whole answer. As feminists have pointed out, he went in several false directions.[15] A particularly important question is how far the relationships that Freud identifies are a product of the particular family structure and culture of modern capitalist society. When Freud referred to the repression and transferences involved in these relationships as culturally induced he used culture in the broadest sense of human civilization. Detailed studies of differential socialization could usefully complement the more Freudian emphasis on the studying of infants' emotional responses to their first pattern of human inter-relationships. Different forms of play encouraged for boys and girls, different characteristics praised or condemned, the different use of language to boys and girls, probably all provide clues to the precise mechanisms whereby definitions of what is socially unacceptable − so crucial to the Freudian theory of repression − enter consciousness.

EDUCATION AND THE SEXUAL DIVISION OF LABOUR

The relationship between education and the sexual division of labour can best be understood in terms of the general purpose of the education system in preparing each generation for the social division of labour as a whole. This process of pre-paration can be broken down into three important components: the way the educa-tion system trains the future labour force in basic skills such as literacy and numeracy, and gives them some grounding in scientific and humanistic knowledge in order to prepare them for learning more occupationally specific skills; the way in which fifth and sixth forms, colleges of further education, polytechnics, technical colleges and universities meet the needs of the occupational structure more specifically by providing specialized guidance and teaching. Finally there is the way that, at all levels, the education system provides ideological support for the division of labour, and for institutions like the state and the family which guarantee and reproduce this division. The mechanisms of this general ideological support include the content of curricula, the organization of teaching, discipline, and forms of selection. In all these ways the distinct destinies of girls and boys within the division of labour are reflected and actively reinforced.

However, education's role in producing generations of women who as mothers, teachers, nurses, housewives, social workers, service workers and secretaries, will privately and publicly perform the tasks of socializing the young, caring for the sick, the old and exhausted, is not without contradictions. There is not necessarily a harmonious relationship between the needs of the family and domestic labour, and the requirements of employers and of the state. For example, the decreasing rate of a real increase in expenditure on the welfare state in the last few years, and changes in the organization of welfare facilities, have put more of a burden on the family and therefore on the housewife, e.g. for the care of the old and the handicapped. Within the lower levels of the education system the indirect effect of this has been pressure for more time and resources to be spent on developing domestic science teaching; on the other hand the needs generated by industrial reorganization and technological advances for selective increases in non-manual skilled labour have produced a demand for more scientifically and mathematically skilled women and thus for more equal resources to be allocated to training such women. In many schools two distinct images of women are therefore beginning to emerge. A further contradiction arises from historical factors that have produced schools and colleges partially in conflict with the division of labour: for example, the feminist energies of education reformers like Frances Buss and Emily Davies achieved a standard of education for middle-class girls in the early twentieth century almost equal to their brothers'.[16] Many of these reformers' achievements have been undermined, but their heritage is partly responsible for the conflict between expectations engendered by a relatively egalitarian ethos in the higher levels of the education system and the reality of limited job opportunities. This conflict has been one cause of an increasing consciousness among women within higher education of their secondary position.

These and other contradictions will be looked at in more detail in the course of analysing the different levels of the relationship between education and the sexual division of labour.

EDUCATION IN BASIC SKILLS AND KNOWLEDGE

In 1864 the first Schools Enquiry Commission asked if girls were capable of learning Latin and mathematics. In the early twentieth century the headmistress of one of the most advanced centres for girls' education, Manchester Girls' Grammar School, said: 'Mathematics should be kept at a minimum for girls, it does not underlie their industries as it does so many of the activities of men.'

Comparable judgments have an active influence in present-day education. They are, for instance, reflected in the subjects chosen by, or for, girls in the majority of schools, as in figure 3.2 and table 3.20.

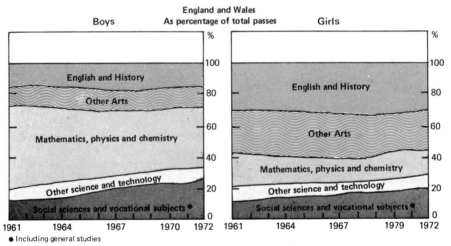

Figure 3.2   Subjects Chosen by, or for, Girls in the Majority of Schools
Source: *Social Trends* (1974), p. 152

TABLE 3.20

GCE 'A' level entries

Comparison of Subjects Studied by Girls and Boys at 'A' level

		All maintained schools		
		Pupils following GCE 'A' level courses in:		
		Mathematics/ science subjects only	Other subjects only	Subjects in both groups
As a percentage of all sixth-form pupils on 'A' level courses				
1965	Boys	50.9	36.8	12.3
	Girls	19.6	66.4	14.0
	Total	37.8	49.2	13.0
1966	Boys	49.9	37.1	13.0
	Girls	17.9	67.8	14.3
	Total	36.3	50.2	13.6
1967	Boys	47.0	37.9	15.1
	Girls	16.4	68.1	15.5
	Total	33.8	50.9	15.3
1968	Boys	44.9	38.2	16.9
	Girls	15.3	68.3	16.4
	Total	31.8	51.5	16.7
1969	Boys	43.9	37.8	18.3
	Girls	15.3	67.6	17.1
	Total	30.9	51.3	17.8
As a percentage of all pupils on 'A' level courses				
1970	Boys	44.2	36.8	19.0
	Girls	15.5	66.4	18.1
	Total	30.9	50.5	18.6
1971	Boys	43.5	36.1	20.3
	Girls	15.7	66.0	18.4
	Total	30.6	50.0	19.4
1972	Boys	43.6	35.4	21.0
	Girls	15.9	65.1	19.0
	Total	30.6	49.3	20.1

Source: *Social Trends* (1974)

An analysis by the ILEA Research and Statistics Group shows a similar disparity in the numbers of boys and girls choosing various 'A' level subjects in the sixth form in 1970–1:

TABLE 3.21

	Maths	Physics	Chemistry	Biology	Eng. Lit.	History	Total
Boys	1,922	1,526	1,098	783	1,271	977	7,577
Girls	784	546	638	989	2,653	1,343	6,953

Table 3.21 indicates that when girls do turn to science, the majority of them take biology, the science with the least abstract and the most humanistic image. Further evidence is provided by the statistics of those sitting the General Certificate of Education examination at 'O' level in 1972: 164,000 girls took biology but only 88,000 took physics and chemistry, whereas 88,000 boys took biology and 285,000 took physics and chemistry. However, the combined pressures brought about by the growing involvement of women in social production and the increasing complexity of the roles of wife and mother as these roles become integrated into the welfare state, have begun, however unevenly, to undermine some of these discrepancies. The percentage increases in table 3.22 indicate that the gap between boys and girls passing GCE examinations in scientific subjects is diminishing.

TABLE 3.22

Percentage changes in numbers of GCE passes, 1960–70

Actual numbers of passes in 1970 are given in brackets

	Maths	Physics	Chemistry	Economics	English Language	English Literature	All subjects
'O' Levels							
Boys	24.1	46.1	34.6	254.1	28.7	36.1	34.7
	(101,557)	(47,846)	(36,156)	(20,852)	(94,074)	(52,104)	(669,580)
Girls	61.1	119.4	137.4	378.2	65.0	46.6	52.3
	(56,053)	(11,997)	(14,711)	(14,508)	(112,950)	(82,945)	(656,239)
Total	35.1	63.6	53.8	296.3	46.2	42.3	42.9
	(157,610)	(59,843)	(50,867)	(35,360)	(206,664)	(135,049)	(1,325,819)
'A' Levels							
Boys	49.7	29.7	15.9	311.9	–	147.4	79.5
	(34,866)	(23,350)	(16,136)	(19,659)		(15,041)	(180,673)
Girls	141.0	86.6	97.2	653.4	–	210.3	168.2
	(8,603)	(4,684)	(5,301)	(6,042)		(26,331)	(122,653)
Total	61.8	36.6	29.1	361.0	–	184.1	107.2
	(43,469)	(28,034)	(21,437)	(25,701)		(41,372)	(303,326)

Source: Extracted from Statistics of Education (1970), Vol. 2, tables 31 and 32

But the changes in table 3.22 must be treated with caution, first, because the numbers from which the percentages are drawn are too small for them to be reliable indicators of a continuing trend. For example, although there is an increase of 86 per cent in the number of girls passing in physics, the total number of these girls is only 4,684. Secondly, the way that the statistics are presented does not take into account the hierarchy of the education system and the consequent possibility that such overall statistics might cover up divergent trends. Diminishing sexual differentiation at 'A' level streams might make up statistically for continuing differentiation at 'O' level. The CSE figures certainly indicate a slower rate of change over the period 1960–70, and this might also apply to the 'O'-level statistics.

Further evidence of the consolidation of sexual differences among those whose lot, in addition to housework, will be the clerical, semi-skilled and unskilled job market, comes from the educational advisors themselves: the Crowther Report (1959) argues that the more able girls, who should qualify for a career before getting married, will not have time for education oriented towards their role as wives and mothers, but it goes on to say: 'With the less able girls, however, we think that the schools can and should make more adjustments (not more than all but a handful have yet done so) to the fact that marriage now looms much larger and nearer in the pupils' eyes than it has ever done before.' The Report concludes that 'the prospect of courtship and marriage should rightly influence the education of the adolescent girl'. It goes on to propose that their education should concentrate on dress, personal appearance and human relations.

The explanation of these continuing sexual differences lies in a combination of girls' own conceptions of their femininity and future aspirations, the assumptions and expectations of many of their teachers and parents, and the prevailing images of love and marriage reflected in the media and popular culture, together with the institutional constraints of restricted curricula, inadequate science teaching, and the channelling of any available facilities and resources into domestic science and home economics. The last aspect of the explanation, which concerns government education policy, can only be fully understood in the context of the needs of industry, the general pattern of which will be analysed in the next section.

In the first element in this explanation one sees the consequences of the formation of the female identity discussed in the last section. Many studies have revealed that girls are particularly prone to 'under-achievement' in relation to their measured IQ. This under-achievement tends to come to the fore during puberty. Before puberty girls tend to do better than boys, especially in linguistic/verbal subjects but also in mathematical subjects. This greater achievement is itself probably related to the initial formation of female identity in the sense that girls' tendency towards passivity and conformity will make them more attentive pupils than boys who are likely to have developed stronger tendencies towards aggression and autonomy. Around puberty many girls find themselves in the situation of wanting to do well academically but having a sneaking feeling that intellectual dominance in relationships with men contradicts their femininity; or, less crudely, they experience a conflict between the active autonomous impulses of work and achievement and the passive impulses of normal sexual relationships. The momentum of emotions whose basis has been structured in early socialization tends to drive women towards sexual relationships of subordination. Thus intellectual effort appears as an obstacle to emotional satisfaction. The other half of this process is of course male socialization and the often unconscious male desire to dominate and prove himself vis-à-vis women.

TABLE 3.23

CSE all modes results; pupils achieving grade 5 or better, 1965–72

	1965[1]	1966	1967	1968	1969	1970	1971	1972
English								
Boys	22,646	50,614	65,049	76,672	88,582	95,855	102,124	116,921
Girls	17,456	41,801	56,668	68,214	79,060	84,551	90,626	103,571
Total	40,102	92,415	121,717	144,886	167,642	180,406	192,750	220,492
History								
Boys	8,787	18,234	24,123	29,269	33,606	36,281	38,749	45,181
Girls	6,744	14,951	20,559	25,758	30,023	32,954	35,263	40,456
Total	15,531	33,185	44,682	55,027	63,629	69,235	74,012	84,637
French								
Boys	3,439	8,967	12,625	15,796	18,688	20,790	24,244	27,718
Girls	4,484	11,665	16,028	20,892	26,578	30,587	34,485	40,411
Total	7,923	20,632	28,653	36,688	45,266	51,377	58,729	68,122
Art and craft								
Boys	5,838	12,771	18,090	21,904	26,290	29,525	31,867	35,679
Girls	4,049	9,618	14,788	19,101	23,455	25,999	28,134	31,680
Total	9,887	22,389	32,878	41,005	49,745	55,524	60,001	67,359
Other arts subjects								
Boys	4,198	8,986	12,597	14,263	16,230	17,045	18,090	20,461
Girls	5,877	12,092	17,414	21,572	25,193	27,537	29,524	33,798
Total	10,075	21,078	30,011	35,835	41,423	44,582	47,614	54,259
Mathematics[2]								
Boys	23,655	51,153	64,275	74,283	81,724	89,582	95,424	107,588
Girls	15,507	38,523	49,128	59,755	68,182	76,294	83,655	95,844
Total	39,162	89,676	113,403	134,038	149,906	165,876	179,079	203,432
Physics								
Boys	9,209	21,096	29,019	35,307	41,850	46,180	50,520	58,721
Girls	587	1,240	1,815	2,613	3,431	4,181	5,154	6,900
Total	9,796	22,336	30,834	37,920	45,281	50,361	55,674	65,621
Biology								
Boys	2,113	5,216	7,107	9,630	12,514	14,558	17,260	21,445
Girls	5,559	13,206	18,662	25,427	32,444	36,576	40,753	47,888
Total	7,672	18,422	25,769	35,057	44,958	51,134	58,013	69,333
Technical Drawing								
Boys	13,706	28,176	34,527	39,746	44,223	47,356	49,818	55,356
Girls	54	135	227	268	303	358	462	593
Total	13,760	28,311	34,754	40,014	44,526	47,714	50,280	55,949
Metalwork and woodwork								
Boys	12,661	26,823	35,554	41,803	48,544	52,027	56,078	63,233
Girls	7	31	54	61	84	96	169	213
Total	12,668	26,854	35,608	41,864	48,628	52,123	56,247	63,446

TABLE 3.23 (continued)

	1965[3]	1966	1967	1968	1969	1970	1971	1972
Other science or technical subjects								
Boys	10,771	25,393	32,395	37,934	44,010	48,922	53,720	62,862
Girls	2,373	5,630	8,727	10,111	12,474	14,943	17,762	22,022
Total	13,144	31,023	41,122	48,045	56,585	63,865	71,482	84,884
Geography								
Boys	12,494	25,699	33,671	39,491	45,771	49,165	52,455	59,204
Girls	6,966	15,245	21,318	26,690	30,854	33,303	36,248	40,617
Total	19,460	40,944	54,989	66,181	76,625	82,468	88,703	99,821
Domestic subjects[3]								
Boys	89	223	365	522	822	1,111	1,541	1,901
Girls	9,945	22,119	31,994	40,038	49,405	54,653	60,038	66,161
Total	10,034	22,342	32,359	40,560	50,227	55,764	61,579	68,062
Commercial subjects								
Boys	988	2,496	3,560	4,229	5,044	5,609	6,078	7,011
Girls	5,340	12,801	18,573	22,122	24,424	27,318	28,934	32,439
Total	6,328	15,297	22,133	26,351	29,468	32,927	35,002	39,450
Other social science or vocational subjects[4]								
Boys	528	2,164	3,848	4,926	7,114	9,326	11,216	13,509
Girls	269	1,910	3,549	4,581	6,796	8,972	10,933	13,530
Total	797	4,074	7,397	9,507	13,910	18,298	22,149	27,039
All subjects[5]								
Boys	131,122	288,011	376,805	445,775	515,012	563,332	609,184	695,790
Girls	85,217	200,967	279,504	347,203	412,706	458,322	502,130	576,123
Total	216,339	488,978	656,309	792,978	927,718	1,021,654	1,111,314	1,271,913
of which								
Mode 1	186,835	425,500	569,139	680,807	784,155	855,783	923,614	1,042,362
Mode 2	11,345	17,541	21,840	24,063	29,681	31,565	33,860	35,842
Mode 3	13,159	45,937	65,330	88,108	113,882	134,306	153,840	193,709

Notes:

[1] Only nine of the 14 Regional Boards were operational in 1965, the first year the examinations were held

[2] Including Arithmetic

[3] Including Cookery and Needlework

[4] Including English Economic History, Economics and Social Studies

[5] Excluding Shorthand, Typewriting and related subjects

Source: *Social Trends* (1974)

The majority of girls are aware that attempts to keep up with boys do not provide any escape from the dreary destiny of unskilled, low-paid work. Romance, marriage, jobs connected with the world of femininity — hairdressing, boutiques, secretarial work — seem to offer the best option. An illustration of this can be seen in a study carried out in the early sixties on the attitudes to work and marriage of 600 adolescent girls. This showed that in the age range of 14–17 the vast majority had no ambition or goal other than marriage and homemaking. In essays about their future lives, 90 per cent wrote of marriage, while 53 per cent mentioned paid work as something that their husbands would oppose or as a way of saving money to buy a house. There is however strong evidence that among girls facing the possibility of the career level of the job market there is greater resistance to the female stereotype. We shall return to this crucial explanation of women's continued complicity in their subordination. It has far-reaching implications for trends towards divergence between the position of women with the realistic prospect of *individual careers* and the position of women likely to become part of our undifferentiated mass work force.

Girls have their traditional aspirations reinforced or their resistance to stereo-typed choices constrained by severely restricted curricula. Sometimes this is a result of explicit assumptions about what is relevant for girls and what for boys. In many mixed schools the timetable is organized so that girls do needlework or domestic science while boys do metalwork or woodwork. Other restrictions, particularly in girls' schools but also in mixed schools, are due to a serious shortage of adequate facilities and teaching staff for mathematical courses. In 1972 the ILEA Standing Committee on Careers Opportunities for Girls reported the evidence presented to them on this problem: 'In most schools there are difficulties in the recruitment of maths and science teachers and although girls' schools may be particularly affected, we noted that girls in some mixed schools also suffered when it came to the alloca-tion of scarce resources. There are very few girls' schools equipped with any form of workshop facilities other than for needlecraft and home economics.'

In 1973 a study was carried out by HM Inspectorate which looked at the extent to which curricular differences and customs contributed to the inequality of opportunity for boys and girls. The prevailing picture was that traditional assump-tions were being worked through the curricular patterns of secondary schools; and that there was support and acceptance of these patterns by the majority of teachers, pupils and parents.

The significance of this sexual differentiation in the learning of basic skills is not only that it prepares the way for a more rigid division of learning within specialized training, it also has a direct bearing on the occupational division of labour. Lack of mathematical competence is a major obstacle to wider job choices for women because of the range of jobs closed to those without 'O' level maths. These closed options now include not only the sciences but many branches of commerce, administration and even the social sciences. The careers ruled out by not having 'O' level math-ematics include, accountancy, architecture, advertising, astronomy, banking, bio-chemistry, cartography, computer programming, dentistry, economics, engineering, horticulture, laboratory technology, land management, market research, optics, park administration, patent work, the Post Office (technical), printing, the police, radio-graphy, statistics, surveying, textile technology, town planning. The role of the educational system in nourishing the sexual division of labour thus becomes all too clear when one sees that the number of girls who have this key to wider opportunities is only half the number of boys (see table 3.23).

TABLE 3.24

Analysis by type of employment entered and age of entry

		Males				Females			
		15	16	17	Total	15	16	17	Total
Apprenticeship or learnership to skilled occupation (including pre-apprenticeship training in employment)	1973	5.9	51.0	9.1	66.0	0.6	3.3	1.1	5.0
	1972	52.2	40.7	7.3	100.2	14.0	3.0	1.0	18.0
		−46.3	+10.3	+1.3	−34.2	−13.4	+0.3	+0.1	−13.0
Employment leading to recognized professional qualifications	1973	0.1	1.6	1.6	3.3	0.1	2.2	1.7	4.0
	1972	0.5	1.3	1.5	3.4	0.3	2.0	1.6	3.9
		−0.4	+0.3	+0.1	−0.1	−0.2	+0.2	+0.1	+0.1
Clerical employment	1973	0.8	10.2	6.6	17.8	5.1	40.6	16.6	62.3
	1972	3.3	8.9	6.2	18.4	20.3	33.9	15.1	73.6
		−2.5	+1.3	+0.6	−0.6	−24.2	+6.7	+1.5	−16.0
Employment with planned training, apart from induction training, not covered above	1973	2.3	13.2	4.9	20.4	1.2	8.2	3.0	12.4
	1972	26.4	12.1	4.1	42.6	30.7	7.0	2.7	40.5
		−24.1	+1.1	+0.8	−22.2	−29.5	+1.2	+0.3	28.1
Other employment	1973	5.9	20.9	6.2	33.1	3.5	15.1	4.7	23.3
	1972	68.7	19.9	5.7	94.3	69.3	13.9	4.3	87.5
		−62.8	+1.0	+0.5	−61.2	−65.8	+1.2	40.4	−64.2
Total	1973	15.0	96.9	28.6	140.5	10.5	69.4	27.2	107.0
	1972	151.2	82.9	24.8	258.9	143.6	59.9	24.8	228.2
		−136.2	+14.0	+3.8	−118.4	−133.1	+9.5	+2.4	−121.2

Source: Department of Employment, *Gazette* (May 1974)

TRAINING FOR FUTURE WORK

We have seen that sexual differentiation is particularly marked in the lower streams of the education system. This is partly because within the division of labour the likely destiny of children is more apparent at the lower level. This is one indication of a pattern in which the degree of sexual differentiation varies directly with the extent to which parts of the educational system are integrated with the occupational structure. Where the function of education is directly tied to an occupation sexual differences are most extreme. For example, in the case of day-release courses – which is the most widespread form of industrially-backed part-time education – only 13.3 per cent of the students for 1970–1 were women, and this figure has been virtually static for the last few years. Of the 16–19 age group of employees 40 per cent of men and only 10 per cent of women at present obtain release from employment for further education. Table 3.24 indicates this asymmetry in relation to apprentice-ships. (The actual entry figures are down because of the raising of the school-leaving age.)

This lack of training, education facilities, and encouragement closes the trap which restricts the majority of women to the unskilled low-paid job market des-·cribed in the first section. This in turn reinforces the sexual division of labour in the home. Wages are so low that going out to work does little to reduce woman's economic dependence on her husband. The nature of the work is either an extension of housework or is completely without interest and so in many cases it does little to change a woman's attitude towards her home.

Within full-time further education the situation is not much better. From the 1970–2 statistics of the London and Home Counties Regional Advisory Council for Further Education it would seem that the trend towards diminishing sexual differences – which the DES optimistically infer from the GCE results – is not carried through into further education. Girls are still concentrated in traditional areas and there is no sign of a move across to science/technology-based subjects. In the Schools Council Working Paper No. 45 on the education of 16 to 19-year-olds there is clear evidence of the direct pressure of the poor job market in producing this situation. This points to the fact that in areas where women form the majority of students, as in OND Business Studies, the education on these courses is often adapted to the lower level of work opportunities for girls: 'It is noteworthy that in many colleges girls taking OND in Business Studies are expected to acquire shorthand and typewriting skills. This suggests that the colleges do not expect these young women to be offered managerial openings and therefore advise them to take the secretarial skills in order to get into business at the level of personal assistant rather than trainee manager . . .'[17]

At the highest level there has been a very slight increase in the proportion of women getting into university but it is significantly below what would be expected on the basis of the sex distribution of 'A' level grades. Analysis of the annual statistics for London 'A' level exams shows a higher percentage of girls in the top three grades and yet table 3.25 shows that in 1970–1 only 57 per cent of all girls with three 'A' levels went to university compared with 67 per cent of all boys.

Table 3.25 indicates the continuation at university level of the pattern of differentiation of subject choice, in relation to secondary education.

The extent to which colleges of education are predominantly a female option is clearly reflected in these figures. A teacher writing about her experience of one of these colleges vividly describes the main theme of their culture: 'My college, like most, had academic pretensions but underlying and undermining it was an environment which cocooned you securely from any real mental effort. Right from the beginning we accepted that marriage would be on the agenda long before a teaching job. Student culture, from "freshers week" and the emphasis on that all too familiar song "How do you feel when you marry your ideal . . ." to the spoon-banging crescendo like some primitive initiation rite, only emphasized it more strongly.'[18] The implications are backed up by a survey of the attitudes of female teachers by the National Institute of Industrial Psychiatrists. They found that the majority of women thought that men were better in authority, fairer, more patient and generally more respected. One third of the sample admitted they thought that men were generally superior. In the light of this it comes as no surprise that teachers tend to reinforce sex roles.

EDUCATION AND THE IDEOLOGY OF SEXISM

When a girl goes to school her vague consciousness of what it means to be a girl is developed into a concrete shape by the models presented of her future destiny. They include reading-books where boys always appear to have the monopoly of adventure and naughtiness, where adult women are engrossed only in housework and never appear in the world of work and activity outside the home (other than shopping); science textbooks which in their illustrations show a few pictures of girls doing things like tending plants, stroking kittens or blowing bubbles and numerous pictures of boys demonstrating 'energy' by chopping wood, kicking footballs and having pillow fights, or using torches, magnifying glasses and other technical instruments. They include, too, the structure of the school itself in which women are almost invariably in subordinate positions to men: women are the assistant teachers, secretaries, auxiliary workers, cooks and cleaners; men are most frequently the headmasters, the heads of departments.[19]

The strength of these models of behaviour and aspiration does not derive from their being consciously taught as the ways in which girls ought to behave. Their power lies in the appearance that they present of the complete naturalness and inevitability of women's secondary position. There appears to be no way out except to refuse to identify with one's own sex. A partial solution therefore for girls who react negatively to the limp and passive bystanders or the happy plastic figures doing the washing up, is to identify with the active, interesting images of the opposite sex. But to be a tomboy is to be in limbo. A girl is expected to 'grow out of it', and consequently is not related to herself as she is and wants to be, but only to the hints of femininity that fit into what she ought to be. On the other hand boys will not easily accept her. It is a solution she knows can never work. Apart from this ambiguous solution the shape of the images that most girls absorb appears to point to becoming a wife and mother as the main goal in life. There are very few reading-books for children, even among the newest series, that present different images of girls.

The idea that women's present subordinate position is natural and inevitable is not, in general, consciously constructed to inculcate sex roles. Most writers probably think they are presenting real life; in fact a lot of effort has gone into making children's reading-books more realistic by not restricting them to a middle-class

TABLE 3.25

Male and female full-time students: comparison of subjects chosen for study, 1970–2

The distribution of the 234,985 full-time students in 1971–2 by subject of study is summarized below, with the 1970–1 figures shown for comparison

Subject group	1970–1				1971–2			
	Men		Women		Men		Women	
	Number	Percentage of total	Number	Percentage of total	Number	Percentage of total	Number	Percentage of total
Education	4,673	2.9	4,487	6.8	4,571	2.8	4,018	5.8
Medicine, Dentistry and Health	16,368	10.1	6,491	9.9	16,405	9.9	7,206	10.3
Engineering and Technology	35,475	21.9	817	1.2	35,978	21.8	965	1.4
Agriculture, Forestry and Veterinary Science	3,689	2.3	853	1.3	3,475	2.1	912	1.3
Science	43,253	26.7	13,274	20.2	44,696	27.0	14,277	20.5
Social, Administrative and Business Studies	31,927	19.7	14,474	22.0	33,236	20.1	16,006	23.0
Architecture and other professional and vocational subjects	3,146	1.9	769	1.2	3,586	2.2	878	1.3

(continued)

Language, Literature and Area Studies	11,944	7.4	14,531	22.1	12,104	7.3	15,541	22.3
Arts, other than languages	11,650	7.2	10,135	15.4	11,227	6.8	9,904	14.2
Total	162,125	100.0	65,831	100.0	165,278	100.0	69,707	100.0

Source: Education Statistics for the UK (1974)

TABLE 3.26

Destination of school leavers by type of school, England and Wales, 1971–2

	Universities	Colleges of Education	Polytechnics	Other full-time further education	Employment[1]
Boys:					
Grammar	23.3	4.4	7.2	10.0	55.0
Comprehensive	4.5	1.5	1.7	5.8	86.5
Modern	0.1	0.2	0.2	8.4	91.1
Other secondary	3.7	0.8	1.6	6.8	87.1
Direct grant	37.6	2.9	7.5	13.4	38.6
Independent	28.1	1.3	5.8	23.3	41.5
Girls:					
Grammar	12.8	15.3	4.1	19.0	48.8
Comprehensive	2.5	4.5	0.8	9.7	82.4
Modern	0.1	0.5	0.1	13.3	86.0
Other secondary	1.7	3.5	0.7	10.6	83.5
Direct grant	25.3	15.3	4.8	20.7	33.9
Independent	14.3	6.8	4.3	39.3	35.3

Note:

1 Includes those entering temporary employment pending entry into full-time further education not later than September–October 1973, and those who left for other reasons and whose destinations were not known

Source: *Social Trends* (1974), p. 154

life-style. But they are still only presenting an idealized form of the real situation of women, and are not describing the contradictions. And it is only an awareness of these contradictions which can give girls the tools with which to construct an alternative. The fact that women *do* get out to work, that women *do* organize against low pay and bad conditions, that there *are some* women doctors, scientists, politicians, artists and poets, that girls *do* feel like having adventures, and taking the initiative, all provide holes in the smothering blanket of domesticity.

Women and the Economy

Earlier in this chapter the position of women within the labour market was presented in terms of what is in effect a dual market. The main point of this description was to show the ways in which the chief feature of women's paid work did not directly clash with the sexual division of labour. The analysis went on to show how the socializing institutions through which social values regarding the division of labour are acquired and skills and capacities are learnt, reflect and reinforce this. The relation of the state to the family guarantees it materially. Is it the cultural and official reinforcement of women's role which prevents a general erosion of accepted attitudes? Or is there a sense in which modern capitalist industry also depends on and sustains the dual labour market? If this is the case, the cultural and political processes already traced have a strong material basis, not easily weakened, as far as the majority of women are concerned, by egalitarian cultural pressures stemming from the formal granting of equal economic and legal rights.

In order to understand the present distribution and the future of women as wage labourers, we must not be content with the relatively equal situation of some women (despite their dual role as domestic labourers) in parts of the professional sector. Instead, we should identify those features of a capitalist economy which thrive on the sexual division of labour and thereby endorse it. Only in this way will it be possible to explain why women are concentrated in certain sectors of the economy and to evaluate fully the strength of processes tending to erode women's unequal position.

There are two main processes which are relevant: capitalism's tendency to create a section of the labour force which is sufficiently manoeuvrable to be easily expelled from employment during periods of recession or of increased capital intensity, and to be drawn rapidly into employment when there is fresh investment and new sections of industry are opened up; secondly, the tendency towards a dual economy in which the large, corporate, high labour-cost sector comes to *depend* on, rather than to squeeze out, small firms running on low labour costs, producing components and acting as sub-contractors to the large corporations.

To consider the first: in the past capital has relied on agricultural labour, immigrants, or a high rate of native male unemployment, to provide the necessary surplus labour. In the course of the post-war boom these sources reached their political and economic limits. And yet the need for new sources of labour grew fast; particularly for new industries, new services and new administrative extensions to the production process for which no existing section of the labour force was available or trained. The expansion of the welfare state, combined with the increased revenue which the state gained from the expansion of the economy, led to an unprecedented growth in the need for clerical and other service workers throughout government departments. A similar demand for clerical and administrative workers increased with the growing need of large corporations to monitor, plan and control the production process as its size and complexity grew and as the processes of coordination, skill and planning had been transferred from the shop floor to the office.[20] The growth in advertising and related marketing processes which has followed the increased power of the large corporations reinforced this need. Along with this growth in the service and clerical sectors there has been a simultaneous mushrooming of new light industries, made possible by the technological advances preceding and during the expansion of the economy. These light industries needed a rapid influx of unskilled and green labour which could be easily fitted into the new assembly-line techniques unacceptable to many workers in the traditional industries. Moreover this labour force had to be expendable. Corporate investors rarely considered new plants to be permanent. Plants were subject to changes in multi-national plans and possibilities, or were highly tactical operations geared to utilizing government subsidies and ready to move at the slightest sign of trouble or greener fields elsewhere. And even if a plant was stable the technology utilized within it was not. New combinations of machinery and labour need to be continually tested and, in the eyes of management, the 'Luddite' restrictive practices of the unions would hold back progress.

Married women, with initially low wage expectations, negligible traditions of organization, no established work customs and with an alternative life to return to, provided the ideal work force.

If capitalism were a stable economic system this basis on which married women have been drawn in to meet capital's new labour needs during the boom period would not produce any strong tendency towards reinforcing the division of labour. Married women would develop high wage expectations and become strongly organized in the same way as other groups who have acted as sources of surplus labour in England, such as ex-agricultural workers, Irish and, increasingly, Asian and West Indian workers. But given the increasingly lengthy periods of recession which periodically and unpredictably afflict the capitalist economy, the sexual division of labour provides a unique advantage to capitalism. No other group is so well situated from capital's point of view. The sexual division of labour and the ideology that justifies it ensures that women are not dependent for their subsistence on wage labour. Among workers in a capitalist society they are unique in having access to a means, or a partial means, of livelihood on the basis of social relations other than economic exchange relations. It is almost as if capitalism was able to preserve a rural economy for workers to return to, and could yet make use of them whenever necessary. The situation of 'guest-workers' in France and Germany is the nearest equivalent.[21]

The unique feature of married women as wage labourers has become increasingly important in a context where employers face growing uncertainty combined with successful attempts by unions to protect job security and to raise the cost of redundancies. The Redundancy Payment Act, the Employment Protection Act, and the successful occupation of factories during the early 70s, all contribute in different ways. In this context the advantage of employing women is that they can work part-time. In consequence the costs and problems of making redundancies are evaded. This is becoming more attractive as the size of investment projects and the growing uncertainty of general economic conditions increases the risks facing the multi-national companies. Not surprisingly there has been a significant growth in the number of part-time married women workers. The Counter Information Services report, 'Women Under Attack', describes it as follows:

> Between 1961 and 1971 full-time employment (both sexes) in the manufacturing sector fell by 405,000, while part-time employment increased by 85,000. In the year June 1971 to June 1972 full-time male employment in all industries fell by 106,000, and full-time female employment fell 14,000. Part-time female employment, however, rose 120,000 in the same period. Obviously employers have become willing to employ part-time workers, and part-time women workers in particular, at times when full-timers are losing their jobs and there is plenty of full-time labour available on the market. This is not to say that part-time women are not susceptible, in employment terms, to market cycles. In the manufacturing industries they numbered 470,700 in September 1973, rising to 504,900 in December of the same year as the boom was reaching its peak, and falling to 494,800 by June 1975 in the course of the long rundown to the present slump.[22]

This increase in part-time women workers is the clearest expression of a general feature of the position of the majority of women workers. British capitalism's increasing need for a manoeuvrable section of the labour force, the political and economic limits on previous sources of such labour, and the uniquely accommodative nature of family relations outside of direct exchange relations, reinforces the position of women as a distinct and subordinate caste. Part-time work visibly illustrates the way in which the sexual division of labour is built into the strategies of management to meet their fluctuating labour needs. Part-time work on wages lower than subsistence is *only possible* because of women's domestic obligations and dependence. In this way, far from a steady *erosion of* the sexual division of labour, sections of the production process are organized on the basis of compromise. The general fluctuations in women's employment as compared to men's are shown in figure 3.3.

The way in which the sexual division of labour and the fluctuating labour requirements of the economy interlock to keep the majority of unskilled and semi-skilled women in their subordinate position contrasts sharply with the position of women in the 'career' sector of the job market. In this sector the specific capacities of each individual are central to the needs of the employer. Once women have been drawn into this sector because of shortages, and once the women involved have through their relatively high income transferred their domestic commitments to private services, bought on the market, there is no basis other than overt discrimination on which they can be treated differently. In this sector of the job market where workers are hired for their individual merits as distinct from being units of un-differentiated labour power, tendencies towards meritocracy are strong. There is little to be gained from treating women differently. Prejudice still exists but it is becoming increasingly anomalous. It is at this level of the job market that the Sex Discrimination Act is likely to have some effect. In the unskilled/semi-skilled labour market the individual capacities of each worker are irrelevant. They are selling a general capacity to work which the employer will then control and use. What is important is the controllability of this capacity to work. If certain groups of workers have particular characteristics which enhance the ability of management to control when and how their work capacity is utilized, these characteristics will be harnessed to the production process. This is what has happened to the present family system and women's dependent position within it. It is the way that this has become

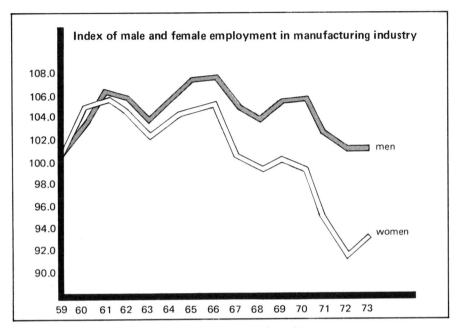

Figure 3.3   Index of Male and Female Employment in Manufacturing Industry
Source: CIS Report, *Women Under Attack* (1976), p. 11

integral to employers' labour needs that gives the lie to optimistic generalizations from the increasing presence of women in the higher echelons of British society.

THE HISTORICAL ROOTS OF THE PRESENT DIVISION OF LABOUR

So far we have concentrated on the problem of how the sexual division of labour is reproduced. Our analysis does not imply that these processes *caused* the division of labour. It merely implies that there is no automatic tendency towards its erosion within the institutions of modern capitalism. To explain the basic features of women's position we need to re-examine the transition from feudalism to capitalism. How were relations between the sexes transformed in the course of this transition between two modes of production?

Historians argue correctly that a major consequence of the industrial revolution was the destruction of the family as a unit of production. As one historian describes it: 'Each stage in industrial differentiation and specialization struck also at the family economy, disturbing customary relations between man and wife, parents and children, and differentiating more sharply between "work" and "life".'[23] But this was not simply a change whereby all those processes which in pre- and early industrial Britain came under the category of production were, in the course of industrialization, transferred from the family to the factory or office. The pre-industrial, predominantly family-based form of production involved the fusion of what later became two distinct aspects: that is, a fusion of production for some sort of exchange with production for the maintenance of the family. The dairying, care of poultry and pigs, brewing, growing of vegetables and fruit, spinning of flax and wool and other similar work that was done within the family in varying degrees, was done both for exchange and for the family's direct consumption. Similarly, future generations of producers were reared and were taught their trades in the place where those trades would be practised: within the family. They also received medical care from inside the family, usually from the mother.

For the feudal family the consequences of the growth of capitalism were not simply an increasing differentiation between 'work' and 'life'. They can be more accurately described in terms of the severing of this feudal fusion between labour involved in the production of goods and the labour required for the maintenance of human life. But factory production did not permeate the whole sphere of family production, nor did it entirely strip the family of its economic functions. In varying degrees it left the labour involved in the reproduction and maintenance of the family outside wage labour and exchange relations. This aspect of production remained within the private sphere of the family, to be carried out on the basis of the sexual division of labour in which the man — because of a pre-existing sexual division — was the main wage-earner and the woman the housewife. The housewife occasionally became a wage-earner, but this was only when the insufficiency of the man's wages coincided with employers' needs for more labour.

The fact that this sphere of housework and child-rearing was not itself directly organized according to the laws of the market and wage labour does not mean that it was not integrated into, and at various times modified by, the emerging capitalist relations of production. Essential to the wage system is the fact, referred to above, that it is the individual worker, and not the family unit, who is directly involved in the productive process. In general the family was not recognized as in any sense an economic unit. At times this was the case: wages were so low that wives and children frequently had to become individual wage labourers and the family's role in the maintenance of the labour force came near to collapse. However it was soon realized by employers and those concerned with the long-term development of their own enterprises and the economy as a whole, that this virtually complete destruction of the working-class family without alternative institutions (apart from the stopgap measure of the workhouse), undermined the health and work capacity of the present and future workforce. This realization, combined with innovations in machinery that periodically reduced employers' labour needs, led to pressures on women to give priority to their domestic obligations. These pressures included legislation which made it difficult for women to opt for a more independent existence. Between 1802 and 1898 a series of Factory Acts at first protected and then drastically reduced the employment of women. Parallel with this, and resulting from the increasing strength of the organized working-class, wages began to be successfully demanded to cover the cost of subsistence of both the worker and his dependent wife and children. The possibility of women becoming dependent home labourers was given a further material boost after the First World War by the successful campaigns for family allowances in the 1920s and 30s. But as labour needs remained either static or even below the supply of male labourers, there was very little possibility for women to break out of their position as housewives. Nor was there any impetus for the traditional role and skills of the housewife to be supplanted by labour-saving food and appliances, familiar to us since the post-war boom created a demand for labour. Similarly there was no pressure on the state to provide nursery or other facilities, until, for the duration of the Second World War, women's labour was required on a massive scale. Because of the relationship between the position of women and the rate of industrial growth the productive capacity of a family of the pre-industrial era eventually became integrated into the industrial economy. In the course of this integration the subordination of women, which in the feudal family had been characterized by authority relations rather than the nature of work, took the form of a rigid division of labour.

The above is only a brush-stroke picture of the division of labour as expressed in the division between domestic and wage labour. These processes of industrial development also shaped the division expressed within the labour market. Before the development of modern production methods women worked in almost every type of trade, industry and agriculture. For example, until the Colliery Act of 1842 women worked in the mines, pushing wagonloads of coal along the underground rail track to the bottom on the shaft, or landing, weighing, picking and screening, although not hewing, the coal. Until the decline of family industry in the course of the seventeenth and eighteenth centuries women were working as blacksmiths, metal workers, printers, bakers, millers, brewers, spinners and many other crafts, trades and professions in whose modern workshops women play little or no role. Through this productive activity they made their independent contribution to the prosperity of their families. The idea that a man should maintain his wife through his own work, while she was restricted to production purely for domestic consumption, was rarely accepted. The business responsibilities that women in Tudor England took on in the absence or incompetence of their husbands, the skilled work that craftswomen performed in a variety of fields, the heavy manual work carried out in agriculture and mining, all demonstrate the historically specific nature of the present division between the sexes.[24]

What precisely were the processes which in the course of industrial development laid the foundations of the present occupational division of labour by both squeezing women completely out of particular trades and by relegating them to unskilled work through which it was impossible to earn sufficient for an independent life? The expansion of the productive forces and the disruptive effects of this on feudal family relationships had differing consequences for the situation of women according to the economic position of the family. In the case of the wealthiest families who, through an intermixing of political position and landed wealth with merchant prosperity and business acumen, were in the vanguard of capitalist expansion, the energetic life of the Elizabethan business partner and wife gave way to the leisurely, ornamental existence of the Restoration lady. The growth of surplus wealth meant that owners of large amounts of capital were no longer themselves required to engage in the productive process. Women were therefore no longer needed to fulfil the managerial functions that they had previously performed *on the basis of their marriage.* They were replaced by men who were hired *on a commercial basis* to manage estates and finances. The possession of a purely decorative wife, or in less wealthy families a wife solely engaged in feathering the domestic nest, gradually became an important symbol of wealth and success; in fact so much so that not only capitalists but also higher-paid wage-earners became proud to have a wife whose energies were devoted primarily to strengthening the family as a private haven.

Just as in the case of wealthy families the downfall of the woman was primarily a result of work deriving from a marriage relationship being replaced, in all but an increasingly narrow domestic sphere, by work performed through commercial relationships, so it was in the case of the craftswoman. Whereas in the past marriage had involved her directly in production, with the spread of hired managerial skill her marriage relationship became an obstacle to any involvement. There were three main aspects of this change: first, because a woman's involvement in the craft or trade was generally dependent on the possibility of work in the home, the move towards factory production made it more and more difficult for her to undertake many types of work. The constraining effects of domestic commitments were reinforced by the fact that it was her husband who had learnt the craft through an apprenticeship and therefore had the formal qualifications required by the employer for skilled work. The woman had usually only learnt from experience, and the replacement of rules of custom by formal rules of capitalist production meant that she could not enter the skilled sectors of production. For example, even in the case of baking where in the past women's domestic experience stood them in good stead as skilled workers, it became increasingly rare to find women involved except at the most menial level. A second factor, closely related to the customary way in which women learned their trade through family relationships, was that when craftsmen began to organize themselves in order to protect their interests from encroachment by employers, they made use of the remains of guild organization to restrict their numbers and therefore to force wages up. This involved tightening the rules governing skill qualifications, and lengthening the period of apprenticeships. This further strengthened the process whereby, when trying to maintain some degree of economic independence, women were faced with increasingly limited, unskilled and unlucrative options. The effect of this pressure is further demonstrated by the fact that the few crafts which were initially dominated by women, such as upholstery, millinery and brewing, had particularly weak forms of guild organization. Thus, in general, by the beginning of the nineteenth century a woman in a skilled job was a rare exception. Furthermore, the higher wages that skilled male workers obtained through increased organization gave their wives a means of subsistence through dependence on the husband's wage, which in the past would have been inconceivable. This materially aided their subjective adaption to, and acceptance of, the job market which could give them neither the monetary nor the psychological satisfaction necessary to make working outside the home a permanent part of their lives. So the elimination of the craftswoman laid foundations for women becoming a flexible, unskilled reserve labour force.

In the case of the poorest families who even before the spread of mass wage labour, being unable to sell the products of their labour directly on the market, were partially dependent on wages, the effects of capitalist development depended on the position of their industry in the British economy. The different industries, of which spinning was a necessary part, illustrate this relationship well. As a result of the Industrial Revolution the linen and the silk industries declined and it was no longer possible for a large number of female spinners, who had earned at least part of their living, to secure a subsistence wage from working in these industries. The women who had previously gained some minimal independence through their spinning joined the growing numbers of paupers dependent on the parish and on their husbands and were obliged to act as a reserve labour force for employers wanting sweated labour or menial domestic servants. However, in the wool industry, the major growth-point of early British capitalism, the situation was very different. Here there was a high demand for labour and although wages were not commensurate with this demand, nevertheless it was possible for women to earn a living wage for themselves and their children from spinning wool.

These factors constitute the beginnings of the sexual division within the occupational structure, the continuity of which has not been persistently challenged until now. These divisions arose, not from some egalitarian Golden Age but from a society in which patriarchy was deeply entrenched. However, the economic relations of which this patriarchy was a part did entail the involvement of women in all levels of production even though it was on the basis of their marital relationship. The new economic relations of capitalism undermined the productive relevance of this relationship and as a result women were squeezed out of business, out of the majority of skilled trades, and out of the professions whose new scientific basis undermined the custom-based medical and teaching practice that were almost exclusively women's role in pre-capitalist Britain. These were the foundations of man's world and woman's secondary place within it. The continuity underlying this emergence and consolidation of the division of labour is that whereas the growth of capitalism broke the direct connection that women, on the basis of familial relationships, had with all levels of production, it never permanently upset the way in which those same relationships tied women to private domestic labour. The commitments of this labour have therefore persistently constrained women from any thoroughgoing challenge to the dominant position that men achieved in productive work after the disintegration of family industry.

CONTRADICTIONS AND ALTERNATIVES

The central argument of this chapter has been that the unequal position of women in modern Britain is a product of the division, on a sexual basis, between social labour for the market and private labour for immediate consumption within the family. This sex-based separation has its roots in the transition from feudal to capitalist Britain. More specifically the basis for the *present form* of women's subordination (the argument does not imply that this is the only form, or that sex inequality is unique to capitalist societies) was established with the growth of an economy in which the capacity to work became a commodity, controlled by those with the wealth to buy it. The crucial link between this and the sexual division of labour is that employers have only been concerned about the workers' capacity to work; as long as this is adequate they, and the state also, have no interest in how the commodity is reproduced. This is left to the private labours of women within the family; others only intervene when the quality and supply of labour power require modification. The analysis has briefly sketched the origins of these structures and the ways in which they transformed the lives of women in all classes. It has also traced the different ways in which this basic sex division has been reinforced by the contemporary institutions which shape people's day-to-day choices. In conclusion, the analysis will now identify the sources of conflict in these relationships and the growing challenges and alternatives which women are creating out of such conflicts.

The fundamental source of instability lies in the breakdown of the sex boundaries between social and domestic labour; that is, the mass entry of married women into the labour market. (The boundaries were never entirely complete but were sufficient to appear natural.) The destabilizing effects of this breakdown are not immediately apparent: they do not lie in obvious institutional clashes nor simply in the strains and tensions experienced by women engaged in both forms of labour. On the contrary, as already noted, the organization of industry, backed directly and indirectly by the state, has been able to base its requirements for female labour on women's commitments in the home. The partial breakdown of the separation appears only to have produced a new harmonious articulation, inherent in capitalism's use of women as a source of cheap flexible labour.

The contradiction lies in the fact that, on the one hand, employers can only have women's labour on essentially the same contractual basis as men's, that is they have to turn women into wage labourers, free to sell their labour power to the highest bidder and with access to all the political and economic rights of wage labourers; while on the other hand, employers depend on the specific obligations and constraints which women face outside of production and which partially negate their position as wage labourers. The significance of this is seen by contrasting the position of women with that of migrant workers, the other major source of reserve labour for European capitalism. Capitalism has been able to deny to the migrant worker, implicitly or explicitly, all the citizenship and trade union rights which have been conceded to other wage labourers. It has been able to separate migrant workers socially, culturally and industrially from the traditions and organizations which have established these rights.[25] Thus not only is the migrant worker's freedom to sell his labour power constrained by relations extraneous to his relation with his employer, but his relationship to his employer is itself only formally one of a wage labourer to a buyer of labour power. The employer's control is over the *labourer himself*, not merely over his labour power. This makes the relationship closer to one of short-term slavery. Thus the relations involved in the migrant's situation have tended to be one unbroken set of unfree relations. In the case of women, however, there is a greater disjuncture created between her rights as a wage labourer and the constraints she faces as a housewife. In spite of all the obstacles from employers and trade unions alike, as a wage labourer she has begun to utilize her trade union and political rights to make the elementary demands which are almost inherent in the condition of being a wage labourer: the demand for a living wage and secure employment. The rising rate of increase in the number of women involved in strike action is an illustration of the over-riding strength of the pressures, expectations and traditions that induce women to make these demands and thus prevent employers from having the best of both worlds.

The assertion by women workers of their basic rights and necessities as individual wage workers and the implied challenge to the assumption that natural family commitments make women a special and subordinate group, have not automatically produced a direct questioning of the conditions for these commitments. But the widespread and increasingly intransigent fight for equality at work has made the sex-based nature of housework and child care increasingly seem an anomaly within many working-class families. This has not radically altered the peripheral involvement of men in domestic labour but it is beginning to encourage the treatment of housework and child care as a social problem of concern to the labour movement as a whole. An equal distribution of housework within the family is not a realistic solution. The work involved is too great for two full-time wage-earners — or even one part-time — to share. Consequently a new need, the need for resources to reorganize housework on a more collective social basis, is being defined and expressed; new demands are found on the agenda of the labour movement. Almost all the major unions, on paper, support demands for day nursery facilities in addition to demands for equality at work. About ten unions have given support to the

Working Women's Charter which contains demands for freely available abortion facilities on the NHS and for full maternity and paternity leave.

This slowly-increasing trend towards treating housework as in some sense a collective responsibility is also indicated at a practical level by the way that child-care facilities are now provided as part of the normal arrangements for conferences and meetings. But this is not enough. The reorganization of housework is low on the list of priorites for the labour movement; it is not thoroughly integrated into pay demands, into struggles against unemployment and into programmes for a welfare state qualitatively transformed to meet social needs. Resistance by the Government to such demands is increasingly strong now that the British economy faces the long-term prospect of chronic economic crisis. Yet at the same time women are becoming increasingly confident in fighting for social solutions to the problems which used to drive them to tranquillizers and other personal solutions. Women have therefore been taking independent action and dragging others behind them. Council offices, university and polytechnic administration blocks have been occupied by women demanding nursery facilities. Centres have been created in almost every major town through which women have coordinated their struggles, supported each other and reached out to women just beginning to reject their traditional position. The increasing consciousness among women has generated alternatives at an ideological level, in literature — including school books — history, films, music and in personal relationships.

Once their domestic role is questioned by women themselves all the institutions and assumptions which have historically given it credibility begin to be revealed and confronted. A central assumption is that of a necessary bond between sexuality and procreation, enforced practically in abortion legislation and the organization of contraceptive facilities. The bond is no longer primarily biological; it is based on the moral and social relations of family and marriage. The demand of women to control their own sexuality and fertility involves a direct rejection of the bond. The growing number of women who are making this rejection is indicated by the size of the movement which mobilized demonstrations of 20,000 against recent attempts to strengthen this bond by further restrictions on abortion facilities.

Within every area of social life, from nursery and primary schools to the health service, housing, the unions and political organizations, women are identifying and challenging all the ways in which everyday activities and institutions are based on the secondary position of women. This challenge is organized through networks of loosely linked groups and journals. Its strength is diffused but this is partly a function of the ways in which the sexual division of labour is sustained. That is, it is not sustained only by the institutions of the state. The terrain is therefore not one for a focused political movement in the normal sense.

The above analysis implies that political transformation is a necessary condition for the elimination of the sexual division of labour. But for such a transformation to be effective it can only be a culmination of resistance to institutions and ideas deeply rooted in areas of private and social life which, until they are challenged, appear unconnected with politics. It is partly for this reason that the Sex Discrimination Act is having little impact. It only skims the surface. It does not entail a threat to the groundwork of sex inequality which it has been the purpose of this chapter to understand.

Notes to Chapter 3

1 This is documented in detail in Ann Oakley, *The Sociology of Housework* (London 1974), ch. 1.
2 *Social Trends* (HMSO 1972 and 1974).
3 J.S.Mill, *The Subjection of Women* (1869, Everyman edn. 1970).
4 This approach was not shared by an important section of the suffragette movement, notably the East London Federation of Suffragettes, led by Sylvia Pankhurst. Their demand for the vote entailed a more thoroughgoing challenge to the secondary position of women.
5 See Jean Coussins, *The Equality Report* (London 1976) for a thoroughly documented analysis of the inadequacies revealed in the implementation of this legislation. See also P.Ashdown-Sharp, 'Women's Rights: the missed opportunity' in the *Sunday Times* (20 February 1977).
6 F.Parkin's *Class, Inequality and Political Order* (London 1971) provides the clearest illustration of this.
7 The analysis of J.Westergaard and H.Resler in *Class in a Capitalist Society* (Penguin edn. 1975) starts from this limitation. It therefore concludes that sex inequality merely 'accentuates class divisions' (ch. 6). There is no hint that sex inequality is a product of social divisions which are distinct from, though related to, class divisions; its basis is referred to merely in terms of 'handicaps' and 'sex discrimination'.
8 This involves a contrasting emphasis to that of Engels in *The Origins of the Family* (London 1940). Engels stresses the process of inheritance through the male line as the basis of women's subordination. He traces this back to the origins of surplus wealth and class divisions. Surplus wealth developed in the sphere of male labour in primitive society. It consequently gave men the power to overthrow the matriarchal and matrilineal family relations which according to Engels characterized pre-class societies. This overthrow of inheritance according to the female line of descent was thus, in Engels' words 'the world historical defeat of the female sex'. Our analysis would imply, in terms of a debate with Engels, that the 'world historical defeat of the female sex' came with the *separation of the labours of production for immediate need from those of production for exchange*. (See pp. 197–201). This would tend to entail inheritance through the male line because only the man would usually be directly involved in the processes of investment and accumulation. But patrilineal inheritance would thus only be a product of a more basic structure — a structure which is most apparent among those directly involved in production.
9 M.Young and P.Wilmott, *The Symmetrical Family* (London 1973), p. 183.
10 Office of Manpower Economics, *Report on Equal Pay Act* (1972).

11   This rule, according to calculations reported in *Women's Report* (March–
     April 1976), deprives at least 8,000 mothers and 1,000 widows of their
     benefits and pensions every year. Moreover, there is little sign that the rule
     will be modified: the Supplementary Benefits Commission has just produced
     a defence of the basic principles behind it in *Living Together as Husband and
     Wife* (HMSO 1976).

12   William Beveridge, *Report on Social Insurance and Allied Services,* Cmnd 6484
     (HMSO 1968), pp. 49, 52–3; for a fuller analysis of the welfare state's relation
     to women, see Elizabeth Wilson, *Women and the Welfare State* (London 1977).

13   M.Mead, *Male and Female* (Penguin edn. 1962).

14   R.Hartley, 'A developmental view of female sex-role identification' in J.Biddle
     and E.J.Thomas (eds) *Role Theory* (Chichester 1966); J.Kagan and H.A.Moss,
     Birth to Maturity: a study in psychological development (Chichester 1967).

15   A very clear and sympathetic account of Freud's theory of femininity and
     masculinity – from one feminist viewpoint – is given by Juliet Mitchell in
     Psychoanalysis and Feminism (London 1974).

16   See J.Kamm, *Hope Deferred: girls' education in English history* (London
     1965).

17   Schools Council Working Paper, No. 45 (London 1972).

18   Maria Loftus, 'Learning, Sexism and Femininity' in *Red Rag,* 7 (June 1974).

19   For a fuller description of the patterns of sexist ideology in education see
     ch. 4 of Sue Sharpe, *Just Like a Girl* (Penguin 1976).

20   For a detailed discussion of this see H.Braverman, *Labour and Monopoly
     Capital* (New York 1974), especially ch. 15.

21   For a vivid and detailed description of the relations of unfreedom enslaving
     the migrant worker, see J.Berger and J.Mohr, *A Seventh Man* (Penguin edn.
     1975).

22   Counter Information Services, *Women Under Attack* (London 1976).

23   E.P.Thompson, *The Making of the English Working Class* (Penguin edn. 1968).

24   Alice Clark, *The Working Life of Women in the Seventeenth Century* (1919,
     reprinted London 1968). Most of the information in this section comes from
     this invaluable book.

25   See J.Berger and J.Mohr, *A Seventh Man.* This situation is also being challenged
     as migrant workers become organized, catalysed by the political struggles of
     their fellow workers and peasants at home in Portugal, Spain and Greece.

4

Elites and Privilege

INTRODUCTION

The term 'elite' retains a distinctively Gallic ring even when printed in English without its accent (a practice that has only quite recently become usual). The importation of the term was an indirect one, however, since it was the Italian writers Pareto and Mosca who more than any others were responsible for popularizing it as a concept in social and political analysis. In the works of these two authors, the notion of elite was introduced to support a critique of Marxist theories of class and class domination. Such theories tie together economic and political power in a way which Pareto and Mosca found unacceptable, and, moreover, they envisage the coming of a form of society in which, through the transcendence of classes, the domination of man over man will be overcome. Against these views they developed the thesis that in all societies, apart from perhaps the most simple and small-scale, there exists an irremediable division between those who exercise power — political elites — and those who are subjected to it; while the composition of elites may change, the domination of the mass by a minority of power holders is as inevitable in a socialist society as it is in a capitalist one.

It is not the purpose of this chapter to examine such all-embracing issues; we refer to them here only briefly in order to trace some main strands in the history of the concept of elite, and thereby to develop a clear framework within which to analyse elites in British society. For while they made use of the notion of elite in order to criticize class theory, the classical elite theorists also retained the terminology of class, using 'political class' as equivalent to 'ruling elite', thereby helping to propagate conceptual confusions which have dogged work in this field for decades.

Following the classical elite theorists, the notion of elite has been used in three contrasting contexts. First, the concept has been adopted and adapted by numerous authors of the 'pluralist' persuasion who have used it to make arguments which diverge substantially from those involved in both classical elite theory and in Marxism. In their writings, elites appear as fragmented groups each of whose power is limited by that of the others. Some of these writers recognize that a ruling class existed in nineteenth-century capitalism, but hold that it has long since become splintered into a series of distinct and often competitive elites. Second, the concept of elite has been taken up by certain authors — most notably C. Wright Mills — who have retained the idea of a unitary, dominant elite, but have given this quite a different moral thrust to that of classical elite theory, the implications of which were expressly reactionary.[1] Mills, however, explicitly distinguished his 'power elite' from the Marxist 'ruling class' on the same sort of grounds that the classical elite theorists had done, namely that the latter notion assimilates political and economic power.[2] Finally, the term elite has been used by some Marxists themselves to refer to sectional groups within the ruling class.[3]

If all this were not confusing enough, the notion of elites has also been at the centre of a debate of a methodological kind: that concerned with problems arising from the empirical study of power. Writers of all persuasions have been interested in examining elite formations in order to analyse the distribution of power within national or local communities. But there has been no clear consensus as to how this should be accomplished. Many studies depend upon the so-called 'positional' method, in which elites are simply defined in terms of formal positions of authority, e.g., cabinet ministers, directors of large companies, high-ranking civil servants, etc.[4] Others have been strongly critical of this sort of approach, and have insisted that authority must not be defined as power, and that elites should be regarded as clusters of effective power-holders, regardless of whatever formal authority they may hold.[5]

The controversies generated by elite studies have often been obscured by conceptual ambiguities, and in the face of these it is important to insist upon a number of elementary distinctions. In what follows we shall use the term 'elite' in a very general sense to refer to those occupying high positions of authority within an organization, without in any way prejudging the issue of how far that authority reflects the actual power they may wield. Elites thus defined may be examined from three angles. First, in respect of processes of recruitment to elite positions: the kinds of social background from which the members of elite groups are drawn, and the factors that characteristically influence the progress of their careers. Second, in respect of the integration of elites: which includes an examination not only of the interconnections that exist between the members of particular elites and between different elite groups, but also an inquiry into the extent of ethical or ideological solidarity within and between elite groups. Finally, it is important to seek as far as possible to analyse in a direct way whatever types of power may rest in the hands of those in elite positions. The latter implies studying the capability of such individuals to take or to influence major decisions in conformity with definite sets of interests. But it is a mistake to suppose that this exhausts the study of power relations. Power is mediated not only through decision-making, but through structures which express asymmetries of life chances, and which form the parameters within which certain issues are 'decisionable', and others are not.[6] This reunites 'elite' and 'class', which in this discussion we shall treat as independent but equally useful concepts: the recruitment, integration and power of elite groups represent important aspects of class structuration, and it is fundamental to connect them with the reproduction of privilege in the class system.[7]

In this chapter, we shall concentrate upon certain major themes suggested by the foregoing remarks: starting with a discussion of wealth and property, then proceeding to look at aspects of elite recruitment, integration and power in some key spheres of British society.

THE DISTRIBUTION OF WEALTH AND PROPERTY

Personal Wealth in General

Trends in the distribution of income between occupations are discussed elsewhere in this book but income is not as relevant to the study of elites as is wealth. To begin with, wealth is a main source of income for the most affluent sections of the population — much more so than vice versa. But more important than this, wealth in the form of property in the means of production is central to any examination of the relationship between elites and classes.

The total personal wealth in Britain in 1973 was estimated at something over £163,000 million.[8] This overall stock of wealth divides about equally into physical and financial assets. Most of the former consists of housing and land. The latter is composed of shareholdings, savings in banks and building societies; and pensions and life insurance policies. If the total of personal wealth as identified in 1973 had been allocated equally among adult members of the population, the average holding would have been £4,000. In fact the actual distribution of wealth contrasts dramatically with such a hypothetical state of affairs: a small fraction of the population owns a very substantial proportion of the overall amount of personal wealth in this country.

While there is no dispute that the general pattern in the distribution of wealth is one of concentration, there is, however, considerable controversy about the precise facts of the matter, and especially about whether or not there has been a trend towards the diffusion of wealth downwards from the most privileged groups over the past several decades. All analyses of the distribution of wealth in Britain rest upon estimates from inadequate evidence — a major reason why a Royal Commission has been established recently to examine wealth-holding in detail. Two modes of estimating the distribution of wealth are ordinarily recognized: one depending upon information derived from estate duties at death, the other using projections from investment income. The first is perhaps the more adequate, although it still involves difficulties.

Even if the calculations involved in fig. 4.1 are only roughly valid, it is clear that personal-wealth-holding is very highly concentrated. According to official estimates published by the Inland Revenue (Series B), the top 1 per cent of the adult population (those having £44,000 or above in 1973) own nearly 30 per cent of the total personal wealth; the top 5 per cent (those having £15,900 or more) own over 50 per cent. The vast majority of the population, 80 per cent of the people in this country, have at their disposal little more than a third of its wealth. It is possible that such estimates exaggerate to some degree the level of concentration among top wealth-holders, since among other factors they exclude pensions and life insurance benefits, which are important sources of wealth for the less privileged majority. The effects of these factors are also shown in fig. 4.1. But such effects are at least partly counterbalanced by the capacity of top wealth-holders to escape the full force of estate duty — legally, by the setting up of trusts (recently foreclosed), the making of gifts, etc.; and illegally, through modes of tax evasion more accessible to the wealthy than to the mass of the population. The investment income method of estimating the spread of wealth in fact seems to suggest a higher concentration among the most privileged minority than the first, more usual method of making such calculations. The investment income method involves making projections from known income from capital. According to one such study, in the financial year 1959–60, the top 5 per cent of the population possessed over 70 per cent of the total personal wealth, and the top 10 per cent owned over 90 per cent.[9]

The staggering economic inequalities which these figures indicate would perhaps come less abruptly into opposition with the widespread assumption that the variety of taxation and other measures introduced by successive governments over the

Alternative estimates of the percentage shares of personal wealth owned by given quantile groups of the total population aged 18 and over

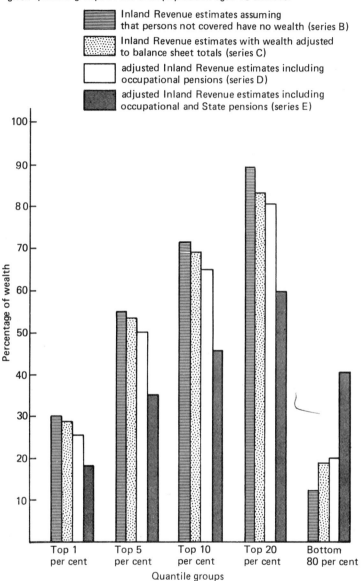

Figure 4.1   Distribution of Personal Wealth on Alternative Bases, GB, 1972
Source: Royal Commission on the Distribution of Wealth, Cmnd 6172, p. 144

course of this century have stimulated a process of levelling, if it could be shown that there has been a long-term trend for the concentration of wealth to become less pronounced. Whether or not such a trend is discernable has been hotly debated. Available information is so inadequate that the issue cannot readily be settled.

TABLE 4.1

Trends in the distribution of personal wealth up to 1973, England and Wales

Percentage shares of personal wealth owned by given quantile groups of the population aged 25 and over, assuming that persons not covered by the estate duty returns have no wealth; at specified dates between 1911 and 1973

(Series B)

Quantile group	Percentage share of personal wealth					
	1911–13	1924–30	1936–8	1954	1960	1973[1]
	%	%	%	%	%	%
Top 1 per cent	69	62	56	43	42	27.6
2– 5 per cent	18	22	23	28	33	23.7
6– 10 per cent	5	7	9	8	8	15.9
11–100 per cent	8	9	12	21	17	32.8
(Cumulative basis)						
Top 1 per cent	69	62	56	43	42	27.6
Top 5 per cent	87	84	79	71	75	51.3
Top 10 per cent	92	91	88	79	83	67.2

Note:
1 The figures for 1960 and 1973 are, strictly speaking, not comparable but they do not alter the gist of the argument
Sources: J. Revell, 'Changes in the social distribution of property in Britain during the twentieth century', 3rd international conference of economic history, Munich 1965; and Royal Commission on Wealth and Income, *Report No. 1*, p. 102

On the face of it there would appear to have been a marked diffusion of wealth downwards: the figures in table 4.1 indicate that the share of the wealthiest 1 per cent has declined substantially over the period of the last sixty years. The three sets of figures in the middle of the table suggest, however, that most of the wealth lost by the leading 1 per cent has not been redistributed broadly, but remains heavily concentrated among the top 5 per cent. Their share has markedly increased over time up to 1960 at least; the share of the top 2–10 per cent until very recently accounted for virtually all of the wealth spread downwards from the richest 1 per cent. Between 1911 and 1960 the share of wealth held by the top 1 per cent fell from 69 per cent to 42 per cent, the share of the next 9 per cent of wealth-holders rose from 23 per cent to 41 per cent. Between 1960 and 1973 the share of the top 1 per cent fell to 27.61 per cent and that of the next 9 per cent to 39.6 per cent. As Atkinson says: '. . . it seems therefore that what redistribution there has been is not between the rich and the poor, but between the very rich and the rich'.[10] The significance of this is a matter of some dissension. The most obvious and likely explanation of a substantial proportion of this transfer is that it reflects the passing on of wealth *inter vivos*, to heirs or relatives. Some indirect evidence supports this view which if correct would imply that the seemingly greater spread of wealth expressed in the statistics represents in large part only its diffusion among families prior to inheritance. The proportion of younger men among the top wealth-holders has risen in recent years, as one would expect on this interpretation: and so has that of women, which suggests that property may be settled upon wives by the wealthy as well as distributed among heirs. Inheritance nevertheless clearly remains of central importance in the continuing concentration of wealth. Recent studies indicate that about three-quarters of those leaving estates of £100,000 or more had inherited at least £10,000 from their fathers and about half had inherited £50,000 or more. Judged by the criterion of estates of £100,000 or more, very few of the wealthy are self-made men, although many began with only a modest amount of inherited wealth, i.e., one-tenth or so of the sum they themselves bequeathed. Over the past few decades there has been no tendency for the proportion of self-made men to increase.[11]

Sources of Capital Investment

A discussion of the distribution of wealth would be incomplete if it did not include an analysis of capital investment — the key form of private property tied into economic power. Investment may be of various kinds: deposits in banks and building societies, insurance policies, government bonds or shareholdings in companies. As the foundation of private enterprise capitalism company shareholdings are of crucial significance, and these represent by far the most concentrated form of wealth. According to the research of Lydall and Tipping, the top 1 per cent of the rich in 1954 owned over 80 per cent of privately owned corporate shares: the top 5 per cent owned 98 per cent.

TABLE 4.2

Concentration of ownership of different assets, 1954

	Percentage owned by top:		
	1%	5%	10%
Cash and bank deposits	23	48	64
Government securities	42	71	83
Land, buildings and trade assets	28	58	74
Company stocks and shares	81	96	98
Total personal wealth	43	68	79

Source: H.F. Lydall and D.G. Tipping, 'The distribution of personal wealth in Britain', *Bulletin of Oxford University Institute of Economics and Statistics*, 23 (1961) table V

Levels of concentration fall considerably when we look at other types of assets listed in the table: these are distributed more comparably to wealth as a whole. Studies concerned with the examination of the relative possession of different types of assets in the portfolios of various categories of wealth-holders, show that the wealthier groups have a higher proportion of their assets as shares. Those having between £5,000 and £10,000 in personal wealth, for example, in 1973 had only 4.5 per cent of their assets in the form of company shares and securities, and 53.2 per cent as cash and bank deposits, building society deposits and National Savings. On the other hand, persons having £54,000–100,000 had over 32.4 per cent of their assets in shares and securities, and only 20.7 per cent in cash and bank deposits.[12]

It is often argued that even if wealth in Britain remains highly concentrated, this is not of great consequence for other aspects of privilege, since property ownership has declined significantly in importance both in the means whereby individuals reach elite positions, and in relation to the power they are thus able to command. This view is expressed in various convergent threads of social theory that centre on the idea of the *obsolescence of private property* in advanced, industrialized countries. It is not that property disappears, but, it is claimed, it becomes progressively less salient to the central features of the social organization of the advanced societies.[13] We believe, however, that the unequal concentration of private wealth remains of basic importance in the social structure of Britain, with respect to each of the aspects of elite formation: recruitment, integration and power – and that these in turn reflect broader aspects of the class structure that also depend upon the continued significance of private property.

ELITE RECRUITMENT

Studies of the social background of elites in British society traditionally focus on the proportions of those in elite positions who were educated at public schools and Oxford or Cambridge, or both, as compared to those having other types of educational experience. The method has received a considerable amount of criticism, some of it justified. It has been rightly pointed out that shared educational experience in a particular type of school does not necessarily generate a coherent ethos or culture among elite groups; nor on the whole does it follow that because individuals are drawn from a common and distinctive sort of background they will necessarily promote qualities that favour the interests of the social groups to which they belong. But despite these qualifications the study of the educational background of the members of elite groups is still highly important. If it does not prove an overall coherence of views and interests, the demonstration of shared educational experience is certainly relevant to a possible coherence.

But quite apart from this, available material about the social origins of the members of elite groups is often sketchy. The differentiation of public school education from the state sector of education provides a useful complement to whatever direct information about social origins is available. There is only a tiny minority of non-fee-paying boys in public schools, and we can be confident that a public school education usually indicates that a person is not of lowly social origins, especially if he or she was educated at one of the more prestigious public schools. Since a high proportion of Oxbridge students have traditionally been drawn from the public schools, it can be presumed that attendance at Oxford or Cambridge (especially prior to 1939) is also a general indicator of social background, although as a criterion this is obviously more fallible than attendance at public school.

There is available a range of studies of recruitment to elite positions in the major institutional spheres in Britain: the church, the armed forces, the judiciary, Civil Service, Parliament and banking. Comparable information on business elites has hitherto been lacking, but we are now able to draw upon new material collected in the Cambridge Elites Study.[14]

The Church

The most detailed study of the social origins of the higher clergy in the Church of England is by Morgan. Surveying the background of diocesan bishops over the years from 1940–59, he concluded that 64 per cent were of aristocratic origin, the higher ranks of industry and the professions, or were from ecclesiastical families.[15] A longer-term study giving the social origins of bishops from 1860–1960 shows, as would be anticipated, that the proportion coming from aristocratic or landed families declined markedly from over one-third in 1860 to 2 per cent in 1960. But this is counterbalanced by the rise in the proportion of those drawn from a professional or higher administrative background. These figures also show that the percentage of bishops whose fathers were clergymen has substantially increased over the period.[16] It would seem fairly clear that as the church has moved nearer to the margins of secular power in its recruitment its elite has become more specifically ecclesiastical. Yet it has nevertheless retained a strong exclusiveness. Thus there has developed a more marked contrast between the episcopate and the lower clergy; only just over one quarter of the latter (1960–2) have been educated at public schools, compared to 85 per cent of the bishops.[17]

The Armed Forces

One of the difficulties in examining the social origins of members of different elites is that the available studies often use discrepant classifications of occupational or class backgrounds. While such research demonstrates very strikingly that the elite in all the major British institutions are drawn overwhelmingly from privileged strata, direct comparisons are usually impossible. Thus Otley's study of the recruitment of army officers of the rank of lieutenant-general or above shows that in 1959 39 per cent were the sons of 'land-owners or entrepreneurs', and an additional 44 per cent were the sons of higher professionals and managers. Before the Second World War the proportions were 40 per cent and 54 per cent respectively so there has been little change.[18] An overlapping study by Abrams found that 32 per cent of lieutenant-generals or above in 1960 were either 'upper' or 'upper-middle class' in origin, including in the first category those from titled families or first-generation relations of such families; and in the second those from families listed in *Burke's Landed Gentry* or from a 'high professional' background. A further 28 per cent, however, were traced to other professional or managerial origins.[19]

The army elite is dominated by those of public school education. In 1970 86 per cent of officers of the rank of major-general or above had attended public school, a notably higher proportion than in 1939 (64 per cent). The percentage of officers educated at Oxford or Cambridge also rose from a mere 3 per cent in 1939 to 24 per cent in 1970. Only 8 per cent were graduates of other universities in 1970 – most of Scottish universities. The internal career provided by the Royal Military Academy, Sandhurst, has however retained the pre-eminent position. In 1970 about one-third of major-generals or higher had been educated there.[20] Sandhurst seems to be undergoing a definite widening of its recruitment base at the present time, a trend which is too recent to be reflected yet in the highest ranks, but is probably associated with the declining attractiveness or prestige of a military career.[21]

The highest levels of the navy and air force are less solidly recruited from those of public school or Oxbridge background than the corresponding ranks in the army.

Nevertheless, in 1971 two-thirds of the air force officers of the rank of air vice-marshal and above had attended public schools — a proportion virtually unchanged since 1939. Public school education is much less prominent in the navy, largely it seems because of the influence of Dartmouth Naval College, through which over half of the top leadership has passed.[22]

The Judiciary

Assessed in terms of social origin and educational background the judiciary is probably the most exclusive of all elite groups in Britain. A recent study shows that over the period 1951—68 77 per cent of judges were recruited from what the researcher called 'upper class' and 'upper middle-class' backgrounds. Since the relevant information was unavailable for 14 per cent of the total, this leaves only 9 per cent who originated from what were designated as of 'lower middle-class' (8 per cent) and 'working-class' (1 per cent) origin. If these proportions have changed over the years, it is towards a slight increase in exclusivity of origin rather than the reverse. Over the five decades from 1876 to 1920, for example, 72 per cent of judges were drawn from the upper or upper middle classes as identified in the study, 8 per cent from the lower middle class, and 1 per cent from the working class, with the remainder unknown.[23]

There is an extraordinarily high level of internal recruitment between the generations within the judiciary and the legal profession as a whole; this has increased across the years. In 1900—9, 18 per cent of judges were from families in which either their father or an uncle had been a judge; in 1960—9, 29 per cent were from such families. This tendency is highest for the elite within the elite — principal judges. Fully 20 per cent of these men in 1960—9 had fathers or uncles who had been judges before them. The level of internal recruitment is much higher still if analysed in terms of the legal profession in general, and also rises in this century. Thus in 1900—9, 43 per cent of judges (principal and High Court judges) had fathers in the legal profession; by 1960—9 this had risen to 52 per cent![24]

In 1960—9 well over three-quarters of judges had received their education in public schools. 81 per cent of the principal judges were of public school background — a figure which has remained fairly stable since the 1920s, although climbing to a peak of 92 per cent in 1940—9. A notable phenomenon is the number of the judiciary who were educated at one of a handful of major public schools: In 1960—9 over 40 per cent of the principal judges had been to one of these so-called 'Clarendon Schools'.[25] In 1960—9 about 80 per cent of judges had studied at Oxford or Cambridge.

The Civil Service

Alone among the institutions discussed here, entry to the Civil Service is based upon success in public examinations. There used to be two methods of entry. Method 1 was the more traditional, and consisted of a written examination plus an interview. Method 2 was created after the Second World War, and involved a series of interviews and other techniques of evaluation; it has now wholly replaced method 1, following a period in which they operated side by side.

Whether or not this is due to the use of examinations as a method of selection, the Civil Service elite does emerge as the most open, or it would be more apt to say, the least closed, of any of the professions we are analysing here. In 1967 17 per cent of civil servants of the rank of Under Secretary or above were from manual work backgrounds; almost one-third had fathers in either manual or routine non-manual occupations. The proportion of higher civil servants from such relatively humble origins has risen steadily over the past half century or so. Thus in 1929, 7 per cent of civil servants of equivalent rank to that just mentioned (Assistant Secretary and above) were from manual backgrounds, 12 per cent from manual plus non-manual origins combined.[26] The success of those from lowly backgrounds seems to be due mainly to promotion from the lower levels of the Civil Service, rather than a consequence of the examination system as such. There is some indication, however, that method 1 favoured those from less privileged backgrounds, and that therefore the abandonment of this method of entry will in some part diminish the chances of those from less privileged backgrounds.[27]

The increasing penetration of the higher echelons of the Civil Service by those from less well-to-do homes has accompanied a decline in the proportion having a public school eduction. In 1939 84 per cent of Under Secretaries or above had attended public schools; the comparable figure for 1970 was just over 60 per cent. The contribution of the grammar schools (which however underwent considerable reorganization after 1944) over this period rose from 6 per cent to 28 per cent. The influence of Oxford and Cambridge diminishes much less than that of the public schools, however, which indicates that a grammar school plus Oxbridge education is a considerable advantage in entering the Civil Service elite: with the exception of London, other universities barely appear in the picture. In 1970 2 per cent of Under Secretaries and above had attended provincial universities, 10 per cent London University, and 69 per cent Oxford or Cambridge.[28]

Unlike other professions, the Civil Service has a more limited type of elite, but this does not seem to restrict recruitment to those with a privileged social background.

TABLE 4.3

Education of Permanent Secretaries, 1900–63

	1900–19 (n53)	1920–44 (n 62)	1945–63 (n 83)
All public schools	64.2	61.3	54.2
Public school and private	73.6	80.7	74.7
Other schools or no information	26.4	19.3	25.3
Oxford Univ.	61.8 } 91.2	66.7 } 79.7	53.1 } 84.4
Camb. Univ.	29.4	13.0	31.3

Source: J.S. Harris and T.V. Garcia, 'The Permanent Secretaries: Britain's top administrators', *Public Administration Review* (March 1966), pp. 31–44

Table 4.3 shows that the proportion of Permanent Secretaries who went to public school reflects the same trend towards a diminution in exclusive recruitment as appears at the lower level of the Civil Service hierarchy. There has occurred a marked dropping-off in the percentage of Permanent Secretaries coming from the leading public schools, and the proportion with a public school background declines from 64 per cent in the 1900–19 period to 54 per cent in the post-war years. However, the role of Oxford and Cambridge appears to be more important here than in the lower ranks: the proportion of Permanent Secretaries who went to one or other of the ancient universities has consistently been between 80 and 90 per cent.

Parliament

A much greater variety of studies of the political elite has been carried out than of any of the other groups analysed in the preceding sections, and the material available on the social and educational background of politicians is more complete and detailed than any referred to so far. In discussing this, we shall consider the social backgrounds of parliamentarians as a whole and also of the elite within a parliamentary party, the Cabinet.

There have of course been massive changes in the nature of British politics since the last two decades of the nineteenth century, and we shall confront some of these more directly later in this chapter. Their basic pattern is clear enough: the decline of the landed interests in the face of the ascendancy of commercial and industrial ones, and a counterbalancing of the latter by the labour movement, which led to the enfranchisement of the working class. A graphic account of landed interests is provided in table 4.4 which illustrates the economic interests represented by MPs in the nineteenth and early twentieth centuries.

TABLE 4.4

Economic interests represented in the House of Commons, 1868–1910

Percentages

	Land-owning	Commerce and industry	Legal and professional	Others	Total (in Nos)
Conservatives					
1868	46	31	9	14	477
1874	36	38	13	13	635
1880	35	42	11	12	446
1885	23	50	16	11	442
1886	23	50	18	9	767
1892	24	49	18	9	679
1895	20	52	19	9	833
1900	20	52	18	10	832
1906	17	64	11	8	377
Jan. 1910	26	53	12	9	644
Liberals					
1868	26	50	17	7	756
1874	21	55	19	5	614
1880	20	55	19	6	786
1885	15	57	23	5	640
1886	13	58	25	4	453
1892	9	60	27	4	565
1895	9	58	29	4	371
1900	9	58	29	4	372
1906	8	65	23	4	766
Jan. 1910	7	66	23	4	541

Source: Table VIII in W.L.Guttsman, *The British Political Elite* (London 1968), p. 104; based on J.A.Thomas, *The House of Commons 1832–1901* (Cardiff 1939) and *The House of Commons 1906–11* (Cardiff 1958)

The decline in the representation of land-owning interests, and the growth of commercial and industrial ones is clear in each of the parties. But the process affected the Liberal Party most of all, which by the turn of the century had been abandoned by most of the land-owners. At this time the Liberals seemed to be at the height of their success; by just after the end of the First World War, however, the number of Liberal MPs had dropped to 115, by 1924 to 40, and by 1945 to 10. The growth of the Labour Party introduced major changes in the social composition of the House of Commons. Both Tory and Liberal MPs up to and after the turn of the century were drawn almost entirely from landed, entrepreneurial or professional backgrounds. But the first cohorts of Labour MPs were of very different origins. All 29 Labour members elected in 1906 were from a manual, working-class background – as were with one exception the 57 who entered Parliament in 1918. Ever since, there has been a marked contrast – much less notable in recent parliaments – between the backgrounds of Tory and Labour politicians; on the other hand, the distinctively working-class character of Labour parliamentary recruitment began to disappear from the middle of the 1920s onwards, as the Party came to replace the Liberals as one of the two major parties vying for office.

Table 4.5 shows the occupations followed by MPs before their election to the House of Commons. The figures indicate that while there is still a major disparity between the two parties in terms of recruitment from manual or routine non-manual jobs (1 per cent in the Conservative Party in 1970, 28 per cent in the Labour Party), between 1951 and 1970 the proportion of MPs in the Labour Party with such a background has continued to drop. An increasing proportion of Labour MPs come from professional occupations – in 1970 not far short of half of the total. The figures in table 4.5 do not adequately disclose, however, the degree to which Conservative MPs are still drawn from more privileged backgrounds than Labour MPs; if Labour is not any longer a specifically 'working class party' judged by its patterns of recruitment, it has become a 'middle-class' rather than an 'upper-class' one. Conservative members having professional careers, for example, tend to be more frequently from one of the older prestigious professions than are their Labour counterparts.

Analysis of the educational backgrounds of MPs in the two major parties shows the same trend as their occupational origins. There still are major and quite striking differences between Conservative and Labour MPs in terms of educational background. A much higher proportion of Labour than Conservative MPs have been educated within the state system; but the educational backgrounds of MPs in the two parties are nevertheless today more similar than they were fifty years ago. This can be demonstrated by comparing the educational background of MPs over the period 1918–35 with that between 1951 and 1970. In the earlier period 76 per cent of Labour MPs had only had an elementary school education (compared to 3 per cent of Tory MPs), 9 per cent were educated at public schools and no more than 8 per cent had attended Oxbridge. In the second period, the majority of Labour members (52 per cent) were grammar school educated; but 20 per cent had been to public school, and the same proportion had been at Oxford or Cambridge. Of Conservative MPs over the same period, (1951–70) 76 per cent were educated at public schools and 53 per cent at Oxbridge.[29]

The pattern of working-class recruitment among the early Labour MPs was partly reflected in Cabinet membership, but all Labour Cabinets from 1924 onwards have included a substantial proportion of individuals from the higher socio-economic

TABLE 4.5

Occupational background of Conservative and Labour MPs[1], 1951–70

Percentages

	1951		1955		1959		1964		1966		1970	
	Con.	Lab.	Con.	Lab.	Con.	Lab.	Con.	Lab.	Con.	Lab.	Con.	Lab.
Armed forces	10.0	0.7	13.7	1.0	9.9	1.2	9.2	0.6	7.5	0.8	7.2	–
Farmers	4.6	0.7	9.0	1.7	10.5	1.2	11.5	0.6	10.7	0.5	9.4	0.3
Professions	30.5	30.8	29.3	34.2	33.1	35.6	36.2	38.2	36.4	40.8	36.1	45.6
Commerce and industry	37.0	12.8	32.6	13.3	33.5	11.2	28.3	12.3	32.0	10.2	32.4	11.8
Politicians and journalists	7.8	13.2	10.5	12.2	10.2	12.4	10.2	10.7	7.5	10.5	12.1	13.2
Workers and white collars	1.5	40.6	1.4	36.7	1.4	37.2	2.3	36.0	3.6	36.1	0.9	27.5
'Private means'	8.4	–	3.2	–	1.1	–	1.3	–	2.0	–	–	–
Others	–	0.2	0.3	0.7	0.3	1.2	1.0	1.6	0.4	1.1	1.2	1.4
Total	321	295	344	278	365	258	304	317	253	363	330	287

[1]Based on statistics in respective Nuffield election surveys but occupations regrouped to allow for separate enumeration of armed forces, farmers, politicians (political organisers) and *rentiers*

Source: W. L. Guttsman, 'The British Political Elite and Class Structure' in P. Stanworth and A. Giddens (eds), *Elites and Power in British Society* (Cambridge 1974), p. 34

strata. Virtually all of those from working-class origins in Labour Cabinets have risen through the trade union movement. In the 1924 Cabinet, for example, 11 of the Ministers came from a manual working background, of whom 9 were ex-union officials; this applies to all those of working-class origin (9 again) in the 1950 Labour Cabinet of 18 members. In recent Labour Cabinets there has been a pronounced tendency for the proportion of working class members to fall as the life of the government has been extended. Johnson has noted that though working-class members were well represented in 1964, they were gradually replaced until the 1970 Cabinet comprised a much more homogeneously middle-class body of parliamentarians. Tory Cabinets by contrast have been very restricted indeed in terms both of the social and educational origins of their members.[30] Of Conservative Cabinet Ministers and others of ministerial status in 1951, for example, 36 had attended Eton or Harrow (35 per cent in the 1961 Conservative administration), and a further 34 per cent had been to one of the other 'leading 20' public schools, (32 per cent in 1961). These patterns were repeated between 1970 and 1972 when 77 per cent of Cabinet members were of public school background, and 77 per cent had attended Oxford or Cambridge University.

Industry and Finance

In the course of the Cambridge Elites Study, we have gathered material on the social and educational background of directors of the largest industrial and financial organizations in Britain over the years 1906–70. The companies studied include firms from each of the major sectors of industry (general manufacturing, shipping, oil, brewing, iron and steel and retail), the largest clearing and merchant banks, and the major insurance companies (the latter after 1946 only).[31] Table 4.6 offers a representation of the class origins of the business elite thus defined.

TABLE 4.6

Social origins of directors, 1906–70

Percentages

		1906	1920	1946	1952	1960	1970
Upper class	I	62	61	53	48	50	39
	F	78	73	71	48	69	55
Middle class	I	21	24	32	32	39	45
	F	14	17	18.5	24	24	35
Working class	I	1	0.3	3	2	2	3
	F	–	0.5	1	1	2	1
Upper Middle	I	6	10	17	16	22	27
	F	7	9	13	15	15	25
Lower middle	I	15	14	15	16	17	18
	F	7	8	6.5	9	9	10
Unknown	I	17	14	12	12	9	12
	F	8	11	9	7	6	9

Source: A. Giddens and P. Stanworth, Cambridge Elites Project (1971–4)

The financial directors are more consistently drawn from the 'upper class', as we use that term,[32] than their equivalents in industry. In both cases there occurred a decline between 1906 and 1970 in the proportion of individuals of upper-class origin, but the trend is more consistent for industrial directors. Most of the change is accounted for by the increase in the percentage of directors, both industrial and financial, drawn from 'upper middle class' backgrounds: particularly important here is a rise in the proportion of those whose fathers were in professional occupations. There is little indication of any growth in long-range mobility into the business elite over the sixty or so years covered by the study. A more detailed breakdown of the origins of those ranked as upper class in background shows that there is a fairly consistent proportion of directors of aristocratic descent during the present century (that is the sons or grandsons of Barons, Viscounts, Earls, Marquesses, and Dukes) although there has been a considerable change in the composition of the nobility since the latter part of the nineteenth century when truly industrial peers were first admitted to the House of Lords. Approximately 11 per cent of the industrial directors and 15 per cent of the financial directors in each annual sample prior to 1970 had such a family background. Similarly the proportion of directors who have inherited titles (not necessarily from their fathers, or grandfathers) remains at around 12 to 13 per cent for industrial directors and 13 to 17 per cent for financial directors. Only in 1970 is there any evidence of a decline in the proportion of directors with aristocratic origins.

There is also some evidence of a decline in the proportions of directors whose fathers had themselves sat on the boards of, or were proprietors in large businesses. Given the poor quality of information available in publicly available sources with regard to the comparative sizes of nineteenth-century industrial and financial enterprises, only data relevant to directors holding seats in the period after the Second World War is presented in table 4.7. From this fragmentary information it appears that the boardrooms that constitute the apex of the private sector of the economy are more broadly recruited in the sense that their fathers are less likely to have been on the boards of major corporations themselves. As with other elites, the elite within the elite, in this case company chairmen, have more select social backgrounds than those of their less exalted colleagues.

It seems reasonable to conclude that boardrooms have been rather more widely recruited in recent years than in the past. However the broadening of recruitment has been largely restricted to the upper echelons of the class structure. There is little evidence that this elite has opened to men whose origins are to be found in the working- or lower middle-classes.

TABLE 4.7

Directors with fathers who were directors, proprietors or partners in 'large' businesses			
	1946	1952	1960	1970
I	32.0	24.4	25.8	19.7
F	38.3	36.3	35.9	23.1

Source: A. Giddens and P. Stanworth, Cambridge Elites Project (1971–4)

Analysis of the educational background of the business elite shows an overall trend towards the increasing significance of public school and Oxbridge education

TABLE 4.8

Percentage of directors educated at various types of school and Oxford or Cambridge Universities (Birth cohorts)

		1820–39	1840–59	1860–79	1880–99	1900–19	1920–39	Total sample
Unknown	I	43.8	26.5	20.5	14.8	8.9	11.1	16.7
	F	50.0	19.2	18.0	9.0	6.8	5.2	
Local grammar Proprietary and Elementary	I	3.1	5.4	3.9	13.3	10.5	13.3	7.1
	F	7.1	3.3	1.0	8.1	9.8	5.2	
Total Public School	I	31.2	44.7	58.3	62.3	72.6	73.3	62.5
	F	32.1	47.5	75.9	76.3	78.1	79.9	
Total Clarendon	I	28.1	31.8	35.7	33.4	35.5	35.5	37.9
	F	28.6	40.8	46.5	50.7	46.5	46.6	
Privately	I	7.8	11.3	6.0	2.3	0.7	0.0	3.9
	F	3.6	10.0	2.6	1.4	0.7	0.0	
Other School	I	6.3	8.8	6.4	4.9	6.6	2.2	5.9
	F	3.6	10.0	5.2	3.8	3.4	7.8	
Oxford or Cambridge University	I	22.0	28.0	32.9	33.1	48.3	42.2	40.2
	F	24.9	39.2	44.8	47.4	58.0	52.6	
Numbers of Directors	I	64	204	283	263	304	45	1163
	F	28	120	194	211	295	116	964

Source: A. Giddens and P. Stanworth, Cambridge Elites Project (1971–4)

among both industrial and financial directors. Table 4.8 represents the distribution of types of school and university in the educational background of cohorts of directors born within the discreet periods indicated. The proportion of directors attending public schools has risen from about one third in the first cohort to three quarters in the most recent one. There is some evidence of the social differentiation of the City and industry in the consistently higher proportions of financial directors attending a Clarendon school in all cohorts but that of 1820–39. The position of Eton is particularly notable, accounting as it does for approximately one third of City directors in each annual sample taken this century. As in the case of public school education an increasing proportion of each succeeding cohort of directors attended either Oxford or Cambridge. Similarly there has been a tendency toward an education embracing both public school and Oxbridge. For instance in 1906 36.8 per cent of financial directors attended both a public school and Oxford or Cambridge, in 1970 the figure was 51.9 per cent. The chairmen of these boards have an even higher proportion of public school educated men among their number and Oxbridge scholars than do the bulk of the already selectively educated directors.

Therefore, despite the huge expansion of state education during the period after 1870, and the increase in the number of places at 'redbrick' universities, the directors in our sample have been drawn increasingly from the narrow confines of the public school system and the universities of Oxford and Cambridge.

Summary: Elite Recruitment

The material described in the preceding sections is deficient in certain respects, and does not provide a basis for any sort of precise comparison between the elites in different institutions. Nevertheless, a number of unequivocal conclusions can be drawn from it:

1. Elite positions in the major institutions in Britain are dominated by persons from privileged social backgrounds.
2. The public schools and Oxbridge continue to play a pre-eminent role in elite recruitment: in most elites between 60 per cent and 80 per cent have been educated at public schools.
3. It is generally, though not universally, the case that the higher the level of what is to count as the 'elite' is placed in any institution, the greater will be the proportion having public school and/or Oxbridge backgrounds.
4. In most elites, the proportion of individuals drawn from public school and/or Oxbridge backgrounds has remained stable or has actually increased over the past several decades.

THE INTEGRATION OF ELITES

The Centralization of Economic Life

In order to analyse the integration of elites, it is not enough to discuss the ties which may exist between the members of different elite groups today; any discussion must take into account the sweeping social changes during this century which have brought about the centralization of the economy and the polity.

The level of economic concentration in this country today is very high: it is higher than in the United States, for example.[34] Industrial concentration increased gradually in Britain from the later decades of the nineteenth century to the end of the 1930s. Most of this seems to have been due to the internally generated growth of the larger firms rather than to mergers or take-overs. In this early period Britain contrasts with the United States. In the United States towards the end of the last century, a flurry of merger activity gave rise to a level of concentration considerably higher than that existing in Britain at the same period. During and after the Second World War, the degree of concentration in the British economy dropped off, but since the middle of the 1950s it has climbed steeply. The top eighty companies by asset size in 1957 accounted for 53 per cent of the total net assets of publicly quoted industrial companies; ten years later, this proportion had increased to 62 per cent: the top three hundred companies accounted for some 85 per cent of the total. Much of this growth in concentration in recent years is accounted for by take-over activity.[35] Within the financial sector, the same process has occurred even more markedly. Between 1880 and 1917, the steady consolidation of the leading banking organizations and their absorption of smaller ones created the eleven clearing banks dominated by the 'Big Five'. With the merging of the National Provincial and Westminster Banks in 1967, banking is now largely centred around four major organizations: Barclays, National Westminster, Lloyds and Midland.[36] The increasing centralization of the economy has been matched by the ever-expanding role played in economic life by the state. At the turn of this century, only 2 per cent of the civilian labour force was employed in national or local government service. This had risen to 17 per cent by 1971 — if the nationalized industries are included, to fully one-quarter of the labour force.[37]

Analysis of interlocking directorships gives some sort of index, although an inherently crude and limited one, of the degree to which the rising level of economic concentration has been accompanied by the burgeoning of connections among large corporations, and between industry and the City. In the Cambridge Elites Study, we attempted to map the directorial connections between the top fifty quoted companies, leading banks and insurance companies between 1906 and 1970. The results certainly indicate a steadily increasing range of interconnections between the major organizations. In 1906, less than half of the 85 corporations in the sample were connected by shared directorships, 34 organizations joined by 41 links making up the major network (6 other companies were linked in 3 separate pairs). The banks figured fairly prominently in these connections; hence only 16 of the top 50 industrial companies entered any of the networks. In 1970, by contrast, 29 of the industrial firms in the top 50 were linked with one another by at least one shared directorship. Moreover the banks and insurance companies had sprouted a whole series of new links with industrial firms as well as with each other. In the 1970 sample, 73 out of 85 organizations in the study appeared in the network.[38]

The Centralization of Government

The growing centralization of political life over the course of the past century is demonstrated in various ways: in the detachment of MPs from their roots in the local constituency, in the 'professionalization' of politics, and in the consolidation of the organization of the major party 'machines'.

Since most MPs have had prior experience in local politics and remain at least nominally responsible to the interests of their constituencies, the connections between local and national politics cannot become completely severed. But the relations between these levels have changed with the changing nature of political careers. In the nineteenth century, those who rose through local politics to enter Parliament frequently maintained a close involvement in the affairs of the locality from which they came. This was true even of those with a more aristocratic background, although in a different sense, in that they often were more concerned with regional matters, or the protection of their own landed interests, than with national issues. In the present day, MPs perhaps spend more time in dealing with constituency affairs than they did in previous times, owing to the expansion of governmental intrusion into a wider range of areas in the life of the citizenry; but their connections with their constituencies are for the most part more 'distant' than they used to be. Few MPs were born in the constituency they represent.

The process can be fairly easily traced. In *The English Constitution*, Bagehot wrote: 'The counties not only elect landowners, which is natural, but also elect landowners from their own county' and went on to add, 'Each county prohibits the import of able men from other counties'.[39] The decline of landed groups in the House of Commons has largely, although not totally, eliminated the influence of political families which played such a major role in British politics in the eighteenth and nineteenth centuries. Those who increasingly took over from landed groups in the Commons in the nineteenth century were characteristically men prominent in their local communities in industry or trade, and who continued an active involvement in local organizations after being sent to Westminster. But this type of MP and this sort of dual involvement in local and national administration has again largely disappeared in modern times — partly as a result of internal changes in politics, but partly also because of the growth of the large corporations described earlier. Many large firms are administered from the capital, and their regional organizations are often controlled by managers who were not born in the locality.[40]

Over the course of the present century, politics has become more professional in two senses: being an MP is a more full-time occupation than it was formerly; and both the skills and tasks of politicians have become more specialized. The two types of MP mentioned above — those from a landed background or with local business interests — each included men who devoted much of their energies to involvements outside Parliament. But although nearly all MPs retain outside commitments of many kinds, politics is no longer an amateur pursuit of gentlemen or ambitious local entrepreneurs. It would certainly not be true to say that involvement in national politics is the only, or even the main, career of all contemporary MPs; but those who live 'off' rather than 'for' politics are today in the majority — certainly in the Labour, if not in the Conservative, Party.

Something of an index of the internal consolidation of the parties from the latter part of the nineteenth century up to the present day is provided by the incidence of 'Whip divisions' on Parliamentary legislation in the Commons. Thus, in 1836, when the Liberals formed the government, the party put its Whips on in less than 50 per cent of the divisions in the House; in 1908, when the Liberals were again in power, this had risen to 96 per cent. A similar rise is manifest for the Tory Party.[41] The proportion is marginally higher today in both Tory and Labour Parties. Whereas a century ago a considerable proportion of legislative proposals in Parliament were drafted and introduced privately, today private members' bills are unusual. Moreover, the work of preparing legislative action has become largely

bureaucratic and operates through the Civil Service. Within the Parliamentary
Party organizations, the Cabinet and Shadow Cabinet have come to assume more
and more pre-eminence — although as we shall indicate below, the power of
Cabinet Ministers is a matter of some controversy.

Interconnections between Polity and Economy: the Business Interests of MPs

In the nineteenth century, and at least up to the First World War, the connections
between property and political power were naked and direct. In both Tory and
Liberal parties more than a few MPs were wealthy men. The 1895 Parliament contained thirty-one millionaires as well as others nearly as wealthy. Rubinstein
remarks: 'Since there were probably at that time 200 living millionaires in Britain,
many of whom were members of the House of Lords, it seems likely that any State
opening of Parliament during the period saw a greater concentration of Britain's
economic wealth in one place at one time than ever in British history, and possibly
in the annals of any legislature anywhere'.[42] Those in the Commons included a
substantial number of the 'regional entrepreneurs' referred to above: Brunner and
Mond represented Cheshire constituencies; Spencer Charrington, Mile End,
Stepney; Harland and Wolff, Belfast North and Belfast East respectively. Today
there are certainly fewer of the very wealthy who sit in the House of Commons;
although since estimates of wealth depend upon the tracing of estates, it is not
possible to build up an accurate picture for recent years. Of the post-war MPs for
whom Rubinstein was able to gather information, none were millionaires, and
only two (both members of the Conservative Party) left over £500,000: in spite
of the fact that the numbers in the country as a whole owning this much wealth
or more have risen since the turn of the century. The advent of the Labour Party
has obviously had an effect. Labour MPs are overwhelmingly of modest circumstances, even if they have included a few individuals of moderate wealth: four
Labour members of the 1922 Parliament, for example, left estates of £50,000 or
more.

It would be a mistake to suppose that the fact that there are fewer wealthy
MPs today than there were a hundred years ago means that the erstwhile connections
between political and economic elites have become severed, or that such connections
are no longer important in the distribution of power in British society. Rather, they
have become altered and ramified as a consequence of the twin processes of
centralization of the political and economic orders. Of course, even in the nineteenth
century the ties between political and economic elites were often indirect, or
mediated through other institutions. One should not over-emphasize the
significance of the presence of the wealthy in the forum of politics itself. Most
played only a minor role themselves in parliamentary affairs, and very few rose to
positions of any eminence in the Commons.[43]

Studies show that a complex series of direct ties exist between members of the
Commons and industry in recent Parliaments. For instance in the 1960—6 House
of Commons MPs held 770 directorships and 324 posts as chairman, vice-chairman
or managing director of an industrial or financial organization. The vast majority —
in the order of 90 per cent — were held by Conservatives. Within the ranks of the
Tory businessmen, there were elements of what Roth calls 'Political Lysenkoism' —
on leaving the House of Commons, a person passes on directorships in politically
sensitive companies to fellow MPs. Thus, when the chairman of the Wellman Smith

Owen Engineering Corporation planned to retire from the House, Quintin Hogg became a director of the company; Daniel Awdry, Conservative MP for Chippenham, became a director of the BET Omnibus Co when Sir Hubert Butcher, another member of the board, was defeated at the polls. Findings such as these support the conclusion that the proportion of Conservative MPs who 'live off' politics is much lower than is the case with their Labour counterparts. According to Roth, only 12 of the 250 Tory MPs elected in 1966 apparently had no remunerative occupation outside politics; and of these dozen, for whom politics seemed to be a full-time pursuit, at least two had inherited wealth.[44] The links between major companies and banks and the House of Commons are examined in more detail below (see pp. 230 ff).

The Broader Scope of Interconnections: Personal and Kinship Ties

In any context, the integration of elites depends upon two elements: the existence of direct ties of association, friendship or kinship that can be called upon to fulfil obligations; and the existence of a common culture of belief, habit, and outlook that mediates and facilitates new social contacts. We have noted earlier that a shared type of social or educational background does not in itself generate shared interests. But it is difficult not to accept that shared backgrounds provide a basis for ready communication for those exposed to them, and that the pre-eminence of the public schools and Oxbridge, whose students only constitute a small minority of the total school and university populations, is the medium of the perpetuation of an 'elite culture'.

Three principal means have been used in the literature on elites in an attempt to examine the forms of direct connection that exist between members of elite groups; each is only partially satisfactory. One method is to treat membership of private clubs as a mode of indexing personal networks and ties. Another is to calculate how far close kinship connections exist between elite members. However these only indicate potential types of association and influence that may be developed rather than showing whether such connections are mobilized in any significant way by those involved. The third method, which is to study the patterns of interaction among elite members in particular sets of circumstances in which nominally hidden ties become revealed, turns up more detailed information than the other two, but one cannot be certain how 'typical' the specific situation studied is.

Whitley studied club membership among directors of a sample of large industrial and financial corporations.[45] He found that 28 per cent of the 261 directors about whom he was able to gather information were members of one or more of eight 'prestigious and aristocratically connected clubs' (the Carlton, Boodle's, Brook's, Buck's, the Beefsteak, Pratt's, the Turf, St James' and White's). 46 per cent of the financial directors were members of one or more of these clubs. Analysing this membership as a network between the industrial and financial companies showed a very high meshing of connections between the firms studied. The clubs perpetuate into adult life the atmosphere, and even the style of physical surroundings, of the leading public schools and the Oxbridge colleges; and they help to bring together the members of different elite groups. A study of top civil servants, ambassadors, judges, bishops and ministerial politicians found that three-quarters belonged to one or more London clubs.[46] Whitley's research also included an analysis of kinship connections[47] between, rather than within, companies. He found that 15 of the 40 industrial companies studied were connected through directors mentioned in *Burke's Peerage* and *Burke's Landed Gentry*. This was only a loosely connected network, compared to that existing among financial organizations. In the case of the latter, 26 out of the 27 firms were thus connected, forming a highly integrated network of ties. Taking the two types of organization together, 18 industrial firms joined the network with the financial companies. The studies showed that those industrial firms dominated internally by kinship networks — 'family firms' — stand apart from the networks that link most of the other organizations. It should be noted that this type of research, which depends on the two source-books of the aristocracy and landed gentry, is only likely to provide a minimal estimate of the extent of kinship networks.

One of the very few pieces of research that attempts to develop an analysis of kinship connections from an examination of a particular set of circumstances involving 'top decision-makers', is Lupton and Wilson's study of the Bank Rate Tribunal.[48] The Tribunal was set up to report in 1956 on allegations that an impending change in the bank rate had been leaked prior to the event. Lupton and Wilson tried to show how evidence given at the proceedings of the Tribunal indicates the importance of a 'culture of expectations' within which the everyday interactions between individuals prominent in finance, politics and public administration is carried on: shared beliefs and confidence in customary procedures gear to a range of informal contacts that cut across formal allegiances and relations of authority. A good example came out during the examination of witnesses. The Attorney General asked Lord Kindersley (a director of the Bank of England) why he, and not Mr Cobbold (the Governor of the Bank of England), had gone to see Lord Bicester about the possible effect of the bank rate rise on the Vickers issue and on relations between the 'City and the Bank of England'. Lord Kindersley replied: 'I consider it perfectly natural that I should be allowed to go and talk to a colleague at the Bank of England . . . I do not think that Lord Bicester would find it in the least surprising that I should come to him and say to him: "Look here, Rufie, is it too late to stop this business or not?"; and: "I have discussed this with Jim — with the Governor — and I am coming on to see you" '.[49]

Lupton and Wilson attempted to document in some detail the kinship connections of leading figures appearing in the Tribunal proceedings, for example Lord Kindersley and Cobbold. By tracing through parents, siblings, spouses and children they were able to build up 'family trees' that often joined up with one another. The categories represented include Cabinet Ministers and other Ministers of the Crown (A); senior Civil Servants (B); directors of the Bank of England (C); directors of the Big Five clearing banks (D); directors of merchant banks or discount houses (E); directors of insurance companies (F). In fig. 4.3 appear some of the connections of C.F.Cobbold, a man with a background in the landed gentry. Through the paternal line he is related to Lieutenant Colonel John Cobbold, who was in turn married to a daughter of the ninth Duke of Devonshire. John Cobbold's sister married Sir Charles Hambro, a member of the famous banking family — and a director of the Bank of England. Figure 4.4 shows some of the ties developed through the marriage of Sir Everard Hambro with a relative of Lord Norman, a former Governor of the Bank of England. One of Lord Norman's cousins married an uncle of the then Home Secretary, R.A.Butler. A director of the Bank of England, Sir George Abell, married a daughter of the above marriage; Abell's brother-in-law, N.N.Butler, married into the Hambro family.

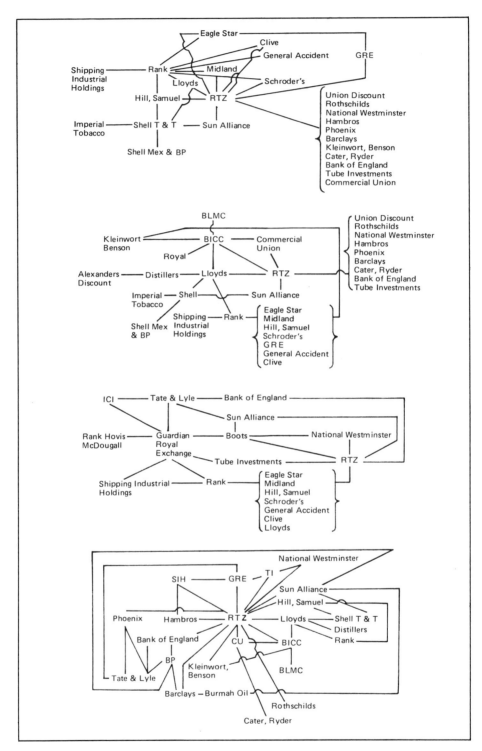

Figure 4.2   Kinship Relations of Hill, Samuel, Lloyds Bank, GRE and RTZ, omitting
connections between financial institutions

Source: R. Whitley, 'The City and industry', in P. Stanworth and A. Giddens, *Elites and Power in British Society* (Cambridge 1974)

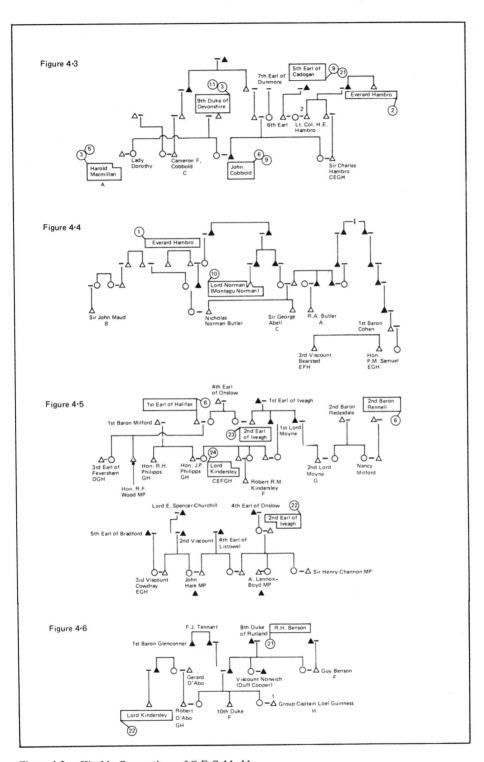

Figure 4.3   Kinship Connections of C. F. Cobbold
Figure 4.4   Social Ties Developed by Sir Everard Hambro through Marriage
Figure 4.5   Social Connections of Lord Kindersley (1)
Figure 4.6   Social Connections of Lord Kindersley (2)

Source: T. Lupton and C. Shirley Wilson, 'The social background and connections of "top decision makers" ', The Manchester School, 27 (1959)

Figures 4.5 and 4.6 represent some connections of Lord Kindersley. The second Earl of Iveagh, the father-in-law of A.Lennox-Boyd, erstwhile Minister of State for Colonial Affairs, had a niece who married Kindersley's brother. A sister of J.Hare, also a former Conservative Minister, is the daughter-in-law of the Earl of Iveagh. Hare's wife, in turn, is the sister of Viscount Cowdray (who is mentioned in the proceedings of the Tribunal).

The Overlapping of Elite Groups

One cannot leave the topic of the integration of elites without considering, despite the lack of data, first, how far the interlocking of elite positions extends beyond the spheres of the political and economic elites themselves and, second, what degree of individual movement there is from one elite group to another. At least two methods of examining elite linkage by way of multiple position-holding may be distinguished: first, that based on comparing annual samples which illustrate the extent of elite interlocking for particular years, and therefore when compared give an indication of how the pattern of interlocking has changed over time. The concern in this case is to discover those individuals who hold more than one elite position at a particular time. This method, however, fails to pick up those individuals who may never have held more than one elite position at any particular time, but who have held several such positions at different points in their career. Thus, while the first method might reveal the links current between the boards of large banks and the House of Commons in, for instance, 1906, it would not indicate the number of MPs who had once held seats on major boards, or vice versa. Similarly, it would not show the number of High Court judges for that year who had formerly sat as MPs. This latter type of information can only be revealed by the second method which concentrates on the careers of individuals holding elite positions and reveals the extent to which elites have been joined through the movement of individuals from one sphere to another over a period of years. Given the lack of any comprehensive study for elite groups as a *whole*, there is no clear indication of how, and to what extent, the patterns of linkage of either type have changed over the years. However, though a comprehensive study is not yet available, there are data which relate to certain distinct elites and illustrate their links with other elites in both the senses mentioned.

Some of the most recent information emanates from work done in the Cambridge Elites Study. Changes in the pattern of interlocking between the companies and the banks themselves have been indicated above.[50] Data dealing with the links between the boards of major companies and other elites is shown in table 4.9.

This documents a cohort analysis, taking the careers of individual directors in order to compare the extent to which they entered other elites during the course of their working lives (the figures for the last two cohorts are almost certainly underestimates, since some of the directors included have not yet completed their careers and may still 'accumulate' other elite positions). It is apparent that the proportion (and number) of directors also taking a seat in the House of Commons has declined during the present century, a trend which undoubtedly reflects the increasing full-time, professional, nature of both pursuits. This form of institutional separation is reflected in the figures for particular years. For instance, in 1906 90 of the directors of the major industrial corporations sampled for that year had been, or still were,

TABLE 4.9

Elite interlocks: percentage of directors of large industrial and financial institutions with links to other elite sectors (Birth Cohorts)

		1820–39	1840–59	1860–79	1880–99	1900–19[1]	1920–39[1]
House of	I	40.6	34.4	23.7	13.4	5.9	6.7
Commons	F	39.2	22.5	18.6	13.3	5.1	0.9
House of	I	11.0	23.2	21.1	24.3	15.2	8.8
Lords	F	7.2	15.0	22.7	24.1	17.3	6.2
Govt. advisory	I	4.7	6.4	7.4	8.8	4.7	4.4
councils etc	F	0.0	2.5	8.2	10.4	5.4	0.9
Higher Civil	I	3.1	1.5	2.8	0.8	1.6	0.0
Service	F	0.0	2.5	3.6	1.9	4.8	1.7
Nationalized	I	–	–	0.7	6.9	12.9	8.9
industries	F	–	–	0.5	6.6	13.2	8.4
Military	I	0.0	1.0	0.7	2.7	0.3	0.0
Elite	F	0.0	0.0	0.5	3.3	0.0	0.0
Univs. board	I	4.7	6.4	7.8	11.0	14.8	4.4
of govts.	F	10.7	4.2	7.2	13.8	16.3	6.0
Royal	I	15.1	16.1	27.5	24.8	27.6	4.4
Commissions	F	10.7	17.5	26.8	27.5	29.5	6.0

Note:
1 The careers of some of the directors in these cohorts have yet to be completed and the
  figures for the various linkages may yet rise
Source: A.Giddens and P.Stanworth, Cambridge Elites Project (1971–4)

Members of Parliament. In 1970 the equivalent figure was 16. Among directors of the main banks sampled in 1906, 26 had been, or still were, MPs. In 1970 only 13 bank directors had this kind of connection with politics. It is interesting to note, however, that the cohort analysis reveals that the proportion of both financial and industrial directors who actually served in a government administration in a ministerial rank rose for those born in each successive decade of the nineteenth century. Only for those directors born in the twentieth century do the figures reveal a fall in the 'ministerial connection', and as pointed out earlier, these latter figures are under-representations.The figures for connections between the economic and other elites may be briefly summarized. A higher proportion of each succeeding generation of directors have served on government advisory councils, commissions, etc. Likewise, service on the boards of universities and nationalized industries has become more common, both among succeeding cohorts of directors, and for annual samples taken over the last seventy years for universities, and since 1945 for nationalized industries. As universities have proliferated, so business has maintained its links with the academic world. Similarly, the public sector of the economy has drawn increasing numbers of board members from among the directors of the larger industrial corporations and banks. The numbers of directors who had achieved

positions of Under-Secretary or above (or equivalent) in the higher Civil Service
and similar posts in the Foreign Service and Diplomatic Corps, though always very
low, have also increased. In 1906, 2 financial directors and 2 industrial directors
had served in such a capacity; in 1970 8 industrial directors and 12 financial
directors (18 different men, since 2 had directorships in both the financial and
industrial samples) had reached senior appointments in the higher Civil Service
(or equivalent) prior to their directorships. Details for directors who achieved or
inherited peerages reveals a rise and then a fall in the proportion entering the
House of Lords, both in the cohort analysis and in the series of annual samples.
The military elite has always had weak links with large-scale business.

The data for the links between the Cambridge sample of directors and other
elite sectors between 1906 and 1970 are summarized in figure 4.7. Table 4.10
illustrates the extent of multiple interlocking between directors who held at least
three elite positions.

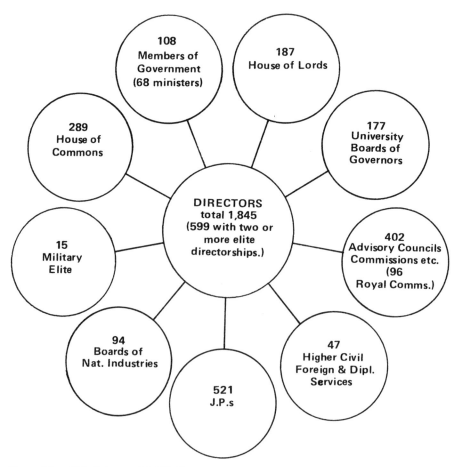

Figure 4.7   Elite linkages of 1,845 directors, 1906–70
Source: A. Giddens and P. Stanworth, Cambridge Elites Project (1971–4)

TABLE 4.10

Multiple position by directors holding at least two other elite positions, 1906–70

n.	House of Commons	University Governors	Government Administration	House of Lords	Higher Civil Service	Nationalized Industries	Military Elite
(289) House of Commons		27	89	63	2	4	1
(177) University Governors	27		18	25	6	18	1
(108) Government Administration	89	18		52	4	5	0
(187) House of Lords	63	25	52		3	11	3
(47) Higher Civil Service	2	6	4	3		4	0
(94) Nationalized Industries	4	18	5	11	4		2
(15) Military Elite	1	1	0	3	0	2	

Note: Of 289 directors who sat in the House of Commons, 27 were also on University Boards' of Governors, 89 served in Governments and so on
Source: A. Giddens and P. Stanworth, Cambridge Elites Project (1971–4)

There appears to be no long-term study of links between the House of Commons and other elite groups. The work of Guttsman, Johnson and others has provided an enormous amount of information on the political elite, but we still lack a comprehensive account of the extent to which the patterns of linkage between political and other elites have changed. Our data on directors illustrates a sharp decline in multiple position-holding between Parliament and the top boardrooms. However, Guttsman's analysis of cross-membership of elite groups between 1945 and 1955, in which members of the Labour and Conservative administrations figure prominently, demonstrates that the political elite was far from 'isolated' at that time.

TABLE 4.11

Cross membership of elite groups

Affiliations with other elite groups	Lab. Gov't, 1945–51	Cons. Gov't, 1951–5	Directorate of culture	Scientific directorate	Government committee men
None	56	45	25	26	57
One	36	22	17	25	61
Two	14	15	11	8	47
Three	6	4	8	10	21
Four	1	2	1	2	8
Five or more	–	–	3	3	6
Total	113	88	65	74	200
Total of Memberships	86	76	84	100	284

Source: W.L.Guttsman, *The British Political Elite*, p. 361

One type of linkage particularly subject to comment in the early decades of the twentieth century was that between the Bench and Parliament.

TABLE 4.12

High Court Judges who had sat as Members of Parliament

Percentages

on bench	1900–9	1910–19	1920–9	1930–9	1940–9	1950–9	1960–70
all high court judges	44.2	43.6	39.4	30.0	22.6	13.4	9.5
Principal judges	52.9	46.5	44.8	36.7	29.7	18.8	15.4
number	57	69	61	70	80	82	128

Source: A.Giddens and P.Stanworth, Cambridge Elites Project (1971–4)

Laski observed that 80 of the 132 High Court judges who occupied a position
on the Bench between 1832 and 1906 had also been MPs.[51] Table 4.12 shows that
this 'channel of entry' is much less common than once was the case. The proportion
of judges with parliamentary experience in the House of Commons has fallen for
each succeeding decade of the present century. The actual numbers, as opposed to
percentages, show a rather less dramatic decline, with a rise in the most recent
decade (25, 27, 24, 21, 18, 11 and 18 for each respective decade). In the earlier
part of the century some of the judges had shown little inclination for a continuous
involvement in the processes of law until elevated to the Bench. Some appointments were notoriously political; at the present time appointments are monopolized
by practising members of the legal profession. Just as judges are less likely to have
parliamentary experience, so too the number holding high office in a government
administration (usually Solicitor General, or occasionally Home Secretary) has
fallen from 17.6 per cent (10 in number) for 1900–9 to 4 per cent (5 in number)
for 1960–70. Of those High Court judges who did sit as MPs, between one-half
and two-thirds sitting in each decade investigated had been Conservatives. These
figures present further evidence of a demographic separation of two elites, in this
case the House of Commons and the High Courts. However, just as many MPs
retain links with business (often with the top firms and banks) so too the legal
profession is extremely well-represented in Parliament. In the 1971–2 session, for
instance, 101 barristers and 26 solicitors were to be found in the House (over 40 per
cent of these had business connections).

A CASE STUDY OF THE INTERPENETRATION OF GOVERNMENT AND INDUSTRY: THE INDUSTRIAL REORGANIZATION CORPORATION

The growing significance of state activity in the economic sphere over recent
decades is easily documented. In 1914 public expenditure represented 14 per cent
of GNP; by 1918 as a consequence of war expenditure the figure had risen to
27 per cent; by 1948 there had been a further rise to 42 per cent of GNP; in 1974
the figure passed 50 per cent. Though the output of nationalized industries recently
accounted for only 11 per cent of GNP, the public sector as a whole employed 25
per cent of the nation's labour force (60 per cent of those with higher degrees).
State purchases from the private sector amounted to £5,000 million in 1970 (12 per
cent of total output) and current and capital expenditure of central and local
government on goods and services at factor cost amounted to 25 per cent of GNP.
Between 1936 and 1970 taxation as a percentage of GNP rose from 23.2 per cent
to 48 per cent.[52] With one or two short-term reversals, the growth in the role of
the state has continued since 1945 both as a general orchestrator of the economy
as well as a direct participant, whichever political party has been in power.
Perhaps the most notable examples of government incursion into economic
activity itself is the nationalization of the coal, rail and steel industries. A wide
range of public utilities are now operated by publicly owned enterprises and the
nationalization of Rolls-Royce and British Leyland extended the hand of the state
into sectors of the largest and most important of British manufacturing industries.
In most of these cases of nationalization the industries involved suffered chronic
economic ailments which would probably have led to their collapse, or severe

diminution in size, but for government interference.[53] The state has also recently concerned itself with attempts to 'modernize' British industry, not merely by encouragement and inducement, but by the creation of agencies directly involved in industrial reconstruction.

Between 1964 and 1970 two Labour governments implemented a number of policies which expressed their particular brand of managerial capitalism. These policies further advanced the increasingly close relationship that had developed between the representatives of large corporations and banks on the one hand and government and Civil Service on the other. Thus British economic policy was advancing towards the pattern already well-established in West Germany, France and Italy, with government at the very centre of industrial and commercial activity. The broad aim of these policies was to encourage the modernization of British industry in the hope that the performance of the whole economy might be improved and growth rates achieved comparable with those of other advanced capitalist societies. A particularly controversial aspect of these policies was the creation of the Industrial Reorganization Corporation (IRC) in 1966.[54] Extensive powers were vested in the new organization although its precise role was never defined beyond that of promoting industrial efficiency and profitability. It is clear however that the case for the IRC rested on the assumption that the units of production in British industry were in many cases too small to compete effectively on the international market. The intention was to create higher levels of concentration, despite the fact that the firms dominating the British economy were on the whole larger than their European rivals. As the actual practice of the IRC evolved throughout the four years of its existence, it shifted from being a catalyst for mergers between willing partners towards a more assertive policy in which it attempted to revitalize and even remove poor management; to encourage a more active involvement of institutional investors in companies in which they had an interest; and even to thwart or promote mergers 'in the national interest' regardless of the resistance of some of the participants. This change in policy reflected in part variations in the personal inclinations of the different managing directors, but one consistent theme that did develop was the role of the IRC as the government's merchant banker. As such it was deeply implicated (in some cases as a prime mover) in a number of significant mergers. In June 1967 the IRC provided £15 million to facilitate the merger between English Electric and Elliot Automation and later in the year, after an earlier failure, it succeeded in a similar move involving Associated Electrical Industries and the General Electric Company.

In January 1968 the take-over of British Motor Holdings by Leyland Motors took place with the support of the IRC, which loaned £25 million to finance the operation. Later in 1968 the IRC intervened in the take-over battle between Rank and Kent who were both attempting to acquire Cambridge Instruments. As a result of IRC support Kent were successful, though only after the Corporation had acquired Kent and Cambridge stock on the open market. In September of the same year Plessey attempted a take-over of English Electric and the IRC countered by encouraging the acquisition of English Electric by General Electric. Seven months later, in April 1969, the Corporation played an important part in bringing about the merger between Rowntrees and Mackintosh after the former had been subject to a bid from General Foods. It thereby fulfilled another part of its evolving programme – the protection of British companies from foreign capital. This principle was further implemented in May when the IRC sought successfully to create a major British ball-bearings company and thereby thwarted the take-over activity of Skefke (the British subsidiary of a Swedish company). In January 1970 the Corporation established various guidelines for the merger of Reed and the International Printing Company (IPC), thereby protecting the newsprint interests of Bowater, Reed's principal competitor in this field. Later in the same year funds were loaned to Rolls-Royce, to BLMC — in order to purchase advanced machine tools — and to Cammell Laird who were assisted during a liquidity crisis. This list includes only the most notable of the IRC activities; Young and Lowe in their study of the IRC describe many other examples. It is also apparent that the Corporation acted confidentially on a number of occasions, settling commercial disputes, promoting the standardization of products, encouraging the modernization of machine tools, and, through the CBI, urging institutions to be more active in companies in which they were major investors. During its short life the IRC represented the merging of business, government and Civil Service in a particularly notable form, and as later developments have shown (the National Enterprise Board for instance) its demise did not represent the end of the inter-penetration of these spheres.

The IRC was formally independent of government, though in practice this independence was reliant upon political support. Once the Corporation had settled down, and especially after the merger between GEC and AEI, its relations with its sponsoring department, the Ministry of Technology, were generally harmonious. Suggestions for inquiries which required a commercial and independent appraisal were received from both Civil Servants and politicians, though the IRC itself came to value its own initiative most highly. It was this potential for independent action, and the feeling that the corporation was 'out of control' that led to its abolition by Heath's Conservative Government in 1972. Since the IRC operated within the business world and could not, except in exceptional circumstances, enforce cooperation, there was an effort to cultivate understanding of the benefits it might bring to industry. This seems to have been in the main successful, for the suspicions felt by the business community were gradually replaced by cooperation, trust and mutual respect. The composition of the board of the IRC must have encouraged these attitudes, for during its existence it included in its number 9 industrialists, 3 bankers, 1 lawyer, 1 business academic and 1 trade union leader. Furthermore, the Corporation was a source of funds for capital investment when capital itself was in short supply and expensive, therefore it might not only provide valuable advice but also the wherewithal to achieve rationalization and greater efficiency. There were of course exceptions: 'Because the IRC seems to have articulated a particular brand of enthusiastic, radical change-promoting attitude to industry, it was most warmly received by those individuals with similar views. On the other hand, a state of almost non-communication probably existed with more conservative businessmen.'[55]

It would be a mistake to regard the development of the IRC and other similar institutional arrangements as examples of 'creeping socialism'. The extension of direct state involvement in the economic sphere does not represent, in itself, any negation of capitalism as such. Indeed it may be argued that the increasing role of the state is a logical concomitant of capitalist development, essential to the continuation of profitable enterprise in the private sphere, and therefore indicates not the degeneration of capitalism, but its evolution to a further stage. Attempts by recent governments to regulate both the price of labour and the cost of living represent not an attempt to transcend the categories of labour and capital, but a further effort to institutionalize their potential for conflict without altering the fundamental nature of the socio-economic context in which they operate.[56]

ELITES AND THE DISTRIBUTION OF POWER

The study of social power poses notorious conceptual and methodological difficulties. Power, in a certain sense, only comes to light when used, although it nonetheless refers to a 'capacity'; it is not a constant, and can be 'expanded' by the development of new resources at the disposition of individual or collective actors. We think it is important to distinguish two aspects of power that are immediately relevant to elite studies. The first is what one of us has referred to as the 'institutional mediation of power', meaning by this the structure of power as represented by asymmetries in the reproduction of life chances across the generations.[57] This refers above all to the general form of state and economy within the context of which elite groups operate, and we shall return to problems raised by this at the conclusion of the chapter. The second, the 'mediation of control', refers to the capability of members of elite groups to take or to influence policy decisions, and it is this we shall concentrate upon in the current section.

Power in Industry: the Impact of 'Managerialism'

The thesis of managerialism has a curious history in the literature dealing with corporate power. In the third volume of *Capital*, Marx discussed the rise of the joint-stock company and the concomitant 'obsolescence of the capitalist'.[58] The fragmentation of shareholding in public companies, according to Marx, means that the control of the affairs of the firm passes out of the hands of the owners of property into the hands of managerial executives. For Marx, this signals incipient socialism within capitalism: the joint-stock company, although necessarily still operating within a framework of capitalist production, shows that the functioning of modern industry has no need of the capitalist. In Marx's writings, the internal transformation of capitalism is due to be complemented by the accession to power of a socialist labour movement that will complete politically the socio-economic changes that have already in substantial part transformed the system from within.

In more recent writings on the topic, the presumed transfer of power to the managers is presented from a different aspect – not a socialist revolution as anticipated, but on the contrary as undercutting the possibility of such an occurrence. The modern debate over managerialism dates from the publication in 1932 of *The Modern Corporation and Private Property*,[59] and James Burnham's account of the 'managerial revolution'.[60] Most of those who have contributed to the controversy from the non-Marxist side have (unlike Burnham himself) held that the coming to prominence of the propertyless managers produces a dispersion or fragmentation of economic power. Later Marxists who have entered the debate have mostly done so with the object of showing that the proportion of large companies that are dominated by their managers rather than their shareholders is much lower than that claimed by 'managerialist' authors.

The following points are relevant in assessing the issues involved in the protracted controversy over the internal distribution of corporate power, insofar as it relates to Britain:

1   Even among very large corporations, family companies are far from having completely disappeared: not all the mega-corporations are public joint-stock enterprises.

2   In public companies in which stock ownership is widely dispersed, ownership of relatively small blocks of shares can be sufficient to allow those who own them to intervene effectively in the running of the corporation. Moreover, forms of corporate control exist whereby such minority interests can yield a ramified set of powers extending through various companies: as where a minority shareholding controls a parent company that in turn holds interests which effectively dominate other subsidiary firms.

3   There is a difference between 'power' and 'administration'. It is certainly the case that among the large corporations the old-style entrepreneurial company is rare, and that day-to-day administration of the firm is in the hands of directors and executives. But it still may be the case that propertied interests can intervene when they feel it necessary to do so, and thus that they ultimately control the policies followed within the company.

4   Not all stock carries voting rights, and there may be concentrated ownership of voting shares where non-voting stock is dispersed among a large number of unenfranchized shareholders.

5   There is a growing amount of institutional stock-ownership in large companies in Britain, especially insurance companies. The intertwining of firms through institutional ownership is very difficult to trace out, but may represent one of the most significant mechanisms in the modern economy whereby ownership of private property is tied directly to economic power.

The nature and forms of economic control obviously are likely to vary by type of company and perhaps by industrial sector. But some general conclusions seem warranted as outcomes of the debate on managerialism. The original claims of those who, following Berle and Means, have held that the ownership of private property is now only of marginal significance to corporate power within large companies, can really no longer be sustained. It seems undeniable that the picture is more complex than such authors tend to suggest: and indeed that managerial positions can be used to accumulate property that can then yield an extended range of power. Certainly the advent of the large corporations and the fragmentation of shareholding does not express a movement beyond the capitalistic structure of the enterprise itself, as is frequently suggested.[61] If, in many large companies, directors are not themselves major shareholders in those companies, nevertheless most own shares in some form which ensures that their interests are not too discrepant from those of property owners in the means of production as a whole. And the companies whose fortunes they direct necessarily operate within a framework of profit-making and the sustaining of levels of investment.[62]

The voluminous literature dealing with managerial themes rests on insecure foundations. Most of the discussion depends upon inferences from statistical materials; there are few studies of the actual operations of power inside companies. One such piece of research, however, is that reported by Pahl and Winkler.[63] These authors concentrate on relations between the board-room and other managerial staff rather than on those between shareholding interests and managers as such. Pahl and Winkler are particularly concerned to point to the insufficiencies of previous research, arguing that it has typically identified the holding of office with effective power, and contacts between the members of elite groups (e.g. inter-locking directorships) as signifying mutual influence. In analysing decision-making at board level, they distinguish two types of boards of directors – 'pro forma boards' and 'functioning boards'. The first has only a nominal existence, in accordance with legal requirements; it plays no part in the actual running of the company and may perhaps not even meet at all. Pro forma boards are characteristic of business organizations dominated by a single individual or a tiny minority of oligarchs – who may be members of the same family in a family firm, a block of shareholders, or a small group of managerial executives. A functioning board is one which does not participate as a collective entity in the government of the affairs of the corporation. But Pahl and Winkler emphasize that functioning boards usually possess only limited power. 'Any group which purports to be an instrument of decision-making in any institution, yet only meets once a month or less, as most boards do, is inevitably cast in the role of a gatekeeper, weighing proposals for future action, letting some go through, rejecting others. Unless it organizes and exerts itself in a way we never observe, the initiative passes over to individuals or to a permanent secretariat/management.'[64] Most of the matters that come before the board are 'pre-packaged' by managers and executive directors in such a way as to manipulate the information available about the proposals; thus, what the board tends to do is merely to ratify decisions that are actually taken from below. 'Inter-locking' directors, Pahl and Winkler say, are typically the least influential of all, because they usually know less than the others about the affairs of the companies on whose boards they sit. 'Ironically, the more boards on which an interlocking director sits, the more influential he is thought to be in many conventional studies of elites, yet the easier he is to manipulate because he has less time to devote to each.'[65]

Pahl and Winkler argue that their research carries direct implication for the managerialism debate. Most contributors to the controversy, they claim, have treated property rights as equivalent to control, without differentiating between such rights. They suggest a distinction between 'allocative' and 'operational' control. The first refers to the power to distribute economic resources, the second to what we have earlier called the 'administration' of such resources. Allocative control may derive from ownership of capital, but need not do so. It is particularly important, they point out, to notice that not only managers but also propertied interest may take advantage of the diffusion of shareholding within large public companies. Thus, asset-strippers deliberately buy up scattered holdings in such a way as to enforce take-overs; and institutional investors, whose allocative control is now very considerable indeed, come to dominate companies in which their actual stock-holdings are relatively small.

Power in Politics: Parliament, Cabinet and Civil Service

Bagehot's celebrated portrayal of government in *The English Constitution* has for many years provided a focus for analyses of the distribution of power within Parliament. Bagehot diagnosed as the 'efficient secret' of British politics the signifi-cance of the Cabinet as fusing legislature and executive. The role of the Cabinet and the power wielded by its members as contrasted with that of MPs in general on the one hand, the Prime Minister and the Civil Service on the other, have remained subjects of chronic dispute. The growing pre-eminence of the Cabinet after the

closing decades of the nineteenth century was clearly in substantial degree the outcome of the internal consolidation of the parties within Parliament, and the
strengthening of party discipline. The Cabinet has become not a committee in and
of the legislature as a whole, as Bagehot represented it, but the apex of the party's
organization – 'a committee of the party chosen by the Prime Minister from
Parliament'.[66] A Cabinet secretariat, responsible to the Prime Minister, was only
created for the first time during the First World War.

No one now doubts that the power of the ordinary MP to influence government
policy, whether his own party is in or out of power, is limited indeed. But there is
considerable disagreement as to how far the power of Cabinet Ministers themselves
has been eroded by the twin-influences of Prime Ministerial and Civil Service power.
It is difficult to deny that the dominance of the Prime Minister within the Cabinet,
although of course always subject to variabilities of personality, has grown over the
past seventy years. Lord Morley's much quoted characterization of the position of
the Prime Minister in the Cabinet – 'primus inter pares' – today appears less than
adequate. The formal authority and certainly the effective power of the Prime
Minister has expanded with the centralization of party politics. The range of the
Prime Minister's patronage within Parliament includes not only the twenty or so
Cabinet Ministers themselves, but also about sixty junior ministerial posts. The
number of ministerial appointments have grown steadily over the decades of this
century. In the Conservative administration of 1900, 42 of the 402 Tory MPs
held ministerial positions, in the Labour government of 1967, 122 members of the
ruling party – one-third of its complement of MPs –held ministerial positions.[67]

So long as he retains the general support of the Parliamentary party, these
rights of patronage enable even a moderately forceful Prime Minister to wield a
great deal of power over the formulation of general policy. Surveying the role of
the Cabinet, the most plausible conclusion, at least in the post-World War Two period,
is that policy is dominated by what Crossman called 'Prime-Ministerial government'.
Crossman quoted Lord Home: 'Every Cabinet Minister is in a sense the Prime
Minister's agent – his assistant. There is no question about that . . . If the Cabinet
discusses anything it is the Prime Minister who decides what the collective view of
the Cabinet is. A Minister's job is to save the Prime Minister all the work he can.
But no Minister could make a really important move without consulting the Prime
Minister . . . '[68] The Prime Minister not only is able to control the organization of
the Cabinet through his rights of patronage, he is also able to determine the agendas
in Cabinet meetings. The 'Information control' that Pahl and Winkler speak of in
regard to board meetings in business organization is applied from two directions so
far as Cabinet Ministers are concerned – from 'above' through the control of the
Prime Minister, and from 'below' through the channelling of information on the
part of Civil Service advisers.

Until well into the nineteenth century, the higher posts in the Civil Service
were patronage appointments, staffed by relatives or friends of Ministers and other
MPs whose political support was deemed necessary to the government. The fall of
the government was likely to mean that some leading Civil Servants lost their
appointments; also promotion within the Civil Service was in some degree tied to
the success or otherwise of the political parties. As a consequence, the Civil Service
was dependent upon Parliament and in terms of the formation of policy decisions,
undoubtedly very largely subordinate to it in terms of power. The modern Civil
Service, as a professional organization, dates effectively from the reforms instituted

by Robert Lowe in 1870, which replaced patronage by competitive examinations administered by the Civil Service Commission, and formally separated off the members of the 'administrative class' from those at lower levels. As the Civil Service has become more professional, it has increased enormously in size, while the Cabinet has remained virtually the same size. Between 1929 and 1966 the number of persons in the administrative class grew from 1,100 to 2,500; those in the executive class expanded five-fold to 83,600; and those in the professional, scientific and technical categories rose to 84,900.[69] The stability and permanence of the Higher Civil Service today contrasts with the transitional status of Cabinet Ministers, who are reshuffled fairly frequently and may lose their Cabinet membership even when their party is in power.

A letter to *The Times* written in 1954 by R.H.Dorman-Smith, a former Conservative Cabinet Minister, aptly expresses this contrast:

> One of the very first lessons my Permanent Secretary thought fit to teach me was 'whatever you may think of me or any other Civil Servant here, you cannot sack us'. I had no desire whatever to sack any of the Ministry of Agriculture Civil Servants, all of whom I had learnt to admire. But I was amazed to find that in fact a Minister had no individual control over his staff, from the newest joined junior clerk or typist right up to the top.[70]

The limited range of knowledge most Ministers possess of technical aspects of matters with which they must deal and the shortness of time in which they are in charge of particular departments, drastically confines any initiatives they might be able to take in modifying pre-existing viewpoints or policy orientations in Whitehall. The possibility of Ministers becoming anything remotely approaching 'tycoons' in the sphere of business is negated by these elements; unlike business leaders, a Minister has no authority to either promote, transfer or dismiss the staff with whom he works. The range of 'information controls' used to present issues in specific ways seems to be potentially much greater than is possible in most industrial settings. Moreover, a Minister simply cannot devote most of his time to the administration of the affairs of the Department which he leads, as an executive director in business enterprises can do, since he must spend a considerable time in the House of Commons replying to questions, and dealing with his general duties as an MP. It is contact between Civil Servants, rather than between Cabinet Ministers as such, that preserves cooperation between different Departments in Whitehall — such contact often being mediated through the Treasury which, as the Department most responsible for economic questions, has become central to the coordination of the Civil Service as a whole.

So far as the distribution of power in the higher circles of the British polity is concerned, then, it would seem most plausible to conclude that power is normally concentrated in the hands of the Prime Minister, often acting in conjunction with an 'inner circle' of trusted advisers, usually drawn from the Cabinet but not operating significantly within the sphere of official Cabinet meetings, and associated with small numbers of Civil Service officials. This is not to suggest, of course, that these constitute an integrated circle with an internally consistent outlook; the power of Whitehall may be used to blunt ministerial initiatives that emanate from the Prime Minister. But the Cabinet functions more as what Headey has termed an 'inter-departmental battleground' rather than as 'a forum for collective deliberation on policy'.[71] As Crick has remarked: 'The evidence is great that the Cabinet no longer makes policy and that, in any case, little reliance is to be put on the old concept that the Cabinet represented a kind of coalition of the diverse forces from a great party and was, therefore, in itself an effective check on the powers of the executive.'[72]

CONCLUSION: CLASSES AND ELITES

Debate on the usefulness of the term 'elite' has recently been renewed in a well-known exchange between Poulantzas and Miliband.[73] In *The State in Capitalist Society*, although concerned with a broad range of Western countries, Miliband attempts to rebut the idea that the property-owning ruling class of nineteenth-century capitalism has become displaced by an amorphous set of elites. It has never been true, Miliband argues, that in modern capitalism the capitalist class has actually 'governed', and he quotes Kautsky to the effect that 'the capitalist class rules but does not govern' since 'it contents itself with ruling the government'.[74] In this way modern industrial capitalism differs from earlier types of society where the dominant class actually ruled directly. Thus while businessmen have often themselves participated, and still do participate quite extensively, in the immediate exercise of governmental power, political and economic elites have largely separate personnel. But the social composition of these and the other major elite groups, judged in terms of similarity of background, experience and values, shows that elites in the advanced societies today still compose a unitary dominant class. 'In an epoch when so much is made of democracy, equality, social mobility, classlessness and the rest', Miliband says, 'it has remained a basic fact of life in advanced capitalist countries that the vast majority of men and women in these countries have been governed, represented, administered, judged, and commanded in war by people drawn from other, economically and socially superior and relatively distant classes.'[75]

For Miliband, therefore, the concept of elite is not incompatible with that of a 'ruling' or 'dominant' class, but can in fact be used to underpin the latter, by showing that elites have a similar class background and display a general unity in outlook or beliefs. Poulantzas on the other hand argues that a satisfactory analysis of problems of class domination, in relation to the state, can only be undertaken if the elite concept is criticized and abandoned. In Poulantzas' words, social classes and the state are 'objective structures' which cannot be reduced to inter-relations between individuals or even groups. Miliband, for example, criticizes managerialist theories by indicating that managerial executives, even where nominally 'property-less', are still profit-seeking in their actions. But, says Poulantzas, neither the existence of capitalism, nor of a dominant capitalist class, are predicated upon the actions or the motivations of individuals; they concern instead structural properties of the social system. In the same way, similarities in the social composition of elite groups, divisions and conflicts between elites, and the degree of participation of industrialists in the operations of government, do not establish the existence of a dominant class: that class is an expression of the overall structure of society as a totality. The state in fact may serve the interests of the capitalist class most effectively when the 'ruling class' is not the 'politically governing class', since the ambitions of particular groups, for example, of industrialists, may be inimical to the interests of the survival of the system as a whole.[76]

Miliband's reply to this critique is to suggest that the concept of elite can be detached from the perspective of those who have made most play with it (the original elite theorists and the political pluralists), and turned back against them. Moreover, he adds, Poulantzas still talks about elites, albeit within a different terminology, referring to 'fractions of the dominant class'. It is important, when examining the claims of managerialists, to analyse the behaviour and motives of managers precisely to show in what ways these are constrained by the broader imperatives of the society of which they are a part. Poulantzas dismisses the composition of elites, and what their members do, as of no account; but if we do not study them, we will have no way of analysing the dynamic character of class relationships. We have to avoid a 'structural super-determinism'.[77]

This debate raises general questions of social theory that cannot be tackled here: such as how ideas like 'structure' and 'structural effects' might be most appropriately understood. So far as the use of the term 'elite' in relation to that of 'class' is concerned, it seems perfectly possible to accept Miliband's points without denying the significance of the substance of those made by Poulantzas. Classes are correctly regarded as properties of the social totality, insofar as they express definite forms of alignment between economy and polity: 'private property' here is of fundamental importance both for supplying a legitimating framework of contract and exchange, and for providing the material medium of investment, price and profit in the economic system. But the particular form of the groups and group relations that become consolidated round class divisions, i.e., the nature of class structure, is influenced by a variety of factors, including ones specific to the particular development of a given society. These have to be studied directly, at any level of the class system. The dimensions of elite group formation analysed in this chapter thus represent basic aspects of the structure of the dominant class, but are not by any means exhaustive, since a more comprehensive account of class domination in British society would have to relate them to a broader institutional setting.

Notes to Chapter 4

1 For an examination of the changing use of the term 'elite' see P. Bachrach, *The Theory of Democratic Elitism* (Boston 1967). The conservative implications of classical elite theory are most methodically developed in Pareto's work, especially *Les systèmes socialistes* (Paris 1902). Pluralist elite theory may be found exemplified in Clark Kerr et al, *Industrialism and Industrial Man*, 2nd edn (London 1973); Daniel Bell, *The End of Ideology: on the exhaustion of political ideas in the fifties*, rev. edn (New York 1962). For a collection of reactions to C. W. Mills, *Power Elite* (London 1953) see W.G. Domhoff and H. Bullard (eds), *C. Wright Mills and the Power Elite* (Boston 1968).

2 Mills, *op. cit.*, p. 277.

3 R. Miliband, *The State in Capitalist Society* (London 1969). Poulantzas criticized Miliband's use of the term 'elite', preferring the term 'fraction of capital' as a replacement notion. See N. Poulantzas, 'The problem of the capitalist state' in R. Blackburn (ed.), *Ideology in Social Science*. The ensuing debate has been summarized and extended by E.L. Laclau, 'On the specificity of the political', *Economy and Society* (Spring 1975).

4 Positional studies include W. L. Guttsman, *The British Political Elite* (London 1963); R. K. Kelsall, *Higher Civil Servants in Britain* (London 1955); C. Otley, 'The educational background of British army officers' in *Sociology*, 7, 2 (May 1973), and D. Boyd, *Elites and their Education* (Windsor 1973).

5 These issues are discussed at length in A. Giddens, 'Elites in the British class structure' *Sociological Review* (1972), and the same author's *Class Structure of the Advanced Societies* (London 1973).

6 Giddens, *Class Structure of the Advanced Societies*, ch. 9.

7 The concept of structuration is elaborated in Giddens, *Class Structure of the Advanced Societies*, ch. 6.

8 Royal Commission on the Distribution of Wealth, *Report No. 1*, Cmnd. 6172 (1976) p. 139.

9 Quoted in A. B. Atkinson, *Unequal Shares: Wealth in Britain* (Penguin edn. 1974) p. 15. Atkinson's argument has been criticized by others who claim to discern a far more radical redistribution of wealth in recent years; see G. Polyani and J. B. Wood, *How Much Inequality?* (London 1974). For Atkinson's answer see A. B. Atkinson, *The Economics of Inequality* (London 1975), ch. 8.

10 Atkinson, *Unequal Shares*, p. 22. These statistics refer to the distribution of wealth among individuals but sociologically speaking the most significant data would be that (as yet unavailable) referring to the distribution of wealth among families, or economically effective kinship units.

11 C. D. Harbury and P. C. McMahon, 'Inter-generational wealth transmission and the characteristics of top wealth-leavers in Britain' in P. Stanworth and

A.Giddens (eds), *Elites and Power in British Society* (Cambridge 1974); C.D. Harbury, 'Inheritance in the distribution of personal wealth', *Economic Journal* (December 1962).

12   Royal Commission on the Distribution of Wealth and Income, *Report No. 1*, p. 81.

13   For an evaluation of this and similar notions see Giddens, *Class Structure of the Advanced Societies*, pp. 53–81; and P.Stanworth, 'Property and Class in the Corporate Elite' in I. Crewe (ed.), *The British Political Sociology Year Book*, Vol. 1 (London 1974).

14   The Cambridge Elites Study, funded by the Social Science Research Council, concentrated on the analysis of biographical data of persons holding elite positions in Britain 1900–70. Due to the limitations of time and money the main body of data relates to 1,845 directors of leading financial and industrial enterprises; however, a large amount of information relating to judges, Permanent Secretaries, ambassadors, bishops, high-ranking soldiers, etc., was also collected.

15   D.M.J.Morgan, 'The social and educational background of diocesan bishops of the Church of England, 1860–1960', MA thesis (University of Hull 1961).

16   K.Thompson, 'Church of England bishops as an elite' in Stanworth and Giddens, *Elites and Power in British Society*.

17   Thompson, *op. cit.*, p. 202.

18   C.B.Otley, 'Militarism and the social affiliations of the British army elite' in J.van Doorn (ed.), *Armed Forces and Society* (The Hague 1968).

19   P.Abrams, 'Democracy, technology and the retired British officer' in S.P. Huntingdon (ed.), *Changing Patterns of Military Politics* (New York 1962).

20   Boyd, *op. cit.*, pp. 82 and 89. Boyd's book contains a wealth of information on the social background and education of a wide range of elites in Britain. It covers the period 1939–71.

21   See C.B.Otley, 'The educational background of British army officers', *Sociology*, 7, 2 (May 1973).

22   Boyd, *op. cit.*, pp. 82–3.

23   J.Brock, 'The social class origins of the judiciary of the Superior Courts (1820–1968)', M.Phil thesis (University of London 1972).

24   This data was obtained from sources such as *Who's Who, Dictionary of National Biography, The Times, Burke's Peerage, Burke's Landed Gentry*, and reports in the judicial press.

25   The Clarendon Schools, so named after the Clarendon Commission of 1851–4 (the Public Schools Commission), are Charterhouse, Eton, Harrow, Merchant Taylors, Rugby, St Paul's, Shrewsbury, Westminster and Winchester.

26   R.K.Kelsall 'Recruitment to the higher Civil Service: how has the pattern changed?' in Stanworth and Giddens, *op. cit.*, p. 172.

27   *Ibid.*, p. 177.

28   Boyd, *op. cit.*, p. 104.

29   W.L.Guttsman, 'The British political elite and the class structure' in Stanworth and Giddens, *op. cit.*, p. 35.

30   R.W.Johnson, 'The British Political Elite 1955–72', in *European Journal of Sociology* (Summer 1973).

31   The lists of companies were compiled from various sources, including different editions of the *Stock Exchange Yearbook*; P.L.Payne, 'The emergence of

large-scale companies in Britain, 1870–1914' in *Economic History Review*, XX (1967); *Company Income and Finance 1949–53* (National Institute of Economic and Social Research, London 1956); and various editions of *The Times '500'* and *The Times '1000'*. The last are annual reports which have appeared since the mid 60s on Britain's largest companies. Due to the limitations of available sources, information was obtained on 44 per cent of the directors who sat on these boards, and who held 50 per cent of the directorships. Such a sample clearly over-represents the 'well known', 'public figures' and the 'titled'. It thus represents a 'prestige' elite within the business elite.

32   We use the term 'upper class' to include industrialists, land-owners, bankers, and others who possess substantial property or wealth.

33   Cf. P.Stanworth and A.Giddens, 'An economic elite: a demographic profile of company chairmen', in Stanworth and Giddens, *op. cit.*

34   For a useful summary of data and issues, see M.A.Hutton, *Industrial Concentration* (Penguin edn. 1970); a more complex treatment can be found in P.E.Hart, M.A.Hutton and G.Walshe, *Mergers and Concentration in British Industry* (Cambridge 1973).

35   G.Whittington, 'Changes in the top 100 quoted manufacturing companies in the UK 1948–68' in *Journal of Industrial Economics*, XXI (November 1972).

36   For a summary of the growth of large banks in Britain see Monopolies Commission, *Report on the proposed merger of Barclays, Lloyds and Martins Banks*, Report 19 (HMSO July 1968).

37   A.Gamble and P.Walton, *Capitalism in Crisis* (London 1976), p. 27.

38   P.Stanworth and A.Giddens, 'The modern corporate economy: interlocking directorships in Britain, 1906–70', in *Sociological Review*, 23 (1975).

39   W.Bagehot, *The English Constitution* (Fontana edn. 1963), p. 164.

40   Guttsman, *op. cit.*, pp. 25 ff.

41   S.H.Beer, *British Politics in the Collectivist Age* (New York 1967).

42   W.D.Rubinstein, 'Men of Property: occupations, inheritance and power', in Stanworth and Giddens, *op. cit.*, p. 168.

43   Rubinstein, *op. cit.*, pp. 168–9.

44   A.Roth and J.Kerbey, *The Business Background of MPs* (Parliamentary Profiles) (London 1972), p. 12.

45   R.Whitley, 'The City and Industry: the directors of large companies, their characteristics and connections' in Stanworth and Giddens *op. cit.*

46   J.Harvey and K.Hood, *The British State* (London 1958) pp. 86 ff. Our own study of directors (based on a different sample of London clubs than that chosen by Whitley) produced the following figures: Proportion of all directors who are members of one or more London clubs (Athenaeum, Boodle's, Brook's, Carlton, White's, Junior Carlton, Reform and City of London)

1906	1920	1938	1946	1952	1960	1970
56·7	54·6	57·0	52·7	51·8	51·0	35·2

47   Using five criteria of kinship connection based on common great-grandparents, Whitley, *op. cit.*, pp. 73 ff.

48   T.Lupton and C.ShirleyWilson, 'The social background and connections of "top decision makers" ' in *Manchester School*, 27 (1959).

49   T.Lupton and C.Shirley Wilson, *op. cit.*

50 Stanworth and Giddens, *op. cit.*, 'The modern corporate economy'.
51 H.J.Laski, *Studies in Law and Politics* (London 1932), p. 168.
52 The data on the growing economic significance of state activity may be found in various sources, see particularly, Walton and Gamble, *Capitalism in Crisis*; S. Brittan, *Steering the Economy* (London, 1974); and London and Cambridge Economic Service, *The British Economy: Key statistics 1900–70* (London 1972).
53 Government participation in the North Sea oil bonanza represents something of a departure from this pattern.
54 For a detailed examination of the history of the IRC see S.Young and A.V. Lowe, *Intervention in the Mixed Economy* (London 1974).
55 Young and Lowe, *op. cit.*, p. 83.
56 See Giddens, *Class Structure of the Advanced Societies*, pp. 275–94.
57 Giddens, *Class Structure of the Advanced Societies*, pp. 156–76 and passim.
58 Karl Marx, *Capital*, Vol. 3 (New York 1967), pp. 436–41.
59 A.A.Berle and G.C.Means, *The Modern Corporation and Private Property* (Chicago 1932).
60 J.Burnham, *The Managerial Revolution* (New York 1941). For a useful summary of the ownership and control debate, see J. Child, *Business Enterprise in Modern Industrial Society* (London 1969).
61 For the argument that fragmentation of shareholding represents an important step towards a 'post capitalist' society, see R. Dahrendorf, *Class and Class Conflict in Industrial Society* (London 1959). A contrary view is presented in R.Miliband, *The State in Capitalist Society*; and in P.Burch, *The Managerial Revolution Reassessed* (Lexington 1972). Burch also argues for the continued significance of family holdings in large American corporations and challenges Berle and Means strongly on this point.
62 See Stanworth 'Property and Class and the Corporate Elite' in Crewe, *op. cit.*, and C.S.Bond, 'The Separation of Ownership and Control' in *Journal of Economic Studies*, I (2) (1966).
63 R.E.Pahl and J.T.Winkler, 'The economic elite: theory and practice' in Stanworth and Giddens *op. cit.*
64 Pahl and Winkler, *op. cit.*, p. 108.
65 Pahl and Winkler, p. 111. The actual power held by interlocking directors has never been systematically studied.
66 B.Crick, *The Reform of Parliament* (London 1968), p. 34.
67 R.Rose, 'The making of a Cabinet Minister' in *British Journal of Political Science*, I (1971).
68 R.H.S.Crossman, 'Introduction' to Bagehot, *The English Constitution*.
69 R.Rose, *Politics in England Today* (London 1974), p. 85.
70 *The Times* (25 June 1954), quoted in Harvey and Hood, *op. cit.*, p. 189.
71 B.W.Headey, *British Cabinet Ministers: the roles of politicians in executive office* (London 1974).
72 Crick, *op. cit.*, pp. 37–8.
73 Reprinted in John Urry and John Wakeford, *Power in Britain* (London 1973).
74 Ralph Miliband, *The State in Capitalist Society* (London 1973).
75 *Ibid.*, p. 62.
76 Poulantzas, *Political Power and Social Classes* (London 1973).
77 Miliband, 'The capitalist state: reply to Nicos Poulantzas', in Urry and Wakeford, *op. cit.*, p. 312.

5

Deviance and Deprivation

TABLE 5.1

Persons found guilty of indictable offences or crimes per 100,000 of the population: by age and sex, GB

Numbers per 100,000 population

	1972	1973	1974	1975
England and Wales				
Males aged:				
Under 14	1,229	1,246	1,406	1,291
14 and under 17	4,597	4,738	5,418	5,229
17 and under 21	5,475	5,522	5,952	6,428
21 and under 30	2,427	2,349	2,509	2,714
30 and over	567	543	587	642
All ages	1,484	1,464	1,603	1,694
Female aged:				
Under 14	124	129	152	151
14 and under 17	490	505	626	656
17 and under 21	639	659	745	831
21 and over 30	368	356	400	462
30 and over	137	126	151	172
All ages	219	210	247	278
Scotland				
Males aged:				
Under 17	790	845	892	886
17 and under 21	4,663	4,248	4,642	5,005
21 and under 30	2,337	2,106	2,225	2,377
30 and over	585	535	603	633
All ages	1,181	1,102	1,206	1,273
Females aged:				
Under 17	64	74	83	98
17 and under 21	380	434	510	565
21 and under 30	297	294	280	365
30 and over	125	122	141	167
All ages	155	157	175	209

Source: *Social Trends* (1976): Home Office: Criminal Statistics (Scotland), Scottish Home and Health Department

What are tables like these telling us? It looks as though there are an awful lot of people committing indictable offences in the United Kingdom — more now than there were in 1972 — and also an awful lot of people who, if the receipt of

TABLE 5.2

Persons receiving Supplementary Benefit[1], UK

Thousands

	National assistance			Supplementary benefits				
	1951[2]	1961	1965	1966	1972	1973	1974	1975
Retirement pensioners and National Insurance widows 60 years and over	767	1,089	1,258	1,668	1,857	1,796	1,761	1,635
Others over pension age	202	234	212	203	112	107	106	104
Unemployed with National Insurance benefit	33	48	35	79	91	50	76	138
Unemployed without National Insurance benefit	33	94	85	111	320	242	240	418
Sick and disabled with National Insurance benefit	121	138	153	161	142	122	98	80
Sick and disabled without National Insurance benefit	98	142	147	151	171	175	175	175
Women under 60 with dependent children	41	78	110	128	232	233	250	281
National Insurance widows under 60	86	60	58	62	65	55	44	32
Others	81	18	17	17	24	24	27	27
Total persons receiving Supplementary Benefit	14,162	1,902	2,075	2,580	3,014	2,772	2,778	2,891
of whom wage stopped (unemployed)		15	19	25	27	12	10	

Notes:

1 The figures in the table relate to times close to the ends of the years shown.

2 GB only

Source: *Social Trends* (1976): Social Security Statistics. Department of Health and Social Security

Supplementary Benefit is any guide, are living in some degree of deprivation – and again a good many more than in 1972. So are deviance and deprivation on the increase? Are they at a disturbingly high level? What do the figures mean? The plain fact is that tables like these tell us a much smaller proportion of the facts about deviance and deprivation than they appear to do. The task of applying sociology to the discussion must first and foremost be a matter of learning to question the things that seem true, that official statistics seem to present and that most policy-makers take for granted. We are in the elusive area of the sociology of moral life. One thing we can be sure of is that statistics about behaviour and people's contacts with the official world of the police and the welfare state will at best tell us a tiny fraction of the sociological truth about moral life.

We must begin by trying to combat the tendency to see such matters in terms of absolutes. In the statistical tables produced by the Home Office and the Department of Health and Social Security deviance and deprivation appear to be fixed and objectively determined features of our social life. They tell us that badness, madness, and poverty are determinate conditions, specified by strong moral rules and equally strong statistical indicators. From year to year and from decade to decade the poor and the wicked seem to be ever-present as sinister lumps in our social structure. We worry because tables like those above suggest that the lumps are growing. Other tables (*Social Trends*, 1976, p. 186) tell us that the number of people in prison who have not been tried by a court has increased by 25 per cent since 1970 and the more sensitive of us worry about that – why, they ask, on an average day are three and a half thousand unconvicted people in prison in this country. But they, too, are being naive. The 'scandal' of the untried prisoner is just another aspect of the application of power in our society which also gives us the statistics of crime and dependency. The initial sociological task must be to escape from the simplistic, absolute modes of thought that produce data like this.

Nevertheless, our commonsense picture of deprivation and deviancy builds on just those assumptions of determinate, absolute patterns of behaviour and determinate, absolute knowledge about that behaviour which conventional official statistics embody and encourage us to accept. Consider table 5.3. This is the kind of data which year after year give rise to alarms and panics in Parliament or the press about crime waves, declining moral standards, problem families, welfare scroungers and the other familiar bogies in terms of which the comfortably-off picture the lives of those outside their own prosperous and tightly regulated universe. The statistics themselves and the values used in these reports are never questioned; their meaning is unambiguous; they are self-evidently 'the facts'. But what will be argued in this chapter is that information of this sort is *not* reliable about either deviance or deprivation – that the special contribution of sociology in this field is to challenge rather than to affirm the data on which conventional wisdom is built. It will be argued that the simplistic, naive, or as I shall call it, 'absolute', acceptance of crude statistical information about deviance and delinquency needs to be replaced first by a more *relative* and then by a more *relational* understanding if these moral dimensions of contemporary UK society are to be adequately grasped. To put it another way, what we make of deviancy and deprivation in modern Britain will depend on whether we adopt an absolute, a relative or a relational view of our society as a whole. So the chapter begins with an attempt to identify the nature of each of these perspectives and the contrasting views to which they give rise.

TABLE 5.3

Crime: types of offence, England and Wales[1]

Thousands

	1951	1961	1966	1971	1972	1973	1974
Offences recorded as known to the police							
Murder, manslaughter and infanticide	0.3	0.3	0.4	0.5	0.5	0.5	0.6
Wounding and assault	6	16	25	45	51	59	62
Other offences of violence	1	1	1	1	1	2	1
Sexual offences	15	20	21	24	24	26	25
Robbery	0.8	2	4	7	9	7	9
Larceny and receiving	365	545	798	–	–	–	–
Breaking and entering	96	165	276	–	–	–	–
Fraud and false pretences	27	40	51	–	–	–	–
Burglary	–	–	–	452	439	393	484
Theft and handling stolen goods[2]	–	–	–	1,004	1,009	999	1,190
Fraud and forgery	–	–	–	100	108	111	117
Criminal damage[3]	–	–	–	27	42	53	67
Other offences	14	17	23	6	7	8	8
Total	525	807	1,200	1,666	1,690	1,658	1,963
Total per thousand population	*12.0*	*17.5*	*25.0*	*34.1*	*34.5*	*33.7*	*39.9*
Percentage recorded offences cleared up	*47.1*	*44.8*	*40.2*	*45.2*	*45.8*	*46.6*	*44.2*
Persons proceeded against							
Indictable offences	144	193	250	351	373	366	406
Non-indictable offences	626	1,014	1,269	1,445	1,569	1,674	1,645
Total	769	1,206	1,519	1,796	1,942	2,040	2,051
Persons found guilty							
Indictable offences:							
Murder, manslaughter and infanticide	0.1	0.1	0.2	0.3	0.3	0.3	0.4
Wounding and assault	4	11	15	25	27	32	32
Other offences of violence	0.2	1	1	1	1	1	1
Sexual offences	5	6	6	7	6	7	7
Robbery	0.4	1	2	3	3	3	3
Larceny and receiving	93	116	149	–	–	–	–
Breaking and entering	22	36	49	–	–	–	–
Fraud and false pretences	5	7	8	–	–	–	–

(*continued*)

TABLE 5.3 (*continued*)

Thousands

	1951	1961	1966	1971	1972	1973	1974
Burglary	–	–	–	65	61	54	64
Theft and handling stolen goods	–	–	–	193	189	181	204
Fraud and forgery	–	–	–	16	18	16	18
Criminal damage	–	–	–	4	27	33	36
Other offences	5	6	5	8	8	10	10
Total	133	182	233	322	340	338	375
Non-indictable offences:							
Assault	12	12	11	12	12	12	12
Drunkenness	51	72	67	83	88	97	98
Motoring offences	291	655	898	988	1,089	1,192	1,173
Malicious damage	9	15	17	20	–	–	–
Motor vehicle licences	6	21	40	85	93	88	83
Wireless and Telegraphy Acts	3	10	21	27	47	43	34
Other offences	213	187	159	152	157	159	157
Total	584	970	1,213	1,366	1,486	1,591	1,559

Notes:
1 The figures reflect changes affecting the statistics in legislation and recording practice. The major changes in legislation were the Theft Act 1968 and the Criminal Damage Act 1971. Figures for the years 1972–4 are on a comparable basis
2 Thefts under £5 are included throughout
3 Figures for 'criminal damage' have been adjusted in 1971 to include offences of malicious damage valued at over £20 but under £100 to facilitate comparability with 1972 onwards
Source: *Social Trends* (1975)

We must begin, then, by breaking down as best we can the commonsense attitudes that define both deviance and deprivation. Take a simple but critical example: in 1975 five million people in the UK visited their doctors with problems that were diagnosed as various forms of mental illness; 600,000 of these people then found themselves passed on to specialist psychiatric services for treatment. A very substantial body of sociological work has shown that whatever else mental illness may be it is not just a simple medical condition. Much more importantly it is a way of defining social relationships, a method by which some people manage to exclude others from the rights and freedoms that go with ordinary social relationships by getting them defined as 'ill'. More specifically still, people without power who are rash enough to object to the way those with power wish social life to be conducted, are peculiarly likely to find themselves redefined as mentally ill. In more extreme cases they will of course find themselves redefined as criminal. That is why so many students who object to examinations and so many wives who object to being mere appendages of the lives of their husbands find themselves being treated as mentally ill rather than as people with reasonable objections to an unreasonable world. They come to be deprived (of the rights of 'normal' people) because those with power over them see them as deviant. But in what objective sense is their refusal to go along with the demands of others really deviant? Is not their deprivation best understood as a concomitant of someone else's power? If we were considering the hospitalization of dissidents in the Soviet Union few British readers would find it hard to agree that deprivation and deviance are closely linked aspects of the victimization of some by others with power to impose definitions on them. But the vast majority of those readers would strongly resist any suggestion that deprivation and deviance might have essentially the same meaning in the UK. The fact that large numbers of people are put into the situation of being mentally ill, or unemployed, or criminal, in our society is certainly some sort of social problem; it is not necessarily a problem objectively rooted in the nature or behaviour of those people though. If sociology has any general lesson to offer about deprivation and deviance it is that the real social problems of deprivation and deviance are not those of the 'criminal classes', the 'poor', the 'problem families' and all the others who are officially identified as deviant or deprived but the social construction of definitions like that which some members of society impose on others.[1] There is little reason to suppose that the 39,000 men sentenced to imprisonment in the UK in 1974 (*Social Trends*, 1976, p. 41) were in any sense indicative of the level of deviance in the country at that time. All we can really say is that that number of people were effectively deprived of their freedom for actions which others judged deviant; the statistics tell us nothing about the immediate causes or meaning of whatever it was they did; nor of course about the ones who got away. And what does table 5.4 on the incidence of poverty tell us about what poverty is like or how people come to be in that condition?

In sum, we can make no progress until we have decided whether to adopt an absolute, a relative or a relational perspective on the problems involved.

THE ABSOLUTE PERSPECTIVE

The Absolute perspective has the great advantage of simplicity. It denies that the understanding of deviance and deprivation is socially problematic: deviance is a matter of the violation of given moral codes and laws; deprivation is the condition of life below certain objectively determined standards. The criminal law determines deviance; measures of intelligence determine sub-normality; the poverty line determines poverty. The tasks of social science are also simplified by this approach: the problem is to know how many people commit 'bad' acts or fall below certain standards and what individual characteristics explain their doing so. There is no problem as to why some acts rather than others are treated as bad, or whether the distribution of conditions is a matter of social relationships rather than of individual characteristics. From a sociological point of view, therefore, the absolute perspective may have some advantages in establishing rule-of-thumb measures of deviance and deprivation. There is, for example, a useful simplicity in the suggestion made by the Low Pay Unit in 1975 that a family of four with one wage-earner could be regarded as 'in poverty' if the wage-earner's weekly income was less than £40 because after deductions such wages would put the family below the official poverty line.[2] But it has overwhelming disadvantages in that it encourages the policy-maker and the ordinary person alike to take social relations out of the explanation of social phenomena.

An extreme, early, and now totally discredited, version of this attitude in the field of deviance is to be found in the work of Cesare Lombroso. Carrying out a

TABLE 5.4

Families[1] and persons normally with low net resources, GB, December 1974

Thousands and percentages

	Family resources					
	Below supplementary benefit level and normally not receiving supplementary benefit		Normally on supplementary benefit		Above supplementary benefit level but within 20% of it	
	Families	Persons	Families	Persons	Families	Persons
						Thousands
Families under pension age						
Married couples with children	90	390	80	390	120	580
Single persons with children	20[2]	70[2]	260	760	20	60
Married couples no children	30	70	80	150	30	70
Single persons no children	330	330	300	300	100	100
Families over pension age						
Married couples	90	200	320	650	330	660
Single persons	350	350	1,480	1,480	700	700
All families	920	1,410	2,530	3,730	1,300	2,160
					Percentage of all families of each type	
Families under pension age						
Married couples with children	1	2	1	2	2	2
Single persons with children	4	4	1	4	3	3
Married couples no children	1	1	2	2	1	1
Single persons no children	5	5	4	4	1	1
Families over pension age						
Married couples	5	5	15	15	16	16
Single persons	9	9	36	36	17	17
All families	4	3	10	7	5	4

Notes:
1 Families are included in this table if the head is either normally receiving Supplementary Benefit or if the family's net income less net housing costs less work expenses is less than 120% of their supplementary benefit scale rate
2 Subject to considerable sampling error

Source: *Social Trends* (1976); Analysis of the Family Expenditure Survey, Department of Health and Social Security

post-mortem on a famous brigand Lombroso came across a curious hollow in the man's skull which reminded him of similar features on the skulls of lower animals. This led him to study the skulls of many criminals and he found in them striking resemblances to those of apes and primitive man. Eventually he concluded that the impunity of the criminal to remorse as well as his cynicism, cruelty and violence were all attributable to his primitive physiological make-up. Lombroso can be treated as something of a joke in the textbooks of today but in fact the method represented in his work remains very much alive. It is essentially a matter of treating the determinants of deviance and deprivation as moral properties of the individual rather than as relational features of a society. Social work in this country, for example, developed on the basis of a clear and strict distinction between the character of the deserving poor who were to be helped to help themselves, and the undeserving on whom help would be wasted. And as Jones has recently shown, virtually the same moral distinctions that underlay the beginnings of social work in 1900 have sustained and shaped its dramatic development since 1950.[3] Indeed, in an exceptionally thorough review of the literature on so-called 'problem families' Rutter and Madge conclude that emphasis has actually tended in recent years to shift from social conditions to personal problems.[4] All that has really happened is that instead of the residuum of feckless, idle and drunken individuals of the past we hear about the residuum of feckless, violent, child-neglecting families of the present; the root problem is still seen just as clearly as a matter of the attributes of persons not of the structure of society. And in the field of deviance most police practice rests as firmly on absolutist conceptions of personal villainy as most social work practice rests on notions of personal inadequacy. Like the problem family, the 'villain' is known by his objectively observed way of life and still more by his record – by what is officially on file about him. But what does the 'fact' (*Social Trends*, 1975) that 2 per cent of the population are annually proceeded against for theft tell us about the social meaning of property in our society?

Nevertheless, commonsense left to itself tends also to adopt an absolute conception of deprivation and deviance. Of course, in practice commonsense is not left to itself but is constantly bombarded by plausible interpretations of badness and inequality through the media of mass communication – which means that it is now very difficult to tell how far the attitudes recorded in opinion polls are natural or induced. But however that problem is resolved it is clear that on a day-to-day basis our tendency to treat *conventional* moral and social standards of badness, oddness and wretchedness as though they were absolute, objectively certain measures, is very strong. Just as Lombroso 'knew' unthinkingly what sort of acts constituted delinquency and was able wholly to ignore what we might regard as the highly delinquent behaviour of many of nineteenth-century Italy's most prominent politicians and businessmen, so we all tend to judge the world in terms of ready-made stereotypes of right and wrong, good and bad, respectable and disreputable. We have off-the-peg notions of the sorts of people we would not want our daughters to marry; we can tell the bad guys from the good guys when we see them – why else should the commonest source of domestic friction in Britain in 1976 have been the length of children's hair?

In the study of deprivation the same attitude has persisted. Throughout the latter part of the nineteenth century social scientists sought to map the extent of poverty in Britain and to do so by identifying a clearly and objectively defined standard, the poverty line, below which people were poor and above which they were not. The results of these studies, especially those of Charles Booth and Seebohm Rowntree, surprised contemporaries by demonstrating that up to a third of the population were 'in poverty'. The force of their findings was closely related to the way they had chosen to define deprivation – in terms, that is, of an apparently unassailable absolute criterion. As Rowntree wrote, 'my primary poverty line represented the minimum sum on which physical efficiency could be maintained'. It was a standard of bare subsistence based on nutritional research, not a standard of living related to conceptions of social acceptability: 'a family living upon the scale allowed for in this estimate must be . . . governed by the regulation, nothing must be bought but that which is absolutely necessary for the maintenance of physical health, and what is bought must be of the plainest and most economic description'.[5] Application of the standard led Rowntree to find that while certain people were indeed 'without the minimum necessaries for the maintenance of mere physical efficiency' that is, there was not enough money coming into the household to provide for the bare needs of its members however carefully they managed, there were others who had sufficient funds but spent them inappropriately – they bought vegetables at the wrong time of year, cooked them wastefully, spent money on trade unions, newspapers, holidays or beer – one way or another failing to provide themselves with the necessary intake of calories. The first type of poverty, that deriving from an inadequate income, Rowntree called primary poverty; the second, deriving from the 'misuse' of income, he called secondary poverty. Both notions immediately called in question the adequacy of any absolute concept of poverty. The problem of primary poverty directed attention to the kind of social relations that produced incomes insufficient to maintain the worker's basic physical health. And the problem of secondary poverty directed attention to the kind of social standards which refused to recognize people as genuinely poor if they used any part of their modest incomes for even the least of the 'unnecessary' items wealthier families took for granted: 'they must never spend a penny on railway fares or an omnibus . . . never purchase a halfpenny newspaper or a ticket for a popular concert . . . they cannot save . . . the children must have no pocket money . . . the father must smoke no tobacco'. So the application of an absolute measuring rod had the effect of throwing into relief both the relative and the relational nature of poverty.

Other forms of deprivation proved even more difficult to measure, let alone to explain in absolute terms. Writing in 1914 about the mentally defective and the Poor Law Geoffrey Drage observed:

> Classification is difficult, as the line of demarcation between sane and insane, feeble-minded and normal, has not yet been satisfactorily defined. In the present instance the definition has been criticized as likely to be uncertain in application for two reasons, (a) that incapacity to manage their own affairs is a matter of degree; and (b) that having been 'normal' and become 'abnormal' they may conceivably recover, or so much so as not to merit detention any longer. This last aspect of the case is important in view of the *Mental Deficiency* Act which has just become law. The difficulty as regards the exact amount of incapability in managing his or her affairs which shall be deemed feeble-mindedness will have to be left to the discretion of the doctors. A method is at present being developed in France by which the account of a person's intelligence can be gauged with mathematical exactitude, so that this difficulty may before long cease to exist.[6]

For Drage, the need for an absolute definition was about to be met across the Channel. The tests he referred to were IQ tests and once their scientific credentials had been accepted they did indeed dominate legislation and policy in the field of mental health, and also in that of education, for fifty years. Policy and practice alike in both fields were founded on the assumption that there was an absolute solution to the problem of determining mental capacity and mental health. It took thirty years of conscientious, detailed research to convince policy-makers that intelligence tests were not measuring some absolute, psychologically-given human capacity and that differences in intellectual performance were related in complex and variable ways to social circumstances and experiences. Once again it did eventually come to be seen that the apparently absolute standard was in fact a standard based on the relative performance of particular social groups and that the problem of mental ability was in large measure a problem of social relationships. Once more the real value of the absolute approach was in indicating the relative and relational problems beneath the surface. Meanwhile in the field of mental health thousands of people found themselves shut away for life in lunatic asylums because they had committed a petty theft or become pregnant and were then judged to be mentally subnormal. And in the field of education the application of intelligence tests to entry to secondary education served not to separate the clever from the stupid but to segregate the middle classes from the working classes — and to do so on a basis which had no foundation in objective distributions of ability.

The best that can be said for absolute approaches to deviance and deprivation is, then, that they can often in a basic, sociographic manner, indicate the existence of a relative or relational problem. They are a tool of descriptive social reporting and sometimes a very useful one. Sally Holterman, for example, has used absolute indicators of deprivation — measures of unemployment, overcrowding and lack of basic amenities — in a highly effective mapping of 'multiply deprived' districts throughout Britain which brutally documents the spatial concentration of the victims of deprivation in certain, mainly inner-city, areas.[7] But sociography and sociology are very different; sociology seeks to explain what sociography can only indicate; and in the explanation absolute approaches lose their value, even when they do not become a positive obstacle. In practice the seemingly objective standards on which absolutist conceptions and policies are based are forever awkwardly changing. New laws make new crimes or abolish old ones. It becomes clear that the incidence of deviance or deprivation is dramatically influenced by where and how you look for it.[8] Worst of all, the quality of deviance or deprivation is constantly being found to vary according to its social location. Working-class offenders, for example, are sentenced more severely for crimes committed in middle-class settings than for the same crimes committed in a working-class background.[9] Middle-class people with emotional troubles go to psychiatrists for help; working-class people with similar problems often find themselves referred to social workers. In other words, for all the convenience and apparent scientific toughness of the absolute approach the relative and relational essence of deviance and deprivation constantly break through the facade.

THE RELATIVE PERSPECTIVE

Not surprisingly the last twenty years have seen a massive onslaught on what has been called the 'absolutist monolith' in the study of deviance and deprivation.[10] The first victories were won by social scientists adopting a relativistic perspective and in general that perspective now dominates mainstream sociological accounts of deviance and deprivation and is increasingly coming to influence liberal social policy. Yet oddly enough the great value of the relative perspective has been to open doors to uncertainty and to let in a quantity of healthy doubt about things that used to be taken for granted, rather than to establish a new body of knowledge. The advocates of this perspective start with powerful criticism of the very idea of absolute standards of deviance and deprivation. They point to the covertly relative nature of supposedly absolute social standards and emphasize the importance of subjective socially and historically conditioned definitions in determining what particular people at particular times and places regard as wrong, weird or intolerable. Evidence from cross-cultural or trans-historical studies is cited to draw attention to the constantly changing nature of both deviance and deprivation — indeed, of all social standards. Shooting German soldiers was heroism for Britons in 1940, murder in 1970; meticulous observation of kerb drill is good sense in a city centre but could be paranoia in a deserted country lane; regular use of drugs now proscribed in Britain was an essential feature of the way of life of other societies. The important point that relativists draw from such observations is that what constitutes deviance and deprivation is in a decisive way a matter of social judgment and social choice — hence of subjective circumstance and subjective responsibility because social judgment is not externally fixed but is historically fluid and variable; it is ultimately what we choose, or allow others to choose, to make it.

In the field of deviance this tends to call the very concept of deviance into question. The resulting sociological problem concerns the way such a concept is constructed socially. The object of study ceases to be those who are identified as deviant and becomes instead those who do the identifying and the ways in which they do it. The important data do not concern the commission of 'deviant' acts but are those which locate the social creation and the imposition of definitions of deviancy; statistics are hard to come by and the argument tends instead to be constructed through case studies and historical accounts. A classical relativistic analysis of deviance is provided in Howard Becker's studies of marihuana users, which are based on the idea that 'social groups create deviance by making the rules whose infraction constitutes deviance'. A parallel British study more sharply focused on the way in which official ideas and theories of deviance are imposed on the actions of others is Jock Young's 'The Role of the Police as Amplifiers of Deviancy' — although as we shall see Young develops an important relational analysis as well; it is not just police definitions but the power of the police over drug-users that is decisive.[11]

However, it is in the field of deprivation that the relative perspective has had its most profound influence. The attack on absolute perspectives centred initially on their operational difficulties. It was all very well for Rowntree to say that a certain calorific intake was essential to subsistence and that poverty was the condition of having less than that intake, but in the real world people do not take-in calories; they eat food. It was not difficult to show the unreality of Rowntree's assumptions about the nature of the process by which cash becomes calories. How sensible was it, for example, to assume that people had or could have the sort of detailed nutritional knowledge needed to absorb calories efficiently? And quite apart from the question of what people could realistically be expected to know, there was the more serious doubt about the reasonableness of expecting them to behave as though food was merely calories. A meal is a social activity shaped as much by the expectations and standards of the culture in which one lives as by economic resources or nutritional knowledge. There are elements of convention and culture in social life which make the attempt to apply absolute and externally derived criteria of deprivation completely meaningless and irrelevant to the individual. People eat not what is best for them but what is socially defined as conventional, acceptable and tasty: overcooked meat and vegetables; too much tea and white sugar; puddings instead of citrus fruit. Unfortunately for the absolute approach, people do continually behave as though there were socially-formed necessities in their lives as well as physical necessities; it is as essential to have enough fuel to make a fire around which the family can sit in a pleasant, cosy atmosphere, as to have simply the amount needed to keep the blood circulating – once again a possibility denied in the absolute approach of Rowntree's regime. Need, the relativists were able to show, is relative in many different directions and ways; but above all human need is shaped socially, in terms of standards derived from society; and the poor, too, live socially. Perhaps the major impact of the relativist studies of deprivation has been in spelling out some of the implications of that fact. For example, that societies change over time; yesterday's luxuries become today's necessities; circumstances that were thought tolerable in 1900 are intolerable in 1970; deprivation is relative to cultures, conditions and points of view. What people need, and therefore what makes them deprived, is related to what is normal at least as much as to what is necessary. Only, it is argued, when these relativities are taken into account can genuinely objective measures of deprivation – as distinct from the spuriously simplified measures typical of the absolute perspective – be achieved. For example, Peter Townsend, one of the strongest and most influential advocates in the UK of the relative approach, says quite bluntly that 'poverty can be defined objectively and applied consistently only in terms of the concept of relative deprivation'.[12] I shall consider the nature and impact of Townsend's work in more detail shortly. Essentially, the approach has revolutionized the discussion of deprivation in the UK by proposing that deprivation must be judged as a condition relative to what is normal for the society at a given time: 'Individuals, families and groups in the population can be said to be in poverty when they lack the resources to obtain the types of diet, participate in the activities and have the living conditions and amenities which are customary, or are at least widely encouraged or approved, in the societies to which they belong.'[13] The crucial statistics therefore are those that tell us what is the average or mean distribution of selected living standards or conditions, and then about the distance between that average and the actual standards or conditions of sections of the population at the bottom of the national distribution. Details like those presented in table 5.5 become the basis for discussion because deprivation has been made a problem of equity and it is the gap between the condition of the most favoured and that of the least favoured members of society that now matters; the social problem has been made relative – one notes that in 1953 television was a luxury but that by 1977 the absence of television in a household can reasonably be taken as one index of deprivation for the members of that household.

For all its strengths, however, the relative perspective runs into difficulties of its own making. If deprivation is a matter of social definition how do we determine the level of deprivation in any particular setting? Recent work has tended to be trapped by its own relativism; perhaps everyone is deprived; or perhaps no one is. It can be argued that according to the standards of contemporary Western Germany almost everyone in the UK is deprived; or that hardly anyone is by the standards of contemporary India; that by the standards of the seventeenth century we are all very well off; that many people are badly off by the standards of a few; that relative to our expectations yesterday most of us are badly off today. Relativism opens a hazardous chasm of subjectivity here. In order to avoid it advocates of the relative perspective have tended recently to seize upon some objectively measurable and conveniently available yardstick – the lowest 10 or 20 per cent of the income distribution, say, or the ad hoc poverty line created by the levels at which Supplementary Benefit is fixed – and to base their arguments on the relativities

TABLE 5.5

Gross weekly earnings of full-time workers[1], GB

£ and Percentages

	Men aged 21 and over					Women aged 18 and over				
	1968	1970	1972	1974[2]	1975	1968	1970	1972	1974[2]	1975
Manual workers £										
Highest decile	33.1	37.7	45.9	60.3	76.9	16.0	18.5	23.9	32.5	43.8
Upper quartile	27.4	31.3	38.3	50.6	64.5	13.1	15.4	19.9	27.2	37.1
Median	22.4	25.6	31.3	41.8	53.2	10.8	12.8	16.4	22.7	31.0
Lower quartile	18.2	20.8	25.5	34.4	44.1	9.0	10.6	13.5	18.8	25.8
Lowest decile	15.1	17.2	21.2	28.7	36.8	7.7	8.8	11.3	15.7	21.2
As percentage of median										
Highest decile	*147.8*	*147.2*	*146.6*	*144.1*	*144.4*	*148.3*	*144.8*	*145.9*	*143.4*	*141.4*
Upper quartile	*122.3*	*122.3*	*122.3*	*121.0*	*121.3*	*121.1*	*120.1*	*121.6*	*119.8*	*119.6*
Lower quartile	*81.0*	*81.1*	*81.3*	*82.2*	*82.8*	*83.4*	*83.0*	*82.5*	*83.0*	*83.3*
Lowest decile	*67.3*	*67.3*	*67.6*	*68.6*	*69.2*	*71.1*	*69.0*	*68.9*	*69.1*	*68.4*
Non-manual workers £										
Highest decile	49.6	55.0	66.8	83.1	103.1	24.8	27.6	34.4	42.3	61.6
Upper quartile	36.5	41.1	50.5	63.1	80.2	18.3	20.6	26.0	33.4	45.7
Median	27.8	31.4	38.5	48.5	61.8	14.1	15.9	20.1	26.1	35.9
Lower quartile	21.1	24.2	29.6	37.6	47.9	11.1	12.4	15.8	20.7	28.8
Lowest decile	17.0	19.4	23.7	30.5	38.7	9.3	10.2	12.9	17.4	23.9
As percentage of median										
Highest decile	*178.5*	*175.1*	*173.7*	*171.6*	*166.7*	*175.5*	*173.7*	*170.9*	*162.0*	*171.5*
Upper quartile	*131.1*	*130.8*	*131.3*	*130.2*	*129.6*	*129.3*	*129.4*	*129.1*	*127.9*	*127.2*
Lower quartile	*75.9*	*77.1*	*76.8*	*77.6*	*77.5*	*78.8*	*78.3*	*78.2*	*79.4*	*80.3*
Lowest decile	*61.2*	*61.8*	*61.7*	*62.9*	*62.6*	*65.4*	*64.2*	*64.0*	*66.5*	*66.5*

Notes:

1 These figures relate to men aged 21 and over and women aged 18 and over whose pay for the survey period was not affected by absence. The survey period was in September in 1968, and in April in 1970 and subsequent years

2 Estimates for 1974 were affected by under-representation of local authority and National Health Service employees in the New Earnings Survey sample

Source: Social Trends (1976); Department of Employment New Earnings Survey (1975)

that then emerge; for example, the inequity implicit in the fact that the poorest 10 per cent of the population receive a mere 3 per cent of total personal income while the richest 10 per cent enjoy 25 per cent. While this procedure gives relativists an important ability to claim objectivity for their arguments it also of course marks a retreat from the full implications of relativism. It would seem more honest to recognize that the difficulties of the relative perspective can really only be resolved by concentrating on the ways in which deprivation and deviance are produced through the workings of specific social relationships — hence the relational perspective.

THE RELATIONAL PERSPECTIVE

It has always been implicit in both absolutist and relativist treatments of deviance and deprivation that the problems of each are embedded in social relationships — that low incomes somehow implicated those who bought labour as well as those who sold it and that squalid housing had something to do with those who owned houses as well as with those who lived in them. But these implications tend to remain beneath the surface of absolutist and relativist analyses. The distinctive feature of the relational perspective is precisely that it sees deprivation and deviance first and foremost as predicaments created dialectically in the structured relationships of the deviant or deprived individuals to the rest of society. The relative approach certainly often points that way, as when it emphasizes low earnings as a cause of poverty, or the imposition of middle-class standards of judgment on working-class children as a source of their educational 'under-achievement'. But the tendency has been to concentrate on subjective definitions and experiences or at best to treat the sources of deprivation as facts of life rather than features of a dynamic relationship which might themselves be open to criticism and alteration. By contrast the relational perspective suggests that it is impossible to understand, let alone to do anything much about, people living on a low income unless we know how that small income is *made* small by the bigger incomes of other sections of society; and that it is impossible to understand or alter the ways in which certain activities and persons come to be seen as deviant without looking at the ways in which normalcy *creates* deviancy. This approach forces us to look away from the deprived or the deviant as special, isolated or peculiarly problematic segments of our population — however defined — and to attend to the processes and relationships in society as a whole which generate deprivation and deviance as ways of life imposed on some people through their involvement with others.

To use an analogy: if we are presented with a picture of a man reeling back and collapsing we can perhaps comment on the distance he has to fall or the extent of his proneness, but without further information we cannot begin to explain what is happening to him; we need other figures in the picture, or a relational story to accompany it, before we can tell whether he is the victim of a heart attack or an assault, or whether he is simply fooling around. Only then will his odd behaviour and parlous position become fully intelligible. In the same way it is the relational context of deviancy and deprivation that sociology has to bring to light. Applied sociology is not just a matter of amassing information in a form that is relevant to policy; more fundamentally it is a question of making sense of information about social problems by translating facts and figures about incomes, benefits, activities, conditions, back into the dialectical language of social relationships. But having said that, the advocate of a relational perspective has a problem. How in a necessarily restricted discussion of deviance and deprivation is the involvement of the deviant with the normal, and of the deprived with the privileged, to be made clear? Exactly what features of British society should I discuss in the rest of the chapter? In a sense the whole point of the relational perspective is that there ought not to be a separate chapter on deviance and deprivation in a book like this one; it is precisely the cutting-off of the vanquished from the victors in a social system that the perspective criticizes. Arguably the tables in the chapter on elites tell us more about the causes of deprivation than all the information that can be gathered in surveys of the poor.

However, deviancy and deprivation do exist as commonsense categories of everyday life and are to that extent realities of the social world of the people who find themselves thus classified and cut off. So I shall select four from the many sub-worlds of British society that are created by that type of classification and in each case I shall aim to build a relational account of why such sub-worlds exist. The four categories I have chosen are poverty, vagrancy, the one-parent family and juvenile delinquency. These are not necessarily the areas that would immediately spring to mind when deviancy or deprivation are mentioned. They do not include the more glamourous forms of deviancy (such as drug use or pornography) nor the more politically troublesome forms of deprivation (like squatting and unemployment). What they do include though are the day-to-day lives of millions of people trapped by social categorizations — and more powerfully by social relationships over which they have no control — which lock them into the predicament of being deviant or deprived, or both. Indeed, one of the most striking aspects of these four categories within contemporary UK society is the way in which all of them in some degree challenge and confuse the distinction between deviance and deprivation. The people who do this most spectacularly are of course political prisoners — who directly challenge the claim that their deprivation (of liberty) is legitimately grounded in the suggestion (made by the police and the courts) that their actions are deviant. But in less dramatic ways each of the four categories of our society that I have chosen to look at also threaten the convenient idea of a neat distinction between deviance (morally reprehensible behaviour to be punished) and deprivation (a morally lamentable condition to be remedied).

The poor have always been much more pitiable or unfortunate than merely deprived; for hundreds of years they have also been described and discussed by the non-poor as a sinister as well as a pathetic element of society, a uniquely potent source of deviance, the dark side of society from which both crime (above all crime against property) and socialism (the political crime against property) are liable to erupt.[14] Vagrants are in many ways merely the extreme examples of the poor; that is to say they are treated variously as ill, muddle-headed, outsiders, criminals, dangerous, down-on-their-luck, misfits and enemies of society.

The one-parent family seems to be a more straightforward case. At first sight the presentation of the children and mothers (or fathers) who find themselves lacking in the full complement of members of the 'normal' British family is a simple matter of deprivation. In fact, close study of the ways in which one-parent families are discussed in the media and by government, suggests that a quite powerful tendency to identify these families as deviant, as failures, as centred on one or more 'inadequate' personalities, even as threatening, is also quite an important component of the social definition of their situation. Why didn't she have an abortion? Why couldn't she keep her husband? Why can't she get a job? Why does she have to have new boy-friends? Why doesn't he let her have the children? These are the questions that lurk beneath the surface of the social definition and social construction of the one-parent family.

As for juvenile delinquents, they are the most ambiguous category of all. Juvenile crime is widely regarded as 'not really' crime at all; it belongs in a special category called 'mischief'. At the same time juvenile delinquency is generally recognized as a 'serious' social problem. It occupies a great deal of time and space in the mass media and in political argument. The actual treatment of the young criminal is equally ambiguous. There is normally a long process of treatment by social workers — based on the assumption that the child is deprived rather than 'really' deviant — before the offender is frankly handed over to the criminal law. Nevertheless, at the end of the day, after all attempts to explain the young person's aggression in terms of deprivation — broken homes, difficult circumstances and so forth — have failed to actually stop his or her annoying behaviour, no difficulty is experienced so far as the relevant educators, social workers, lawyers and policemen are concerned in quickly redefining the poor child as a villain. In each of these cases, then, we should consider the ways in which deviance *or* deprivation is selected by powerful persons as the appropriate label to apply to certain powerless persons. Over and above that, however, we need to understand that for certain groups in contemporary UK society deviance *or* deprivation is the only career choice allowed to them by other groups.

POVERTY

In taking a relational and dialectical view of poverty it is essential and unavoidable that we see it at the outset in the context of social and economic inequalities within UK society as a whole. To understand poverty, therefore, we must look at the full range of social, economic and cultural inequalities in our society from the top to the bottom.

In writing about poverty at the end of the 1970s it is sometimes hard to realize that less than twenty years ago most people in Britain believed that poverty had been eliminated from our society. The late 1950s were not only a time when we could believe that we had 'never had it so good'; it was also a period when the creation of the welfare state was fresh in public memory and when Labour Party intellectuals like C. A. R. Crosland, to say nothing of American sociologists such as S. M. Lipset, could confidently tell us that the traditional problems of inequality created by the industrial revolution had been successfully mastered.[15] It was with something of a sense of shock therefore that poverty was rediscovered in the 1960s. The excellent study of poverty in Nottingham by Coates and Silburn is representative of that period in the way it opens with a stark characterization of the complacency of the immediate past:

> During the fifties the myth that widespread material poverty had been finally
> and triumphantly overcome was so universally current, so widely accepted by

politicians, social commentators and the general public alike, that for
and more public controversy and political discussion were engrossed b
(and fundamentally more encouraging) problems of what people are st
to call the 'affluent society'. The age-old malaise of poverty, far from b
endemic problem facing a mass of the population, was felt to be a slight social
hangover, a problem affecting tiny groups of people who through their incompetence or fecklessness were failing to share in the new prosperity.[16]

Yet it is difficult in the late 1970s to persuade young people that the late 1950s
ever existed; that people really did believe that poverty had been done away with.
Each year in my lecture course on the welfare state, as the students' birth dates
creep up to and past 1960, they look more and more incredulous about that
decade. There has been a revolution of consciousness about poverty. The mystification achieved in the 1950s is a worthy subject of analysis in its own right. But
what is important here is the fact that the poverty which we now know to
surround us is essentially a rediscovered poverty, a poverty highlighted in the mass
media and in our own minds precisely against the background of the affluence of
the rest of society, a poverty therefore which appears all the more out of place,
unfortunate and problematic. For the sociologist, moreover, its rediscovery
represents one of the few passages of post-war British history in which academic
social science can be held to have played a significant constructive role in the
course of events — albeit a small and peripheral role in relation to the major
political struggles of the time. Academic social science may not be able to change
the world but at least when mystification is deep-seated we can sometimes
effectively interpret it. And that appears to have happened in the rediscovery of
poverty.

Symbolic of the rediscovery was the publication in December 1965 of *The Poor
and the Poorest* by Brian Abel-Smith and Peter Townsend. Based on very
thorough analysis of the Ministry of Labour's *Household Expenditure Surveys* and
comparing household incomes in 1953 and 1960 the paper forcibly injected the
relative approach into a discussion previously conducted in complacently absolute
terms. The authors accepted as the basis for determining poverty the standard
applied by the government in determining National Assistance (now Supplementary
Benefit) scales, at the same time pointing out that this was essentially a conventional
not an absolute yardstick: 'Whatever may be said about the adequacy of the National
Assistance Board level of living as a just or publicly approved measure of "poverty"
it has at least the advantage of being in a sense the "official" operational definition
of the minimum level of living at any particular time.'[17] They then went on to
demonstrate that on the basis of the best available figures, and using the official
minimum criterion of acceptability, 3.8 per cent of the population, or 1,990,000
people, were in poverty in 1960. However, because the criterion *is* relative and
because in practice various additions are commonly made to the scale to meet
special needs Abel-Smith and Townsend chose to set their own poverty line at the
National Assistance level plus 40 per cent and calculated that on that basis 14.2 per
cent of the population, or 7,438,000 people, could be said to be living in poverty.
Other studies published at that time suggested that if anything these estimates were
too modest; and A.B.Atkinson surveying the field as a whole in 1969 reached the
view that: 'It seems fair to conclude that the proportion of the population with
incomes below the National Assistance/Supplementary Benefit scale lies towards

the upper end of the range 4–9 per cent. In other words, around 5 million people are living below the standard which the government feels to be the national minimum.'[18]

Evidence of this sort had a dramatic impact on public opinion, especially when taken up by the Labour Party in successive election campaigns. But looking back now on that period it is clear that although the issue was raised little was done to solve the problem. Many publicized reforms, such as the abolition of National Assistance and the introduction of Supplementary Benefit, proved little more than window-dressing. Looking back in 1970 on six years of Labour government the Child Poverty Action Group could conclude that 'poverty remains on a con- siderable and perhaps even greater scale than when the government assumed office'.[19] One of the most alarming findings of the poverty debate of the 1960s, though, was the powerful confirmation from virtually every form of research of the point initially made so clearly by Abel-Smith and Townsend – that the numbers of the poor increased hugely if one took the most generous rather than the meanest view of how the official poverty line might apply. Two million people in poverty is just conceivably a social problem with which existing government machinery – including 60,000 officials administering Supplementary Benefit – and existing patterns of social policy could hope to deal. But the persistent presence of five million or more people in a socially acknowledged condition of poverty suggests, as Kincaid wrote in 1973, that what we are faced with is not some unfortunate residue from a harsh but vanishing past but rather a 'massive and structural charac- teristic' of UK society.'[19] As table 5.6 shows, the gap between the poorest tenth of our population and society as a whole has remained virtually unchanged over the last ninety years so far as male wage-earners are concerned and it has improved only marginally for women. As the CPAG have noted, in 1972 the Department of Health and Social Security itself acknowledged that there were in fact almost six million

TABLE 5.6

Lowest decile's wages as a percentage of median earnings, 1886–1974

| Year | As percentage of the median for male and female employees | |
	Male lowest decile	Female lowest decile
1886	68.6	
1906	66.5	
1938	67.7	64.3
1960	70.6	72.0
1965	69.7	66.5
1970	67.3	69.0
1974	68.6	69.1

Sources: CPAG, *Poverty: the facts* (1975); *British Labour Statistics; New Earnings Surveys*

people living on incomes at or below the official poverty line.[20] And the Depart- ment has found that the number rises as its own thinking becomes more relativistic. By 1974, as table 5.4 indicated, the Department – although still not willing to go as far as Abel-Smith and Townsend – was contemplating a poverty line set 20 per cent above the Supplementary Benefit level, and the effect of that was to suggest a possible total of 7,300,000 people in poverty. Moreover, all these figures, although based on the actual numbers of those claiming and receiving benefit, are only estimates of the numbers of those who are entitled to benefits but are deterred by the stigma of poverty or other reasons from actually taking them up. And some case studies have strongly suggested that those numbers are quite a lot higher than the official estimates.[21] How is this massive and structural characteristic of UK society to be understood?

Poverty, Welfare and Wages

The answer, I suggest, lies in the three-way relationship between poverty, social welfare and the wage-economy. At one time that relationship would have seemed perfectly obvious to every informed enquirer: the wage economy needed poverty and welfare policies worked to ensure that this need was met. But surely it is not like that today?

Since 1900 successive governments have made strenuous efforts to change that relationship — primarily through the introduction of social insurance. But their continuing failure to do so attests to the strength of the relationship; and the new institutions that mark the latest version of the British welfare state, like the Supplementary Benefits Commission, have their roots firmly embedded in the nineteenth century Poor Law. In implementing the first measures of social insurance the Liberal Governments of 1906–14 had sought to escape from the influence of the Poor Law, but in the event they failed to create institutions capable of doing so. In 1919 when the Coalition Government found itself faced with the prospect of millions of unemployed workers the full implications of social insurance became apparent — namely, that the level of benefit provided in return for insurance contributions should at the very least be enough to keep the beneficiary out of poverty (however that was defined). No government between the two World Wars was prepared to face up to that implication. But it was of course boldly and explicitly faced in 1942 in the Beveridge Report, *Social Insurance and Allied Services.* Officially implemented in 1948 and still the ostensible framework of social policy in this country the Report was founded on the cardinal principle that insurance should henceforth replace means-tested doles, reliefs and assistance as the distinctive instrument of welfare. The object was to ensure 'at all times to all men a subsistence income for themselves and their families as of right', and through insurance.[22] In other words, as Beveridge himself said later on, the central idea was 'the subsistence principle, the guaranteeing to every citizen in virtue of contribution and irrespective of need or means, of an income in unemployment, sickness, accidental injury, old age or other vicissitudes *without further resources* to provide for his basic needs and those of his dependents'.[23]

Against that background it was only reasonable to assume that any system of means-tested, ad hoc supplementary relief would come to an end. National Assistance was accordingly envisaged as a minor, subsidiary, background element of social policy designed to mop up the left-over problems of the past and therefore with a steadily diminishing role in the future. Thus, the National Assistance Act of 1948 opens with the resounding words 'the existing Poor Law shall cease to have effect'.

In practice the means-tested National Assistance/Supplementary Benefit element of the welfare state has played a steadily larger, not smaller, part in the relief of poverty since 1948. Even before Beveridge himself died in 1953 the real pattern was becoming clear and he was calling on the government to admit that 'they have formally abandoned security against want without a means test'.[24] Yet as table 5.2 showed, by 1975 1,885,000 of the 2,891,000 people receiving Supplementary Benefit were also National Insurance beneficiaries. Or to put it the other, and more telling, way round, one in five National Insurance beneficiaries were also receiving Supplementary Benefit — their insurance benefits had failed to keep them out of poverty. The attempt to use the wage-economy, via insurance, as a basis for preventing poverty had once again proved a disaster and as a result it seemed that the Poor Law was still very much with us. Again, table 5.2 indicates just how far we remain from realizing Beveridge's ideal. And so long as social insurance cannot lift people out of poverty — an inability which is of course itself closely linked to distributions in the wage and profit economy — so long as we are unable to run an insurance system at an adequate level, the cruder mechanisms of the means-tested hand-out will continue to be the distinctive feature of UK social welfare. It is in those mechanisms that the legacy of the Poor Law is most evident.

The Poor Law of 1834 was meant specifically to act as a deterrent, to discourage the poor from applying for relief by making the conditions associated with it as unpleasant as possible. The point of the law was to force people to work:

> In all extensive communities, circumstances will occur in which an individual, by failure of his means of subsistence, will be exposed to the danger of perishing. To refuse relief, and at the same time to punish mendacity when it cannot be proved that the offender could have obtained subsistence by labour, is repugnant to the common sentiments of mankind.
>
> But in no part of Europe except England has it been thought fit that the provision, whether compulsory or voluntary, should be applied to more than the relief of indigence, the fate of a person unable to labour, or unable to obtain in return for his labour the means of subsistence. It has never been deemed expedient that the provision should extend to the relief of poverty; that is, the state of one who in order to obtain a mere subsistence is forced to have recourse to labour.
>
> The first principle is that his situation on the whole shall not be made really or apparently as eligible as the situation of the independent labourers of the lowest class. In proportion as the condition of any pauper class is elevated above the condition of independent labourers the condition of independent labourers is depressed; their industry is depressed, their employment becomes unsteady, and their remuneration in wages is diminished. Such persons are therefore under the strongest inducements to quit the less eligible class of labourers and enter the more eligible class of paupers. The converse is the case when the pauper class is placed in its proper position, below the condition of the independent labourer.[25]

The plain aim of the law, then, was to ensure that the living standard of those on relief was appreciably worse than the standard of those who were receiving the lowest wage from work. Conditions in the workhouse and the tests governing entry were explicitly designed to realize this relationship between pauperism and the labour market. And it is that relationship — essentially the relationship between poverty and the wage system — that has dominated the social treatment of poverty in the UK ever since and which persists today.

Creating a system of social security which made life on relief deliberately and palpably worse than life on the lowest available wage was not an act of punitive nastiness on the part of the Poor Law authorities. Rather, it represented the creation of conditions which allowed a wage economy to function effectively. The Poor Law served to create and maintain labour mobility on a national scale: by making life on relief a degrading, desperate last resort it ensured that all those on relief, and the vast majority of those who might otherwise be tempted to apply for relief, would be prepared to take work at the lowest possible wage. Thus the powerlessness of the wage-earner in the supposedly 'free' labour market was ensured. It was that function that the creation of the workhouse served so efficiently:

> Into such a place none will enter voluntarily; work, confinement and discipline will deter the insolent and the vicious and nothing but extreme necessity will induce any to accept the comfort which must be obtained by the surrender of their free agency, and the sacrifice of their accustomed habits and gratifications. Thus, the parish officer being furnished with an unerring test of the necessity of applicants is relieved from his difficult and painful responsibility; while all have the gratification of knowing that while the necessitous are abundantly relieved, the funds of charity are not wasted by idleness and fraud.[26]

The barbarities of the workhouse have not survived into the present day; but the reasoning behind them is still evident in the way poverty is constructed and then relieved in Britain in the 1970s. Listen to Professor David Donnison, the progressive and enlightened Chairman of the Supplementary Benefits Commission, lecturing on his responsibilities in 1976 and the echoes of the Poor Law Commissioners are not far below the surface:

> The SBC must show that it is not soft on fraud, particularly for the sake of the millions of people entitled to every penny of Supplementary Benefit they get. If the public comes to believe that the whole system is a racket, our political leaders will ultimately be compelled to impose crippling restrictions which will punish those who depend on it. We can and must report that the Department of Health and Social Security detected about 16,000 cases of suspected social security fraud in 1975 and prosecuted in about 15,000 of these — succeeding in nearly every case.[27]

The crucial application of Poor Law thinking is the presence of tests (backed if necessary by prosecutions because the line between deprivation and deviance is a slender one and it is the privileged and normal who decide where it is to be drawn), based on the belief that the individual or family should in principle be in the labour market as a condition of relief. Thus the 1920s saw workers having to prove that they were 'genuinely seeking work' before they became eligible for benefit. The 1930s saw workers having to undergo a test of their means to ensure that they were genuinely in need. In the words of Ramsay MacDonald addressing the nation in 1931, 'Unemployment benefit is not a living wage; it was never meant to be that'. In effect, in both periods the lowest available wage determined social policy, not any sense of the needs of individuals or families separate from the logic of the labour market. The decisive consideration was the need of the wage economy for a supply of very low wage-earners, not the needs of those wage-earners for any particular standard of living.

In the period since 1948 the most obvious manifestation of the link between social security and the wage economy was the 'wage-stop' clause attached to National Assistance and Supplementary Benefits until the summer of 1975. The wage stop was quite simply a device which required the SBC, unless there were exceptional circumstances in a particular case, to adjust the allowance so that the claimant's income could be no greater than it would have been had he been engaged in full-time work in his normal occupation. In other words, if one's normal wage was too low to secure a reasonable standard of life the choice offered by the welfare state was not one that included the possibility of escaping from poverty. It was merely a choice between being poor on the wages of a rotten job or on the charity of the state. In other words the post-war system of social security was just as deeply entangled with the wage economy as its predecessors. Indeed, Beveridge had been adamant that the system should not be seen as a disincentive to work, that it should not give the poor the freedom to opt out of the labour market.

Yet the Beveridge scheme did represent an advance on earlier policies for poverty insofar as it included a series of benefits for spouses, dependent children and rent and thus recognized variations in the personal circumstances of claimants as a legitimate source of variation in need and as a proper basis for varying the level of relief. In that respect it also differed of course from the wage economy which operates with no reference to that sort of variation at all. As a result of this step away from invariant levels of assistance, however, unskilled — low-paid — workers with large families were bound to be a problem of a special sort for the post-Beveridge welfare state. In order to ensure that such workers received less on National Assistance/Supplementary Benefit than they would at work it was essential to create devices that would ensure payments at lower levels than those to which they would otherwise have been entitled. That was what the wage stop was about. The abolition of the wage stop was therefore a major attempt to break the power of wages over welfare and to move towards a more independently political relationship between the state and poverty. Ironically, however, a main effect of the reform was to make it rather clearer than before just how thoroughly poverty as a whole was a product of the wage system. As Professor Donnison said early in 1976:

> When Parliament abolished the wage stop last July the Commission knew perfectly well that . . . this would expose the fact that benefits sufficient to support a large family will sometimes provide a larger income than an unskilled worker can earn for himself. The wage stop did not solve that problem; it simply swept it under the carpet — at the cost of advertising to the world that the Commission's benefits would never exceed the wages offered by employers no matter how low those wages might be.[28]

Since 1975, in other words, although the relief of poverty has been put on a slightly more generous basis, the root cause of poverty, the relation between poverty and the labour market, has been more rather than less apparent. That relationship expresses itself directly through low pay, and indirectly through the inability of governments to fix the benefits of social insurance at adequate levels. Table 5.7 indicates in a quite uncompromising way just how far poverty springs from these sources.

TABLE 5.7

Relative contribution of selected causes of poverty

Cause of poverty	Percentage of total of those in poverty[1]		
	1899	1936	1960
	%	%	%
Unemployment[2]	2	29	7
Old age and sickness[2]	5	19	40
Inadequate wages[3]	52	42	40
Fatherless families	16	8	10

Notes:

1 The first two columns derive from Rowntree's surveys in York; the third from *The Poor and the Poorest*. The first two columns therefore refer to an absolute standard — Rowntree's subsistence criterion; the third to a relative criterion — the current level at which people become eligible for national assistance/supplementary benefit

2 In the 1960 data these figures are of course indicative of poverty caused by inadequate insurance benefits

3 Abel-Smith and Townsend include in this category all those whose income is below the poverty line either because of an absolutely low wage or because of a wage that is low in relation to the size of the family it has to support — the so-called 'large-family' problem which is merely another form of wage-induced poverty

Before looking into the role of inadequate social security and low pay in constructing poverty, however, we should note that even in its post-1975, reformed, condition the Supplementary Benefit system is itself not all that independent of the wage economy. The various 'control procedures' and tests applied to claimants by the SBC to discourage what the Commission regards as fraud are still rooted in the assumption that eliminating poverty is a matter of getting people into the labour market, or at least into relationships in which they can be defined as dependent on people in the labour market, rather than a question of eliminating those features of the labour market that produce poverty in the first place. In the areas where the Commission exercises discretion the old Poor Law principle of less eligibility is still all too evident. The logic of the 'work-shy' control procedures which gives the Commission's officers discretion to withdraw benefits if they judge that the claimant is fit for work and that work is available, the parallel logic of the 'voluntarily unemployed' procedure which allows benefits to be reduced if the Commission judges that a claimant is out of work without good reason, and the logic of the 'cohabitation rule' which provides for the reduction or withdrawal of benefits from women claimants believed to be living as the common law wives of men with jobs, all rest on the same fallacy. In each case it is assumed that full-time work is in principle an adequate source of livelihood for all and that it is therefore reasonable to make welfare systematically less eligible than work — even the work of a common law spouse. In 1973, 13,700 claimants were judged to be voluntarily unemployed and had their benefits reduced accordingly. In the same year 8,700 claimants suffered the indignity of being investigated as possible cohabitees.

The Commission's policies are thus at best ambiguous; its officers frequently use their discretion generously in making decisions on cases; but the system as a whole inexorably pushes the claimant on to the defensive in asserting the reality of his or her need against the natural workings of the labour market. From the claimant's point of view it also works to preserve the distinction between work (good and natural) and welfare (regrettable and abnormal) by blurring the distinction between deprivation and deviance. The procedures of control, investigation, means-testing and punitive deductions all contrive to make poverty an offence. Having been made poor by economic 'necessities' which the state is powerless to redress, one is then made deviant by the efforts of the state to embody those necessities in its own policies. Benefits are kept as low as possible; extreme vigilance is maintained in holding them low and guarding against frauds. And the very business of applying for and receiving benefits becomes an arduous and degrading experience. A mass of research now suggests that a distinctive feature of the social relationships of Supplementary Benefit offices and of the whole world of the 'beneficiary' is the aura of stigma associated with being a claimant and the discovery that as a claimant one is the bearer of a 'spoiled identity', to use Goffman's apt term.[29] Throughout, the system seems to work as though it was essential for the claimant to be as financially and socially ill-at-ease, uncertain and embarrassed as possible, ensuring perhaps that he or she thus feels impelled to seek other kinds of less demeaning income, to take any sort of work rather than to persist in the enigmatic, unpredicatable and totally awkward role of welfare beneficiary.

National Insurance

The causes of poverty are, then, twofold: inadequate wages and inadequate insurance against the hazards of the labour market and the life cycle. So far as the insurance aspect is concerned the problem is compounded by the fact that since 1911 at least the state has been heavily committed to the attempt to insure people against the risks associated with poverty. In the event of unemployment, sickness, widowhood or old age, National Insurance schemes are designed to produce returns for the insured that guarantee that they are protected from poverty. The thinking behind these schemes is quite simple — the immediate causes of poverty are the various traps and disasters that can befall working-class families and interrupt the normal flow of earnings. This interruption is not seen as a cause of poverty in its own right: the problem is held to be the inability of the working-class family to insure itself privately against such interruptions and exigencies. The state therefore sets out to ensure that appropriate protection is nevertheless provided.

However, in the period since 1948 an important irony has emerged in the relationship between insurance and poverty. The National Insurance benefits which were meant to guarantee that individuals and families would now be able to live above the poverty line as of right, have been allowed to fall in value to a level well below the scales worked out by the National Assistance Board and the Supplementary Benefits Commission as the criteria for eligibility for their benefits. Thus substantial proportions of the people in receipt of National Insurance benefits also *have* to claim Supplementary Benefits in order to achieve even the standard of living represented by our official poverty line. Tables 5.2, 5.4 and 5.7 all indicate the existence and extent of this problem. And the DHSS Annual Report for 1974 concedes that in 1973 24 per cent of those receiving unemployment benefit, $10\frac{1}{2}$ per cent of those receiving sickness benefit, 28 per cent of those receiving retirement benefit and 14 per cent of those receiving widows' pensions were also receiving Supplementary Benefits. These figures pose brutal questions about the nature of our National Insurance system, and confirm that it is itself a direct cause of poverty.

One of the fundamental aims of National Insurance was to guarantee that families would not have to undergo means tests in order to obtain a decent standard of living — would not in fact have to apply to the state for relief. In the event this has proved impossible. If you are entitled to the old age pension and have *no* other private pension or income then the only way you can obtain the income needed to reach the poverty line is to apply for Supplementary Benefits as well. Table 5.4 indicates that 920,000 families who for this reason are eligible for Supplementary Benefit do not actually receive these benefits — either because of the stigma associated with dependence on the state or because no one has told them they are eligible.

How did this situation arise? It originates in the very nature of the insurance principle. Private insurance is based on the calculation of 'risks' worked out actuarily. Rather like betting, this necessitates an analysis of the likelihood of suffering these eventualities in proportion to the amount staked. Thus, if you were betting on the likelihood of a car-worker and a university lecturer being made redundant and needing unemployment benefit, on the existing evidence you would conclude that the car-worker ran a much greater risk. Consequently you would ask for a much higher premium in insuring the car-worker than you would in insuring the university lecturer. If you fail to apply market probabilities in this way your scheme will go bust. However, if you were to carry out this exercise for all workers, all occupations and all risks (which is essentially what National Insurance seeks to do), a number of further problems arise. There is a very wide range of risks and costs to be considered. Since there are great many car-workers and only a few university lecturers — that is to say, an overall high level of risk — premiums need to be set at a fairly high level if the scheme as a whole is to be viable. But the high-risk members of the scheme are also typically the low income ones. So the 'natural' premium level is likely to be too high for the majority of wage-earners to pay. Other means of obtaining finance are therefore essential. And this is where the employers' contribution and the state's contribution come in. It is only if these are real and substantial contributions that a three-way contributory system such as our own can adequately insure all its members against the risks to which they are exposed.

The original National Insurance scheme of 1911 met these problems by restricting membership to certain forms of occupation, the better risks, as well as by requiring relatively modest contributions from the employer and the state. A large proportion of the population were left outside the scheme but for those within it the scheme was actuarially sound; the contributions received were sufficient to meet the demand for benefits being paid out. But the delicate balance of contributions and benefits achieved for the original group of low-risk workers failed to survive the political and industrial demand generated during the First World War and its aftermath for the inclusion of millions of other workers. Once the total work force of low-paid, high-risk families had to be included the viability of the scheme collapsed. Faced with the massive unemployment of the 1920s and 1930s the idea of effective National Insurance was reduced to a romantic memory. The Beveridge plan was accordingly designed with the failures of the past very much in mind; its central purpose was to build up an actuarially sound National Insurance fund to provide adequate benefits for all. But to do this without a huge assault on the existing distribution of income (which was regarded as politically unacceptable) Beveridge felt obliged to allow a period of twenty years during which the fund would accumulate, through contributions being paid in and no benefits being paid out. Only after that time would the resources available be sufficient to counteract the fact that many high-risk members of the scheme could not afford high premiums.

Alas, the political consequences of not paying out benefits until 1968 were more than the Labour government of the day was prepared to face. So the insurance principle was written-in to the National Insurance scheme essentially as an ideal — perhaps merely as a convenient myth. The funding of the scheme was put on a year-by-year basis, treating the contribution purely as a form of regressive taxation. The level of benefit is similarly tied to the level of contribution in only the most formal way; in practice, especially in the case of old age pensions, it is varied in the light of political pressures and opportunities whenever and however the party in office sees fit. The paradox is that the contributory principle is vehemently maintained as the official *account* of the system even though it is perfectly well understood that contributions cannot in practice produce adequate benefits. In 1954 the Philips Committee, set up specifically to limit the amount the contributory income of the insurance fund could be increased by additions from taxation, fixed a ceiling of 18 per cent. Since this limit has been respected the scheme as a whole is doomed to inadequacy, based as it is on flat-rate contributions which are determined by what the poorest can be made to pay. Without massive additions from general taxation, which successive governments have refused to contemplate, the level of benefit remains below the poverty line and National Insurance becomes a major contributory factor in the making of poverty in the UK. The number of National Insurance beneficiaries eligible for Supplementary Benefit increases steadily. By insisting that rights have to be bought — that pensions must be paid for by contributions — National Insurance guarantees that a wage economy characterized by a vast number of small incomes will be matched by a welfare state characterized by a vast number of inadequate benefits. It simply transfers the wage-relationship to the field of social welfare.

The failure of the state to provide adequate insurance benefits has been high-lighted and aggravated by the continued reliance of governments upon the application of means tests. This has become one of the most distinctive features of contemporary poverty. At the time of writing there are 42 means-tested benefits, which represent a huge maze of interference into people's lives. The experience of being poor becomes one of constant form-filling, endless trips to Supplementary Benefit offices, Job Centres, housing, Health and education departments, permanent vulnerability to the visits of social workers, SBC inspectors and the like. Once again these experiences are created: they are not accidental. Consequently it takes a great deal of courage, energy and persistence for someone whose poverty results from the inadequacy of the benefits to which he or she is entitled to fight their way back up to the poverty line. If they have in the first place accepted the official doctrine that benefits should be something earned, not handed out — 'a benefit in return for contributions rather than free allowances from the state is what the people of Britain desire', as Beveridge put it — then they are trapped ideologically as well as materially.

Poverty and Low Pay

If the oblique relationship of the state social security system to the wage economy
is one major cause of poverty there is nevertheless a much more direct and
immediately material relationship between wage levels and poverty as well: namely,
low wages themselves. Coates and Silburn identify very clearly what is involved:

> The second largest category of poor households we interviewed included by far
> the largest number of persons (accounting for 50 per cent of the poorer
> population). This consisted of those families with breadwinners at work whose
> incomes did not entitle them to receive public relief. As Townsend has explained,
> there are two elements here, which alone or in combination cause poverty. The
> first is found where the breadwinner's wage is very small, too small perhaps to
> support even the smallest family. The second is seen when the numbers of
> dependents in the family stretch the income further than it can go. Of course,
> both elements combine in the case of a large family trying to live on a very
> small income.[30]

The same effect emerges in many other studies — for example in Hilary Land's
analysis of large families in London. In a complex and revealing table (table 5.8)
Land shows the way in which the basic wage of a large family, or the basic level of
state benefits, leaves the family well below the poverty line. The study is of 86
families with five or more children. The line across the table marks the median
point in each column. As we go across the columns of this table and add on
dimensions of income for the large family we see that even in column 6 with all the
additional income of different kinds added on the median point is still below the
poverty line, if we accept the Abel-Smith and Townsend definition of poverty as
140 per cent of the Supplementary Benefit basic rate. Looking at column 1, though,
we can see that only 14 per cent of Land's sample were above the poverty line
when they had only their basic wage to live on. This provides yet another example
of the way in which the wages system is organized on the basis of systematically
providing insufficient resources.

The relationship between low wages and family size is an obvious one, but one
that is usually noted in only one respect — poor people have too many children. In
looking at the issue in this way we fail to grasp the more important point — the
inability of the wage economy to provide for the needs of even some quite small
families. To quote Coates and Silburn once more:

> The argument is not only about the families of eight, nine or ten children, but
> in a depressingly large number of cases it is about the families with only two or
> three children. Thus in St Ann's, nearly one in five of the one-child families,
> over a third of the two-child families, and approaching half of the three-child
> families were in poverty.[31]

This sort of proportion must bring into question the whole issue of the relationship
between family size and poverty and certainly forces us to abandon any simplistic
notion that having too many children is a root cause of poverty. Instead, it
directs our attention once again to the wages system as the Invisible Hand behind
the social construction of the poor. For if low wages cause poverty, what causes
low wages?

The Report of the National Prices and Incomes Board on low pay attempted to

TABLE 5.8

Cumulative income of large families

% of NAB scale + rent	Basic wage or benefit	Plus overtime	Plus wife's earnings	Plus children's contributions	Plus welfare and education in kind	Plus irregular money income	Plus income in kind
	1	2	3	4	5	6	7
Under 80	29	9	6	5	–	–	–
80–89	29	16	12	8	6	6	4
90–99	13	11	11	10	12	10	12
100–109	5	9	8	9	12	14	14
110–119	5	6	12	10	10	8	3
120–129	3	13	12	14	12	11	15
130–139	2	4	2	6	6	10	11
140–159	3	15	12	10	11	10	9
160–199	2	6	14	17	18	16	17
200 Plus	9	11	11	11	11	15	15
Total	100	100	100	100	100	100	100

Source: H. Land, *Large Families in London*, Occasional Papers in Social Administration no. 20 (London 1969)

answer that question, adopting − in line with most official thinking nowadays − a fairly naive relativistic view of the problem:

> The following propositions may be said to underlie the approach to low pay developed in the White Papers:
> 1 A significant number of workers have low pay
> 2 This is inevitable in an increasingly affluent society
> 3 Low pay is moreover a cause of poverty though by no means the only one
> 4 It is therefore desirable both to enable those with low pay to have bigger pay increases than other workers and to tackle other causes of poverty through changes in tax and social security arrangements.[32]

Just as the kind of figures presented in table 5.5 make poverty inevitable by making it relative − that is, the poor are the 'lowest decile' and any distribution of the population into deciles is always going to have a lowest decile − so the thinking that lies behind this sort of statement at once relativizes the issue of low pay and evades it. People are poor because they get less than other people in wages; the solution, equally relativistic, is that these people should have bigger pay rises. This fails to recognize the actual social process through which wages are determined. The amount paid out at the end of the week is the result of a complex relationship between the powers of the employer and of labour. Those who receive less than others do so because of their weakness in this relationship, a situation that can change rapidly under the influence of changing markets − as the experience of the coal miners since 1970 demonstrates. The miners moved from a low to a high pay condition because their economic and political bargaining power was transformed. Inadequate bargaining power is one cause of low pay and hence of poverty; and that leads us back to consider the social relationships prevailing between workers and employers in the particular sectors of the economy in which low pay is concentrated. The general distribution of low pay in the economy is discussed in detail earlier in this volume by Richard Brown. It will suffice to remember here that the decisive causes of low pay are not the personal attributes of individual workers but the structural characteristics of certain employment relationships. So far as bargaining power is concerned, the concentration of low pay in agriculture, among women workers, in small firms and in the Wages Council industries, is perhaps evidence enough of the direct connection between a weak bargaining position and an inadequate income.

But the bargaining power of given groups of wage-earners is only one cause of poverty: the larger context of wage bargaining must also be taken into account. Labour bargains with capital and capital attempts to ensure that it retains as much surplus value as possible. The resulting bargains are struck over the whole range of industries and occupations and all relate to each other. Within this process the maintenance of a low-wage sector is important not only because of its internal value to the employers who pay low wages, but also because this sector relates to all others and constitutes a base in terms of which employers' costs in those sectors, too, can be held down. In this way the low-wage sector is functional if not crucial to the maintenance and profitability of the whole fabric of any capitalistic wage economy. This in turn means that when we talk of low-wage poverty we are not talking of an isolated sector which can in some simple administrative way be brought up to the income level of others. Attempts to force companies to pay higher wages in the low-wage sector would certainly result in numerous bank-ruptcies, not just among those companies but also among the much greater number of firms that depend on cheap labour-intensive industries for their part-made materials and services.

Where does this leave our understanding of poverty? A Supplementary Benefits scheme which measures need in terms of the availability of the lowest-paid work; a National Insurance system so dependent on the wage economy that it must pay inadequate benefits in order to avoid relieving poverty through progressive taxation; a plethora of stigmatizing and often crudely administered means tests, and a low-wage sector that must be maintained to ensure the overall viability of the economy. Those are the sources of poverty in contemporary UK society. Each creates a group of people who are socially and economically isolated in terms of their own experience, but are nevertheless indissolubly linked to the social relationships of our wage economy as a whole.

ONE-PARENT FAMILIES

Perhaps the clearest finding of recent research into one-parent families is that there is no such thing as *the* one-parent family. Rather, there are a great many different ways in which a mother or a father can come to be living alone with her or his children, and even more different ways in which people in that situation can be treated socially. But what I am particularly concerned with here is the way people in that situation have the category 'one-parent family' imposed on them as the effective account of their social reality, the way they are made deviant or deprived.

Let us start by considering the ways in which each of the three perspectives I outlined at the start of the chapter might, stereotypically, view such people. From an absolutist point of view the one-parent family is self-evidently deviant because the two-parent family constitutes an absolute norm of proper family life; con-comitantly, the members of the one-parent family are also deprived because the emotional and material support provided by the missing spouse and parent is denied them. The one-parent family is therefore a social problem to be treated and controlled. From a relative point of view there is of course nothing intrinsically deviant about one-parent families; they are merely another way of living. But because they are commonly treated as deviant and because conventional family arrangements involve two parents and a division of labour in terms of breadwinning and housekeeping, they can be seriously disadvantaged in practical terms. There is therefore a problem of relative deprivation to be solved through financial and other forms of support. A relational analysis would start from the observation that one-parent families are in practice treated as both deviant and deprived in our society and that as a result of that treatment they are indeed deprived of a wide range of the pleasures and amenities of life enjoyed by two-parent families. It would go on to ask how that treatment is brought about, assuming that the answer is to be found in the institutions to which they relate.

The figures in table 5.9 provide some picture of the number of one-parent families in our society, but the reality of the issue they present goes much deeper than one million children. The Finer Report is remarkable for the way in which it attempted to make sense of that deeper reality. Consider the following passages:

8.9 We have been struck by the evidence of how universally the division of labour is taken for granted by which mothers and fathers in the two-parent family seek to enrich the upbringing of their children by extending their range of activities – especially in their educational and leisure activities. The handicaps of the one-parent family in this respect have been continuously emphasized. Even at the level of disposing of everyday chores, and despite the degree of merger between the traditional roles of the male and the female which has taken place in the last decade, many household tasks still tend to be allocated sexually. Men mend fuses and women do the ironing. The necessity for the lone parent to take on both roles may arise suddenly, leaves no alternatives, and often is not satisfactorily achieved.

8.10 One of the main personal problems in one-parent families is the parents' social isolation. They suffer from loneliness – not only of surroundings but also of unshared difficulties. They are lonely in their responsibility for the physical care of their children – a responsibility which often robs them of sleep and makes demands on them beyond their physical stamina. They carry the entire burden of responsibility for the social, emotional and moral up-bringing of their children, and for that part of their education which has to take place outside of school. They suffer all the strains of being compelled, as one parent, to play the part of two, in order to create within the home a microcosm of the society in which children will become adults.

8.11 On top of these stresses often comes the frustration of foregoing sexual relations or conducting them clandestinely so as to avoid the notice of children or the neighbours or arousing the suspicions of the officers of the Supplementary Benefits Commission.[33]

Contained within these three paragraphs are three principal elements of the experience of one-parent families which lead to their being seen as deprived and deviant. One element springs from the social 'normalcy' of the two-parent family; a second from the sexist character of the society as a whole; and the third from the way state organizations, such as the SBC, have chosen to treat single parents.

TABLE 5.9

Estimates of the number of one-parent families, GB, April 1971

Sex and marital status of parent	No. of families (thousands)	% in receipt of Supplementary Benefit	No. of children (thousands)
Female			
Single	90	68	120
Married	190	54	360
Widowed	120	21	200
Divorced	120	33	240
Total	520	44	920
Male	100	7	160
Grand Total	620	38	1080

Source: *Report on One-Parent Families* (Finer Report), Cmnd 5692 (HMSO 1974), Appendix 4

The Family, Sexist Roles and One-Parent families

We are only too prone to think that the children of one-parent families are victims of an absolute deprivation; taking the two-parent family as a given, natural phenomenon we see single parents as deprived of the natural support of a spouse and worst of all their children as deprived of the natural attachment of two parents. The studies of maternal deprivation carried out at the Tavistock Institute in the 1950s powerfully reinforced our readiness to make such judgments. In these studies Bowlby and others raised a body of folk commonsense to an apparent level of scientific certainty. The whole series of studies took the given social organization of the family for granted as well as the culturally given modes of bringing up children in a sexually differentiated society.[34] The commonsense knowledge which these studies reaffirmed rested on more than a century of social, religious and economic policy towards the family. That history is touched on elsewhere in this book; it is its effects on our view of one-parent families that is important here.

The deprivation of the one-parent family comes, then, from the relationship of that form of social grouping to the 'normal' nuclear family. The missing element of the 'other parent' becomes a shattering socially-created deprivation in the face of a world organized on the basis of that standard of normalcy. Of itself, in a society created around many diverse types of familial relationships the one-parent family would not embody the concentration of multiple deprivations it suffers as a result of being the glaring exception to a powerfully asserted rule. If we look, for example, at the specific role of social policy in this context we can see the ways in which the whole experience of single parenthood is discouraged and made exceptional; it transforms an experience that is merely different into one that is both deviant and deprived. Yet one can imagine societies in which there are many different modes of bringing up children and where, accordingly, single parenthood was no more than just something different: one difference among many. In other words, the specific deprivation and deviance of UK one-parent families are socially created by the attitudes and practices of the wider society and especially the state towards family life in general.

The situation of women in UK society is discussed by Hilary Wainwright in another chapter; what matters here are the results of that situation for the single mother or father who is in charge of a family. She or he has to go through a maze of difficulties which are not simply a matter of deprivation. In a sexually divided society it is a problem for one person of either sex to meet the requirements of that society in bringing up children. Again this is not a matter of absolutes: women are not *necessarily* softer, more interested in cooking, sewing and shopping; men are not *necessarily* tougher, more interested in woodwork, painting and mending the car. Yet these are the roles assigned to the sexes in the domestic division of labour, and a household which exists without an adult of one sex or the other has to confront the difficulties of the situation while learning the role of the missing sex. Thus, the father in the single-parent family has quickly to learn to cook, to look after the house, to give the children the more tender forms of love 'normally' provided by mothers as well as those 'normal' to fathers. For the single mother the problem is reversed. And all this happens at the worst possible time. Lacking any early training or teaching in the roles of the opposite sex these must now learn them at a time when there is no easy apprenticeship and no one close at hand to help. Moreover, the father who succeeds in acquiring the skills and roles of a

mother and the mother who succeeds in acquiring those of a father then face a
further problem — that of seeing themselves, or being seen by others as losing their
'natural' sexual identities. Thus the rigid sexual differentiations of our society
compound the predicament of single parenthood.

The Role of Social Security

The contribution of our system of social security to this multiply created
deprivation is crucial. The Beveridge Report has a number of seemingly generous
provisions for women in charge of one-parent families. The important thing to
note, though, is that once again Beveridge was as much concerned with morality
as with welfare; and once again the determination to impose a particular moral
system ended up by undermining the provision of welfare:

> Divorce, legal separation, desertion and voluntary separation may cause needs
> similar to those caused by widowhood. From the point of view of the woman
> the loss of her maintenance as a housewife without her consent and not
> through her fault is one of the risks of marriage against which she should be
> insured; she should not depend on National Assistance. Recognition of house-
> wives as a distinct insurance class, performing necessary services not for pay,
> implies that if the marriage ends otherwise than by widowhood she should be
> treated as insured, unless the marriage maintenance has ended through her fault
> or voluntary action.[35]

Beveridge argued specifically for a form of social security which secured the
housewife, and hence the one-parent family, as an insured category. But he
qualified this by making it the responsibility of the social security officer to decide
whether the woman herself had been responsible for the break-up of the marriage.
It was important for him that the insurance system should not be seen as
'encouraging adultery', or as paying women who had chosen to break with their
husbands for whatever 'voluntary reason'. The two-parent family was in effect
treated as an absolute moral norm, and social security was designed in such a way
as to punish those who voluntarily departed from it.

To the average National Insurance Inspector in the post-war period it would
have been a nightmarish if not an impossible task to differentiate accurately
between those who had left their husbands 'voluntarily' and those who had left for
reasons of mental cruelty or a host of other good reasons. Since the practical
implementation of a distinction between innocent and guilty women was impossible
the whole conception of insuring women against single parenthood was dropped.
The Government played safe and decided that if the woman's need was seen as
real (that is if she fell below the official poverty line) her case would be dealt with
by the National Assistance Board. At a stroke single parents were thus deprived,
with all the associated stigma of that condition. The National Insurance scheme
was left entirely linked to contributions made during employment, thereby
ensuring that millions of women would be dependent upon their husbands'
entitlement and have no social existence in their own right. The ability of women
to acquire an adequate contribution record was profoundly and persistently
hampered by the ways in which the employment patterns of women had to be
worked out in the context of culturally defined rules for the reproduction and

socialization of children. The effect of those rules is to shorten and interrupt the contribution pattern of nearly all women, thereby ensuring that they fall outside the National Insurance system if they ever have to exist independently of their husbands. Thus, the contribution element in the social security system makes sure that for most one-parent families the form of social security on which they depend will be Supplementary Benefit.

Benefits from the SBC are means-tested and are also complicated by the liability of the father to maintain his children. In the case of Supplementary Benefit this means that the Commission will attempt to recoup payment from fathers for the maintenance of children, which in turn necessitates tracking down the father and the often tortuous extraction of payment. No one subjected to this can survive with their dignity intact. This sort of liability is one more way in which the 'normal' view of the family is imposed forcibly and by law on those whose lives are 'abnormal'. The 'abnormal' family with a low income is immediately subject to a whole apparatus of scrutiny and control which offers financial support only on condition the proposition is accepted that one is really abnormal and deviant. The most savage expression of this effort to make the one-parent family deviant is the cohabitation rule.

Over the past few years claimants' unions throughout the country have brought the attention of the public to the way in which this SBC control procedure is used to reinforce the stigmatized condition of the single mother. If a man is living with a woman who is on Supplementary Benefit then he becomes liable to maintain her and her children. The problem for the SBC officer is to find out when a man is actually living with a woman. Does spending a night count, or two nights, his washing on her line? Do the neighbours know the man? Is his underwear in her wardrobe? Such questions are the stock-in-trade of an officer trying to prove cohabitation, and consequently for a woman anxious to protect the family income she receives from the SBC the practical alternatives are either promiscuity, in which case no one responsible male can be made liable to support her, or sexual abstinence. In either case the woman's attempts to rebuild the sort of long-term relationship (to say nothing of the financial security), which the 'normal' family is generally thought to be about, is systematically undermined by her relationship to the state. The use of social security as an instrument of moral regulation combined with the refusal of successive governments to recognize that looking after a child is a job of work, ensures that the mere 'difference' of a one-parent head of a household is made deviant and incurs the full measure of stigma and intolerance. Here again the social security system draws the boundaries of what is and is not normal for our society; in such ways, too, did the workhouse ensure that the individual who entered it would be stripped of the habits and gratifications that they enjoyed outside, would be made deviant as the price of securing the benefits held out to them as a compensation for having first been made deprived. Like poverty the social problem of the one-parent family thus emerges as one that is specifically *created*: created by the interaction of that form of living with a sexist society and with a series of state policies that reinforce the exclusive normalcy of the two-parent family.

VAGRANCY

Vagrancy may seem an odd example to include in an analysis of deviance and deprivation in the UK. Odd, because it affects only a few people; and odd because it is surely the archetypical 'rump' problem which will 'always be with us'. Yet in some ways a society's treatment of vagrancy tells us a great deal about its treatment of deviancy and deprivation as a whole; it is one of the ways in which the distinction between normal and abnormal social relationships tends to be most clearly created and most ruthlessly imposed.

The sturdy beggars of the distant past, typically bands of unemployed workers fighting for some form of decent living, the vagabonds of the sixteenth century, the migrant labourers of the eighteenth and nineteenth centuries and the homeless men of the present, have presented a constant challenge to the norms of property, work and domesticity on which UK society is founded. And the way they have been treated has constantly revealed the close connection between social welfare and punishment, between relieving poverty and policing it. One way and another, from the time of the old Anglo-Saxon laws which provided that the traveller who was allowed to stay in any one place for more than three nights then became the responsibility of his host, the effort has been to eliminate the vagrant or failing that to build a wall of massive social isolation, stigma and control round his existence. Both responses are embodied in the series of late sixteenth-century laws passed in both England and Scotland following the Act of 1572 'for the Punishment of Vagabonds and for Relief of the Poor and Impotent'. On the one hand 'masterful idle beggars' were to be branded, flogged, imprisoned and then banished unless 'some respectable citizen should take them into service for a year'.[36] On the other hand parishes were to identify their poor and raise funds to support them. The English but not the Scottish laws also provided for able-bodied vagrants to be put to work. Thus the vagrant was doubly stigmatized. Branding — on the right ear and the size of the iron to be used was specified in the Act — manifestly set the vagrant apart from his fellows, ostracizing him by a permanent, visible symbol. And the subsequent linking of poor relief to 'settlement' similarly stigmatized the whole vagrant way of life as outside normal society. The vagrant thus acquired the peculiar form of identity with which he has been burdened ever since; denied membership of society he is redefined as the 'scrounger on society'.

It has not always been the simple fear of unrest or crime that has caused this stigmatization. Rather, there have been two over-riding principles. First, that the 'settled way of life' of a society should be protected from alternatives which if they became too inviting might lead to the collapse of normal respectable life; so vagrancy or the unsettled life must be made to seem positively uninviting. And secondly, as a capitalist labour market developed, the need to regulate and limit the mobility of labour and to maintain a steady, productive, dependent workforce grew with it. Hence the need to harass and punish those who would not be part of that workforce. It is this combination of moral and economic imperatives that has created the condition of vagrancy. It is not that the mobile labourer is 'work-shy' or disreputable; but that he rejects the *mode* of work and the *mode* of respectability that have progressively been imposed and institutionalized as normal for industrial capitalist society. For these two reasons the vagrant cannot be left alone. In the past he was harried and starved; now he must be 'resettled' into society. In either case the experience of a different way of life is turned by the state into one of deviancy and deprivation.

Each year the Department of Health and Social Security includes in its annual report two or three paragraphs on the running of 'reception centres'. This represents the way in which the Department meets the duty laid upon it by the

Supplementary Benefit Act of 1966 'to make provision whereby persons without a settled way of living may be influenced to lead a more settled life'. Thus:

> There are now 14 reception centres directly administered by the Commission and 4 administered on the Commission's behalf by Local Authorities.
>
> London has only one reception centre, at Camberwell. This has a nightly population of between 500–600 men, of whom about half arrive on a casual basis and half are residents on the resettlement side of the centre. The very large influx of men each night prevents more from being done by the way of resettlement.
>
> DHSS, *Report*, 1968, p. 254.
> 'During the year an average of 1,125 men were accommodated each night.'
> DHSS, *Report*, 1969, p. 99.
> 'The average number of persons accommodated nightly during 1970 was 1,273.'
> DHSS, *Report*, 1970, p. 99.
> 'The nightly average number of persons accommodated during 1973 was 1,704.'
> DHSS, *Report*, 1973, p. 84.

The way in which the Department implements its duty varies a great deal but in nearly every case the reception centres are run with considerable kindness and with thought and sympathy for those entering them. This is in itself a deliberate feature of the overall attempt to influence the vagrants back into a more settled way of life. The approach is clear: vagrancy is officially reprehensible and to be discouraged. The fact that the discouragement is in personal terms often kindly and sympathetic does nothing to make the vagrant way of life any more socially legitimate.

A report published by the Home Office gives us further evidence of the official view:

> Many vagrants today may be said to belong to the periphery of society – they are socially displaced, often with mental disorders and often with criminal records. A recent survey by a psychiatrist and a sociologist of men using the Camberwell reception centre suggested that about one in five had some form of mental disorder; one in seven of the newcomers and four out of ten of the rest were alcoholics or other addicts; about 6 per cent and 10 per cent respectively suffered from physical illness or infirmity; only a small number were migrant workers, but *job problems* accounted for the destitution among three out of ten of the newcomers and one out of ten of the rest, while for about one in ten of the newcomers and one in fifty of the remainder the cause of destitution was a situational factor, e.g., the break-up of a home or the death of parents. As to their background the researchers said: 'In terms of the number of beds occupied we calculate that in the year before their attendance all the men visiting the Centre collectively used on any given night approximately 580 prison bunks, 260 mental hospital beds, 660 places sleeping out, 350 reception centre beds and 1,880 beds in common lodging-houses.[37]

The official picture, then, is one which highlights the individual inadequacies of a vagrant, in terms of moral, social or legal failure. These are seen as the *causes* of his vagrancy; for instance, a record of mental disorder is held to have made the individual a vagrant. The reverse proposition — that the activity of being vagrant has led to his being identified as having mental problems — is not contemplated, although a mass of sociological research and the practical experience of many old people who have had to live out their lives in hospitals for the mentally subnormal because of some minor criminal offence or moral lapse perpetrated in their youth, powerfully suggest its plausibility. But if we look at some of the biographies of vagrants outlined in the Report of the National Assistance Board for 1965 we see that it was not so much any condition of mental disorder that led to the initial decision to turn to a vagrant way of life, but rather an attempt by the individual to escape from what was being experienced as an intolerable situation. Typically, we find middle-aged men who had been looking after their parents and were suddenly orphaned; victims of chronic unemployment; widowers; and people evicted by landlords or planners from sub-standard housing. All these experiences represent predicaments in which lack of support from the community at large resulted in massive strain for the individual, leading in turn to a decision to opt for an 'unsettled way of life'. Vagrancy is resorted to as an escape from an intolerable situation within 'normal' life; the world closes in on the individual and, since the pressures induced by normal life cannot be dealt with, the only rational course is to get out. Such situations are in fact very common in our normal social life; people have to drive themselves to get through examinations, to bear all sorts of personal crises with decent reticence — that is, on their own — to continue day after day doing boring and meaningless work. If the vagrant life were an easily available alternative, an inviting prospect for the victims of such pressures, there would be many individuals opting for it.

So vagrancy is made into a harsh, lonely, awful option to take. One way or another it must be discouraged. Discouragement can be achieved by violence or, as is now the case, by a massive denigration of the whole experience — choosing that sort of escape is in itself treated as evidence of mental disorder — and structurally by the destruction of the casual labour market that could provide a material base for vagrancy. The condition of vagrancy is thus made into a marker for the boundaries of normal life; time spent as a vagrant is time out of society. To be 'of no fixed address' is still one of the most damning pieces of evidence that can be used against anyone; to have no fixed address is still one of the ways in which people can fall through the safety net of the welfare state and be made ineligible for many benefits. The state continually offers vagrants the option of returning to its approved 'settled way of life' but *never* recognizes the fact that it was the settled way of life that created the problems from which the individual had to escape in the first place.

The Home Office working party did not confine its interest to the 'unsettled' aspects of vagrancy. They had interesting things to say, too, about begging;

> Few people are likely to be annoyed or embarrassed by a child asking for money for his fare home, or by a single polite beggar; but to be accosted by a dirty, unkempt and aggressive beggar (perhaps calling at the house when the housewife is alone) can be frightening, and to be accosted by a large number of beggars, even though they might be polite, would be a real nuisance. If begging ceased to be a specific offence there is a danger that the number of beggars would increase, that they would tend to congregate in certain public or semi-public areas, and that the mode of begging would in consequence tend to become importunate or outright aggressive.[38]

So the laws against begging, the criminality of asking for money instead of working for it, is justified in this sort of official thinking. A single, polite beggar is acceptable in a welfare state world; but a collection of beggars gathering together to press their case is a threat to public order, now as for the past four hundred years. The social treatment of vagrancy is not just a matter of defining the boundaries of what is an acceptable way of life in UK society: it also reflects an abiding fear, the Great Dread as it used to be called, of unrest among the poor; a dread that the poor might one day collectively refuse to go on being made poor.

JUVENILE LAW-BREAKING

The alarm and hysteria with which juvenile law-breaking is discussed in contemporary Britain might make us think that both the activities and the panic are new. That is far from the case. In 1818 we learn that 'The lamentable depravity which, for the last few years, has shown itself so conspicuously amongst the young of both sexes in the Metropolis and its environs has occasioned the formation of a Society for investigating the causes of the increase in Juvenile Delinquency'.[39] And a few years later discussing 'juvenile depravity' Henry Worsley wrote: 'The number of juvenile offenders has gradually and progressively increased. Juveniles aged 15 and under 20 form not quite one-tenth of the population but they are guilty of nearly one-fourth of the crime . . . The period which shows the blackest, whether we look at the proportionate amount of crime or its progressive increase, is comprised between 15 and 20 years of age'.[40]

These remarks could be echoed continuously over two centuries; panic about the activities of the young is an enduring state of mind among the old. And such an historical perspective is important here because we can too easily form the impression that post-war UK society has collapsed beneath an unprecedented wave of vandalism, hooliganism, skinheads, hell's angels and the rest. That indeed is what we are encouraged to think. And to discover the extent of the reality of juvenile law-breaking is no easy matter. There are two sets of figures that we can take as a base line for any analysis: the official ones produced by adding up cautions and convictions; and those produced by independently produced 'self-report' surveys.

The former, shown in table 5.10, provide a picture of involvement in law-breaking that is peculiarly 'refracted'. What do I mean by this? Many of us believe that statistics on activities such as crime actually mirror the world; they *reflect* it. Thus, if we see a statistical table on juvenile law-breaking which says that only twenty-one 10-year-old females out of every hundred thousand in the population were convicted in 1974, we take that figure to tell us what actually happened. There is of course another group who tend to dismiss all statistics as lies, to believe that all data of this sort are concocted to prove partisan arguments. I use the metaphor of refraction to suggest a different analysis of such statistics. A refracting mirror *does* reflect reality but *not* in the way reality actually exists. We have all been to fairground booths and seen ourselves in mirrors as four feet tall or with gigantic foreheads. Yet our hair does not change colour and the mirror does not change our sex. There is still a semblance of reality and if we choose to understand the form of the mirror and how it is made we can reconstruct our true images.

TABLE 5.10

Numbers of individuals convicted and cautioned, by age and sex; per 100,000 of the population, 1973

Age group	MALE		FEMALE	
	Convicted	Cautioned	Convicted	Cautioned
10	315	1,389	21	263
11	780	1,939	54	499
12	1,473	2,506	150	824
13	2,517	2,897	305	1,036
14	3,882	3,017	445	1,005
15	5,071	2,488	540	742
16	5,291	1,479	533	365
17	6,677	452	770	84
18	6,162	289	707	42
19	5,059	221	582	27
20	4,247	175	499	28
25	3,003	86	419	26
30	1,849	48	307	22
40	1,229	33	261	20
50	653	20	171	16
60	334	15	131	17
60 plus	98	28	34	25
Total	1,464	347	210	100

Source: Home Office Statistics (1974)

Thus, with the statistics in table 5.10 we must understand exactly what they stand for, where they are produced, by whom and why. Obviously, the first significant thing that happens in this chain is that the police catch someone, otherwise no charging or cautioning can take place. But the police do not catch and charge people either comprehensively or at random. Several useful research studies of police practice with juveniles have emphasized their different approaches to different groups of children. John Lambert's study of police activity in Birmingham shows that police practice can be highly selective and variable and can have many unintended consequences; which must lead one to doubt the validity of the data on juvenile crime they produce as an accurate account of reality. In the United States Piliavin and Briar have shown how certain people end up being charged while others are simply told to get on their way; such variations depend on the 'demeanour' of the youths after being caught rather than on what they did that lead to their being caught in the first place. And Cicourel has studied the way in which some youths find themselves cautioned by the police while others are immediately charged, and still others never reach the police station at all, although all have engaged in the same actions. Such findings can only lead us to be very sceptical in dealing with official statistics of this sort; what should we make, for example, of the 'fact' that there are 6,677 convictions per hundred thousand male 16-year-olds and only 21 per hundred thousand 10-year-old females? Does this really mean that there is over three hundred times as much crime in one age and sex group as in the other? Or does it reflect different police practice for these two groups?[41]

If we look at the data from self-report surveys we are likely to become even more worried about the picture painted by the official figures. Self-report surveys are very simple: presenting the respondents with a list of activities which includes both legal and illegal actions, they ask them to say if they have carried out any of them. Used by themselves such studies have all the dangers of any form of simple questionnaire research. People make things up, forget or suppress, exaggerate, fantasize, and so forth. But if used with other research methods (such as structured and unstructured interviews, participant observation, personal records and diaries, etc) they can provide a picture of the extent of law-breaking that is much more representative than police statistics. Studies like this have been carried out on a worldwide basis: in Oslo, Stockholm, various parts of the United States as well as extensively in the UK. In nearly all cases they have found that over 80 per cent of the male teenage population breaks the law.[42] My own study of male youth in Sunderland bears this out; nearly everyone had either smashed or stolen something during the previous year. Lynn Macdonald's study in London again supports this picture of near universal male juvenile law-breaking. And if such findings are at all reliable they have one unavoidable consequence for the way we talk about juvenile crime. They surely put a stop to the search for the factors or variables in the experience or background of law-breakers which singles them out from the rest of society; it appears that the rest of society are also law-breakers. Statistically at least the real deviants are the tiny minority who don't break the law. And the presentation of juvenile crime as an isolated minority activity begins to look like one more attempt to impose some people's moral norms as though they were everyone's empirical reality.

But where does this leave our understanding of juvenile law-breaking? Do we simply say that it is a universal phenomenon, a phase through which every young male goes? If we leave it at that, we fail to look at the problem; fail to see that thousands of telephone boxes are smashed, that thousands of kids put on to 'care and protection' orders and that many more have their lives drastically changed by being selected to be labelled deviant in more or less official ways; we fail to grasp the meaning of the ways in which juvenile law-breaking is created as a form of deviance. In other words juvenile law-breaking is too important to be set aside or relegated to a list of routine human activities, like eating bread and jam or going for walks. It is a *significant* activity because the state takes certain forms of behaviour from their natural context and treats them as significantly different. Accordingly, an analysis of juvenile law-breaking must consider both youth and the law as separate entities — entities that come together on the streets and in the courts in such a way that certain items of behaviour become delinquency.

The Context of Youth

Because youth has been made into a major 'social problem' since the Second World War there has been a great deal of research and analysis on the subject. For the most part research has concentrated mainly on juvenile law-breakers, neglecting the larger social context within which youth exists. The study of juvenile delinquency has nevertheless provided some of the most important and character-istic post-war sociological work. A.K.Cohen's *Delinquent Boys* emphasized the relationship between values, social class and law-breaking introducing the idea of a delinquent sub-culture; Cloward and Ohlin further developed this type of analysis in America. In Great Britain David Downes' work on the East End of London attempted to show the relationship between the leisure goals of the young and their law-breaking; and Howard Parker studied in depth the interactions within a group of Liverpool youth. In all these cases, though, youth was looked at with some form of deviance as the principal object of concern. Until quite recently in fact youth as a whole remained unstudied. All of this literature is usefully reviewed in Stuart Hall's collection, *Resistance Through Rituals*, which marks an important step towards opening out the sociology of youth into an analysis of a whole people.[43]

Typically, for example, research on juvenile law-breaking has been about young men and boys, Like most of the rest of our knowledge of society it remains almost totally sexist in the sense of at best ignoring the existence of women. The pattern of course reflects the fact that most social researchers have been male and that their problems, interests and abilities reflect that limitation. For myself I would say that the difficulties of a 28-year-old male trying to understand contemporary male youth culture are already enormous; to add an attempt to understand female puberty would make the research task impossible for me. But whatever the reasons, it is only very recently that research on female youth has started in any serious way; like so much else this is a result of the political efforts of the Women's Movement.

More generally, since the statistics provide us with no real understanding of the extent or meaning of juvenile male law-breaking we must attempt a much closer empirical approach, one that emphasizes the context of action. This is important if we are to get beyond the headlines and the panics; if we are to see over the top of societal fears of rampaging vandals. So let us look at the context of Saturday night out for 14-year-old youth in contemporary UK society and then try to see the ways in which law-breaking emerges.

What do You do on an Average Saturday Evening?

Much of the analysis that follows stems from my own research in Sunderland in the early 1970s. The question above represented my point of entry to spare-time action. The main component of the answer, and of all youth culture and delinquency studies, was 'Spend it with me mates'.

Mates and group action are the only ways to spend Saturday evening and indeed as much time as possible. Most law-breaking and most non-law-breaking takes place in gangs. All the trans-Atlantic classics in the sociology of juvenile crime have underlined the role and importance of the street corner group, the near-group, the gang. Whatever it is called it adds up to a group of lads on a street corner. The group nature of their existence and action becomes reinforced when the boys come into contact with any other organization at all.

The most obvious example is school. In school the teacher and the educational system as a whole try to individualize the group — to a great extent successfully. They, on the other hand, try to treat each other and the system in terms of their own groups. While activities such as truancy and classroom mucking-about may manifest themselves to us as individualized action, the experience of school is so far as possible reconstituted in terms of the group of mates. The groupness of their experience, of their efforts to create their own lives, comes over much more strongly when we look at the kids' reactions to commercial institutions like the football match or the dance hall. It is of course within these contexts that the fears of youths' activities have been at their most melodramatic. The teds started the panics, smashing up cinemas; the mods and rockers continued it with their attacks on each other at Bank Holiday resorts; the skinheads played their part and turned into the newest demon, the soccer hooligan. All these groups would appear to have terrorized a nation. Yet most of their reputation is a matter of the fantasies of the media not of actual social devastation.[44]

Let us take the 'soccer hooligan' as an example. Most people, we are told, go to a football match to watch football and are disturbed by the way in which these boys carry on. Yet this precisely does *not* represent the experience of Saturday afternoon for most football fans. While the treasurers of football clubs might want everyone to walk in as an individual to the ground, to pay their money at the turnstile and walk out as an individual at the end of the game, it just doesn't happen that way. The match for most boys starts midway through the morning. It may mean a trip to the centre of town or to the railway station to jeer at the opposing fans coming up on the train. It would certainly mean meeting your mates at the cafe or at the corner. Then there is the long journey to the ground: the tubes or buses are full of groups, the groups are full of football, last week's game, this game, the lies of the press. You get to the ground about ninety minutes early, join up with other groups and fill up your side's area. Not just an individual, not just a group, not just a train full of groups, but the whole North End or wherever. There is nothing individual in the experience unless the police come in and drag you, personally, out. If that doesn't happen you are in there chanting, singing, waving for over three hours.

Then there is the end of the game, the crowd, the train, the group, and the individual back home in time for the evening paper. If it's a home game it takes nearly six hours; if its an away game it takes all day. In the middle there is a football game for an hour and half; a game which provides the opportunity for everything else to take place; a game which allows you to be part of 5,000. In the middle of this, too, there is 'soccer hooliganism'. Yet every weekend does not see thousands dead and maimed up and down the country's football grounds — even if it does see hundreds arrested; areas of cities are not razed to the ground every Saturday — even if the police do pull in regular contingents of hooligans and the television news shows its quota of pictures of people running around on pitches. There is in fact very little damage done on these occasions. One would think that with the passions of a Cup match, and with what we are led to believe is a mass of monsters in every crowd, that there would indeed be bloodshed. But there is nothing of the sort. The six hours of the day represent a collectively created group experience; the experience of the week, in which you and your mates are able really to do something — especially when compared to the restrictions of school or the rigours of work. It is an experience which has built-in creativity, which seriously and collectively attempts to make rather than just experience life. That is the background to soccer hooliganism: not trouble at the pitches or cheap excursion fares or depraved individuals.

Yet this type of understanding is something which does not fit well into any form of statistical analysis. And the same goes for any really sociological understanding we could obtain of the phenomena identified as 'vandalism'. As something that impinges on the day-to-day lives of millions of people vandalism is a serious social problem in the 1970s. But to try to spot the vandal in terms of some special behaviour pattern, social background or chromosome structure is an impossible task. Vandalism as experienced by working-class parents is a matter of smashed telephone boxes, graffiti, and trodden flower-beds. It makes them bewildered and angry, encouraging them to look for a category of marked-out, deviant individuals on whom to vent their resentment. Yet the context of vandalism is not like that, for most of it springs not from a pit of asocial aggression but from the world of Saturday night, of doing nothing on street corners.[45]

> What sort of things do you do when you are just walking about?
> *John S:* Just talk.
> Talk?
> *John S:* Just talk.
> Does anything ever happen to you?
> *John S:* Nothing much, we keep moving about all the time so someone can't complain.
> Complain?
> *John S:* Well, people complain and we get into trouble. Not for doing owt but for just standing about.

Or again:

> What sort of thing do you do with your mates?
> *Duncan:* Just stand around talking about footy. About things.
> Do you do anything else?
> *Duncan:* Joke, lark about, carry on. Just what we feel like really.
> What's that?
> *Duncan:* Just doing things. Last Saturday someone started throwing bottles and we all got in.
> What happened?
> *Duncan:* Nothing really.

Here, smashing bottles must be seen in the context of doing nothing on Saturday evening; of the way in which street corners become the most welcoming place for working class youth; of the way in which doing nothing is the most meaningful activity. Out of nothing springs the smashing up:

> Do you ever go out and knock about with the lads?
> *Albert:* Sometimes, when I feel like it.
> What do you do?
> *Albert:* Sometimes we get into a bit of mischief.
> Mischief?
> *Albert:* Well somebody gets a weird idea into their head, and they start to carry it out and others join in.
> Weird idea?
> *Albert:* Things . . . like going round smashing milk bottles.

or:

> *Edward:* I've been in trouble recently, because my friends smashed a big shop window, but that's all.

or:

> *Steven:* Well you know the Grand Prix down there, well we duff the machines up and get free goes on them. You know the corporation buses, well they go in for a cup of tea, we'll go and open the doors and kick the buses in.

These boys are out on the street corner on a Saturday night in Sunderland, wanting something to happen. Their activity can best be understood as an attempt to get something, anything, to happen; an attempt to *create* their own activity, create their own lives instead of merely experiencing them. The same is true of many 'fights' that take place:

What do you do on an average Saturday evening?

Fred: I go down the station, you know, in the town centre and shoot through to Newcy; a whole gang of us. Then we walk around Newcy, ready for trouble. We find a few Maggie supporters and kick them in. Have a good scrap we do.

What do the police do?

Fred: They try and stop us sometimes . . . catch us, but I give a false name and address because they think I'm from Newcy.

What sort of fights?

Fred: Well, not real fights, as some of them might be quite matey. But still, when you put the boot in, you put the boot in; but we are quite friendly after, like.

Here, we see the way in which 'fights' are created to provide action and meaning for the kids; we are observing an adventure performed not an attempted murder.

The same is true of a great deal of the property theft in which young people engage. David Downes provides a glimpse into the reality of such theft in the following example. In one northern city he studied there was an outbreak of bicycle stealing and, unusually, the police failed to trace any of the bikes. What was strange about this was that the kids had in the past merely joy-ridden the bikes to another part of town and left them. As the city's bicycle stock diminished there were stories of gangs of youths respraying the bikes and selling them through a network of London contacts: organized crime, no less. Quite suddenly the stealing stopped and the 'problem' accordingly disappeared. Some time later, when the canal was being dredged, the police discovered most of the missing bikes on the bed of the canal. Boys had been joy-riding them as usual and giving themselves the additional thrill of running them into the canal.

In my own research I came across many examples of this apparently 'meaning-less' type of juvenile law-breaking: taking a light-bulb from Woolworths, leaving it at a chemist's shop and taking a tube of toothpaste from there to a clothes shop, leaving that and taking a sweater back to Woolworths. Or again, two boys would put on overalls, steal two boxes of oranges and then drop the lot into the river Wear. It is easy enough to see what the meaning of this sort of thing could be as activity; not so clear that it is meaningful to treat it simplistically as 'crime'. And if we look jointly at all four of my examples — soccer hooliganism, vandalism, fighting and stealing — we see a set of experiences not *in themselves* directed at breaking laws. Rather, they are created activities very different from much adult property crime; the kids are making life for themselves as best they can and in ways which *happen* to run up against the law. They find themselves *incidentally* involved with the law. They do not set out deliberately to smash the moral universe of respectable society, because for the most part they exist outside what are wrongly assumed to be the universal rules and conventions of that society.

But while the boys view the streets as their place, a place in which they can live their own lives, so does another force in our society — the police. To the police the same streets are places they are charged to keep safe for 'the general public' who-ever they are. And typically the behaviour of these groups of kids fails to meet with police requirements for public safety. The interaction of these two groups, both seeking to use the streets for their particular purposes and each intrinsically naive about the motivations and attitudes of the other, creates the delinquency figures cited at the start of this section. The boys see the power of the police as virtually total. Police studies have themselves stressed the arbitrary nature of police power at this level of interaction. Further studies have shown the kids' complete lack of understanding of the courts and the whole apparatus of law and law enforcement. These ignorances combine to provide the kids with a view of the power of the policeman as all-encompassing and absolute. He can hit you, fine you, take your name and address, get you wrong, perhaps get you put away. It is this sense of police power which haunts the lives of the boys, makes them conscious that their streets are not really theirs. It is that power that they try to work their way round, a power which if it corners them, will change their identities and their lives. In the face of that power they are involved in an effort to find space to make their own lives. All the mumbo jumbo about doing wrong, or of ending 'society' is outside their experience, meaningless, a rhetoric in which they cannot possibly share:

Do you ever knock around the streets?
Ian: Sometimes.
What happens?
Ian: Sometimes we have a panda around us for playing football or something like that.
What?
Ian: Well, you know, just hanging around minding our own business.
What happens then?
Ian: Well . . . er (laughs), you've got to run.
Do you like playing footy?
Ian: Well, you see where we play football, like behind the shop, the people that live above the shop complained, then the panda came round.

Or:

Do you ever just knock around the streets?
Jim: Yes, that's what we do every day.
Do you ever get into trouble?
Jim: Yes, I was getting into trouble for playing inside a club. I was getting picked up by the police. Its just because we were on the premises and they caught us.
What else?
Jimmy: Sometimes when you're fighting you get caught by the coppers.
How does trouble start?
Jimmy: Well, we were just playing football, minding our own business and police will come up and argue with you. Sometimes they'll hit you and sometimes they'll just take your name.

Are these boys 'amoral'? Or simply living in a different social world? What is clear is that they see trouble as something connected with the control agencies they encounter not as something intrinsic, let alone intended, in their own action; and certainly not as something connected with an overall sense of right and wrong, or

indeed with a sense of law as a body of relevant moral norms. And if we accept
that that is their reality then our view of juvenile law-breaking has to become one
in which law is relevant as a criterion only in so far as it is the basis on which the
police and other control agencies deploy their power against the boys in an attempt
to suppress certain forms of behaviour which they find unacceptable. In that
perspective the sorts of behaviour that fall into the category of juvenile law-breaking
do so not for reasons inherent in that behaviour but because they are so defined by
the powerful agencies of social control. The sociological 'problem' of juvenile law-
breaking becomes a problem of why the actions of the young are made criminal in
this way by those agencies. Obviously they do not just pick at random on behaviour
to ban; the harassing of youth, the presentation of youth as a special problem from
the point of view of 'public safety', represents the imposition of certain views of
the kinds of behaviour that should and should not occur. Which leads us some considerable distance both from the panic headlines about smashing and thieving and
from the official statistics about juvenile convictions.

CONCLUSIONS

This chapter has attempted to question some commonsense assumptions about
deviancy and deprivation in the UK. It has done so by looking at four specific
examples rather than by trying to cover the whole field of deviancy or every form
of deprivation. In selecting these four examples I wanted to pick things which
people normally do see as deviant or deprived so that the arguments of the
chapter would link up with the things readers will find in their newspapers or
what textbooks about British society will tell them. It is important to try to generalize
this approach to a whole range of activities in society. Initially, readers could try
to look at the way in which other forms of activity that are normally labelled as
deviant are in fact created socially rather than given absolutely as odd or bad.
Equally they can see the way in which the institutions of the state interact with
those ways of life and make them deprived in certain ways; noting all the time that
this relationship is not one brought about by wicked individuals or inadequately
trained Supplementary Benefit officers but rather represents the very nature of the
institutions we have created.

Having generalized in that way, perhaps the reader could then turn to other sets
of activities not connected with what we usually see as deviant or deprived and
look at them: at the activities of employers who make people work seven days a
week one year and the next year allow them to work only two days a week; the
activities of teachers and lecturers who make their students sit through the
idiocy of examinations year after year; at all the experiences that this society
presents as normal. Look at them with some dialectical imagination and see the
way in which 'normalcy' is created as a meaning for absurd activities just as deviancy
is a created meaning for normal activities.

Notes to Chapter 5

1 For a useful review of the way sociology has moved in this direction see S.Cohen, 'Criminology and the Sociology of Deviance in Britain', in P.Rock and M.McIntosh, *Deviance and Social Control* (London 1974).

2 F.Field, *Are Low Wages Inevitable?* (Nottingham 1976).

3 C.Jones, 'The Development of Social Work Education in Britain' (PhD thesis, University of Durham 1977).

4 M.Rutter and N.Madge, *Cycles of Disadvantage* (London 1976).

5 B.S.Rowntree, *Poverty and Progress: a second social survey of York* (London 1941), pp. 102–3.

6 G.Drage, *The State and the Poor* (London 1914), pp. 52–3.

7 See the chapter by Brian Elliott in this volume and also S.Holterman, 'Areas of Urban Deprivation in Great Britain: an analysis of 1971 Census data', in *Social Trends* (HMSO 1975).

8 This point is made rather forcefully by D.J.West and D.P.Farrington in *Who Becomes Delinquent?* (London 1973); and see too, Rutter and Madge, *op. cit.* ch. 6.

9 R.G.Hood, *Sentencing in Magistrates' Courts* (London 1962).

10 See in particular J.Young, *The Drug Takers* (Paladin edn. 1972).

11 H.Becker, *Outsiders* (London 1973), and J.Young, 'The Role of the Police as Amplifiers of Deviancy', in S.Cohen, *Images of Deviance* (Penguin edn. 1971).

12 P.Townsend, 'Poverty as Relative Deprivation: Resources and Style of Living', in D.Wedderburn, *Poverty, Inequality and Class Structure* (Cambridge 1974); and see too, P.Townsend, *The Concept of Poverty* (London 1972).

13 *Ibid.*

14 See, for example, D.Marshall, *The English Poor Law in the 18th Century* (Oxford 1926); and in a different context B.Semmel, *Imperialism and Social Reform* (London 1965).

15 C.A.R.Crossland, *The Future of Socialism* (London 1956); S.M.Lipset, *Political Man* (London 1960).

16 K.Coates and R.Silburn, *Poverty: the forgotten Englishmen* (Penguin edn. 1970).

17 B.Abel-Smith and P.Townsend, *The Poor and the Poorest*, Occasional Papers in Social Administration, no. 17 1965.

18 A.B.Atkinson, *Poverty in Britain and the Reform of Social Security* (Cambridge 1969).

19 J.Kincaid, *Poverty and Equality in Britain: a study of social security and taxation* (Penguin edn. 1973).

20 Child Poverty Action Group, *Poverty: the facts* (London 1975).

21 See, for example, M.Young (ed.), *Poverty Report 1974* (London 1974).

22   Lord Beveridge, *Social Insurance and Allied Services* (HMSO 1942); and
     House of Lords, *Hansard*, Vol. 182, cols 675–6.
23   *The Times* (November 1953), cited in Kincaid, *op. cit.*, p. 59.
24   House of Lords, *Hansard*, Vol. 182, col. 677; cited in Kincaid, *op. cit.*, p. 62.
25   *Report from His Majesty's Commissioners for Inquiring into the Administration
     Practical Operation of the Poor Laws*, 1834 – the Poor Laws Report.
26   *Ibid.*
27   David Donnison, 'Supplementary Benefits: Dilemmas and Priorities' in *Journal
     of Social Policy*, Vol. 5, Part 4 (1976).
28   *Ibid.*
29   E.Goffman, *Stigma: Notes on the Management of Spoiled Identity* (Penguin
     edn. 1968).
30   Coates and Silburn, *op. cit.*, p. 61.
31   *Ibid.*
32   National Prices and Incomes Board, Report 169; *General Problems of Low
     Pay* (HMSO 1971).
33   *Report of the Committee on One-Parent Families* (Finer Report), Cmnd 5692
     (HMSO 1974).
34   See in particular, J.Bowlby, *Child Care and the Growth of Love* (Penguin edn.
     1953) and M.Rutter, *Maternal Deprivation Reassessed* (Penguin edn. 1972).
35   Beveridge, *op. cit.*, p. 134.
36   R.Mitchison, 'The Making of the Old Scottish Poor Law' in *Past and Present*,
     no. 63 (1974).
37   Home Office, Working Party on Vagrancy and Street Offences, *Report*
     (HMSO 1974), pp. 7–8.
38   *Ibid.*
39   *Report* of the Committee of the Society for the Improvement of Prison
     Discipline (London 1818), p. 11.
40   H.Worsley, *Juvenile Depravity* (London 1849).
41   J.Lambert, *Crime, Police and Race Relations: A Study in Birmingham*
     (Oxford 1970); I.Piliavin and S.Briar, 'Police Encounters with Juveniles' in
     E.Rubington and M.Weinberg, *Deviance: the Interactionist Perspective*
     (London 1968); A.Cicourel, *The Social Organisation of Juvenile Justice*
     (Chichester 1968).
42   N.Christie, 'A Study of Self-reported Crime' in *Scandinavian Studies in
     Criminology* (1965), pp. 86–118; D.Farrington, 'Self-reports of Deviant
     Behaviour', *Journal of Criminal Law and Criminology*, 64, pp. 99–100;
     T.Hirsch, Causes of Delinquency (California 1968).
43   S.Hall and T.Jefferson, *Resistance Through Rituals* (London 1975), esp. J.
     Clarke et al, 'Subcultures, Cultures and Class', pp. 9–74.
44   See CCSS Mugging Group, 'Some Notes on the Relationship between the
     Societal Control Culture and the News Media' in Hall and Jefferson *op. cit.*,
     and S.Cohen, *Folk Devils and Moral Panics* (Paladin edn., 1972).
45   All of the following quotations are drawn from my own study, *Schooling the
     Smash Street Kids* (forthcoming) Macmillan; see too P.Corrigan, 'Doing
     Nothing' in Hall and Jefferson.

Select Bibliography

The Bibliography is organized in four sections: *1. General Sources and Works of Reference* concerned with the aspects of contemporary UK society treated in this volume; *2. Cities* — the principal sources used for chapter 1 of this volume together with other major recommended works on urbanism and urban change in the UK since 1945; *3. The Division of Labour* — the principal sources used for chapters 2 and 3 of this volume and other major recommended works on work, occupations and the political economy of gender relationships in the UK in recent years; and *4. Inequality* — the main sources used for chapters 4 and 5 of this work together with major recommended works on elites and deprivation in the contemporary UK.

1. GENERAL SOURCES AND WORKS OF REFERENCE

CENTRAL STATISTICAL OFFICE, *Annual Abstract of Statistics,* HMSO, London.
CENTRAL STATISTICAL OFFICE, *Facts in Focus,* HMSO, London, 1975.
CENTRAL STATISTICAL OFFICE, *Social Trends,* HMSO, London, 1970—8.
DEPARTMENT OF EMPLOYMENT, *British Labour Statistics: Yearbook,* HMSO, London (annual publication).
DEPARTMENT OF EMPLOYMENT, *Family Expenditure Survey,* HMSO, London, 1971.
DEPARTMENT OF EMPLOYMENT, *New Earnings Survey,* HMSO, London, 1969.
DEPARTMENT OF THE ENVIRONMENT, *Census Indicators of Urban Deprivation,* HMSO, London, 1975.
DEPARTMENT OF THE ENVIRONMENT, *Trends in Population, Housing and Occupancy Rates 1861—1961,* HMSO, London, 1971.
DEPARTMENT OF HEALTH AND SOCIAL SECURITY, *Health and Personal Social Services Statistics for England and Wales,* HMSO, London, 1972.
HALSEY, A. H. (ed.), *Trends in British Society since 1900,* Macmillan, London, 1972.
HAMMOND, E., *An Analysis of Regional Economic and Social Statistics,* University of Durham, Rowntree Research Unit, Durham, 1968.
MARSH, D. C., *The Changing Social Structure of England and Wales 1871—1961,* Routledge & Kegan Paul, London, 1965.
MAUNDER, W. F., *Reviews of United Kingdom Statistical Sources,* vols I—IV, Heinemann, London, 1973.
MITCHELL, B. and DEANE, P., *Abstract of British Historical Statistics,* Cambridge University Press, Cambridge, 1962.
SILLITOE, A., *Britain in Figures,* Penguin Books, London, 1971.

2. CITIES

AMBROSE, P. and COLENUTT, B., *The Property Machine,* Penguin Books, London, 1975.

BELL, C. and NEWBY, H., *Community Studies,* Allen & Unwin, London, 1971.

BROADY, M., *Planning for People,* Bedford Square Press, London, 1968.

BURNEY, E., *Housing on Trial,* Oxford University Press, London, 1967.

CASTELLS, M., *The Urban Question,* Edward Arnold, London, 1976.

CASTELLS, M., 'Y-a-t-il une sociologie urbaine?', *Sociologie du Travail,* no. 1, 1968.

CHISHOLM, M. and MANNERS, A., *Spatial Policy Problems of the British Economy,* Cambridge University Press, Cambridge, 1971.

COUNTER INFORMATION SERVICES, *The Recurrent Crisis of London,* London, 1973.

CULLINGWORTH, J. B., *Housing Needs and Planning Policy,* Routledge & Kegan Paul, London, 1960.

CULLINGWORTH, J. B., *Owner Occupation in Scotland and in England and Wales,* NHRBC, London, 1969.

DAMER, S., 'Wine Alley: the Sociology of a Dreadful Enclosure', *Sociological Review,* vol. 22, no. 2, 1974.

DAVIES, P. and NEWTON, K., 'The Social Patterns of Immigrant Areas', *Race,* vol. XIV, no. 1, 1972.

DENNIS, N., *People and Planning,* Faber & Faber, London, 1970.

DENNIS, N., HENRIQUES, F. and SLAUGHTER, C., *Coal is Our Life,* Eyre & Spottiswoode, London, 1956.

DEPARTMENT OF THE ENVIRONMENT, *Census Indicators of Urban Deprivation,* Working Note no. 6, 1975.

DEPARTMENT OF THE ENVIRONMENT, *Inner Area Studies,* HMSO, London, 1977.

DONNISON, D. and EVERSLEY, D., *London–Urban Patterns, Problems and Policies,* Heinemann, London, 1973.

DURANT, R., *Watling: A Survey of Social Life on a New Housing Estate,* P. S. King & Son, London, 1959.

ENGLISH, J. and NORMAN, P., 'One Hundred Years of Slum Clearance in England and Wales', *Discussion Papers in Social Research,* no. 1, University of Glasgow, Glasgow, 1974.

EVERSLEY, D., 'Landlords Slow Goodbye', *New Society,* 15.1.75.

FERRIS, J., *Participation in Urban Planning,* Bell, London, 1972.

FORD, J., 'The Role of Building Society Managers in the Urban Stratification System', *Urban Studies,* vol. 12, no. 3, 1975.

GANS, H., *The Levittowners,* Penguin Books, London, 1967.

GLASS, R., 'The Evaluation of Planning: Some Sociological Considerations', *International Social Science Journal,* vol. XI, no. 3, 1950.

GOODMAN, R., *After the Planners,* Penguin Books, London, 1972.

GREVE, J. and PAGE, D., *Homelessness in London,* Scottish Academic Press, Edinburgh, 1971.

HADDEN, R., 'The Location of West Indians in the London Housing Market', *The New Atlantis,* vol. 2, no. 1, 1970.

HALL, P., GRACEY, H., DREWITT, R. and THOMAS, R., *The Containment of Urban England,* Allen & Unwin, London, 1973.

HAMNETT, C., 'Social Change and Social Segregation in Inner London', *Urban Studies,* vol. 13, no. 3, 1976.

HARVEY, D., *Social Justice and the City,* Edward Arnold, London, 1973.

JACKSON, A., *Semi-Detached London,* Allen & Unwin, London, 1973.

JOHNSTON, R. J., *Urban Residential Patterns,* Bell, London, 1971.

KELLER, S., *The Urban Neighbourhood,* Random House, New York, 1968.

KINGSTON POLYTECHNIC, *The Buxton Report,* London, 1976.

KUPER, L., *Living in Towns,* Cresset Press, London, 1953.

LAMBERT, C. and WEIR, D., *Cities in Modern Britain,* Fontana, London, 1975.

LIPSKY, M. et. al., *Theoretical Perspectives on Urban Politics,* Prentice Hall, Engelwood Cliffs, New Jersey, 1976.

MELLOR, J. R., *Urban Sociology in an Urbanized Society,* Routledge & Kegan Paul, London, 1977.

MITCHELL, C. D., LIPTON, T., HODGES, M. and SMITH, C., *Neighbourhood and Community,* Liverpool University Press, Liverpool, 1954.

MOGEY, J. M., *Family and Neighbourhood: Two Studies in Oxford,* Oxford University Press, Oxford, 1956.

MOSER, C. and SCOTT, W., *British Towns: A Statistical Study of their Economic and Social Differences,* Oliver and Boyd, Edinburgh, 1961.

MUCHNICK, D., 'Urban Renewal in Liverpool', *Occasional Papers on Social Administration,* no. 33, Bell, London, 1970.

MUMFORD, L., *The City in History,* Secker & Warburg, London, 1961.

NORMAN, P., 'Managerialism: a Review of Recent Work', *Proceedings of the Conference on Urban Change and Conflict,* Centre for Environmental Studies, 1975.

ORLANS, H., *Stevenage: a Sociological Portrait of a New Town,* Routledge & Kegan Paul, London, 1952.

PAHL, R., *Readings in Urban Sociology,* Penguin Books, London, 1968.

PAHL, R., 'The Rural Urban Continues', *Sociologica Ruralis,* vol. 6, 1966.

PAHL, R., *Whose City?,* Longman, London, 1970.

PAHL, R., *'Urban Social Theory and Research',* Centre for Environmental Studies, Working Paper no. 5, 1969.

PAHL, R., 'Urbs in Rure: the Metropolitan Fringe', London School of Economics, Geographical Papers, no. 2, 1965.

PAHL, R., *Urban Sociology: Critical Essays,* Tavistock Publications, London, 1976.

PEACH, C., *West Indian Migration to Britain,* Oxford University Press, Oxford, 1968.

Report of the Committee on Housing in Greater London, HMSO, Cmnd. 2605, 1965.

REX, J., 'The Sociology of a Zone of Transition' in R. Pahl, *Readings in Urban Sociology,* Oxford University Press, Oxford, 1966.

REX, J. and MOORE, R., *Race, Community and Conflict: a study of Sparkbrook,* Oxford University Press, London, 1967.

RICHARDSON, H., VIPOND, J. and FURBEY, R., *Housing and Urban Spatial Structure,* Saxon House, Farnborough, 1975.

ROBINSON, F. and ABRAMS, P., *What We Know About the Neighbours,* University of Durham, Rowntree Research Unit, Durham, 1977.

ROBSON, B. T., *Urban Analysis,* Cambridge University Press, Cambridge, 1969.

STACEY, M., 'The Myth of Community Studies', *British Journal of Sociology,* vol. 20, 1969.

Urban Trends, City of Newcastle upon Tyne Household Survey, Newcastle, 1975.

WEBER, M., *The City,* trans. D. Martindale and G. Neuwirth, Free Press, New York, 1958.

WILMOTT, P., *The Evolution of a Community,* Routledge & Kegan Paul, London, 1963.

WIRTH, L., 'Urbanism as a Way of Life', *American Journal of Sociology,* vol. 44, 1938.

YOUNG, M. and WILMOTT, P., *Family and Kinship in East London,* Routledge & Kegan Paul, London, 1957.

3. THE DIVISION OF LABOUR

ABRAMOWITZ, M. and ELIASBERG, V. F., *The Growth of Public Employment in Great Britain,* Princeton University Press, Princeton, New Jersey, 1957.

BAIN, G. S., *The Growth of White Collar Unionism,* Oxford University Press, Oxford, 1970.

BAIN, G. S. and PRICE, R., 'Who is a White Collar Employee?', *British Journal of Industrial Relations,* vol. 10, no. 3, 1972.

BALDAMUS, W., *Efficiency and Effort,* Tavistock Publications, London, 1961.

BANKS, J. A., *Trade Unionism,* Collier-Macmillan, London, 1974.

BARKER, D. L. and ALLEN, S. (eds), *Sexual Divisions and Society: Process and Change,* Tavistock Publications, London, 1976.

BARKER, D. L. and ALLEN, S. (eds), *Sexual Divisions and Society: Dependence and Exploitation,* Longman, London, 1976.

BECHHOFER, F. and ELLIOTT, B., 'An Approach to the Study of Small Shop-keepers and the Class Structure', *Archives Européenes de Sociologie,* vol. 9, 1968.

BELL, C. and NEWBY, H., 'Capitalist Farmers in the British Class Structure', *Sociologica Ruralis,* vols 1 and 2, 1974.

BENDIX, R., *Work and Authority in Industry,* Wiley, New York, 1963.

BEYNON, H., *Working for Ford,* Penguin Books, London, 1973.

BLACKBURN, R. M., *Union Character and Social Class,* Batsford, London, 1967.

BLACKBURN, R. M. and BEYNON, H., *Perceptions of Work,* Cambridge University Press, Cambridge, 1972.

BRANNEN, P. (ed.), *Entering the World of Work: Some Sociological Perspectives,* HMSO, London, 1975.

BRAVERMAN, H., *Labour and Monopoly Capital,* Monthly Review Press, New York, 1974.

BULMER, M. (ed.), *Working Class Images of Society,* Routledge & Kegan Paul, London, 1975.

CARTER, M., *Into Work,* Penguin Books, London, 1966.

CENTRAL OFFICE OF INFORMATION, *Occupations and Conditions of Work,* HMSO, London, 1976.

CHILD, J. (ed.), *Man and Organization,* Allen & Unwin, London, 1973.

COUNTER INFORMATION SERVICES, *Women Under Attack,* London, 1976.

COUSINS, J. M., *Values and Value in the Labour Market,* Working Papers in Sociology, no. 9, University of Durham, Durham, 1976.

COUSSINS, J., *The Equality Report,* National Council for Civil Liberties, London, 1976.

DEPARTMENT OF EMPLOYMENT, *British Labour Statistics: Historical Abstract 1886–1968,* HMSO, London, 1971.

DEPARTMENT OF EMPLOYMENT, *British Labour Statistics Yearbook,* HMSO, London.

DEPARTMENT OF EMPLOYMENT, *Classification of Occupations and Directory of Occupational Titles,* HMSO, London, 1972.

DEPARTMENT OF EMPLOYMENT, *New Earnings Survey,* HMSO, London.

DURKHEIM, E., *The Division of Labour in Society,* Free Press, New York, 1933.

ELDRIDGE, J. E. T., *Sociology and Industrial Life,* Nelson, London, 1971.

ENGELS, F., *The Origins of the Family,* Lawrence & Wishart, London, 1940.

ESLAND, G., SALAMAN, G. and SPEAKMAN, M. (eds), *People and Work,* Holmes McDougall, London, 1975.

FOX, A., *Beyond Contract: Work, Power and Trust Relations,* Faber & Faber, London, 1974.

FOX, A., 'The Meaning of Work' in *Occupational Categories and Cultures,* Open University, Milton Keynes, 1976.

FRASER, R. (ed.), *Work: Twenty Personal Accounts,* Penguin Books, London, 1968.

GARDINER, J., 'The Political Economy of Female Labour in Capitalist Society', *New Left Review,* no. 89, 1975.

GARNSEY, E., 'Women's Work and Theories of Class Stratification', *Sociology*, vol. 12, no. 2, 1978.

GOLDTHORPE, J. H. et. al., *The Affluent Worker – Industrial Attitudes and Behaviour*, Cambridge University Press, Cambridge, 1968.

HALL, J. and JONES, D. C., 'The Social Grading of Occupations', *British Journal of Sociology*, vol. 1, no. 1, 1950.

HUNT, A., *A Survey of Women's Employment*, HMSO, London, 1968.

HUNT, A., *Women and Work: a Statistical Survey*, HMSO, London, 1974.

HYMAN, B. and BROUGH, I., *Social Values and Industrial Relations*, Blackwell, Oxford, 1975.

JAQUES, E., *Equitable Payment*, Penguin Books, London, 1967.

JOHNSON, T. J., *Professions and Power*, Macmillan, London, 1972.

KAGAN, J. and MOSS, H. A., *Birth to Maturity: a Study in Psychological Development*, Wiley, New York, 1967.

KAMM, J., *Hope Deferred: Girls' Education in English History*, Methuen, London, 1965.

KINNERSLEY, P., *The Hazards of Work*, Pluto Press, London, 1973.

KNIGHT, R., 'Changes in the Occupational Structure of the Working Population', *Journal of the Royal Statistical Society*, vol. 130, part 3, 1967.

LOCKWOOD, D., *The Blackcoated Worker*, Allen & Unwin, London, 1958.

MACKENZIE, G., *The Aristocracy of Labour*, Cambridge University Press, Cambridge, 1973.

MANN, M., *Workers on the Move*, Cambridge University Press, Cambridge, 1973.

MILLERSON, G., *The Qualifying Associations*, Routledge & Kegan Paul, London, 1964.

MUMFORD, E. and BANKS, O., *The Computer and the Clerk*, Routledge & Kegan Paul, London, 1973.

NICHOLS, T., *Ownership, Control and Ideology*, Allen & Unwin, London, 1969.

NICHOLS, T. and BEYNON, H., *Living with Capitalism: Class Relations and the Modern Factory*, Routledge & Kegan Paul, London, 1977.

OAKLEY, A., *The Sociology of Housework*, Martin Robertson, London, 1974.

OFFICE OF MANPOWER ECONOMICS, *Report on the Equal Pay Act*, HMSO, London, 1972.

PARKER, S. R., *The Future of Work and Leisure*, MacGibbon & Kee, London, 1971.

PARKER, S. R., BROWN, R. K., CHILD, J. and SMITH, M. A., *The Sociology of Industry*, Allen & Unwin, London, 1972.

POLLARD, S., *The Genesis of Modern Management*, Edward Arnold, London, 1965.

PRANDY, K., *Professional Employees*, Faber & Faber, London, 1965.

ROUTH, G. G. C., *Occupation and Pay in Great Britain, 1906–60*, Cambridge University Press, Cambridge, 1965.

SADLER, P., 'Sociological Aspects of Skill', *British Journal of Industrial Relations*, vol. 8, no. 1, 1970.

SALAMAN, G., *Community and Occupation*, Cambridge University Press, Cambridge, 1974.

SECCOMBE, W., 'The Housewife and her Labour under Capitalism', *New Left Review*, no. 83, 1974.

SHARPE, S., *Just Like a Girl*, Penguin Books, London, 1976.

THOMPSON, E. P., *'Time, Work Discipline and Industrial Capitalism'*, *Past and Present*, no. 38, 1967.

VENESS, T., *School Leavers*, Methuen, London, 1962.

WARR, P. and WALL, T., *Work and Well-being*, Penguin Books, London, 1974.

WEDDERBURN, D. and CROMPTON, R., *Worker's Attitudes and Technology,* Cambridge University Press, Cambridge, 1972.

WEIR, M., *Job Satisfaction,* Fontana, London, 1976.

WILLIAMS, W. M., *Occupational Choice,* Allen & Unwin, London, 1974.

WILSON, E., *Women and the Welfare State,* Tavistock Publications, London, 1977.

YOUNG, M. and WILMOTT, P., *The Symmetrical Family,* Routledge & Kegan Paul, London, 1973.

4. INEQUALITY

ABEL SMITH, B. and TOWNSEND, P., *The Poor and the Poorest,* Occasional Papers in Social Administration, no. 17, Bell, London, 1965.

ABRAMS, P., 'Democracy, Technology and the Retired British Officer', in S. P. Huntington (ed.), *Changing Patterns of Military Politics,* Free Press, New York, 1962.

ATKINSON, A. B., *The Economics of Inequality,* Oxford University Press, Oxford, 1975.

ATKINSON, A. B., *Poverty in Britain and the Reform of Social Security,* Cambridge University Press, Cambridge, 1969.

ATKINSON, A. B., *Unequal Shares: Wealth in Britain,* Penguin Books, London, 1974.

ATKINSON, A. B. (ed.), *Wealth, Income and Inequality,* Penguin Books, London, 1973.

BACHRACH, P., *The Theory of Democratic Elitism,* University of London Press, London, 1969.

BEVERIDGE, W., *Report on Social Insurance and Allied Services,* HMSO, London, 1968.

CHILD POVERTY ACTION GROUP, *Poverty: The Facts,* London, 1975.

COATES, K. and SILBURN, R., *Poverty: The Forgotten Englishmen,* Penguin Books, London, 1970.

DONNISON, D., 'Supplementary Benefits: Dilemmas and Priorities', *Journal of Social Policy,* vol. 5, part 4, 1976.

FIELD, F., *Are Low Wages Inevitable?,* Spokesman Books, Nottingham, 1976.

GIDDENS, A., 'Elites in the British Class Structure', *Sociological Review,* 1972.

GIDDENS, A., *The Class Structure of Advanced Societies,* Hutchinson, London, 1973.

GLASS, D. (ed.), *Social Mobility in Britain,* Routledge & Kegan Paul, London, 1964.

GLASTONBURY, B., *Homeless Near a Thousand Homes,* Allen & Unwin, London, 1971.

GOLDTHORPE, J. H. and LLEWELLYN, C., 'Class Mobility in Britain: Three Theses Examined', *Sociology,* vol. 11, no.2, 1977.

GUTTSMAN, W. L., *The British Political Elite,* MacGibbon & Kee, London, 1963.

HALL, S. and JEFFERSON, J., *Resistance Through Rituals,* Hutchinson, London, 1975.

HARRIS, J. S. and GARCIA, T. U., 'The Permanent Secretaries: Britain's Top Administrators', *Public Administration Review,* March 1966.

HOLMAN, R. (ed.), *Socially Deprived Families in Britain,* Bedford Square Press, London, 1974.

HOLTERMAN, S., 'Areas of Urban Deprivation in Great Britain', *Social Trends,* HMSO, London, 1975.

HOME OFFICE, *Report of the Working Party on Vagrancy and Street Offences,* HMSO, London, 1974.

HOPE, K. (ed.), *The Analysis of Social Mobility,* Oxford University Press, Oxford, 1972.

JOHNSON, R. W., 'The British Political Elite 1965–1972', *Archives Européenes de Sociologie,* 1973.

KELSALL, R. K., *Higher Civil Servants in Britain,* Routledge & Kegan Paul, London, 1955.

KINCAID, J., *Poverty and Equality in Britain,* Penguin Books, London, 1973.

LAND, H., *Large Families in London,* Occasional Papers in Social Administration, no.20, Bell, London, 1969.

LUPTON, T. and SHIRLEY WILSON, C., 'The Social Background and Connections of "Top Decision Makers" ', *Manchester School,* 27, 1959.

LYDALL, H. F. and TIPPING, D. G., 'The Distribution of Personal Wealth in Britain', *Bulletin of the Oxford Institute of Economics and Statistics,* vol. 23, 1961.

LYNES, T., *National Assistance and National Prosperity,* Methuen, London, 1962.

MARSDEN, D., *Mothers Alone,* Penguin Books, London, 1969.

MARSDEN, D., and DUFF, E., *Workless,* Penguin Books, London, 1975.

MILIBAND, R., *Parliamentary Socialism,* Allen & Unwin, London, 1961.

MILIBAND, R., *The State in Capitalist Society,* Weidenfeld & Nicolson, London, 1969.

MILLS, C. W., *The Power Elite,* Oxford University Press, New York, 1956.

OPEN UNIVERSITY, *Patterns of Inequality,* Milton Keynes, 1976.

OTLEY, Ç., 'The Educational Background of British Army Officers', *Sociology,* vol. 7, no. 2, 1973.

PAHL, R. E. and WINKLER, J., *The Corporate State,* Centre for Studies of Social Policy, London, 1976.

PARKIN, F. (ed.), *Class Inequality and Political Order,* MacGibbon & Kee, London, 1971.

PARKIN, F. (ed.), *The Social Analysis of Class Structure,* Tavistock Publications, London, 1974.

POLANYI, G. and WOOD, J. B., *How Much Inequality?,* Heinemann, London, 1974.

PRESTON, B., 'Statistics of Inequality', *Sociological Review,* vol. 22, no. 1, 1974.

REID, I., *Social Class Differences in Britain,* Open Books, London, 1977.

REPORT OF THE COMMITTEE ON ONE PARENT FAMILIES (Finer Report), HMSO, London, 1974.

ROSE, R., 'The Making of a Cabinet Minister', *British Journal of Political Science,* vol. I, no. 1, 1971.

ROWNTREE, S. B., *Poverty: A Study of Town Life,* Nelson, London, 1910.

ROYAL COMMISSION ON THE DISTRIBUTION OF INCOME AND WEALTH, Reports nos 1–3, HMSO, London, 1975–6.

RUBINSTEIN, W. D., 'Wealth, Elites and the Class Structure of Modern Britain', *Past and Present,* no. 76, 1977.

RUNCIMAN, W. G., *Relative Deprivation and Social Justice,* Routledge & Kegan Paul, London, 1966.

RUTTER, M. and MADGE, N., *Cycles of Disadvantage,* Heinemann, London, 1976.

SPIEGELBERG, R., *The City: Power Without Accountability,* Blond & Briggs, London, 1973.

STANWORTH, P. and GIDDENS, A., *Elites and Power in British Society,* Cambridge University Press, Cambridge, 1974.

TOWNSEND, P., *The Concept of Poverty,* Heinemann, London, 1972.

URRY, J. and WAKEFORD, J., *Power in Britain,* Heinemann, London, 1973.

WEDDERBURN, D., 'Poverty in Britain Today–the Evidence', *Sociological Review,* vol. 10, 1962.

WEDDERBURN, D. (ed.), *Poverty, Inequality and Class Structure,* Cambridge University Press, Cambridge, 1974.

WESTERGAARD, J. and RESLER, H., *Class in a Capitalist Society,* Heinemann, London, 1975.

WILLIS, P., *Learning to Labour,* Saxon House, Farnborough, 1977.

YOUNG, M. (ed.), *Poverty Report* (1974 et seq.), Temple Smith, London, 1974, 1975.

Index